- 1462 CL

THE ROUGH

D0637388

Irish Music

by
Geoff Wallis and Sue Wilson

There are more than two hundred Rough Guide titles
covering destinations from Alaska to Zimbabwe
and subjects from Acoustic Guitar to Travel Health

www.roughguides.com

**ROUGH
GUIDES**

Rough Guide Credits

Text editor: Joe Staines; **Series editor**: Mark Ellingham
Production: Michelle Draycott, Julia Bovis
Typesetting and design: Katie Pringle
Proofreading: Russell Walton

Publishing Information

This first edition published April 2001 by
Rough Guides Ltd, 62–70 Shorts Gardens, London WC2H 9AH

Distributed by the Penguin Group

Penguin Books Ltd, 27 Wrights Lane, London W8 5TZ
Penguin Putnam Inc., 375 Hudson Street, New York 10014, USA
Penguin Books Australia Ltd, 487 Maroondah Highway,
PO Box 257, Ringwood, Victoria 3134, Australia
Penguin Books Canada Ltd, 10 Alcorn Avenue,
Toronto, Ontario, Canada M4V 1E4
Penguin Books (NZ) Ltd, 182–190 Wairau Road,
Auckland 10, New Zealand

Typeset in Bembo and Helvetica to an original design by Henry Iles.
Printed in Spain by Graphy Cems.

No part of this book may be reproduced in any form without permission
from the publisher except for the quotation of brief passages in reviews.

© Geoff Wallis and Sue Wilson, 608pp
A catalogue record for this book is available from the British Library.

ISBN 1-85828-642-5

Contents

Introduction

The **Rough Guide to Irish Music** is a comprehensive introduction to one of the world's most vibrant and colourful musical traditions. Still mainly transmitted orally, Ireland's traditional music underwent a major revival towards the end of the twentieth century, and its popularity now extends to countries as disparate as the US, Japan and Germany. The release of huge numbers of CDs over the last ten years – well-known artists, remastered classics plus a significant number of home-produced recordings – is reflected in the hundreds of reviews we have included.

The book is divided into three main sections: "Background", "Musicians" and "Listings". The first begins with a detailed account of the music's origins and development highlighting the key figures, including those collectors whose efforts ensured the music's survival. The background section continues with an exploration of the musical elements that comprise the tradition – its song forms and airs and the various tune types (jigs, reels, etc) which make up its dance music.

People are the lifeblood of any tradition, so the bulk of this guide consists of a biographical directory of musicians – singers, groups and instrumentalists. In compiling this we have attempted to provide a balanced picture of the last hundred years, representing both the enduring influence of older figures and the present cream of the crop. Our choice of entries necessarily reflects the current availability of releases, though, in some exceptional cases, the record reviewed may be a long-deleted LP still awaiting reissue in CD format. Of course, in a guide of this type some of our omissions will inevitably provoke controversy while, equally, some of our inclusions – particularly those musicians influenced by the tradition but not necessarily part of its mainstream – may well engender some heated debate. Future editions may see different emphases and reasoned arguments for inclusion are welcome.

Finally, at the end of the guide our Listings section offers pointers to the best places to find sessions and where to catch the liveliest festivals or enhance your musical skills through attending a summer or winter school. We have also included information on Ireland's best record shops and media coverage of traditional music, plus details of resources for both the newcomer or expert and suggestions for further reading.

Acknowledgements

This book could not exist without the much-valued assistance of a legion of singers, musicians, agents and record companies. Above all, the superb facilities of the Irish Traditional Music Archive were pivotal to the project and our thanks go to its director, Nicholas Carolan, and staff members (especially, Joanie McDermott, Maeve Gebruers, Treasa Harkin and Glenn Comiskey).

In addition, our special thanks to Sarah Allen, Ray Barron, Frank Bechhofer, Lindy Benson, Mary Bergin, Turlach Boylan, Finbar Boyle, Paul Brady, Cormac Breatnach, Máire Breatnach, Gary Brodoff, Éamon de Buitlear, Jeanette Byrne, David Caren, Ciarán Cassidy, Ceol, CCÉ, Verena Commins, Seán Corcoran, John Cosgrove, Andy Cowan, Paul Cranford, Jimmy Crowley, P.J. Curtis, Tom Cussen, Mary Custy, Patricia Daly, Eoghan Davis, Liz Devlin, Eamonn Dillon, Liz Doherty, Dúchas, Eoin Duignan, Seamus Egan, Ninian Fergus, Ciarán Emmett, Brian Finnegan, James Fraher, Patty Furlong, Amy Garvey, Seán Garvey, Kieran Goss, Andy Greig, Kieran Halpin, Frances Hamilton, Mick Hanly,

Tommy Hayes, Win Horan, Islington Library and Information Service, Val Jennings, Eamonn Jordan, Seán and Virginia Keane, Tommy Keane, Malachy Kearns, Paddy Keenan, Alan Kelly, Laoise Kelly, Paul Kelly, Kíla, Larry Kirwan, Christy Leahy, Charlie Lennon, Kathleen Loughnane, Carol Luck, Pat Lyons, Joanie Madden, Tommy Martin, Mick McAuley, Conor McCarthy, Eleanor McEvoy, Michael McGlynn, Brian McNamara, Liam McNulty, Morning Star, Robin Morton, John Moulden, Deirdre and Díarmaid Moynihan, Neillidh Mulligan, Tim Murray, June Ní Chormaic, Mairéad Ní Mhaonaigh and Altan, Deirdre Ní Thuathail, Gerry O'Beirne, Patsy O'Brien, Benny O'Carroll, Bill Ochs, John O'Connor, Eamonn O'Doherty, Ellie O'Hea, Brian Ó hEadhra, Christy O'Leary, Colette O'Leary, Eoin O'Neill, Seámus O'Neill, Caomhín Ó Raghallaigh, Melanie O'Reilly, Jerry O'Sullivan, Tommy O'Sullivan, Kelly Pike, Kevin Rowsome, Paul Ruddy, Karen Ryan, Deirdre Scanlan, Shantalla, Tom Sherlock, Harriet Simms, Mary Staunton, Chris Teskey, Pierce Turner, Seán Tyrrell, Niall Vallely, Michael Ward and Desi Wilkinson.

At Rough Guides we would like to thank Katie Pringle for her conscientious and sensitive typesetting and, last, but, by no means least, our editor, Joe Staines, who provided invaluable insight and expertise throughout.

The Authors

Geoff Wallis is a journalist and editor with a special interest in Irish music. He is the co-author of *The Rough Guide to Dublin*. **Sue Wilson** has been writing about Folk and Roots music since 1992 for, among others, the *Scotsman*, the *Guardian* and *Songlines*.

background

The roots
of the tradition

"...the grand old music – the weird, beautiful, wild and mournful reel tunes that entranced me when a child, a youth and a man, in the street or barn, at the bonfire or on the hill top; the music, the never-to-be forgotten strains that often made my blood alternately flame or freeze..."

Captain Francis O'Neill

Survival and regeneration

Sitting at the eastern edge of the Atlantic Ocean, separated from the main continent of Europe by its centuries-long subjugator, Britain, Ireland remains an island of contrasts and divisions, not least via the continued existence of a demarcation line between Northern Ireland and the Republic. The majority of its people retain a connection with a past draped in myth and legend, yet the Republic's capital, Dublin, possesses all the character (and some of the pretension) of a modern European city. Ireland's history has been coloured for four hundred years by emigration, exacerbated by one of the most devastating human tragedies, the Great Famine of the 1840s. Its language, Gaelic, dwindled into near non-existence and its institutions, both Church and State, are still characterized by an innate conservatism. Yet despite all exigencies, Irish music has not merely survived, but entered the new millennium with a renewed vigour.

The reasons for traditional music's tenacious longevity are multi-form and inter-related. Ireland's geographical isolation is an essential component, but its centuries of colonization are of paramount importance. While the colonizers themselves (whether Viking or Anglo-Norman) may have been absorbed to the extent that they became "more Irish than the Irish", the simple outcome of their rule is that Ireland is one of the most homogeneous and least ethnically diverse countries in the world. Adversity, and the poverty of its predominantly rural population, often socially organized in the near closed community of the clachán, enhanced the strengths of both mythology and the oral tradition central to the maintenance of folklore. Even the recurrent cycles of migration, and a concomitant toing and froing of departure and return, failed to result in any significant infiltration by other cultures. Indeed the process itself reinforced the emigrés own perceptions of the essential nature of "Irishness" and resulted in vibrant Irish communities in countries as far apart as Australia, Canada (notably Cape Breton Island) and the US.

Within this framework of upheaval and deprivation, traditional music was maintained within Ireland's rural heartlands, remaining strongest in those areas where the Irish language itself retained a vital presence. Equally importantly, this inspiring musical vigour evolved as a natural escape valve for communities which passed most of their working week engaged in arduous agricultural labour.

Ironically, while the new nation state which emerged from British Rule in 1921 sought to redefine Irish identity, the policies of its most influential leader, Eamon de Valera – his "frugal economy" – enhanced emigration from those Irish-speaking areas best able to personify the goals of statehood. It took both the emergence in the

1960s of **The Clancy Brothers and Tommy Makem**, themselves emigrants, and a revived economy from the 1980s onwards to reinstate traditional music as a national treasure and establish its credentials as an international commodity.

Ireland's music draws inspiration from many sources. Fundamentally, it remains a music designed for dancing. Indeed the majority of players in the first half of the twentieth century honed their skills by providing accompaniment for house dances, although some of the most influential players have preferred to define themselves as "listening" musicians. So, the question arises, just what exactly is traditional music? Ethno-musicologists differ on the finer points, but generally agree on the major ones. Traditional music involves a continuous link between present and past; incorporates degrees of variation emanating from individuals and within communities; and involves a process of selection by the community determining how the music survives. In simpler terms, this means that music is transferred orally from generation to generation; that different parts of a country will play and sing the music as they like to hear it, and that, above all else, a good tune or song will survive. **Ciaran Carson**, the author of the excellent *Pocket Guide to Irish Traditional Music*, has an even simpler explanation – "since traditional musicians call the music 'traditional music', we might as well call it that too."

Nevertheless, the fundamental ingredient of oral transmission is vital to the continuation of Ireland's musical tradition. While songs and tunes can be learned from books, CDs, radio and even the Internet, knowing how to sing or play them is entirely a matter of personal contact and experience. This does not mean that a musician has to be Irish to play Irish traditional music – indeed there are some outstanding examples to the contrary – but it certainly helps to have been brought up in its midst.

There's an almost stereotypical pattern to the careers of many Irish musicians which begins in infancy – learning songs from parents or listening to music in the family home – and progresses to taking up the tin whistle at aged, say, six or seven. If proficient, the musician next acquires a "proper" instrument, has lessons and enters competitions, learning the "standard" way of playing to satisfy examiners. Most then break free of the competitive constraints and begin to explore their instrument's potential in the company of like-minded souls, usually in the form of a regular session (see p.32). Others come to listen and so the cycle continues.

Is Irish music Celtic?

In recent times Ireland's traditional music has been labelled "Celtic" in some quarters and often bracketed together with the music of Galicia, Brittany, Scotland, Wales and anywhere else similarly defined. While this concept does allow musicians to share some form of kinship, it is largely a marketing ploy utilized by record companies to make their products more commercially attractive or to describe a form of "ethereal" or "haunting" New Age, ambient music beloved by Bord Fáilte (the Republic's Tourist Board) and muzak installers. Yet it does prompt the obvious question of just how "Celtic" Irish music is and to answer that we need briefly to examine its origins.

Apart from numerous archeological remains, a vibrant mythology and, of course, the Irish language itself, little has survived from the Celtic culture which was pre-eminent in Ireland from around 500 BC to the coming of Christianity in the fourth century AD. Through mythology we know a little about the Celts' music, in particular, its division into three forms: related to sleep and meditation (suantraí), happiness (geantraí) and lamentation (goltraí), and a little about its instruments which included various pipes, horns, stringed and percussion instruments. However, no written forms of music have survived so, in this sense, today's Irish music cannot be described as Celtic.

Similarly, the processes of conquest, settlement, intermarriage and emigration mean that it would be difficult for any Irish person to trace their lineage back to Celtic forebears. Furthermore, the substantial body of Ireland's music has evolved from relatively recently imported dance forms, while its instruments, with the exception of the bodhrán and (probably) the uilleann pipes, are also of foreign origin. Yet, these foreign elements or borrowings, as the Belfast-born flute player, **Hammy Hamilton**, has observed, simply demonstrate that the island's dominant musical form, and its innate Irishness, is defined by the process of playing and not its component products.

The harping tradition and the early collectors

Equally, many believe that Ireland's music is directly linked to the harping tradition which flourished from medieval times until the seventeenth century. Every time you purchase a pint of Guinness (or, more especially, Harp), the image of Ireland's national symbol slides subtly into your subconscious. Yet the harp on the glass has little connection with the modern development of Irish music. The image itself is of the Brian Ború harp on display in Trinity College, Dublin, and despite being named after an eleventh century king, is thought to date from the late fourteenth century, and, as such, is Ireland's oldest surviving harp. This was a time when the harper still held an elite status in Gaelic society, receiving privileges, such as land, in return for playing at ceremonial and other occasions and accompanying songs composed by a similarly endowed court poet. Thus the harper was an integral part of the ancient bardic tradition, though little is known about the actual music he played, other than in very general terms.

Following the Flight of the Earls in 1607, when several Irish Chiefs chose voluntary exile in Europe rather than accede to English erosion of their power, England's grip on the country strengthened. It was further reinforced following the defeat of the Catholic King James II by the Protestant William III. Those harpers who had not fled with their chiefs now found a living as itinerants, coming eventually to rely on the patronage of the Ascendancy – the Protestant landowning plutocracy who now controlled Ireland. The most famous of these harpers was **Turlough Carolan** (1670–1738), sometimes known as O'Carolan, from Nobber, Co. Meath, and blind, like many other harpers. Carolan's reputation is grounded on his compositional skills, rather than his playing, and reflects the taste of his patrons, featuring elements drawn from popular sources, including fashionable Italian composers, like Corelli. The Neales' *Collection of the most Celebrated Irish Tunes*, the first work dedicated exclusively to Irish music, published in 1724, included a number of Carolan's compositions and others were contained in further such collections over the next hundred and fifty years.

The most celebrated collection of this period is **Edward Bunting**'s *General Collection of the Ancient Music of Ireland* (1796). Bunting's interest had been stimulated by the 1792 Belfast Harp Festival which he had attended in the role of transcriber, instructed to notate the old melodies played by the harpers without adding a note in order to record the last vestiges of the now almost extinct tradition. Among those who performed was **Denis Hempson** (1695–1807), from Magilligan, Co. Derry, the only harper still using the old playing method of plucking the harp's brass strings with long fingernails. Bunting subsequently paid home visits to Hempson and other harpers in Derry and Tyrone to collect more material and later employed a scribe to record the memoirs of **Arthur O'Neill** (1734–1816) which provide a detailed account of the dying embers of the harping epoch. Despite Bunting's dedication, his ear was classically-trained which, undoubtedly, resulted in "refinements" creeping in to his transcriptions.

From Thomas Moore to Danny Boy

Many of the airs collected by Bunting subsequently appeared in **Thomas Moore**'s *Irish Melodies*, published in ten volumes between 1808 and 1834. Moore, who knew no Gaelic, provided his own highly romanticized lyrics to traditional melodies, with anodyne piano accompaniments composed by the Dublin composer Sir John Stevenson. Moore's songs, such as "The Last Rose of Summer", "The Harp That Once, Thro' Tara's Halls" and "The Minstrel Boy", proved enormously popular, especially in middle-class drawing rooms and parlours. Other writers were to follow Moore's lead and utilize Irish airs as the basis for their own song lyrics, a process which continues to the present day. The most famous example is probably "Danny Boy", the words of which were written by English lawyer and songwriter, **Fred E. Weatherley** in 1912 and fitted – a year later – to the melody "The Londonderry Air" (originally transcribed from a travelling fiddler by Miss Jane Ross of Limavady, Co. Derry, in 1851). Later examples include "She Moved Through the Fair" a traditional melody with words by **Padraic Colum**, and "Raglan Road" written by the poet **P.J. Kavanagh** which employs the air "The Dawning of the Day".

The nineteenth century also saw the composition of completely new, often highly sentimental, "Irish" material, like the immensely successful "I'll Take You Home Again, Kathleen" (words and music by Indiana school teacher Thomas Westendorf). Like "Danny Boy", such popular songs often managed to touch the heartstrings of emigrants without actually mentioning anything specifically Irish, thus guaranteeing wider commercial appeal. This drawing-room ballad "tradition" achieved even greater popularity in modern times through the recordings of Irish opera stars, like tenor **John McCormack** and the soprano **Margaret Burke Sheridan**, and still retains its hold over the dewy-eyed, especially in the US.

Dancing

From the eighteenth century onwards traditional music largely developed as an accompaniment to the dancing of reels, jigs and hornpipes introduced to the country. The dance forms, including set dances were transmitted by a unique profession, the dancing masters, each of whom travelled a local patch, often accompanied by a fiddler (many of whom were blind).

Despite the latitude allowed to contemporary dancers, especially when performing in groups, the original principles of step dancing related closely to confined space with "star" performers being able to contain their movements within the framework of, for example, a half-door laid on the ground. As its name inevitably suggests, the vital elements of step dancing are the legs and feet. The rest of the dancer's body is expected to remain static with the arms pointing downwards (although arm movements do occur in sean-nós step dancing, found in Connemara). The form of the dance itself is not set in stone and consists of improvisation involving raising of the leg and a variety of foot movements, such as kicking the floor with the toe's tip, stamping, shuffling the feet and side-stepping to left or right.

Despite the rigid nature of the dancer's body, the leg movements themselves provide a rivetting spectacle.

Teaching set dances was also once the province of the dancing masters. Mostly of French form, such as the cotillion, minuet or quadrille, these dances reached Ireland through the presence of the British army and most commonly featured a full set of dancers (four couples) or half-set (two). The dancing masters incorporated Irish steps into their teaching and, equally, traditional music was employed further to Gallicize the dances, especially the polka (which later arrived from Bohemia). Equally, already popular step-dance forms, such as the ubiquitous reels, jigs and hornpipes, were conscripted into action.

Sets are commonly named after the area where they were first popular, such as the Valentia set (named after the Kerry island) and are numerically categorized according to their form. So, the "first set" is the oldest immigrant form and consists of quadrilles. The second is based on Lancers, connected to the British regiment of that name, and the third is similarly termed the Caledonian.

As a foreign import, set dancing was regarded as an un-Irish aberration by **The Gaelic League** shortly after its inception in 1893. The League then revived group figure dances, originally taught by the dancing masters to their more adept pupils, in the form of the céilí dance, danced to the melodies of reels, jigs and hornpipes. As a consquence, set dancing declined in most areas, though retained some popularity in Clare and Kerry, counties which formed the basis of its revival in the 1980s.

The Great Famine

One and a half million people died in the Great Famine which struck Ireland between 1845 and 1849 and more than a million more left the country, many risking death in the "coffin ships" which took them to new lives (if they survived) in North America. The impact on music in Ireland is incalculable. While much was irretrievably lost, a chilling legacy of these sombre times remains in the small number of Famine songs which have survived. Unsurprisingly, efforts to collate the music that endured began in earnest. Foremost amongst the post-Famine collectors was **George Petrie**, who co-founded the short-lived Society for the Preservation and Publication of the Melodies of Ireland in 1851, whose only publication was to be *The Petrie Collection of the Ancient Music of Ireland* four years later. Petrie continued to collect music until his death in 1866, though it was to be almost forty years before his labours attained full fruition through **Sir Charles Stanford**'s editing of *The Complete Collection of Irish Music as Noted by George Petrie* which was published in three volumes between 1902 and 1903 and contains more than 1500 tunes.

Other notable nineteenth-century collectors include the clergyman **James Goodman** who transcribed many tunes from the uilleann pipers of Munster. **Patrick William Joyce** published *Ancient Irish Music* in 1873, but his most influential collection, *Old Irish Folk Music and Song*, appeared much later, in 1909. This drew substantially from the Goodman collection and also from the work of the pre-Famine collector William Forde whose own collection, now housed in the Royal Irish Academy, is estimated to have included almost 1900 airs and many other pieces. Joyce's collecting in part reflected continuing concern for the preservation of the Irish language and culture which had already led to the formation of Conradh na Gaeilge (The Gaelic League) and the instigation of an annual Oireachtas competition (including song) in 1897 (still one of the most important events in the Irish-speaking calendar).

Francis O'Neill

In 1903, one Captain **Francis O'Neill**, then Chief Superintendent of Police in Chicago, published *Music of Ireland*, consisting of 1850 airs, jigs, reels and other music collated from Irish musicians in the US, followed, four years later by *The Dance Music of Ireland*. Somewhat overlapping with the former, this latter publication contained 1001 dance tunes and became known amongst Irish musicians on both sides of the Atlantic as "The Book". These ground-breaking collections, specifically focused on dance music and not the airs collated by previous collectors, were inspired both by a dedication to the music and concern that it was withering on the vine. The Chief, as he was known, had himself left his native Cork in 1865 and was well aware of the tragic impact of the Famine, not least from the numbers of Irish in the US, and his efforts helped to secure a future for a substantial body of music, not least because of the relative cheapness of "The Book". His later publications include *Irish Folk Music: A Fascinating Hobby* and the influential *Irish Minstrels and Musicians*, published in 1913, essentially a collection of character sketches of over three

IRISH TRADITIONAL MUSIC ARCHIVE

hundred musicians, mainly uilleann pipers, from the past and from O'Neill's own time.

However, other factors were helping to keep the music alive in Ireland. The process of mass production had made inroads into many walks of life and, from the 1880s onwards, cheap instruments began to become available, including fiddles, concertinas and fifes. The paid professional musicians were gradually being superseded by home-based entertainment while the houses themselves were improving too. Many incorporated larger kitchens whose flagstone floors offered scope for dancing masters to teach a new repertory. So, despite many fears, the great era of the "house dance" had begun and would continue in most parts of Ireland until the 1930s, lingering on in others for another decade or so.

The Irish-American record industry

The presence of so many Irish emigrés in American cities provided a ready market for new forms of mass media. Though some recordings of traditional music had been made on cylinders, most notably by the uilleann piper, **Patsy Touhey**, and the German-American accordionist, **John J. Kimmel**, the technology was being gradually overtaken by the hand-cranked gramophone and its ubiquitous shellac 78 rpm discs. A stream of recordings developed into a full-scale torrent from the early 1920s as fiddlers such as **Michael Coleman** and **James Morrison**, the concertina player William J. Mullally and the flute player **John McKenna** released 78s for the Irish market. Ensemble playing became increasingly common too as groups such as The Flanagan Brothers played for the burgeoning dance halls, while specific Irish radio stations emerged in the major cities. In England too, though the recording industry was slow to catch up, **Frank Lee** had formed a group, calling it a "céilí band" – probably the first to bear such a title – to play at a 1918 St Patrick's Day celebration in London.

From crossroads to dance hall

Ireland, meanwhile, was recovering from the effects of, first, a bloody struggle for freedom from British rule, the War of Independence commencing in 1919, then an even nastier Civil War following the granting of Home Rule for the new Irish Free State in 1921. Such conflicts catalysed waves of emigration from rural areas during the 1920s, including many musicians. Bereft of much music, those remaining rapturously welcomed the arrival of the American recordings: the names of Coleman and Morrison, in particular, acquired legendary status in Ireland with their South Sligo-style fiddle playing establishing a new norm. Such was its influence on Ireland's music that even

NATIONAL LIBRARY OF DUBLIN

today musicians continue to link the same tunes together as they appeared on the original recordings. Radio too began to make an impact with the formation of the national radio station 2RN in 1926 (which became Radio Éireann in 1937) which began to feature traditional music with groups such as the Ballinakill Traditional Players soon becoming household names. Meanwhile, the uilleann pipers **Leo Rowsome** and **Liam Walsh** had recorded for record labels in England.

The house dance, however, was on the wane. The Black and Tans (the British paramilitary police force) had broken up dances during the War of Independence, and now such entertainment faced an onslaught from the Irish clergy, determined to eradicate the new scourge of "jazz dancing". The Fianna Fáil party came to power in 1932 and, thanks to a dispute with Britain, initiated austerity measures which shattered rural communities. Linked to a policy of cultural nationalism and strict codes of censorship, this included the passing of the Public Dance Halls Act of 1935 which sought to restrain jazz music and modern dancing. Only those with a licence could now stage public events and the priesthood now took command, running céilí dances (which involved no physical contact) in village halls. This marked the beginning of the céilí band era as, being barred from playing anywhere else publicly for dancing, musicians grouped together (adding non-traditional components such as the piano, drums and saxophone). Famously described by Seán Ó Riada as "a rhythmic but meaningless noise with as much relation to music as the buzzing of a bluebottle in an upturned jamjar", céilí bands remained a remarkable presence in Ireland until decline set in during the 1960s.

While this period saw the virtual end of the outdoor (known as "crossroads") dance along with the house dance, it also seriously undermined the tradition of playing solo and unaccompanied in public, though a dwindling number of travelling musicians, such as the uilleann pipers **Johnny** and **Felix Doran**, continued to do so.

The field collectors

During the 1940s, the decline in rural life had become so marked, despite a state culture still defined in such terms, that serious efforts were made to record the lingering remnants. From 1942, the uilleann piper and singer, **Séamus Ennis** was employed by the Irish Folklore Commission to travel the countryside, transcribing as many tunes and songs as he could find. More than 2000 such pieces entered the Commission's archives by the time Ennis moved on to Radio Éireann where he instigated a similar process, though this time recording music for transmission. In the same year, the BBC had begun a similar undertaking in Northern Ireland and Ennis was to join the organization for a spell of seven years in 1951, during which time a massive body of field recordings was collected from around the British Isles, some of

Séamus Ennis and Jean Ritchie, 1952

17

which were broadcast on the radio programme, *As I Roved Out*. Irish radio had its own successful shows too during this period, most notably *Ceolta Tíre* and *A Job of Journeywork*, two weekly shows presented by **Ciarán MacMathuna** from the mid-1950s until 1970.

The Fleadh Cheoil

Equally of lasting importance was the establishment of Cumann Ceoltóirí Éireann (The Society of Irish Musicians) in October, 1951, following the mounting of a successful musical gathering earlier that Summer in Mullingar. The organization changed its name the following year to **Comhaltas Ceoltóirí Éireann** (The Association of Irish Musicians), mounting the first **Fleadh Cheoil** (Festival of Music) that year in Monaghan town. From the outset this enabled musicians to come together to play and listen to traditional music and established competitions (and standards for judging) in a range of instrumental, song and dance categories. During the 1960s, these annual events attained such popularity (70,000 people are thought to have attended the 1966 Fleadh in Boyle) and caused much controversy regarding the behaviour of the crowd that subsequent gatherings were moved as far away from Dublin as possible, beginning at Listowel in 1970 and moving on later to further outposts, such as Buncrana. The Fleadh and its preceding music school, Sceoil Eigse, retains its popularity today, involving competitors from all thirty-two counties as well as the UK and US, while CCÉ has remained one of the driving forces behind traditional music's preservation.

Elsewhere, from the late 1940s onwards, the public house had become the major focus for traditional Irish music in London and other British cities, where migrant labourers gathered after work and at weekends to swap yarns and play tunes. Many major names spent temporary or longer sojourns in England's capital and, as emigration became even more intense during the 1950s, the Irish pubs and clubs developed a mighty musical influence. From this period onwards, specialist record labels, such as Topic, began recording traditional musicians and releasing a significant body of material using the new vinyl LP format which had recently emerged. Many of these recordings made their way back to Ireland and joined releases from the Gael-Linn label on the shelves of Irish homes.

The revival years

As ever, events in America were to have an extensive impact. The 1950s had seen the emergence of a folk revival linked to a new political radicalism, inspired by the singer Woody Guthrie's *Dust Bowl Ballads*. Figures such as Joan Baez, Pete Seeger and a youthful Bob Dylan took up Guthrie's mantle and the coffee houses of New York's Greenwich Village became their home from home. Three brothers from Carrick-on-Suir (Tom, Pat and Liam Clancy) joined forces with the Armagh singer Tommy Makem to record **The Rising of the Moon** in 1959, an album of Republican rebel songs. Their playing might have been rudimentary, but their trademark Aran sweaters and songs delivered with zestful exuberance found a huge following in the US and struck a resonant chord when they returned home to tour Ireland.

The folk and ballad revival that ensued dominated the Irish music scene in the 1960s, drawing strength too from a folk-song movement which had similarly emerged in the UK. Ever available to spot a commercial opportunity, Irish publicans opened their doors to the host of sweater-clad imitators who followed in the Clancys' and Makem's wake. However, the most illustrious group to appear, **The Dubliners**, adopted a far more streetwise image based on a hard-drinking, devil take the hindmost attitude. While the ballad boom was relatively short-lived, a number of other significant figures arrived on the music scene during the 1960s, including **Finbar** and **Eddie Furey** and groups such as **Sweeney's Men** and **The Johnstons** all of whom successfully blended folk songs and ballads.

Breandán Breathnach

Of enduring importance was the work of the later twentieth century's most significant collector and musicologist, Breandán Breathnach (1912–85). A Dubliner with a passion for traditional music, who spent his working life as a civil servant, Breathnach devised his own code for analysing the various forms of traditional music. Transcribing tunes from fellow musicians (and paying others, such as Seán Keane, a future member of The Chieftains, two shillings a time for additional transcriptions), Breathnach was able to establish the identity of previously unpublished melodies. Gathering this material, the first volume of his *Ceol Rince na hÉireann* appeared in 1963. Two others followed during his own lifetime and another two have subsequently been compiled from his researches. His book *Folk Music and Dances of Ireland* (see p.590), and its accompanying recording of musical examples, remains a landmark in traditional music's history, while his activities, such as his role in the founding of Na Píobairí Uilleann (the uilleann pipers' organization) in 1968, has ensured lasting recognition for his unswerving dedication to the tradition. Breathnach's traditional music journal, *Ceol*, which he first published in 1963, also formed a major forum for debate and provided much valued information on virtually every conceivable facet of the music until it ceased publication with his death in 1985.

If ensemble playing had now become the norm amongst folkies, then similar developments in traditional music had been initiated by **Séan Ó Riada** who first experimented with traditional forms in his soundtrack for the 1959 film *Mise Éire*. Further studies led him to devise "an ideal type of Céilí Band or orchestra". Working as musical director at the Abbey Theatre, he gathered together musicians from Dublin's growing pool of traditional musicians to form the group **Ceoltóirí Chualann** to accompany the play *The Honey Spike*. The format evolved around small groups of instruments as various as the harpsichord, uilleann pipes, fiddles, flute and – unprecedentedly – the bodhrán (an Irish frame drum). Ó Riada's arrangements were greeted with some acclaim, especially amongst the concert-going middle classes accustomed to formal settings. His own radio series, *Our Musical Heritage*, reached a broader audience and his formation of a local choir in his new home in the West Cork Gaeltacht of Cúil Aodha saw him writing and arranging material based on the sean-nós singing tradition.

Some of the members of Ceoltóirí Chualann formed together in 1963 as **The Chieftains** and, in part inspired by Ó Riada's principles, recorded for the recently established Claddagh label, initiating a process which eventually saw the band garnering huge international success and acclaim as Ireland's most illustrious traditional group.

From the 1970s to Riverdance

First and foremost amongst the new traditional groups which dominated Ireland's musical scene in the 1970s was **Planxty**, followed closely by **The Bothy Band** and **De Dannan**. The rock band **Horslips'** achieved some acclaim for its conceptual experimentations in Celtic mythology, while the idea of blending acoustic and electric instruments took a major leap forwards with **Moving Hearts** (formed by the Planxty backbone of **Christy Moore** and **Dónal Lunny**). **The Pogues**, and their compelling, raucous music, emerged from the wreckage of the London punk scene in the early 1980s while, in complete contrast, the Donegal band **Clannad** transformed itself from a jazz-influenced folk band to pioneers of the sound described in some quarters as "Celtic hush" music. The increasing "respectability" of traditional music in other circles was reinforced by the appearance in 1988 of **Irish Heartbeat**, by the Belfast legend, **Van Morrison**, and The Chieftains. Groups have continued to dominate traditional music since the 1990s and many musicians also prefer to share their music via the ensemble format, most notably, the button accordionist, **Sharon Shannon**.

In determining the cause of the recent resurgence of interest in traditional music some point the finger determinedly at the *Riverdance* phenomenon, the step-dancing spectacular which began as an interlude during the 1994 Eurovision Song Contest and developed into a full-scale international hit show, featuring the dancers **Jean Butler** and **Michael Flatley** with music penned by **Bill Whelan**. That might alone explain a revival in step dancing, but set dancing had already been rejuvenated for a while in Clare in the 1980s. What is certainly true of Ireland is that its enormous economic expansion in the 1990s and the country's wholehearted emergence as a European state was characterized by immigration rather than its opposite.

Accompanying this new national confidence came a more relaxed attitude towards the past and a process of rediscovery. Early generations of city dwellers, especially those arrived from the country, had rejected their rural past, including traditional music. Their children now felt more at ease with a process of rediscovery that coincided with growing international interest in world and roots music. For the first time in its long life, Irish traditional music had become hip.

Forms
and styles

"They played every kind of music – they didn't care, as long as it was a good tune."

Mairéad Ní Mhaonaigh

Song traditions

I reland has many song traditions. Indeed, until recent times every area had its own singers and a local popular song repertoire. It is convenient to consider two broad traditions, defined by the language of the song, Irish or English. It is also worth drawing attention to the curious hybrid known as the macaronic song. Still sung today – notably by Altan's **Mairéad Ní Mhaonaigh** – these are bilingual songs in Irish and English which achieved a degree of popularity during the nineteenth century, emerging at a time when a knowledge of English was seen as increasing one's employment opportunities.

Sean-nós

The oldest form of singing in Ireland is known as sean-nós, a term literally meaning "old-style". It was so applied by The Gaelic League (at a time when the survival of such singing was considerably endangered) to stress its inherent links with the past and to distinguish the form from the stronger, but younger English-language song tradition. As many have observed, the term is something of a misnomer since the unbroken process of transference from one generation to another has ensured that the tradition is both youthful and ancient.

In the simplest of terms, sean-nós consists of (mostly) unaccompanied singing in Irish and the tradition is strongest in those areas of the country where the Irish language has survived as a living tongue (the Gaeltacht areas). Its form and melodies are intrinsically linked to the natural rhythms of the language (and variations in dialect) and to the essential elements of Gaelic poetry, its own metrical shapes and rhythms.

The origins of sean-nós are obscure. Some suggest that the tradition dates back to the bardic tradition which disappeared in the seventeenth century with the demise of the old Gaelic order. Others point to the emergence of popular Irish love-poetry, linked to similar forms in continental Europe, in that same century, while a more far-reaching analysis has suggested strong correlations between the Irish tradition and singing in North Africa and Moorish-occupied Spain.

Whatever the case, there is no doubting that this beautiful, complex form of singing draws much of its material from Gaelic poetry written in the eighteenth and nineteenth centuries by poets such as **Antaine Raifteraí** (1784–1835) whose pieces covered three of the great (and alliterative) subjects of sean-nós singing – love, loss and longing. However, there are many other topics in the typical singer's repertoire, not least humour and sex. Love, however, in its many varied forms, is the major element and forms the basis for many of the "big songs" (such as "Úna Bhán" or "Bean an Fhir Rua") which can be found throughout the Gaeltacht areas.

The songs are concerned with emotions, rather than telling a story, and often employ extremely vivid imagery. Equally, the airs themselves are wonderfully ethereal and allow a great deal of expressive licence on the part of the singer. Different regions have their own styles. Connemara singers are reckoned to employ more embellishments and operate within a narrower vocal range whereas, conversely, Munster singers tend to adopt a broader range while approaching a simpler melodic form. The Donegal style sees more emphasis on rhythmic regularity. One common element, however, is the practice of saying, rather than singing, the last line of a song to indicate completion.

Performance conventions can also vary. Some singers prefer undivided attention from their audience while others enjoy the odd interjected vocal encouragement or are happy for others to join in for parts of the song. Some sit, while others stand, though most remain still throughout a song, rarely employing any gesture or facial expression to emphasise a phrase. In Connemara, a singer's hand may often be held to show support. While some singers may make eye contact with their audience, others may close their eyes completely and, in some extreme cases, stress their detachment by turning away from the spectators.

Singing in English

Singing in English has less intensity than sean-nós but a far greater range of subject matter. Though unaccompanied singing in English can still be heard in pubs and specialist clubs, songs are usually backed by guitar or bouzouki or heard within an ensemble setting. The most common song form is the narrative ballad, though sea shanties are undergoing a small revival along the south coast and it is always possible to hear a "come-all-ye" anywhere in the island. This last type of song always begins with the words "Come all ye" followed by whoever the original songwriter was addressing (e.g "fair maidens") followed by a moral tale of downfall.

Mostly penned by Irish writers, the range of ballads spans more than three hundred years of song. Emigration songs, such as "Paddy's Green Shamrock Shore", form a substantial component while the rebel songs, celebrating Irish resistance and freedom remain popular. Equally, there is a large body of Loyalist (or Orange Order) songs in Northern Ireland commemorating famous events in the Protestant community's history, such as "The Crimson Banner" (also known as "No Surrender").

Many comic and satirical songs exist, like "The Charladies' Ball" or "The Humours of Whiskey", while more modern versions, such as "The Knock Song" or "Lisdoonvarna", feature in the repertoire of **Christy Moore**. Indeed, the place of song in Irish life is no better exemplified than by the sight of an entire audience singing along at one of Christy's gigs and knowing all the words. Less tongue in cheek, are the songs celebrating places, such as "In Praise of the City of Mullingar".

Love and courtship is another popular theme, such as the North Derry ballad "Sarah Jane" in the great **Eddie Butcher**'s repertoire. Indeed, while most rural regions still, to some extent, have their own local favourites, the cities have spawned a huge number of songs too. The most well-known of the Dublin "street songs" is, of course, "Molly Malone", while Cork city has a notable songwriting tradition, whose continued vitality can be heard on **Jimmy Crowley**'s excellent compilation **Sex Sca and Sedition** (see p.49).

Finally, on a more frivolous note, there are a number of songs which celebrate sporting achievement, not least hurling and Gaelic Football, though Association Football gets a look in with another renowned song from the Christy Moore repertoire, "Joxer Goes to Stuttgart".

Tunes

At the last count, there were more than seven thousand known Irish tunes. Many others have also been lost long ago although, in compensation, new compositions appear daily. As a living, oral tradition the number of tunes actually in circulation expands and contracts according to taste and popularity, though the work of the **Irish Traditional Music Archive** (see p.588) has ensured that many long dormant tunes are once again available to musicians.

A musician's repertoire is determined by social circumstances, personal selection and emulation of others and usually consists of several hundred tunes, though many may linger in the memory's recesses until prompted into action. Regional repertoires are a vital ingredient, but equally important are the tunes played at local sessions which musicians will need to know, if they wish to participate. Music may also be learned from the radio or recordings, and be an especial influence if the player admires a particular musician.

The naming of traditional tunes represents an informal, oral system of cataloguing and is by no means an exact science. As most tunes are learned from other musicians, whether in person or from recordings, the name will usually be passed on too. Like any form of oral communication, tune titles may be misheard, misspelt, misunderstood (as in "Ask My Father"), misremembered or even completely forgotten. In consequence, the same tune may be known to different musicians by different names. The hornpipe "The Top of the Morning", for instance, is also called "Come Down and Let Me in" and "Miss Flynn". Of course, many well-known tunes do not possess such variation while a huge number may be named after their composer or player with whom they are most associated, eg "Matt

Molloy's", "Denis Murphy's". Those where no title is known are simply described as "gan ainm" (lit. without name).

Ornamentation

A tune's melody is just a launch pad for individual expression. Through the subtleties of ornamentation and variation, a musician creates a personal rendition, exploring the capabilities of the instrument and the boundaries of his or her imagination. The most common techniques employed are the triplet (an up or down run of three adjacent notes) and the roll (usually involving the insertion of "grace notes" in an up then down melodic pattern). Uilleann pipers have other forms of ornamentation, including popping (stressing a note by lifting the chanter from the knee) and the cran (a staccato effect on the chanter's low D note).

Breandán Breathnach has argued that such individual expression was the defining component of traditional music. Many believe that this tradition of solo expression has been seriously undermined during the twentieth century, first via the céilí bands and later the groups and sessions which emerged from the 1960s onwards. However, while some of the poorer céilí bands may have adopted a melodic rigidity, there is still much scope for manoeuvre. Within these settings the tune functions as a mere footpath and the musicians are free to roam around the adjoining countryside as they please.

Reels

Tastes change and regional variations continue to bear influence, but easily the most common tune form played today is the **reel**, thought to have arrived in Ireland from Scotland towards the end of the eighteenth century. Played in 4/4 time, reels usually consist of two segments (each eight bars or measures), though shorter versions were prevalent in South Leitrim. The first segment is played and then repeated, followed by a similar reiterated rendition of the second segment. This complete melody will then be played again and maybe even a third time before the musicians move on to a new reel and repeat the process. Reels were originally played to accompany the step-dance of the same name and a well-known tune such as "Miss McLeod's" (derived from the Scottish "The Campbells Are Coming") features characteristic accents on the first and third beats.

Jigs

Second in popularity to reels, jigs, which have been around since the seventeenth century, come in a variety of time signatures. The most common is the **double jig**, played in 6/8 time, with each bar containing two groups of three quavers or eighth notes (da-da-da da-da-da). One of the most famous is "The Irishwoman" (sometimes called "The Irish Washerwoman") which was often used to introduce Irish performers on the British or American variety stage. Most jigs follow the same form as reels, though some may have several parts (for instance, "Wise Nora" consists of eighty bars).

A less common form is the **single jig**, a much more bouncy affair, which is typified by a crotchet or quarter note followed by a quaver (dah-da) and may be played in either 6/8 (eg "Ask My Father") or 12/8 ("With All My Heart"). Next up is the **slip jig** (sometimes known as the **hop jig**) rendered in 9/8 time of which probably the most well-known is "Last Night's Fun". Lying between single and double jigs, slip jigs usually combine the rhythmic patterns of both. Last, the **slide** is associated with the music of Sliabh Luachra and the dancing of sets and is essentially a faster version of the single jig. Its most renowned exponent was Pádraig O'Keeffe from whom one of the most familiar slides takes its name.

Hornpipes

Forever associated with sailors, the **hornpipe** arrived from England in the latter half of the eighteenth century and became popular with dancing masters as a means of demonstrating their solo skills. Played at a steady 4/4 time, slower than reels, a hornpipe like "The Rights of Man", stresses the first and third beat and each part ends with a pattern of three heavily accentuated notes (dah-dah-dah).

Marches

Marches derived from the need to ensure that an army travelled at speed and in good spirits, and quick marches are an almost universal part of the Western musical tradition. For a time popular with céilí bands, marches are usually written in duple time (2/4). They are nowadays usually only heard accompanying parades in Northern Ireland where fife and drum bands adapt many melodies to the rhythm of tramping feet.

Set Dances

Set or **long dances** are sometimes performed to tunes which fall outside the categories above, though may involve certain of their elements. Probably, the most famous of these is "The Blackbird" (which is in some ways similar to the single jig). A significant number bear titles connected to historical events and may have been originally written in commemoration (though not necessarily at the same time), such as "The Bridge of Athlone" (which combines a march and double jig) or "Bonaparte's Retreat".

Other dance tunes

A number of other dances of European origin appear in the traditional repertoire. These include the **polka** (in 2/4 time), which originated in Bohemia in the early nineteenth century and is still popular in the southwestern counties of Cork, Kerry and Limerick, especially the Sliabh Luachra area. The **waltz**, a 3/4 dance of disputed French or German origin, is less common though still heard at old-time dances where tunes may be appropriated from popular songs such as "Molly Malone". Visitors to Donegal may encounter another 3/4 dance tune, the **mazurka**, where the second beat of each bar is stressed. Usually these bear the name of the associated fiddler, such as "James Byrne's" or the name of a place, eg "The Kilcar Mazurka". Donegal fiddlers also carry a repertoire of tunes which reached the county via Scotland and are often variants of the 4/4 German dance, the **Schottische**. In Scotland such dances were denoted "Highland Schottisches", the first word being dropped on adaptation to the Donegal style. The **highland**, accentuating the first beat, is played at a much easier pace than the reel, and players might often indeed convert reels to this format to accompany dancing. A variant of the Schottische is the **German**, played at a similar pace to the hornpipe, often with the third and fourth beats stressed. Scotland was also the source for the **strathspey**, though the Donegal version was not actually danced and usually has a quicker, jerky feel (as shown by the repertoires of John Doherty or Tommy Peoples) incorporating plenty of rapid triplets.

Sessions

Despite their informal, sometimes lackadaisical appearance, the majority of sessions are prearranged regular events for which at least one of the participants is paid to attend. Of course, there are many exceptions, like sessions which spring up at any time or place during a fleadh or summer school, but most take place in a pub as part of the publican's entertainment schedule.

When and where sessions began is open to debate. Some suggest the practice first emerged among groups of emigrant musicians in the US while others point to those pubs in North London frequented by the Irish where music began to be played from the late 1940s onwards. Whatever the case, the session, as we now know it, is intrinsically linked to the 1960s musical revival and the rise of the pub as a significant focus for Irish community life.

Sessions may simply consist of a fiddler and accompanist or, conversely, be grandiose celebratory occasions. Unless the pub owner has decreed otherwise, few sessions begin before 9.30pm and, in summer, sometimes much later. A session's length depends on the musicians' enthusiasm, enjoyment and numbers, local licensing laws and the diligence of the police in their enforcement.

No matter how busy the pub may be, the musicians' seats are sacrosanct, even when one remains empty all night. Newcomers wait until invited before participating, though additional guitarists, bouzouki and bodhrán players are best advised to seek an alternative venue unless they can arrange to take turns with existing session members. If you want to play, are sufficiently competent and have a broad repertoire, then an enquiry to the bar staff or one of the musicians should determine whether your participation is welcome.

Usually, sessions are led by a "senior" player, who will select the tunes played and determine the changes, though this mantle may be passed on during a session, especially if someone has a new tune they wish to try. Changes from one tune to the next are indicated by a complex range of bodily movements and gestures, such as a nod by a fiddler or the wild eye movements of a flute player. Solo performances are by invitation only, as in "Come on, Joanie, give us a song".

Newcomers to sessions may be puzzled by the audience. Put simply, a pub where the listeners are all sitting in silent, entranced attention is likely to be inhabited only by tourists, though solo singers usually do receive undivided attention for the duration of the song and some rare "listening" musicians do expect to be heard. Otherwise, applause when it comes at the end of a set of tunes will be brief, though playing may be punctuated by appreciative shouts or whoops of encouragement. As to the best form of appreciation, the advice offered by Ciaran Carson in *Irish Traditional Music* still applies. Ask the bar staff to set up a round of drinks for the musicians – after all, it will still cost you less than a ticket for *Riverdance*.

Finally, most musicians do not like being photographed or videoed without permission and it is not unknown for stout to be "accidentally" spilled on tape recorders placed on the musicians' table by unwitting musical tourists.

Slow Airs

Much beloved by uilleann pipers and flute players in particular, **slow airs** offer the greatest opportunity for individual expression and indeed are virtually always played solo. Unlike dance music, where ornamentation is the norm, a player's tone defines the quality of the rendition. Since slow airs are often derived from elegiac or melancholic songs and laments (though many independent melodies exist), the aim is to replicate the mood of the song. On completing the air, some players sometimes break straight into a dance tune.

Planxties

Largely associated with the harper and composer, Turlough Carolan, a **planxty** was a tune written in honour of a patron and, consequently, bears the benefactor's name. The origins of the word "planxty" itself, are somewhat cloudy. Some authorities have suggested that it derives from the Irish word for "health" (sláinte, pronounced slon-cha) but it also bears a remarkable phonetic similarity to the simple English "thanks to" when pronounced in an Irish accent.

Programme pieces

A few rare pieces of traditional music exist which actually aim to be descriptive. The most well-known of these is "The Fox Chase", sometimes called "The Fox Hunt" or "The Hounds After the Hare". Seeking to replicate the sounds of the hunt, this often features in the repertoires of uilleann pipers, who use the regulators to simulate baying, but was also part of the repertoire of the Doherty family of fiddlers from Donegal.

musicians

Introduction

T he strength of Ireland's musical tradition is exemplified in the hundreds of individual entries for singers, instrumentalists and groups that form this directory of musicians. Not surprisingly, the native Irish constitute the bulk of these entries, but the impact of the Irish diaspora is represented by many entries for the sons and daughters of Irish emigrants in countries as far-flung as Australia, New Zealand, England, the US and Canada. While the criteria for entry are firmly founded on a combination of fame and ability, we have also been keen to ensure that the music listed is readily available worldwide. All the artists included have been significantly involved with Irish traditional music at some point in their careers. Inevitably, there are borderline cases. Thus **Van Morrison**, who identifies an essential Irish quality in his music and has famously collaborated with **The Chieftains**, is in but **Sinéad O'Connor** is not – even though her vocal style owes much to traditional music. Nor do we find room for those great Irish tenors, **John McCormack**, **Josef Locke** and **Frank Patterson**, who included sentimental ballads in their repertoire. The emphasis has been firmly placed on the recorded aspect of Irish music which has meant no individual entries for some of Ireland's most illustrious, but sadly unrecorded, musicians from the past.

As far as possible, individuals have been categorized either as singers or by the instrument with which they are most commonly associated, though, in some cases, we have drawn together related musicians in our "Families" section. Irish musicians are notoriously versatile, so if you cannot find who you are looking for in one instrumental section, try another.

37

The vast majority of traditional singers and instrumentalists are not full-time players. Indeed, many of those who are lucky enough to be so may be working the circuit of ersatz Irish pubs and other venues in continental Europe or employed to sing ballads in an American bar. Despite its many record labels and venues, Ireland's population is too small to support a large caste of professional musicians and only the elite make any real money, though to do so they need to tour extensively and generate success in the American and Japanese markets. Tourism does bring benefits, but mainly to Dublin and the popular destinations in the West of Ireland. So most musicians continue to play for fun and retain their day jobs. What is astonishing, however, is the overall quality of singing and musicianship and you're just as likely to see a virtuoso performance in the local pub as in one of the major venues.

In terms of record production, Ireland is undergoing a boom comparable only to the late 1970s punk explosion in the UK. The

Recommended releases

Virtually every entry in the book includes at least one recommended album. The overwhelming majority are compact discs, while some are in cassette format. In a few extraordinary cases, where notable albums have not been reissued, the original vinyl LP has been referenced. In all cases for CDs and cassettes, the label referenced is that of the record company currently releasing the album in Ireland (licensing deals may mean that the release appears on a different label in the US or Canada). The original label is provided for LPs. In order to provide a historical reference, the date referred to in each recommendation is the original date of the recording's release (or a range of such dates in the case of compilations) or the original date of a field recording.

introduction of CD writers and their gradual fall in price means that (like the abundance of punk 7" singles) anyone can produce their own release at relatively low cost. Though Ireland's majors continue to issue exceptionally high-quality recordings, the bulk of new releases over the last couple of years have been self-produced and issued on the performers' own labels. The timelessness of much of the music they offer means that it does not really matter if sales are slow, just stick a copy behind the bar where you play and wait.

Compilation Albums and Series

The Irish music market has been plagued by a plethora of compilation albums in recent years, including many of dubious quality. Virtually any album with the word Celtic, Gaelic, ancient, soul, spirit or roots in the title should be viewed with suspicion. The following are all either general compilations of dance music or a mixture of music and song. You'll find recommended collections of singers and instrumentalists in their appropriate sections.

An instant Irish record collection

For a historical and comprehensive introduction, the Globestyle series cannot be surpassed. Ron Kavana's trawl through the Topic label's extensive archive produced eight themed collections. Those on uilleann piping, the Irish in London, the music of Sliabh Luachra and the song tradition are described elsewhere. As a good starting point **Treasure of My Heart** introduces the whole series, while **I'm**

Leaving Tipperary celebrates the great Irish-American recording era of the 1920s and 1930s. The two general collections are **Happy to Meet, Sorry to Part** which focuses on recordings from the 1960s and 1970s (and features major figures such as Willie Clancy, John Doherty and Séamus Ennis) and **A Living Thing** which covers a similar period but includes leading lights from subsequent generations, such as Patrick Street, Cathal McConnell and Kavana himself.

⊙ Treasure of My Heart	Globestyle, 1920s–90s

This impeccable introduction offers a plenitude of music spanning eight decades.

⊙ I'm Leaving Tipperary	Globestyle, 1920s–30s

Despite the absence of fiddler Michael Coleman, this is a remarkable taster of a still influential era.

⊙ Happy to Meet, Sorry to Part	Globestyle, 1967–84

Largely 1970s-based introduction to another classic era of Irish recordings.

⊙ A Living Thing	Globestyle, 1963–93

More stunning samples from the Topic archive, focused on new developments, but with the light still shining bright.

The 78s Era

Ron Kavana also compiled the excellent-value four-CD **Farewell to Ireland** set from Proper Records, a stupendous, bargain-priced introduction to classic recordings from the 78s era which includes many famous names plus obscure musicians who recorded under such names as "The 5th Avenue Busman" and "The Singing Insuranceman". Others to look out for from this period include Topic's **Irish Dance Music** and its companion **Past Masters of Irish Dance Music** (both

of which have some real rarities) and Rounder's **From Galway to Dublin** featuring one of fiddler Neillidh Boyle's few recordings and the wonderfully named Murty Rabbett singing "Molly Durkin". Moving on to the 1950s, one essential recording is Saydisc's **Traditional Dance Music of Ireland**, collated from Peter Kennedy's Folktrax recordings, containing a mixture of Irish and London tapes, including the marvellous flute player Paddy Taylor.

⊙ Farewell to Ireland — Proper Records, 1920s–30s

A stupendous (and budget-priced) boxed set of classic Irish-American recordings

⊙ Irish Dance Music — Topic, 1920s–50s

⊙ Past Masters of Irish Dance Music — Topic, 1920s–50s

Two excellent collections from the 78s era.

⊙ From Galway to Dublin — Rounder, 1926–50s

Another classic compilation worth acquiring simply for the Neillidh Boyle track.

⊙ Traditional Dance Music of Ireland — Saydisc, 1950s

A fabulous collection from Peter Kennedy's field recordings.

Vinyl times but CD reissues

Serious record companies began operating in Ireland during the 1950s and 1960s and two of the grandest compilations come from Claddagh and Gael-Linn (the latter in conjunction with Hummingbird). The two-disc **Claddagh's Choice** is an exemplary archive collection running from a 1960 recording of uilleann piper Leo Rowsome up to the mid-1990s and musicians such as the concertina player, Mary Mac Namara. Gael-Linn and Hummingbird's **Ór** runs right through from Seán Ó Riada and Ceoltóirí Chualann to the Bumblebees, while not forgetting classic music from piper

Paddy Keenan and one of Ireland's greatest song interpreters, Frank Harte. **Folk Music and Dances of Ireland** (issued to accompany Breandán Breathnach's book of the same name – see p.590) is a marvellous demonstration of the breadth of traditional music from the plaintive voice of Seán 'ac Dhonncha to the magical piping of Pat Mitchell. One relative oddity from this era which should not be ignored is the magical **The Lark in the Clear Air: Irish Traditional Music Played on Small Instruments**, originally recorded in 1974, and featuring piccolo, whistle, flute, spoons and mouth organ plus a unique jew's harp trio!

⊙ Claddagh's Choice	Claddagh, 1960–95

Not just an introduction to the label, but a glorious summation of its role in releasing many of Irish music's classic albums.

⊙ Ór	Gael-Linn/Hummingbird, 1969–97

From Ó Riada and Ceoltóirí Chualann to Dónal Lunny's Coolfin, this makes a splendid entry point into Ireland's music.

⊙ Folk Music and Dances of Ireland	Ossian Publications, 1971

The companion to Breandán Breathnach's book of the same name is also an excellent introduction to traditional music.

⊙ The Lark in the Clear Air	Ossian Publications, 1974

Small instruments rule on this unique and thoroughly enjoyable album.

The last decade

The compilation industry really took off in the 1990s with a welter of releases often simultaneously containing some of the same tracks. There are simply too many to list, but here are two outstanding collations. Dónal Lunny's **Sult**, commissioned for the Irish language TV station TnaG (now TG4) and containing a host of major names (though Mark Knopfler's execrable rendition of "Raglan Road" is guaranteed to send Patrick Kavanagh's corpse a-spinning). Also of great interest is the illustrious bodhrán and assorted percussion player Tommy Hayes's compilation, **Síol**, supporting the cause of ecological biodiversity, and featuring a number of new recordings, including the fiddler Martin Hayes and singer Karan Casey.

⊙ Sult	Hummingbird, 1996

Lunny and the Sult Houseband provide the bedrock for stars such as Sharon Shannon, Matt Molloy and Liam O'Flynn.

◉ **Síol**   Magherabaun Records, 2000

A more than worthy cause and a tremendous collection from some of today's finest musicians.

Live compilations

Lovers of live recordings should head for **Ceol na hÉireann**, a collection of rare live cuts from RTÉ's gargantuan archive. Among the gems are the legendary Castle Céilí band from 1964, an early Planxty recording of "The Raggle Taggle Gipsy", Joe Cooley taking a break from the US in 1963, a classic Paul Brady rendition of "Arthur McBride" and John and Simon Doherty duetting on "The Pigeon on the Gate". Others to hunt down include **Sessions from the Hearth**, the brainchild of Kerry guitarist Benny O'Carroll who brought musicians from all over the country to a fun-packed evening at Tralee's National Folk Theatre. A worthy cause is the restoration of the Crosskeys Inn, one of Northern Ireland's major session pubs, which burned down in 2000. **Live in the Kitchen** features a host of local musicians, including ex-members of Déanta, plus songs from Len Graham. Saving the best till the very end, the spirit of youth is captured on **Cumar**, the name of an annual week-long school for young people centred on the arts and culture of the Gaeltacht regions. The

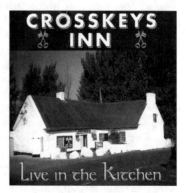

disc gathers nineteen of the singers and instrumentalists who sang or played during the school's concerts and is brim-full with a stupendous range of talent.

⊙ Ceol na hÉireann — RTÉ, 1956–77

A staggering selection from RTÉ's archives, includes tracks rarer than a Finn Harps' away win.

⊙ Sessions from the Hearth — own label, 1998

The combination of ace instrumentalists with singers of the calibre of Deirdre Scanlan and Seán Garvey is predictably compelling.

⊙ Crosskeys Inn: Live in the Kitchen — Crosskeys Inn Heritage Trust, 2000

Some of the cream of the North's musicians feature on this fund-raising venture (available from *www.crosskeys.clara.net*).

⊙ Cumar — Cló Iar-Chonnachta, 2000

Should be number one on your shopping list, if you need reassuring about the tradition's future.

Controversy

Bringing It All Back Home accompanied the much-debated BBC TV series (see p.544) and many of its 37 tracks (spread over two CDs or three LPs) continue to raise eyebrows. What are we to make of The Everly Brothers singing "Rose Connolly" to the accompaniment of Liam O'Flynn's uilleann pipes or a duet between Elvis Costello and Mary Coughlan? Well, as much as we want to and there's plenty here to tickle the senses. 1995's even more controversial **A River of Sound** (see p.544) charted the "changing course of Irish Traditional Music", but, whatever your view, it's worth acquiring simply for the mind-boggling duet between Altan's Ciarán Tourish and Dermot Byrne on "Johnny Doherty's" which doesn't just raise the rafters as suggest the need for a new roof!

⊙ **Bringing It All Back Home**   Hummingbird, 1991

Two remarkable discs. chock-full of classic renditions and intriguing collaborations.

⊙ **A River of Sound**   Virgin, 1995

More in the same vein from Ireland's most controversial traditional music series.

Regional compilations

Most local compilations emanate from the Western coastline. From the far southwest comes **Beauty an Oíleáin**, a lavish collection of music and song from the now-deserted Blasket Islands off the Dingle Peninsula, Co. Kerry. This marvellous collection features former islanders and their descendants, recorded between 1957 and 1991, and offers a tantalizing view of the importance of music on the Blaskets. Clare is well-represented by the tremendous **Farewell to Lissycasey**, virtually a county "greatest hits" compilation, including Willie Clancy, the Tulla CB, Bobby Gardiner and singer Siney Crotty (with whom the title song was always associated). Thanks to the Coleman Heritage Centre in Gurteen, Co. Sligo has produced several fine compilations the latest of which, **The Mountain Road**, is a collection of tunes popular in the south of the county and featuring a host of flute players and fiddlers. For compilations covering Donegal fiddle music, Irish musicians in London, and Sliabh Luachra see pp.308–311, pp.346–349 and pp.355–358 respectively.

⊙ Beauty an Oíleáin   Claddagh, 1955–91

Superbly-packaged homage to the music and song of the Blasket Islands.

⊙ Farewell to Lissycasey   Ossian Publications, 1960s–90s

A splendid introduction to the music of Co. Clare.

⊙ The Mountain Road   Coleman Heritage Centre, 1999

One of the best compilations of the last decade, whisking the listener straight to Gurteen and the sound of South Sligo.

Singers

This section features some of the greatest names in traditional and folk singing, including those who subsequently crossed over into MOR or rock genres. Ireland is also renowned for its contemporary singer-songwriters and a fair few of these are present here, demonstrating yet another diverging strand in the history of Irish song.

The origins and nature of the form of unaccompanied singing in the Irish language known as sean-nós are outlined on p.23. Many sean-nós recordings were produced in a studio and, therefore, lack the essential empathy of an audience. However, there are a number of highly-recommendable sean-nós compilations available, commencing with **Amhráin ar an Sean-Nós**, drawn from the RTÉ archives, which covers singers from all the main Gaeltacht areas, and Raidió na Gaeltachta's **Buaiteoirí Chorn Uí Riada**, showcasing all the winners of the prestigious annual singing competition between 1972 and 1996. Two excellent regional compilations are **Glór Mhaigh Eo**, focusing on the less well-known Mayo song tradition, and **Seoda – Sean-Nois as Tír Chonaill**, featuring some of the most prestigious Donegal singers.

Lilting (or diddling), which uses nonsense syllables to carry a tune, has been around for as long as musicians have conversed about melodies or no instruments were available for dance accompaniment. Songs also include such elements, especially in choruses, and the best exploration of lilting's range is the deeply informative and beautifully presented collection **Celtic Mouth Music**. The lilting theme is continued in **Hurry the Jug**, which also includes some of **Tom Lenihan**'s sto-

ries, and songs from the Ulster and sean-nós traditions, plus the unjustly forgotten **John Reilly** from Co. Leitrim. **Traditional Songs of Ireland** contains a wealth of field recordings from the 1950s, including a rare Donegal keening song. The folk and ballad boom of the 1960s continues to generate a staggering number of compilations of which the most comprehensive is **Folk Heroes**. Moving on to more modern times, the best-selling **A Woman's Heart** spawned its own follow-up album and a host of other collections (whose titles often include the words "Celtic" and "Women"). One collection definitely worth looking out for is **Celtic Voices** which draws on material from Gael-Linn's back catalogue. Lastly, the enduring strength of the Cork ballad tradition is well represented by **Sex Sca and Sedition**, a collection of acutely-penned (and often very funny) songs from the county's singers.

⊙ **Amhráin ar an Sean-Nós** RTÉ, 1948–65

Includes a rare recording of Aodh Ó Domhnaill and a call-and-response rendition of "Cúnla" between Joe Heaney and Séamus Ennis.

⊙ **Buaiteoirí Chorn Uí Riada** Raidió na Gaeltachta, 1972–96

Double-CD featuring all sixteen winners from twenty-five years of the annual singing competition.

⊙ **Glór Mhaigh Eo** Cló Iar-Chonnachta, 1980s–90s

The archives of Raidió na Gaeltachta house a host of field recordings from the Achill Island, Erris and Tourmakeady districts of Co. Mayo.

⊙ **Seoda – Sean-Nois as Tír Chonaill** Cló Iar-Chonnachta, 1960s–90s

A selection from four of Donegal's finest – Éamonn Mac Ruarí, Caitlín Ní Dhomhnaill, Conall Ó Domhnaill and Áine Uí Laoi.

⊙ **Celtic Mouth Music** Ellipsis Arts, 1950–90s

Singers from around the "Celtic" world, including such Irish notables as Elizabeth Cronin, Tommy Gunn and Dolores Keane.

⊙ **Hurry the Jug** Globestyle, 1960s–80s

Another superb collation from the Topic archives, including Sarah Makem, Mary Ann Carolan, Packie Manus Byrne and Joe Heaney.

⊙ **Traditional Songs of Ireland** Saydisc, 1950s

Almost entirely songs in English delivered by a host of great singers, including The McPeake Family, Sarah Makem and Margaret Barry.

⊙ **Folk Heroes** Lunar/RTÉ, 1960s–70s

A double-CD covering some of the best tracks from the folk and ballad heyday, including Emmet Spiceland and The Ludlows.

⊙ **A Woman's Heart** Dara, 1992

This massive-selling album made stars of Eleanor McEvoy, Francis Black and accordionist Sharon Shannon.

⊙ **Celtic Voices** Music Club, 1970s–90s

Features contemporary women singers such as the Ní Dhomhnaill sisters, Dolores Keane and Pádraigín Ní Uallachain.

⊙ **Sex Sca and Sedition** Free State Records, 1999

Probably the only collection to feature songs about computers, Viagra and economics – and great fun too!

Seán 'ac Dhonncha

One of the most celebrated of Connemara's sean-nós singers was **Seán 'ac Dhonncha** (1919–96) from Carna who learned his singing from his parents. Education in Dublin and a subsequent teaching career of his own did not diminish his passion for music and he broadened his repertoire by studying the songs of Munster and Donegal, mainly in the Irish language. During the 1940s he encoun-

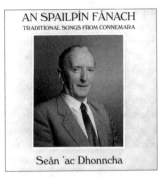

AN SPAILPÍN FÁNACH
TRADITIONAL SONGS FROM CONNEMARA

Seán 'ac Dhonncha

tered Séamus Ennis when the latter was collecting music for the Folklore Commission and, as a consequence, spent much time learning new songs and passing on others from his own storehouse. Winner of the gold medal at the 1953 Oireachtas, for more than twenty years he lived in Ath Eascraigh, East Galway working as a headteacher. On his 75th birthday Cló Iar-Chonnachta issued **An Spailpín Fánach**, a fine tribute to a talented man which, though subtitled "Traditional Songs from Connemara", includes several songs in English ("John Mitchell", "Cathal Brugha" amongst others) and Seán's characteristic use of the slide in his singing. Most of the album was recorded in 1987, but make sure you buy the CD version as it has 8 tracks more than the cassette.

⊙ An Spailpín Fánach   Cló Iar-Chonnachta, 1987

A grand selection demonstrating the sheer versatility of Seán 'ac Dhonncha's magisterial voice.

Balladeers

The rise of The **Clancy Brothers** and **Tommy Makem** inspired the emergence of a host of ballad groups and singers in '60s Ireland. Many were simply Aran-sweatered imitators, belting out traditional folk songs in English to the accompaniment of the ubiquitous guitar, while others followed the lead of **The Dubliners** in presenting a more streetwise image. It was a male-dominated world with groups often stressing their masculinity through adopting the name of a patriot – **The Wolfe Tones** being the most enduring example – and few women dared to raise their voices above the din. Notable exceptions were Margaret O'Brien of The Ludlows, sisters Adrienne and Luci Johnston and the Grehan Sisters. Though fewer in number, solo performers, such as Danny Doyle and **Paddy Reilly** abounded too and for a few brief years folk songs regularly achieved high positions in the Irish charts.

Yet, by 1970, it was virtually all over. First pirate, then mainstream radio had influenced popular tastes and rock began to gain an increasing foothold among the younger generation. Most of the balladeers altered course: some heading for the last lingering showbands, others seizing new opportunities as country and western became increasingly popular. The '70s saw the emergence of Country and Irish and the phenomenal rise in popularity of singers such as Philomena Begley, Joe Dolan, Big Tom and Margo O'Donnell, the elder sister of Daniel O'Donnell (later a highly successful figure himself).

Other balladeers (from the '70s onwards) found lucrative employment entertaining audiences in the Irish bars of the US, where their singalong material went down well with nostalgic audiences, and in turn sparked a mini-revival in Ireland itself. Some singers still have a degree of popularity and in many a small town bar you'll find a man with guitar and beat-box rattling the rafters with "The Wild Rover".

⊙ **Fields of Athenry**   Dolphin, 1984

Paddy Reilly's best album, containing the hit title track plus his version of "The Crack was Ninety in the Isle of Man".

⊙ **Dublin Songs**   Music Club, 1991

Brendan Grace, Paddy Reilly, The Dubliners and The Fureys, all given the Bill Whelan treatment on a set of Dublin's favourites.

⊙ **By Request**   Celtic Connections, 1900

Formerly with The Ludlows, Jim McCann is still making fine music in the folk-ballad tradition almost 40 years on.

Margaret Barry

A colourful, larger-than-life character, **Margaret Barry** (née Thompson) is remembered both as one of the last of the travelling street-singers and a major figure in the London Irish and folk music scene of the 1950s and 1960s. Born in Cork, 1917, Margaret's family were travellers who had settled in the city, and music played a strong role in their lives – her father played in dance halls and accompanied silent movies. Self-taught on the five-string banjo, Margaret first sang on the street at fourteen and began her travels two years later after a row with her stepmother, first touring the country by bicycle and later in a caravan with her husband and daughter. Playing at fairs, football matches and on the street, she built up her repertoire as she travelled, learning from other singers, newspapers, records and, in one legendary case, hanging around outside the doorway of a record shop until she had "My Lagan Love" off pat. Her stomping ground for many years was around the border counties, travelling around from her base in Crossmaglen. Here she was first recorded in 1951 by Alan Lomax and again the following year by Peter Kennedy. Lomax brought her to London in 1953 for a brief appearance in his TV show *Song Hunter*. She was thought to have returned home following the broadcast, but was subsequently found busking in the East End, then began playing in The Bedford Arms where she soon set up a partnership with fiddler **Michael Gorman**, a man with a solid foundation in the music of his native south Sligo. The Bedford became a popular Irish music pub and the fruits of the pair's labours are captured on **Her Mantle So Green**, recorded in part by folk-singer Ewan MacColl in 1955 for the US market and two years later by Bill Leader for Topic.

Margaret's banjo technique was rudimentary (indeed she usually only plucked one string), but the voice that was powerful enough to drown out crowds shines on songs she helped to popularize, such as "The Turfman from Ardee" and "The Flower of Sweet Strabane". Elsewhere, Willie Clancy pops up on a couple of jaunty jigs in tandem with Gorman and there's a previously unissued solo recording by the sweet-sounding Galway fiddler Martin Byrnes. Margaret's partnership with Gorman ended with the fiddler's death in 1970. She later returned to Ireland, occasionally singing in folk clubs, but never reviving her infamous street "request show" when she would ask for requests and then sing the song she'd always intended to. Margaret Barry died in 1989 aged 72.

⊙ Her Mantle So Green   Topic, 1958

Classic performances by the big, clear voice of Barry most notably on the unaccompanied title track.

Dominic Behan

Brother of the more famous Brendan – a fact of which he was often more than a little resentful – **Dominic Behan** nevertheless staked his own, albeit smaller, claim to fame with "The Patriot Game", a song that has taken its place in the canon of Irish rebel songs. Representing his own particular take on Samuel Johnson's dictum about patriotism and scoundrels, while commemorating the death of sixteen-year-old Fergal O'Hanlon during a failed IRA attack in 1956, Behan's song is a bitter warning to would-be Republican heroes not to trust leaders who play the "patriot game". It achieved further immortality when, having been recorded by Liam Clancy during the 1960s, it was used by Bob Dylan as the basis for his song "With God On Our Side" – for which Behan publicly took Dylan to task, until reminded that he himself had lifted the melody, from a popularized version of a traditional Appalachian tune. Though remembered as the composer also of many other songs, often politically topical adaptations of old tunes or words, including "Crooked Jack", "The Leaving Of Liverpool", "McAlpine's Fusiliers" and "Royal Canal", Behan might have received yet more of the recognition he desired if he'd spread himself a little less thinly.

Emigrating from Dublin in 1947, he settled first in London and later in Scotland, collaborating with Ewan MacColl and others in a range of song-collecting and recording projects, notably of Irish and Scottish street songs, for Topic during the 1950s and early '60s. The same period also produced his album **Easter Week and After** (1958), representing a ballad history of the IRA, in terms ranging from the starkly impassioned to the bitingly sardonic. Besides writing the biography *My Brother Brendan* (1965), he worked as a scriptwriter and presenter for the BBC, hosting the music series *A Better Class of Folk* during the '70s and writing a number of plays, probably the best known being 1972's *The Folk Singer*. Through journalism as well as his other writing, he gained a considerable reputation as a satirist, towards the end of his life casting his political lot in with the cause of Scottish nationalism.

⊙ Easter Week and After: Songs of the IRA   Topic, 1958

Behan's thoroughgoing affinity with the material lends this recording a potent authority.

Luka Bloom

Some time in 1987 a passenger on a US-bound Jumbo sat quietly intoning his own personal mantra: "Hi, my name is **Luka Bloom**. I'd like to play here." Or so the story goes. As Barry Moore, younger brother of Christy, he hadn't struck lucky in Ireland, despite a ten-year career spawning three albums. But, adopting Luka from a Suzanne Vega song and Bloom from the protagonist of James Joyce's *Ulysses*, and with new songs and no audience expectations, the singer-songwriter with the percussive guitar style found himself being rediscovered – in Manhattan. Two major tours followed (supporting The Pogues and Hothouse Flowers) before he was signed by Reprise in 1989. The ensuing album, **Riverside**, saw Luka giving full vent to his newfound freedom through the epic voyage of "Dreams in America" while Eileen Ivers' rakish violin on "You Couldn't Have Come at a Better Time" helped to ensure the song's place in the modern Irish canon. More tours ensued, a second album **The Acoustic Motorbike** produced an unexpected cover hit for rapper LL

HEIDI PEARSON

Cool J ("I Need Love"), and the introspective **Turf** marked the end of his American phase. Back in Ireland, Luka spent much of 1995 in a cottage in Co. Offaly penning the songs for **Salty Heaven** and, revitalized by the Irish landscape, produced easily his most expressive album since **Riverside** with an additional ecopolitical edge.

⊙ Riverside	Reprise, 1990

Luka's classy "debut" includes his still most familiar song, "You Couldn't Have Come at a Better Time".

Paul Brady

For some time one of Ireland's most popular singers, songwriters and guitarists, **Paul Brady** was born in Strabane, Co. Tyrone, in 1947 His parents both sang and were involved in amateur dramatics (a possible influence on his stagecraft) and he soon developed a love for music – both the swing and jazz of his parents' generation and his own tastes in blues, R&B, rock, pop and folk song. He learned the piano in childhood, later turning to the guitar and began performing while still in his teens, playing during the summer holidays at a hotel in Bundoran, Co. Donegal.

Moving to Dublin to study at University College in the mid-'60s enabled him to sing and play in a succession of R&B bands, before friendship with traditional musicians – like James Keane and Mick Moloney – drew him to the folk revival. Although he joined Mick in **The Johnstons**, photographs of the time reveal a horn-rimmed Paul seeming to shrink from the camera – an indication of his lack of confidence as a folk musician. By the end of his five-year stint with the group, however, he had developed into a formidable singer and guitarist. Spending time playing music in first London then New York,

Paul returned to Ireland in 1974, replacing Christy Moore in **Planxty**. Sadly, no albums were recorded during this period, though Paul's rendition of the ballad "Arthur McBride" was one of the highlights of the band's performances (and still much requested by audiences). Following Planxty's break-up Paul joined forces with **Andy Irvine,** touring as a duo and recording the superlative **Andy Irvine and Paul Brady** (1976). During this period he was in demand as an accompanist, and appeared backing Tommy Peoples on **The High Part of the Road** (1976) and, with the addition of Matt Molloy, on **Molloy/Brady/Peoples** (1977) an album which featured another classic ballad, "Shamrock Shore". Brady's syncopated and percussive guitar style, was particularly popular with fiddlers and, in 1979, he popped up again, this time supporting **Andy McGann** on **It's a Hard Road to Follow**. One further diversion to note is his multi-instrumental role in the obscure **The Green Crow Caws** (1980) a musical tribute to playwright Seán O'Casey.

By this time Paul had already recorded his own solo traditional album, the seminal **Welcome Here Kind Stranger** (1978) which includes his benchmark versions of "The Lakes of Pontchartrain" and "Paddy's Green Shamrock Shore". Despite many calls to repeat the performance, Paul had already decided to move to a new musical house and, in his own words, "explore those unopened rooms inside". For the last twenty years Paul has navigated an internationally successful career through the choppy waters of rock music, seeing many of his songs covered by performers as diverse as Cher, Mary Black and Bonny Raitt. For an introduction to his work between 1981 and 1995 look no further than the splendid **Nobody Knows: The Best of Paul Brady** (1999), a personally selected compilation of fourteen tracks which also includes a new recording of his Planxty-era barnstormer "Arthur McBride".

Paul has also super-vised the remastering of his entire 1980s/90s back catalogue and the place to begin is the astonishing **Hard Station**. This 1981 album may lack the sophistication of later releases but the songs burst with a raw ferocity, none more so than the epic closing track depict-ing the experiences of Irish migrants in England, the glorious, unequivocal "Nothing But the Same Old Story". The subse-quent **True for You** (1983) saw Paul expanding his rock exploration through raunchy songs like "Steel Claw" (covered by Tina

STEVE GILLETT

Turner) and the tremendous "Not the Only One", featuring guitarist Phil Palmer who became the mainstay of his backing band and fea-tures on the live album **Full Moon** (1984). While the music may have become heavier, Brady's continued to explore the themes of love and longing in his lyrics on the album **Back to the Centre** (1986). This produced an Irish hit in "Walk a White Line" and included a stunning rendition of "The Homes of Donegal", but his song "The Island" was widely construed as an attack on Republican politics and the armed struggle. Though the chorus suggests that this was a misinterpretation, Paul's later work avoided such debates. The following year's **Primitive Dance** included a truly wild solo from Davy Spillane on "Eat the Peach", while increasing interest in Brady's songwriting skills saw the inevitable American album, 1991's **Trick or Treat** recorded with some of LA's best session musicians. By contrast, **Spirits Colliding** (1995) was largely made at home and has a more relaxed feel as a consequence, especially on the tracks featuring bluegrass banjo player, Bela Fleck. Finally, 2000 saw **Oh What a World** which, apart from two tracks, consists entirely of songs co-written with a variety of partners, including Carole King and Boyzone's Ronan Keating. Sadly, the result sounds at best like a second-rate Paul Brady tribute band and the singer's writing strengths seem to have been dissipated through collaboration.

⊙ Welcome Here Kind Stranger | Mulligan, 1978

Brady's only traditional solo album and a masterpiece.

⊙ Hard Station | Rykodisc, 1981

Reborn as a rocker, many still rate this his best to date.

⊙ Nobody Knows: The Best of Paul Brady | Rykodisc, 1981–95

A perfect aperitif for Paul's many courses of musical delight.

Karan Casey

Possessor of one of the most stunning voices in Irish (or any form of) music, **Karan Casey** was lead singer with **Solas** from 1994 until her departure in the Spring of 1999. Born and bred in Ballyduff Lower, Co. Waterford, Karan studied classical music at Dublin's Royal Irish Academy and, after heading for the US, jazz at Long

Island University, New York. You'd never guess either influence from listening to Karan's only solo release to date, the exquisite **Songlines**. Though produced by Seamus Egan and featuring other Solas members, this is Karan's own album from sublime start (the sparkling "Roger the Miller") to haunting finish (the unaccompanied "The Labouring Man's Daughter"). Since leaving Solas, Karan has returned to Ireland and taken a career break to look after her young daughter.

| ⊙ Songlines | Shanachie, 1997 |

The most luscious voice in Irish music delivers an absolute spine-tingler!

Liam Clancy

The youngest of the world-famous Tipperary fraternity which revolutionized Irish music in the 1950s and '60s, **Liam Clancy** can boast some influential names among his fan-base. "Liam was it for me," Bob Dylan has said, having attended many an early Clancy Brothers gig in Greenwich Village. "He was just the best ballad singer I ever heard in my life; still is, probably." Having grown up amidst an all-singing family, Liam's musical appetite was further whetted when he accompanied American musicologist Diane Hamilton on a collecting trip around Ireland in 1955, meeting **Tommy Makem** for the first time en route and contributing three tracks to the resulting album, **The Lark in the Morning** (1955). After emigrating to America later that year, it was during his time with the **Clancy Brothers and Tommy Makem** (see p.167) that Liam first began branching out solo, with a self-titled album released on brother Pat's Tradition label in 1965. Recently rereleased, along with nine new tracks, as **Irish**

61

Troubadour (1999), it includes a stripped-down "Rocky Road to Dublin" with Luke Kelly, a powerful version of Dominic Behan's "The Patriot Game" and the poignant "Black Water Side". Greeted as a classic of Irish balladry, the balance of warmth and gravitas in Liam's singing – its grainy weight beneath the subtleties of his articulation – pack a forceful yet understated emotional punch, which remains the hallmark of his singing today.

After leaving the Clancys in 1973, Liam's second solo recording was **The Dutchman** (1974), a mostly melancholy collection of old and new material including Michael Smith's title track (which would become one of his best-loved duo numbers with Tommy Makem) Ralph McTell's "Streets of London" and Dylan's "Fare Thee Well", alongside traditional songs like "Fiddler's Green" and "Heave Away". His celebrated partnership with Makem (see p.92), following an impromptu performance together at a festival in Ohio in 1975, continued until 1988, during which time the pair released six albums together. After Tom Clancy died in 1990, Liam joined Pat, Bobby and their nephew Robbie O'Connell in the latest version of the Clancy Brothers, which recorded **Older But No Wiser** in 1995. Another familial permutation followed in the shape of **Clancy, O'Connell and Clancy** – Liam, **Robbie**, and Liam's son **Dónal** – which toured extensively during 1996–99, releasing two well-received albums of traditional and contemporary ballads. Now living back in Ireland, Liam continues to perform solo, in between running a recording studio at his home in the Waterford Gaeltacht, and has recently completed his autobiography.

⊙ Irish Troubadour   Vanguard, 1965

All fourteen tracks from his acclaimed 1965 solo debut, together with nine previously unreleased gems including "Dirty Old Town".

Sonny Condell

inger-guitarist **Sonny Condell** (b. 1949, Wicklow) has been one of the most respected figures in Irish music ever since teaming up with **Leo O'Kelly** in the late 1960s to form folk-rock duo **Tír na nÓg**. When the partnership split in 1974, Sonny returned to Ireland from London (his base of several years) and began playing solo and writing the songs which were to form **Camouflage** (1977), regarded by many as one of the most important fusion albums of the decade. Next stop was **Scullion**, formed with Philip King and guitarist Greg Boland, an arrangement which ran on-and-off throughout the 1980s, spanning Condell's reunion with O'Kelly in 1985. Since then Sonny has continued to explore the potential of acoustic rock music from an Irish perspective through two excellent solo albums, 1995s **Someone to Dance With** and, more recently, **French Windows**. The latter amply demonstrates that Condell's voice has lost neither warmth nor strength and his songs continue to incorporate his characteristic melodic twists and his rhapsodic guitar work.

⊙ **French Windows**   Hummingbird, 1998

The old master returns to paint a bright new canvas.

Seán Corcoran

eán Corcoran (b. Drogheda, Co. Louth, 1945) started collecting songs when he was sixteen; his own singing was strongly influenced by the Usher family from nearby Tenure, especially **Mary Ann Carolan** and her brother **Pap Usher**. Since then Seán has forged a considerable reputation as a solo unaccompanied singer apart from a brief spell playing, in his own words, "rudimentary guitar" in the late 1960s band **The Rakish Paddies** (which also featured Paul Brady and Mick Moloney). Subsequently, he was a member of **The Press Gang**, a four-man vocal harmony group influenced by The Watersons which released a successful album on the long-defunct Hawk label. In the 1970s Seán participated in the CCÉ US tour which led to **Sailing into Walpole's Marsh**, where his lyrical, clearly-enunciated voice can be heard on songs such as "Bold Doherty" and the jocose "The Mice Are At It Again". For some years he worked as assistant editor to Breandán Breathnach on the music magazine *Ceol* before embarking on ethnomusicological studies at Queen's University, Belfast. This in turn led to his major research project for the Arts Council of Northern Ireland, **Here's a Health** (1986), a cassette and accompanying book focusing on the Fermanagh song tradition. Seán's interest in vocal techniques and experimentation came to fruition through his long-time friendship with flute player and singer **Desi Wilkinson** and their formation of **Cran**. Here, too, saw the development of his unique bouzouki style, encouraged first by Andy Irvine who gave Seán his first instrument and largely derived from exploring different ways of accompanying Desi's extremely versatile playing.

📼 Sailing into Walpole's Marsh	Green Linnet, 1976

Seán's excellent singing, plus strong support from Mairéad Ní Dhomhnaill, Maeve Donnelly and Eddie Clarke.

Elizabeth Cronin

The undoubted Irish music publishing event of 2000 was the release of *The Songs of Elizabeth Cronin, Irish Traditional Singer*, edited by her grandson, Dáibhí Ó Cróinín. This sumptuous collection of all her songs also includes two CDs of her singing and illustrates why her marvellous voice was so sought after by collectors. The eldest of five children **Elizabeth Cronin** (1879–1956) – known as Bess – was from the Fuithirí (Fuhirees) area of West Cork where her father, Seán Ó hIarlaithe was a local headmaster. Bess first learned songs from her mother, Maighréad Ní Thuama, and from the family servants. This knowledge was expanded when, in her mid-teens, she lived with a paternal uncle and aunt, who, being childless, needed help on their farm.

Bess's first public appearance is reckoned to have been at the 1899 Feis in Macroom where she is reported to have sung two songs in Irish "which were much admired for their beauty and the naive simplicity with which they were rendered". This was at a time when the nearby village of Baile Mhúirne (Ballyvourney) and neighbouring Cúil Aodha (Coolea) had become centres for the revival of the Irish language, stimulated by The Gaelic League. Such rejuvenation inspired song collectors, both local and from abroad, including A. Martin Freeman from London whose *Ballyvourney Collection* is one of the most eminent and widely-known collections from the oral tradition. It was in this vibrant atmosphere that Bess grew up and acquired her songs. Many were local compositions, but others came from beggars who tramped the roads and would often be put up for the night by her uncle. Others came from newspapers and Irish-language magazines or older collections of songs in English, such as Walsh's *Irish Popular Songs*, which explains some of the patriotic songs (like "Seán O'Farrell") in Bess's repertoire.

Bess herself began to be collected in the 1940s, first by Séamus Ennis for first the Irish Folklore Commission in 1947 and subsequently the BBC (with Brian George). Alan Lomax arrived in 1951, followed by Jean Ritchie and George Pickow the next year and, in 1955, by Diane Hamilton. Her voice was regularly heard on BBC Radio's *As I Roved*

Out and began to appear on record in 1955. Previous efforts to produce a collection of Bess Cronin's recordings foundered for a variety of reasons and it was only when Dáibhí Ó Cróinín inherited his father's papers in 1990 that he began researching such a project. Bearing in mind that Bess was in her late sixties when Ennis first came a-calling, the result is nevertheless a magnificent testimony to this most eloquent of singers. All fifty-nine songs featured on the CDs were recorded at her home and there is some variation in sound quality. The first disc contains thirty songs from the BBC and Folklore Commission archives, while the second has another twenty-nine, taken largely from the Ritchie-Pickow collection. There are simply too many highlights to choose, but, plumping for one, Bess's version of the macaronic *Siúil, a Rúin*, dating from 1951, encapsulates all the special qualities of her singing.

⊙ **The Songs of Elizabeth Cronin,**
Irish Traditional Singer   Four Courts Press 1947–55

A book combined with two CDs, this is a stunning and essential addition to the collections of all lovers of traditional song.

Jimmy Crowley

The **Crowley** family have been associated with Co. Cork's music for generations and singer **Jimmy**, from Douglas, has been upholding the clan's reputation for three decades. Both in the 1970s band **Stoker's Lodge** and as a solo guitarist and bouzouki player, Jimmy is one of Ireland's most skilled live performers and possesses a vast range of songs in both Irish and English, complemented by his own articulate songwriting skills. His powerful, emotive voice is capable of expressing both rage and tenderness and been caught on record since 1977's **The Boys of Fair Hill**. Several subsequent releases include his album of

Irish songs, **Jimmy Mo Mhile Stór** (1985) and, in the 1990s, he established his own company, Free State Records. Its releases include his own **My Love is a Tall Ship** and the essential **Uncorked**, recorded live in Cork's Lobby Bar in 1997. Jimmy's on splendid form throughout, particularly on "The Green Island", a grand emigration song from his own pen, and

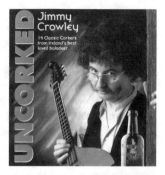

the classic "Johnny Jump Up", the tale of a cider company's mistaken storage of its product in whiskey barrels. Known for his encouragement of songwriters, Jimmy has also compiled **Sex Sca and Sedition** (see p.49), a collection of songs and ballads on mainly contemporary themes written and performed by local Cork singers.

⊙ Uncorked	Free State Records, 1998

Few live recordings are as successful as this encapsulation of the essence of Crowley.

Enya

Among the oddities of 1988s international hit list was "Orinoco Flow", a single issued by the hitherto little-known singer, composer and keyboards player **Enya**. A multitextured, offbeat staccato backing set the tone for the singer's multitracked dulcet voice, intoning a peculiar voyage of exploration: "Let me sail, let me sail, let the Orinoco Flow. Let me reach, let me beach on the shores of

Tripoli". The artiste formerly known as Eithne Ní Bhraonáin (b.1961) was one of the younger members of the **Clannad** family and briefly a member of the band, appearing on 1982's **Fuaim** LP. She next popped up playing synthesizer on a track on the Mairéad Ní Mhaonaigh/Frankie Kennedy **Ceol Aduaidh** LP (see p.141), but her breakthrough came when she was commissioned by the BBC to compose the soundtrack for its 1986 TV series **The Celts**. By then Enya had already begun working closely with lyricist Roma Ryan and her husband, the well-known engineer and producer, Nicky Ryan. Enya's skill was to weave sound textures, often characterized by arpeggio playing, as a backdrop for her delivery of Roma's obscure lyrics, while Nicky adds his studio brilliance to produce an overall otherworldly, but still conceptually Irish, confection. Little changed over four successive albums – **Watermark** (1988), **Shepherd Moons** (1991), **The Memory of Trees** (1995) and **A Day Without Rain**. Newcomers are best guided towards the excellent compilation **Paint the Sky with Stars**.

⊙ **Paint the Sky with Stars**   Warner, 1997

Sixteen tracks (including two previously unissued) spanning the entirety of Enya's career and opening with "Orinoco Flow".

Tommy Fleming

A man who simply loves singing, **Tommy Fleming**, a farmer's son, from Aclare, Co. Sligo has one of the most startling, pure tenor voices in Irish music. His big break came in 1993 when Phil Coulter recruited him for a US tour and he found himself singing in Carnegie Hall. Next a rising reputation as a fine interpreter of songs saw him enlisted by **De Dannan** in 1994, resulting in Tommy's impressive delivery of traditional songs such as "Captain Jack" and "The Mountains of Pomeroy" on **Hibernian Rhapsody**. However, other songs drew on his strengths as a balladeer, and his subsequent solo career has been largely based on his impassioned performances of ballads. The first solo album, **Restless Spirit**, struck a chord in Ireland, and its successor, **The Contender**, continued in the same vein, drawing on songwriters as varied as Jimmy MacCarthy, Christie Hennessy and Stephen Foster (nineteenth-century American composer of "Oh, Susannah"). Confident enough to include even hackneyed ballads such as "Galway Bay" and "Danny Boy" (originally aired on **Hibernian Rhapsody**), this will no doubt sell by the bucketload.

⊙ **The Contender**   Dara, 2000

Immaculately-produced, elegantly-delivered songs, but a mind-numbingly awful waste of Fleming's tremendous voice.

Seán Garvey

S ingers who can single-handedly captivate an audience with a song lasting almost ten minutes are one in a million. One such is **Seán Garvey** (b. 1952, Cahirciveen, Co. Kerry) whose rich, velvet baritone has been enthralling audiences for three decades. Though Seán was a member of the legendary **Pavees** with the Keenan family for four years in the early 1970s, he has generally sung solo, often on radio and television. A fine flute, banjo and harmonica player too, Seán often employs a light finger-style guitar accompaniment, producing an overall effect redolent of the great Scots singer Dick Gaughan, though thoroughly grounded in the Irish tradition. You can hear the results on his superb solo album **Ón dTalamh Amach** (Out of the Ground), co-produced by Eleanor McEvoy's sister Marion who also wrote one track, "Song for the Healing". Seán's song selection is exemplary, including local Kerry songs such as the droll "Haute Cuisine in Cathaír Saidhbhín" and a grand "Sé Oakum mo Phriosún" (learned from Seán 'ac Dhonncha while Garvey was living in Connemara). Elsewhere, Seán multitracks polkas, reels and hornpipes, but the outstanding track is the nine-minute long, but everenthralling "Laurel Hill" where a soldier returns disguised from the Napoleonic Wars to be reunited with his true love.

⊙ Ón dTalamh Amach	Harry Stottle Records, 1998

Measured, eloquent, intense singing and playing of the highest order make this one of the best albums of the last decade.

Kieran Goss

Hailing from Mayobridge, Co. Down, singer-songwriter **Kieran Goss** admits that he was "more influenced by James Taylor and Paul Simon than by The Bothy Band or by Makem and Clancy". He learned his trade as a guitarist plying cover versions in local Belfast pubs while qualifying as a barrister. Resisting the lure of the legal profession he began performing his songs at festivals and released a debut LP in 1988, **Brand New Star**. Mary Black covered two songs from the album and Kieran was soon snapped up by her sister Frances as her accompanist, a role he maintained for four years, releasing an album with her in 1993, **Frances Black and Kieran Goss**. His popularity has been cemented by three further albums, **New Day** (1994) and the marvellous **Worse than Pride** (1997). On the latter, Kieran's clear-as-light voice shines throughout and the production is well-nigh perfect, but what marks it out as a cut above most singer-songwriter albums is the ease with which Kieran can encapsulate a mood, from the stunningly matter-of-fact opener "Waste of Time" to the optimistic "Weight of the World". Progress was maintained with 2000's **Red-Letter Day**, featuring guests Davy Spillane, Máire Breatnach and Gerry O'Beirne, though the starkness of Kieran's photograph on the cover is strangely at odds with the wisely-crafted songs of compassion and reflection on the disc itself.

⊙ **Worse than Pride**   RTÉ, 1997

The album that saw Goss leap from the supporting cast to stardom; consummate singing, fine guitar work and elegant production.

Len Graham and Skylark

Together with his wife, **Padraigín Ní Uallacháin Len Graham** is one of today's leading exponents of the Ulster song tradition. Born in 1944, just a generation or so removed from the last Irish speakers in his native Glens of Antrim, he grew up absorbing the local songs sung by his parents and grandmother, also accompanying his father to meetings of the local Antrim and Derry Fiddlers' Association, a popular focal point for singers as well as fiddlers. His father's trade as a cabinet-maker saw the family moving several times during Graham's childhood in pursuit of work, fetching up in Belfast, from where Graham continued in this itinerant habit during his teens, travelling the length and breadth of Ireland via its An Óige network of youth hostels. This brought him into contact with the full gamut of the country's music and song traditions, although his tireless enthusiasm for sharing and swapping songs wasn't always wholly matched either by the musicians he met or his hostel-mates: "All I can ever remember was singing," he has said. "They used to gag me with a scout scarf to keep me from singing!"

It was through the Antrim and Derry Fiddlers, in 1963, that Graham first met one of his main mentors, the singer and fiddler **Joe Holmes** (b.1909), who had given up singing nearly twenty years previously, until persuaded by Graham to start again. The two formed a close friendship and musical partnership that lasted until Holmes' death in 1978, recording two albums together highlighting the Northern tradition of unison singing: **Chaste Muses, Bards and Sages** (1975) and **After Dawning** (1978). Graham also began attending fleadhanna up and down the country, coming second in his first competition in 1966 before taking first prize, in the English-language song category, in 1971, as well as developing his repertoire and style through numerous all-night singing sessions. Another important influence was Eddie Butcher, from Magilligan, Co. Derry, whose singing was widely broadcast on radio during the 1960s and whom Graham visited regularly towards the end of his life; songs he learned from both Holmes and Butcher feature throughout his own recordings: **Wind and Water** (1976), **Do Me Justice** (1983) and **Ye Lovers All** (1985).

In addition to his solo work, and his earlier recordings with Holmes, Graham is a founder member of the group **Skylark**, formed in 1986 along with fiddler Gerry O'Connor (also of Lá Lugh), multi-instrumentalist Garry Ó Briain and accordionist Andrew Mac Namara, the last being replaced by Máirtín O'Connor after the foursome's self-titled debut album (1987). Combining Graham's rich, warmly authoritative renditions of mostly Northern songs with a widely-sourced range of instrumentals, Skylark have recorded three more albums, most recently **Raining Bicycles** (1996), which wears its many accomplishments admirably lightly, in tracks ranging from a tender parting lovers' song written by Padraigín Ní Uallacháin to an elegant arrangement of Carolan's "Squire Parsons". Graham has also contributed much to the Ulster song revival through his collecting work, including the field recordings compiled as **It's of My Rambles** (1993), for which he was presented with the Seán O'Boyle Cultural Traditions Award in 1992. Many of the songs featured in these projects have subsequently been picked up by bands such as Altan, The Chieftains, De Dannan and the Voice Squad. Although Skylark continues to regroup periodically, for the past decade Graham has performed mostly with Co. Armagh storyteller **John Campbell**, touring on both sides of the Atlantic, while also remaining much in demand as a soloist.

⊙ **Do Me Justice**   Claddagh, 1983

A wide selection from Graham's extensive store, from rousing broadside ballads through seduction ditties to wistful love songs.

Kieran Halpin

Husky-voiced singer-songwriter and song collector, **Kieran Halpin** (born Dundalk, 1955) has been one of Ireland's most prolific recording artists, releasing a dozen albums over the last score of years without squeezing through into the big-time. There's a touch of Tom Waits in his delivery and his finely-crafted songs are reminiscent of another American writer, John Hiatt. His partnership with Tyneside fiddler/vocalist Tom McConville generated two fine early albums which were followed by his 1983 solo debut LP **The Man Who Lives in Bottles**. 1991's **Mission Street** featured notable contributions from Davy Spillane but it's his latest album, **Jangle,** made with former Jethro Tull multi-instrumentalist Martin Alcock, which reaps the richest harvest. Halpin's voice is strongest on the evocative ballad "The Last One Fallen in the War", while the hard-hitting opening track "The Christian Thing" angrily describes the "benefits" brought to the developing world by cultural colonization.

⊙ **Jangle**   SOS Records, 2000

Halpin has produced a grand body of work and this latest album deserves wide exposure.

Mick Hanly

Growing up in Limerick during the 1950s and '60s, **Mick Hanly's** early influences were those of most urban Irish boys and wannabe guitarists of the time – Buddy Holly and Elvis, The Beatles, The Beach Boys and The Shadows – until an encounter with Seán Ó Riada's Ceoltóirí Chualann brought about a quasi-Damascene conversion to folk music. After a few years' strumming along to Clancy-style or Guthrieesque ballads, Hanly met Mícheál Ó Domhnaill, who introduced him to the wider world of fingerstyle playing and non-standard tunings. The two teamed up as **Monroe**, supporting Planxty on their legendary 1973 Irish tour and earning widespread praise for their contemporary treatments of traditional songs, recording one album, **Celtic Folkweave** (1974), before Ó Domhnaill joined The Bothy Band. Following his mostly traditional solo debut, **A Kiss In the Morning Early** (1976), backed by rising stars like Dónal Lunny, Matt Molloy and Tríona Ní Dhómhnaill, Hanly went on to tour with Andy Irvine, a guest on his second album **As I Went Over Blackwater** (1980), before replacing Christy Moore in **Moving Hearts**. His two years with that seminal line-up witnessed his first emergence as a songwriter, with his look back at his dance-hall days, "All I Remember", and the co-written "Open Those Gates", a salute to Irish Republican prisoners in the North, both on the album **Live Hearts** (1983).

Solo again, Hanly shifted his songwriting course into a country/pop vein, eventually hitting the jackpot when first Mary

Black, then up-and-coming Country singer Hal Ketchum covered his song "Past the Point of Rescue", the latter taking it to #2 in the US country charts in 1992. Today, Hanly is rated alongside the likes of Jimmy MacCarthy as one of Ireland's leading contemporary song-writers, while his own most recent recording, **Wooden Horses** (2000), finds him moving fruitfully back into a more acoustic format, in the company of Irish accompanists like accordionist Josephine Marsh, harmonica player Mick Kinsella and fiddler Liam Lewis.

⊙ **Wooden Horses**   Doghouse Records, 2000

Hanly's freshest-sounding album in years is a real delight.

Frank Harte

An architect by profession, **Frank Harte** (b. Dublin, 1933) is also a major figure in the Irish song revival. His interest in traditional songs was sparked by a chance encounter with a travelling ballad-singer and songsheet-seller at a fair in Boyle, Co. Roscommon. Since then Frank has built up his own huge collection of songs, becoming in the process an internationally renowned authority on the Irish song tra-dition, with a special fondness

for Dublin ballads. Many singers owe part of their repertoire to Frank whose recordings since the late 1970s have largely focused on the narrative songs in which his warm, clear voice excels. Unfortunately, none of his early albums, such as 1979's **And Listen to My Song** – where Frank sings "I'm a buxom, fine widow" and you believe him! – and Topic's **Dublin Street Songs** (1981) is currently available, but, fortunately, two more recent releases can be found and are both exceptional. 1987's **Daybreak and a Candle-end** revived Frank's partnership with accompanist Dónal Lunny and includes classic renditions of "Willie Taylor", "Here I Am from Donegal" and an unaccompanied "The Holland Handkerchief". There was also no better person than Frank to celebrate the Rebellion's bicentenary through **1798 – The First Year of Liberty**, again with Lunny's assistance. The package contains Frank's detailed account of the Rebellion and exemplary background information on all seventeen songs. For Harte songs are the expression of the Irish people, no matter where they come from, both geographically and politically, so he's able to sing an Orange song, such as "Croppies Lie Down" and counterbalance it immediately with "The Croppy Boy".

⊙ **Daybreak and a Candle-end**   Phaeton, 1987

Traditional singing at its majestic best.

⊙ **1798 – The First Year of Liberty**   Hummingbird, 1998

A powerful and enduring celebration of the Rebellion's bicentenary by the best man for the job!

Joe Heaney

I t's the kind of story that sounds apocryphal, but **Joe Heaney** himself apparently told of the time when the American chat-show host Merv Griffin, on a visit to Ireland during the 1970s, recognized one of the photographs on the wall of a Dublin pub. "That's my door-man!" he exclaimed. "That," the barman informed him gravely, "is Ireland's greatest traditional musician." Words are cheap, of course, and that fact that Heaney *was* at that time working as a doorman in Griffin's swanky Manhattan apartment building is evidence of how, for most of his life, the disparity between his reputation and financial reward was a glaring one.

Heaney's reputation in the rigorously demanding art of sean-nós singing can hardly be surpassed and he has come to be seen as a defining exponent of the medium in which he operated. In material terms, it was simply his misfortune that that medium, while venerated for its cultural importance, was and is by nature unsuited to the mod-ern record business.

As the musicologist Fred McCormick put it in an article about Heaney's music, the singer's birthplace of Carna, in Co. Galway's Connemara Gaeltacht, possessed "all the qualifications to host one of the greatest folksong traditions on earth, [being] remote, barren and poverty-stricken". It's a landscape inscribed, too, with a long his-tory of injustice and oppression and this legacy forms one among the many layers of emotional and narrative context distilled into the sean-nós tradition. Heaney – Seosamh Ó hÉanaí in Irish, or Joe Éiniú in Connemara – was born here in 1919, encouraged in singing and storytelling from childhood by his Irish-speaking parents and neigh-bours, acquiring the basis of a song repertoire that would later be estimated at some 600 items. He won first prize at the Oireachtas in Dublin in 1942, and the gold medal in 1955, but economic circum-stances saw him emigrating to work as a labourer in Scotland and England. While his gifts certainly came to be recognized by the lead-ing folk revivalists of the day – Gael-Linn bringing him back to Dublin to perform at their traditional music nights during the 1958 National

Tourism Festival, while London's famous Singers' Club awarded him a lifetime resident's chair – it's said that widespread audience indifference to his singing, during the ballad-boom years, was a major factor in his decision to emigrate to the US in 1966. Another may have been the warmly enthusiastic reception that greeted his appearance at the 1965 Newport Folk Festival.

Nonetheless, it was only after nearly fifteen years of working doors and operating elevators, meanwhile coming to be held in increasingly high regard by folksong aficionados both in America and, through his regular visits home, in Ireland, that Heaney achieved a position concomitant with his artistry. In 1980, he was employed to teach Irish folklore at Connecticut's Wesleyan University, soon afterwards being appointed as lecturer and artist-in-residence at the University of Washington in Seattle. He was awarded a National Heritage Award in Folk Arts by the US government in 1982, while his final performance in Ireland that same year took place in Dublin's National Concert Hall. After suffering from emphysema during the last years of his life, he died in 1984, his body being brought back to Connemara for burial.

Heaney has been cited as a major influence by artists as diverse as Luke Kelly and Paul Brady, while Christy Moore, grouping him alongside legendary figures like Seán Ó Riada and Séamus Ennis, credits him with nothing less than having moulded "the way music is in Ireland today – all kinds of music". Heaney himself ascribed the essence of his style to the guidance of his earliest teachers back in Carna: "What they say at home is 'abair amhrán, inis scéal' – say a song, tell a story. They don't tell you to sing a song, but to say it. Without the story, the song is lost."

As well as a consummate storyteller, Heaney was a supreme exemplar of the understated, less-is-more approach to emotional expression that characterizes sean-nós singing, the powerful current of his majestically resonant voice intricately embellished with unerring modulations of tone, precisely applied grace notes and subtly accented timing. Though best remembered for his renditions of the "big" songs and love laments like "Róisín Dubh", "Úna Bhán" and "Eileanóir a Rúin", as well as his unofficial "signature" song, the desolately impassioned "The Rocks of Bawn", he was equally skilled at putting over lighter English-language material, children's songs and several of the few surviving religious songs in the Irish tradition, as well as being an accomplished lilter. A selection from his 1974 Gael-Linn recordings is compiled on **Ó Mo Dhuchás/From My Tradition**, while in 2000, Topic Records, in association with Cló Iar-Chonnachta, issued a magnificent double CD, **The Road From Connemara**, featuring nearly two-and-a-half hours of songs and conversation from a series of interviews with Heaney conducted in 1964 by Ewan MacColl and Peggy Seeger.

⊙ **The Road from Connemara**   Topic/Cló Iar-Chonnachta, 1964

Not just a monumental moment in the recorded history of Ireland's music, but a master class in the art of singing.

Andy Irvine

It's a small and select handful of Irish artists who have had their fingers in as many different musical pies as **Andy Irvine**. Though still associated foremost in many minds with **Planxty**, he had already been performing for a good ten years when they first got together, and has been involved in a continual succession of other projects ever since they split. The son of a Scottish father and an Irish mother, he was born in London in 1942. Though he learned classical guitar in his teens, his initial career ambition was to follow his mother into acting –

then the skiffle boom materialized, followed by the discovery of Woody Guthrie as the UK and US folk revivals hotted up. Irvine adapted his guitar style, taught himself mandolin and harmonica (later also adding hurdy-gurdy, bouzouki and mandola), plied the folk-club circuit and toured with Derroll Adams and Ramblin' Jack Elliott, before moving to Dublin in 1962. A few years' itinerant gigging led to the formation of **Sweeney's Men** in 1966, with singer and multi-instrumentalist **Johnny Moynihan**, and singer-guitarist **Joe Dolan**. Courtesy of Moynihan, it was through this group that the bouzouki made its debut appearance in Irish music, while more broadly Sweeney's Men were among the first to present traditional Irish songs in what we'd recognize today as modern folk arrangements, including the interwoven bouzouki and mandolin picking that would soon become a Planxty hallmark. After Dolan was replaced by Terry Woods (later of Steeleye Span) in 1967, the group recorded a self-titled album (1968), before Irvine too left to travel around Eastern Europe.

Irvine's eighteen months' busking through Bulgaria, Romania and Yugoslavia turned out to be a deeply formative experience. He developed an enduring fascination with East European and Balkan music which has permeated much of his work ever since, while also honing his songwriting skills. Back on Irish soil, Irvine resumed performing solo and toured with Dónal Lunny, whom he first introduced to the bouzouki, this partnership eventually leading on to Planxty. Irvine's input was fundamental both in creating the band's instrumental sound, including the odd East European tune, and in supplying some of their best-known songs, such as "The West Coast of Clare", while his elaborately ornamented, plaintively lyrical vocals lent both freshness and authority to their traditional ballads. During Planxty's hiatus during 1975–78, Irvine briefly joined **De Dannan**, also teaming up with **Paul Brady**, a highly popular pairing that produced an acclaimed eponymous album (1976), featuring mostly Northern-sourced traditional songs, with accompaniment from Dónal Lunny and fiddler Kevin Burke.

Even after Planxty reformed, Irvine continued his own career, releasing his warmly-received first solo album **Rainy Sundays...Windy Dreams** (1980), which combined Irish and Balkan tunes with his own compositions, such as the jazz-inflected title track, highlighting his growing assurance in weaving together Irish and US folk idioms, and in vividly distilling a story into a song. He also recorded a highly-praised album with Scottish singer **Dick Gaughan**, **Parallel Lines** (1982). Following Planxty's final demise in 1983, Irvine founded an ambitious multinational line-up called **Mosaic**, with Lunny and Declan Masterson as well as members from Denmark, Austria, Hungary, Holland and Scotland. Despite a highly successful debut tour, rehearsing and recording proved impossible, and the group disbanded after a year or so. As ever, Irvine returned to solo work, his core fan-base by now extending through Europe, the US, Australia and New Zealand, before being invited to join an American "Legends of Irish Music" tour in 1986, together with fiddler Kevin Burke, accordionist Jackie Daly and guitarist Gerry O'Beirne. Following O'Beirne's replacement by Arty McGlynn, this grouping coalesced into **Patrick Street** (see p.219), now long established as one of Ireland's top traditional line-ups, with Irvine's songs a central plank of their repertoire.

Between tours with the band, Irvine fulfilled a long-held ambition in his 1992 album **East Wind**, with piper Davy Spillane, an ambitious meeting of Irish and East European traditions with a supporting cast including Bulgarian singer Márta Sebestyén, her multi-instrumentalist compatriot Nikola Parov, accordionist Máirtín O'Connor and Bill Whelan on keyboards. Whelan has cited the project as a key influence on *Riverdance*'s musical gestation, a link clearly apparent in **East Wind** arrangements like "Chetvorno Horo" and "Two Steps to the Bar". The year before, Irvine had also recorded his second solo album, **Rude Awakening** (1991), themed as a paean to some of his musical and personal heroes, including Woody Guthrie, the Mexican revolutionary Zapata and a couple of Antarctic explorers. It's since been followed by a third, **Way Out Yonder** (2000), highlighting afresh his distinctive core strengths both as a songwriter and an interpreter of others' material.

⊙ **Andy Irvine & Paul Brady**   Mulligan, 1976

Highlights including Irvine's opening "Plains of Kildare" and Brady's celebrated rendition of "Arthur McBride".

⊙ **Way Out Yonder**   own label, 2000

An album chock-full of stirring stories, including Irvine's sorrowful reflection on the Troubles, "Born in Carrickfergus".

Ron Kavana

To call **Ron Kavana** hyperactive barely covers the range and rate of this Fermoy, Co. Cork-born Londoner's musical activities since the early 1970s. As a singer, songwriter and multi-instrumental-ist (guitar, banjo, mandolin, keyboards, percussion and mandola), he's played with at least a dozen different bands, from Celtic con-cept-rockers **Loudest Whisper**, through R&B and blues outfits with the likes of Alexis Korner and Chris Farlowe, to the various permuta-tions of his own folk/rock/world fusion **Alias** line-up. He's worked as a producer, a record-company director and co-founder of the London Irish Live Trust (LILT) which brought together the cream of London's Irish musicians to record the benefit album **For the Children** (1990) in aid of integrated education in Belfast.

JAK KILBY

Having released three rave-reviewed albums and collected a string of industry accolades with Alias Ron Kavana in the late '80s and early '90s, Ron took time out to study Irish history at university, since when he's initiated and carried through a series of major archive and compilation projects, including the Globestyle series of recordings (see p.39) which drew on the Topic labels archive of Irish traditional music and **Farewell To Ireland** (see p.40). In the meantime, he's maintained his own recording career, his last Alias release being the brashly (and typically) eclectic **Galway to Graceland** (1995), including such treats as the Rolling Stones' "19th Nervous Breakdown" spliced with "The Blacksmith's Daughter", while his most recent solo outing is **Alien Alert**, a forceful live set recorded in San Francisco with Californian band the Resident Aliens.

Deliberately rough-around-the-edges, this covers the whole extent of Kavana's repertoire and stylistic range.

Pat Kilbride

Singer, songwriter, guitarist and cittern player, **Pat Kilbride** (from Castledermot, Co. Kildare) is a man with a pedigree. Learning first classical piano, then a guitar donated by his older brother, Pat at seventeen formed a short-lived band with fellow Kildare man Barry Moore (Luka Bloom) before going to Dublin. Acquiring first a cittern, then bouzouki and bodhrán, he played the city's clubs in the company of Paddy Keenan and Davy Spillane before moving to Manchester in 1975 to study art and design. Having acquired a following in the North of England's folk clubs, he turned professional, first as a soloist then next as a member of **The Battlefield Band**, recording one album with them, **At the Front**. Next stop was Brittany, where he recorded his first album, **Rock and Roses**, before a spell in Brussels, releasing two further solo albums and playing for a while with the band Het Zwarte Goud. Moving to the US in the late 1980s he continued to develop his solo career, releasing two increasingly rock-oriented albums for Green Linnet and forming the **Kips Bay Céilí Band**. By the end of the following decade, the much-travelled Kilbride was now in London and continuing to prove himself a consummate performer. His best album is unquestionably **Rock and More Roses**, a compilation of his original album and later tracks recorded in Belgium. Pat's choice of songs reveals the influence of musicians as varied as Leo O'Kelly, Martin Carthy and The Incredible String Band's Robin Williamson, but the real delight is his marvellous finger-picking guitar which offers a new dimension to a set dance tune like "The Blackbird" or, more uproariously, a couple of wonderful horn-pipes, "Anne's Favourite/Kitty's Wedding".

⊙ **Rock and More Roses**   Temple Records, 1990

Stunning guitar work and eloquent vocals from the globetrotting Kilbride.

Tom Lenihan

The much-collected singer and storyteller **Tom Lenihan** (1905–90) was born into a family of ten in Knockbrack, near Miltown Malbay, Co. Clare. Considered by many to have been one of the most accomplished traditional singers, especially of narrative songs, Tom's family background was intensely musical. Garret Barry, the blind piper, had been a regular visitor, and Tom's father recalled him often playing throughout the night at house dances (or "swar-rys" as they were known in West Clare). Tom himself would recount a story of the piper's method of obtaining porter by ceasing to play and lilting "Hurry the Jug" until it was placed in his hand! Surprisingly, since all his siblings learned at least one instrument, Tom expressed no interest in doing so, compensating by becoming an expert dancer and, in time, an impressive lilter and singer. He spent most of his adult life working as a farmer with his wife Margaret, while amassing a mountainous collection of songs from every available source. A popular singer at both house parties and in pubs (though a teetotaller), increasing interest in the music of Clare led, in his latter years, to appearances at festivals around the country and on radio and television, though many will remember him as the mainstay of the singing event during the Willie Clancy Summer School. During his lifetime Tom released one album for the Topic label, **Traditional Songs from West Clare** (1978). Subsequently reissued as **Paddy's Panacea**, it combines songs and stories (the latter taped in the Lenihans' kitchen) and illustrates the man's utter mastery of his native singing style. Almost confidential in tone, his clearly enunciated delivery for the most part ignores embellishment and tells a tale in a simple, engaging manner, such as the droll "Paddy, the Cockney and the Ass" in which a "naive" countryman outsmarts a city slicker, or, more harrowingly, "The Lake of Coolfin", the tale of a drowning. The stories on the album, along with many songs, were taped by Tom Munnelly, who collected much of Lenihan's folklore over a twenty-year period. This is now archived in University College Dublin's Department of Irish Folklore and a selection, consisting of a book by Munnelly and two cassettes has been issued as the elegantly presented **The Mount Callan Garland**.

📼 Paddy's Panacea	Ossian Publications, 1978

A smashing sample of songs and stories from one of Ireland's greatest traditional singers.

📼 **The Mount Callan Garland**	Comhairle Bhéaloideas Éireann, 1971–90

This stupendous collection (a double cassette plus book) is worth acquiring for Tom Munnelly's enthralling account of Lenihan's life.

Loyalist and Orange Order singers

While Republican songs have a currency throughout the island and a continuing popularity in the US, Loyalist songs are far less well known. Though Orange Order parades are still accompanied by the traditional fife and Lambeg drum bands (see p.190), the singing tradition had virtually died out by the late 1960s. The singer with the widest repertoire was, undoubtedly, **Robert Cinnamond** who knew songs dating back to the early nineteenth century while many Nationalists, such as **Paddy Tunney**, also knew and occasionally sang material from the opposing tradition. However, the onset and prolonged duration of the Troubles in Northern Ireland meant that reviving the songs was seen, in certain quarters, as another means of proclaiming the defence of the Union with the United Kingdom and the assertion of the Loyalist identity. Though some new songs were written in this period, the overwhelming majority date from the nineteenth century and early twentieth century and were originally circulated on broadsheets. Many of these have been collected and published by the Ulster Society. Song titles often typically commemorate key events in Loyalist or Orange Order history or express Loyalist pride – "The Battle of Garvagh", "Derry's Walls", "The Sash My Father Wore", and, of course "The Crimson Banner" (also known as "No Surrender"). The best collection available is **Historical Folk Songs of Ulster** by the **Houl Yer Whisht Folk Group**, led by **Bobbie Hanvey**, who, though born into a Nationalist family, has amassed one of the most comprehensive collections of Orange traditional music in the country.

⊙ Historical Folk Songs of Ulster	Outlet, undated

Not so much a celebration of Loyalism as a judicious selection of songs from the movement's history.

John and Tim Lyons

John Lyons (b. 1934) and **Tim Lyons** (b.1939) are two of Ireland's finest revivalist singers as well as accomplished players of the harmonica, melodeon and accordion. Born into a Co. Cork musical family, they both spent some years in England after the family emigrated in the early 1950s. John returned to Cork in 1955, playing in local céilí bands and beginning his song collection. Since the 1960s, he has been based in Clare where his increasing renown as an expressive singer saw his recording of **The May Morning Dew** for Topic in 1971, which includes a delightful version of the classic "The Maid on the Shore". More recently John released **The Troubled Man**, an album of unaccompanied singing where his colourful voice proves well suited to songs as varied as "The Boys of Mullaghbawn" and "Kerry Hills".

Tim also went back to Ireland in the late 1950s, where he was inspired to study sean-nós singing, but soon returned to England where he became an important figure in the folk revival, singing at folk clubs around the country and playing in Irish pubs and clubs around London. In 1970 he too settled in Clare and recorded the hard-to-find **The Green Linnet** for the Leader label. Fortunately, his second album, **Easter Snow** is still available, albeit only on cassette, and includes his ebullient version of the poteen-praising "The Humours of Whiskey". A spell with **De Dannan** followed. Still a superb interpreter of traditional song, Tim continues to tour and is known as one of the wittiest bookings on the folk and festival circuit, thanks in part to his self-penned satirical songs which he recorded on 1988's **Knock, Knock, Knock** in partnership with flute-player **Fintan Vallely** as the duo **Schitheredee**. Tim can also be heard singing "Henry Joy McCracken" on **The Croppy's Complaint** Rebellion commemoration album.

The Troubled Man   West Winds, 1993

Powerful narrative singing at its best from John Lyons.

📼 **Easter Snow**   Green Linnet, 1978

A splendid rendition of "Lord Gregory" and another strong album from Tim Lyons.

Jimmy MacCarthy

I t's rare for songwriters to be as famous as the singers who perform their songs, but in Ireland **Jimmy MacCarthy**'s reputation stands as high as his brother Seán's famed sculpture of the hurler Christy Ring at Cork Airport. Though he sees himself first and foremost as a singer – his 1991 album **The Song of the Singing Horseman** is well worth hearing – it's as a writer of classic contemporary songs that Jimmy will always be remembered. Since the early 1980s, Irish singers have clamoured to record his works and, fortunately, some of the best interpretations have been compiled on the impressive **Warmer for the Spark** which takes its title from a line in the opening track, "No Frontiers" sung by Mary Black. Here can be found Christy Moore's "Ride On" and "Missing You", Maura O'Connell's "Mystic Lipstick" and Mary Coughlan's "Ancient Rain", all samples of the soft, yet strangely triumphant songs of love and longing that are the Cork man's speciality.

⊙ **Warmer for the Spark:**
The Songs of Jimmy MacCarthy Volume One   Dara, 1997

The best of Irish contemporary songs from the pen of the unique Mr MacCarthy.

Geraldine MacGowan

A fter the break-up of **Oisín**, the band's singer/bodhrán-player **Geraldine MacGowan** and her guitarist husband Shay moved to Germany and, with their two children, set up the MacGowan & Son pub in Hannover. While this became one of Germany's premier Irish music venues, Geraldine has established a solo career which, mirroring Oisín's own successes, has garnered more acclaim in Northern Europe than her native country. Her third and latest album, **Timeless** sees her essaying a trio format with Chris Jones (guitars, keyboards and backing vocals) and Brian O'Connor (flutes and whistles). Still showing a good ear for a song – and a distinct penchant for Sandy Denny's material – the undoubted highlight is her tautly emotive rendition of "The Month of January", the tale of an unmarried mother's abandonment by her family and lover, which was once in the repertoire of Sarah Makem.

⊙ **Timeless**   Magnetic Music, 1999

A heady brew of traditional and contemporary song.

Dolly MacMahon

One of the classic albums of Irish song was recorded by the South Galway singer, **Dolly MacMahon** in the 1960s. Simply called **Dolly**, it still sparkles with a dewy freshness almost forty years on. The oral tradition was strong in Dolly's family and she was blessed with a delightful honeyed voice, capable of a considerable interpretative range. Many of the songs are unaccompanied and in English, for instance the Irish version of one of the classic ballads from the English–Scottish traditions, "Lord Gregory". The two songs in the Irish language are "Brídín Vesey", written by one of Connacht's greatest folk poets, Antaine Raifteraí, and a macaronic ditty, "Dandling Song". Accompaniment, where provided, comes from three of Ireland's greatest musicians, Paddy Moloney, Denis Murphy and Michael Tubridy. Dolly also sang and toured regularly with The Dubliners.

| 📼 **Dolly** | Claddagh, 1966 |

Gorgeous, sweet-toned singing; a lost classic.

Sarah and Tommy Makem

All too many youthful winners of "Most Promising" titles in their field proceed to disappear promptly without trace, but the judges at Newport Folk Festival in 1961 certainly proved their perspicacity when they tipped Joan Baez and **Tommy Makem** for the top. Makem may not have achieved quite the beatified heights of Bob Dylan's ex, but he's certainly borne out that early promise, currently still going strong into the fifth decade of a performing career, during which he's been hailed as a major pioneer of the American and Irish folk revivals of the 1950s–60s, and subsequently as half of one of the best-loved duos in Irish music. Mind you, given his background, to call him a newcomer even in 1961 was something of a misnomer: as the son of **Sarah Makem**, inheritor of a generations-old family song tradition in Keady, Co. Armagh, Makem was singing almost before he could talk. Although Sarah never performed publicly outside her home area, her repertoire of over 500 Irish, Scots and English songs and her eloquently measured, richly evocative delivery won sufficient renown to attract the attention both of the BBC, for whose landmark 1950s folk programme *As I Roved Out* she recorded the title song, and American collectors Jean Ritchie and Diane Hamilton. This wider exposure led in turn to an album on the Topic label, **Sarah Makem: Ulster Ballad Singer** (1968). She can also be heard on two tracks – one solo, one with Tommy – on **The Lark in the Morning** (1955), comprising selected fruits from Hamilton's collecting expedition. That trip was additionally significant in first introducing Tommy to **Liam Clancy**, the youngest of the brothers with whom Makem would go on to achieve international fame, and – looking even further ahead – his future duo partner, who had come along as Hamilton's assistant.

Later the same year, Makem and Liam both emigrated to the US, and after trying their respective hands at acting and song collecting, they hooked up with Liam's elder brothers Tom and Pat, who were beginning to make a name for themselves amidst the emergent folksong revival in New York. Over the next decade, The **Clancy Brothers and Tommy Makem** (see p.167) transformed the profile of Irish music around the world, before Makem left to go solo in 1969. He had earlier recorded a solo album on Pat Clancy's Tradition label, **Songs of Tommy Makem** (1961), an all-traditional set including "The Lowlands of Holland", "As I Roved Out", "The Foggy Dew" and "The Irish Rover". While with the Clancys, Makem was the first to introduce the five-string Appalachian banjo into Irish music, influenced by his enthusiasm for Pete Seeger's band The Weavers, also emerging as a songwriter of distinction, with compositions like "Four Green Fields" and "The Winds are Singing Freedom" having since become standards of the Irish song repertoire.

After several successful years' touring solo, and starring in numerous TV series in Ireland, the UK, the US and Canada, Makem was booked onto the same 1975 festival bill in Cleveland, Ohio, as Liam Clancy, who had himself gone it alone in 1973. Their paths having already crossed on several similar occasions, they decided to perform a short joint set, winning a rapturous standing ovation that marked the start of a thirteen-year duo partnership.

Makem and Clancy recorded six albums together, including their self-titled 1976 debut, which first featured their best-known song together, Eric Bogle's anti-war anthem "And the Band Played Waltzing Matilda", and two live sets. Following their amicable separation in 1988, Makem has remained a perennially popular draw on the international Irish music circuit, continuing to record regularly, his most recent album being **The Song Tradition** (1998), while making further frequent forays into TV work. He has also written a book, *Tommy Makem's Secret Ireland* (1997) and performed in his own one-man theatre show, *Invasions and Legacies*, in 1999, exploring his interest in Irish mythology. His prolific contributions to Irish music and culture have been rewarded with numerous accolades, a place in *Irish America* magazine's Permanent Hall of Fame, and a Lifetime Achievement Award from the World Folk Music Association. Back home in South Armagh, he has established the Tommy Makem International Festival of Song, the first of which took place in June 2000, attracting a large international audience. His sons Shane, Conor and Rory, meanwhile, have earned a growing fan-base on the Irish-American folk scene as The Makem Brothers, continuing the family tradition into another generation.

⊙ **The Lark in the Morning**   Tradition, 1955

Includes Tommy's rich, pliant baritone in "The Cobbler" and Sarah Makem's commanding, delivery of "In The Month of January".

⊙ **The Song Tradition**   Shanachie, 1998

Performing original compositions as well as traditional material, there's an extra maturity and depth to Makem's voice thirty years on.

Eleanor McEvoy

"There's more to this woman than a woman's heart" sings Dubliner **Eleanor McEvoy** on the opening track of her latest album **Snapshots** (1999) in defiance of critics who still associate her only with the massive self-penned hit "Only A Woman's Heart". Eleanor learned piano and violin as a child and played with the National Youth Orchestra before studying for a degree in music at Trinity at the same time supporting herself by busking and playing in pit orchestras for musicals. Graduating in 1988, Eleanor spent three years as a violinist with the National Symphony

Orchestra before joining Mary Black's band as a backing singer and guitarist. "Only a Woman's Heart" came in 1992 and, for a time pigeon-holed Eleanor as a feminist folkie. She's shaken off the image, however, with three increasingly rock-oriented albums – **Eleanor McEvoy** and **What's Following Me?** are the other two – but there's still a lyrical intensity to her songwriting that sets her apart from her contemporaries. **Snapshot**'s subjects, for instance, includes alcoholism ("She Had it All"), lost love ("Did You Tell Him?") and anorexia ("Sophie").

⊙ Snapshots   Geffen, 1999

Bruised and brooding – perfect for bedsitters everywhere.

Sarah McQuaid

Irish-American singer-guitarist **Sarah McQuaid** was born in Madrid, raised in Chicago and discovered Irish traditional music while studying in France. By then she was already writing songs and performing in folk clubs. Back in the US and armed with the DADGAD open tuning she formed **Carnlough**, toured for several years and released a self-produced CD, **The Crooked Road**, in 1993. Moving to Dublin a year later, she became music columnist for *The Evening Herald* and a *Hot Press* contributor while also writing *The Irish DADGAD Guitar Book* (Ossian) and recording the accompanying cassette. Her 1997 debut album, **When Two Lovers Meet**, originally released on her own label, gained considerable airplay and the reason isn't hard to discern. Sarah's voice is both as warm as a turf fire and as rich as matured cognac. Enhanced by Gerry O'Beirne's sparse, but atmospheric production, "When a Man's in Love" (a nineteenth-century "night-visiting" song learned from Seán Corcoran) becomes a sensuous, spine-tingler, while her guitar-playing throughout should be a lesson to anyone unconvinced of the instrument's role in traditional music.

⊙ **When Two Lovers Meet**   Round Tower, 1997

An astonishing debut by a unique talent.

Kevin Mitchell

One of the finest contemporary exponents of the Northern song tradition, **Kevin Mitchell** was born in Derry in 1940, though has lived in Glasgow since 1969. Interest in Irish traditions led him to song and he began to compete in the Derry feis at the age of sixteen, winning the singing title in 1959. In the 1960s he gained an increasing reputation as an excellent come-all-ye singer, reflected nationally by his winning of the John Player Ballad-Singing Prize in 1965. Much of his early repertoire was learned from local Irish language singer Seán Gallagher and his family, though this expanded through singing with **Francie Brolly** of Dungiven and regular visits to Inishowen, Co. Donegal, where he met a number of older traditional singers. Always in demand for festivals, Kevin remains sadly underrecorded – his first LP **Free and Easy** was issued in 1981 and devotees of his spirited style had to wait another fifteen years for his first CD, the wonderful **I Sang That Sweet Refrain**. Virtually all the songs, mostly delivered unaccompanied, come from the northwest of the Ulster province and highlights include splendid versions of "The Rangy Ribs I Bought from Micky Doo" (learned from Francie Brolly) and "The Fanad Mare" (from Jimmy McHugh of Tyrone).

⊙ I Sang That Sweet Refrain   Greentrax, 1996

Indisputably, one of the contemporary greats of Irish song.

Christy Moore

Not content with having co-founded two of the most important bands in Irish musical history, **Planxty** and **Moving Hearts**, **Christy Moore** has also been widely credited with redefining the art of solo live performance. His single-handed ability to hold a crowd of thousands rapt in the palm of his hand, bereft of any props beyond a guitar or a bodhrán, won him a uniquely cherished, even revered place in Ireland's national affections. Deeply held but hard-thought political convictions have always been a key element in Moore's musical make-up, as in that spellbinding stage presence, his

unshakeable though untrumpeted integrity commanding respect even from many who oppose his views.

Born in Newbridge, Co. Kildare, in 1945, Moore grew up largely unschooled in traditional music, listening to early rock'n'roll on the radio "until I heard Liam Clancy, and all the other things were gone". A teenage ballad duo with childhood friend **Dónal Lunny**, **The Rakes of Kildare**, whetted his appetite for performing, and eventually he ditched his job as a bank clerk and headed for London in 1966, guitar in hand. A nomadic existence working the UK folk-club circuit ensued, encountering such revival luminaries as Ewan MacColl, Joe Heaney and Hamish Imlach, a lifestyle reflected in the title of his debut album, **Paddy on the Road** (1969). A mostly traditional collection, produced by Dominic Behan, only 500 copies were issued; those that survive now fetch eye-watering sums on the collectors' market.

The album that really kick-started his career, however, was his second, named with unwitting prophetic insight after the Kildare village where it was recorded. For it's on **Prosperous** (1972) that the line-up of Moore, Lunny, Liam O'Flynn and Andy Irvine first appears, heralding the birth of Planxty and introducing several proto-hallmarks of the band, in the segue from song to tune in the opening number, the vibrant synthesis of instrumental textures, and Moore's sturdy yet richly soulful vocals.

Planxty's giddy rise to fame is detailed elsewhere, but during their split between 1975 and 1978, Moore resumed his solo work, becoming a key fixture in the Anti-Nuclear Roadshow, a campaigning vehicle which contributed significantly towards undermining plans for an Irish nuclear power programme, meanwhile establishing Moore as a compelling political performer. Albums from this time reflect his broadening agenda, in songs like MacColl's classic indictment of anti-traveller prejudice, "The Moving On Song", on **Whatever Tickles Your Fancy** (1975), Guthrie's protest anthem "Sacco and Vanzetti", on **Christy Moore** (1976), "Joe McCann" and the anti-nuclear number "The Sun Is Burning" on **The Iron Behind the Velvet** (1978).

During Planxty's second incarnation, Moore released **Live In Dublin** (1979), which first captured his haunting treatment of the Scottish ballad "Black Is the Colour", but it was after his two years with Moving Hearts that he embarked on what's seen as his solo career proper. The aptly-titled **The Time Has Come** (1983) confidently bridges past and future, including "The Lakes of Pontchartrain" from his Planxty days, reprised versions of "Sacco and Vanzetti" and "The Moving On Song" (as "Go, Move, Shift"), and future standards like "Faithful Departed" and "Don't Forget Your Shovel".

Throughout the rest of the 1980s and the 1990s, Moore's steadily rising profile came increasingly to centre on his live performances; as these gained in power, so his recordings often struggled to match the magic he created onstage. By his own account, he only recently stopped feeling cowed by the studio environment, having previously tended to defer overmuch to producers. This explains the slight excess of pop-style trimmings that smooths the edge off otherwise excellent albums like **Ride On** (1984) **Ordinary Man** (1985) and **Unfinished Revolution** (1987), collectively containing a wealth of all-time Moore favourites including "City of Chicago" and "Natives" as well as the first two title tracks, plus the ebulliently playful "Delirium Tremens" and "Lisdoonvarna", highlighting Moore's distinctive talking-blues style.

A heart attack in 1987 spelled an end to Moore's considerable reputation as a hard-drinking hellraiser, while the Enniskillen bombing that same year saw him renouncing his previous support for the IRA's paramilitary campaign, calling it "an armed struggle in which too many little people are blown away." Perhaps reflecting this period of change and transition, **Voyage** (1989), although heavy on distinguished guests (including Sinéad O'Connor, Mary Black and Mícheál Ó Súilleabháin), was lighter on memorable content. **Smoke and Strong Whiskey** (1991), released on the label he'd set up with his longtime manager Mattie Fox, was another mixed bag, though it did contain the wonderfully mischievous show-opener "Welcome to the Cabaret", and a cover of Shane MacGowan's "Fairytale of New York" – one of several reciprocal compliments in Moore's latter career to the man who once named him as "the greatest living Irishman".

With **King Puck** (1993), Moore began stripping away some of the studio superfluities, opening with his superb cover of Jackson Browne's "Before the Deluge" but also giving his own songwriting, until now a relatively underplayed aspect of his work, greater prominence. As with **Graffiti Tongue** (1996), however, on which he wrote or co-wrote all the material, and performs entirely solo, reviews were more respectful than rapturous. Moore's increasingly soul-searching efforts to translate his peerless live communication skills onto record are intriguingly apparent on both these albums, especially when compared to the triumphant **Live At the Point** (1994), exhaustively culled from 22 concert recordings to depict an artist absolutely in his element, and at the peak of his powers.

The price of operating at such an intense, personally exacting level was brought starkly home in 1997, when Moore suffered what he's frankly described as a "total nervous breakdown". After a year's recuperation, he returned in style with **Traveller** (1999), aligning his characteristically resonant vocals with bold tranches of dance-style production, with surprisingly successful results. Sadly, as soon as he began gigging to promote the album, his old heart trouble resurfaced, forcing his permanent retirement from live performance; the announcement made national headlines in Ireland. With still more recordings up his sleeve, though, not to mention his long-awaited autobiography, *One Voice*, and the boxed set he swears he'll finish compiling one of these days, Christy Moore's magnetic, iconic presence looks set to bestride the Irish music world for a while to come.

⊙ Prosperous	Tara, 1972

The one that started it all; fascinating to hear Moore's developing vocal style, as well as the genesis of Planxty.

⊙ The Christy Moore Collection, Part 1	WEA, 1981–91
⊙ The Christy Moore Collection, Part 2	Grapevine, 1997

These two double albums collate well-nigh all the high points, in all their multifarious glory.

⊙ **Live at the Point**   Grapevine, 1994

Classics old and new the way they were meant to be heard, in the Dublin venue Moore came to regard almost as a second home.

Van Morrison

The ineffable but resonantly suggestive concept of Irishness, or more broadly of a "Celtic" consciousness, has vitally informed a considerable proportion of **Van Morrison**'s prolific musical output over the past four decades. Although the primary bedrock of his sound is a freely adapted amalgam of American styles – blues, R&B, jazz, gospel – it's also frequently been described as "Celtic soul", not least by the man himself, who by "Celtic" consciously alludes to both the Irish and the Scottish aspects of his Northern Irish background.

At different times during his career (consciously or not) Morrison's

Jak Kilby

sense of a "Celtic" heritage has also been specifically influenced by traditional music. While he was growing up in 1950s–60s East Belfast, the old Irish songs of family singalongs, together with the ballads of the McPeake Family, formed as much a part of his musical backdrop as the jazz, blues and country sounds of his parents' and neighbours' record collections – although he's acknowledged that he paid little attention at the time. Early instances of an "Irish" or "Celtic" flavour to Morrison's work can be argued for right back to **Astral Weeks** (1968), whether in its prevailing otherworldly qualities, or the referential specificity of tracks like "Cyprus Avenue" and "Madame George". Others include the version of "Purple Heather" (better known as "Will Ye Go Lassie Go") on **Hard Nose the Highway** (1973), the folk-ballad introspection of "Streets of Arlow" on **Veedon Fleece** (1974), and backing bands' names like the Caledonia Soul Orchestra.

During the 1980s, however, Morrison's return to his roots, both musically and spiritually, became a more explicit journey, or quest. His albums became littered with song titles like "Celtic Ray" (containing the line "I've been away too long"), "Celtic Swing", "Irish Heartbeat", "Tir na Nog" and "Celtic Incarnation", drawing frequently on traditional idioms and suffused with imagery evoking Irish mythology. "I think it can be dangerous not to validate the music of where you're from," he said in a 1982 interview. "For me it's traditional. I'm a traditionalist. I believe in tracing things back to the source and finding out what the real thing was, and how it changed."

For Morrison, this journey of (re)discovery involved such moves as featuring uilleann pipes on the yearning, meditative **Beautiful Vision** (1982) and the mystical, instrumentally-inclined **Inarticulate Speech of the Heart** (1983), and having Moving Hearts guest on **A Sense of Wonder** (1985). **No Guru, No Method, No Teacher** (1986) touched on the archetypal Irish theme of exile in "One Irish Rover" and "Got to Go Back", while the uplifting **Poetic Champions Compose** (1987) marries metaphysical speculation with buoyant melodic simplicity. This phase of Morrison's artistic odyssey reached its logical culmination in **Irish Heartbeat** (1988), recorded with **The Chieftains** – his first album-length collaboration, with Paddy Moloney sharing virtually all the arranging and production credits. After all the spiritual yearning and soulful contemplation of those preceding albums, here he can be heard letting his hair down in highly un-Van fashion on "Tell Me Ma" and "Star of the County Down", while leaving his own arresting blues/jazz imprint on "My Lagan Love", "Raglan Road" and "She Moved Through the Fair".

While Morrison has since moved on to revisit other areas of his musical roots, he has maintained a periodic connection with the traditional world, featuring prominently on The Chieftains' Grammy-winning **The Long Black Veil** (1995), and cropping up regularly in TV/recording projects like **A River of Sound** (1994) and Dónal Lunny's **Sult** (1996). While far too complex and contrary a character ever to be pinned down to any capsule classification, Morrison's embracing of his Irish and Celtic inheritance now forms a key element in his musical iconography.

⊙ **Van Morrison and The Chieftains: Irish Heartbeat**　Mercury, 1988

Morrison's highly individual take on much of the slower material marks this out as a genuinely dynamic and creative collaboration.

Máire Áine Ní Dhonnchadha

Why Claddagh has never reissued **Máire Áine Ní Dhonnchadha**'s 1970 album **Deora Aille** remains an unfathomable mystery for this is one of the classic albums of Irish song.

Máire Áine (1919–91) came from Spiddal and often appeared on radio and TV from the 1950s onwards. The original **Deora Aille** LP was one of the most elaborately packaged of all Irish releases, complete with inset gatefold sleeve and lyrics booklet, and features both a voice as clear as the "water from the rock" whence it derives its title and her rare full-length version of "Úna Bhán", sung with irresistible beauty. In complete contrast, is the jovial "An Faoitín", a song espousing the cause of the whiting as a fish fit for the tables of the nobility.

⊙ Deora Aille   Claddagh, 1970

Utterly gorgeous singing from the incomparable Máire Áine – come on, Claddagh, time for a reissue.

Aoife Ní Fhearraigh

Blessed with a light, pure voice, **Aoife Ní Fhearraigh**, from Luinneach in the Donegal Gaeltacht of Gaoth Dobhair (Gweedore) has been singing from an early age with her local church choir. Like many Gweedore children she was taught fiddle by Mairéad Ní Mhaonaigh's father, Proinsias, while another near neighbour, Máire Uí Bhraonáin – mother of the Clannad family – was her music teacher at secondary school. By then she was singing in local sessions and travelling to competitions, eventually winning the Oireachtas senior singing award in the early 1980s. Aoife's first album, **Loinneog Cheoil** (1991), demonstrated her love of the local singing tradition. Her 1996 album **Aoife**, with its dreamy production by Máire Brennan and Denis Woods, offers an easily discernible Clannad influence which reinforces Aoife's own controlled, tremulous style, typical of the singers of the nearby Rann na Feirste Gaeltacht from which she also draws four songs. Beautifully sung throughout, the album's highlights include a haunting love song "A Neansaí 'Mhile Grá" (from Teelin, Southwest Donegal) and an unusual question-and-answer duet with **Seoirse Ó Dochartaigh** on "Cailin a' tSléibhe Ruaidh". Aoife can also be heard singing live on **Trad Tráthnóna**.

⊙ **Aoife** Gael-Linn, 1996

The "Celtic hush" production may deter some, but there's no disputing Aoife's claims as a singer.

Pádraigín Ní Uallacháin

Thanks in great part to **Pádraigín Ní Uallacháin** (born Co. Louth, 1950) the South Ulster song tradition is alive and well. Now living in Mullaghbawn (in her mother's home county of Armagh) with husband **Len Graham**, Pádraigín was brought up in an Irish-speaking household. Her father's job as a schools inspector meant that house moves were a regular part of her formative years, though at thirteen she gained a scholarship to a Co. Monaghan boarding school with a strong singing tradition. Later, her interest in singing was inspired by hearing Máire Áine Nic Dhonncha and Seosamh Ó hÉanai in Connemara. Subsequently, she worked as a presenter and researcher for RTÉ – she was the first woman to read the news in Irish – before returning to university to take an MA on the Irish song tradition. Marriage to Len in 1982 catalysed her re-emerging interest in singing, though she took time out to raise their two children, while continuing to amass a vast song collection. A specific interest in songs for families has seen her release two superb collections of children's songs **A Stór 's a Stóirín** (in Irish) and **When I Was Young** (in English), the latter with Len and both with Garry Ó Briain. Her own first release, **An Dara Craiceann** (Beneath the Surface), consists largely of previously unrecorded songs from South Ulster and is an evocation of the many facets of love. Pádraigín has composed airs for some songs where the melody has been lost, sings both solo and accompanied with clarity and passion and includes a fascinating booklet featuring notes on the songs' origins and translations. 2000 saw the arrival of **An Irish Lullaby**, Pádraigín's exploration of the suantraí genre from ancient chants to newly-composed material.

⊙ **An Dara Craiceann** Gael-Linn, 1995

The passionate energy of Pádraigín's singing unequivocally conveys the emotions of these South Ulster love songs.

Darach Ó Catháin

The small Gaeltacht of Rath Cairn in Co. Meath was only established in 1935 as part of a government relocation scheme. Among the new inhabitants was **Darach Ó Catháin** (1922–87) who was born in Lettermore, Connemara in 1922. Darach lived for many years in Leeds, England, where he worked as a builder, but he never lost his love for the songs he learned in his childhood nor, on the evidence of his **Traditional Irish Unaccompanied Singing**

Darach Ó Catháin

Traditional Irish Unaccompanied Singing

album, the eloquence of his voice. Perhaps the songs of a migrant possess an additional strength and vitality, animated by estrangement, but, whatever the case, this stands alongside some of the greatest recordings of sean-nós ever made. Compelling, calm and authoritative, Ó Catháin was one of the undisputed masters of Irish song.

⊙ Traditional Irish Unaccompanied Singing   Shanachie, 1975

Joyous, redolent singing from the mighty Darach, including a gorgeous rendition of "Sail óg Rua".

Maura O'Connell

A singer who has made a virtue of falling between musical stools, **Maura O'Connell** has nonetheless steered arguably the surest artistic course out of all the ex-**De Dannan** chanteuses who have progressed to successful solo careers. Originally from Ennis, Co. Clare, O'Connell makes no claim to any traditional background, having grown up listening to pop and country music, learning her craft singing in school choirs and receiving informal tuition from her mother, who sang light opera. Her early folk-club gigs with singer-songwriter Mike Hanrahan resulted in the invitation to join De Dannan in 1980, the sensual, smoky lustre of her voice outweighing her lack of traditional songs, and featuring on the band's American vaudeville-themed album, **Star Spangled Molly** (1981). While touring with De Dannan, she got to know the members of top American roots outfit **New Grass Revival**, including banjo legend Bela Fleck, a developing musical relationship that eventually saw her moving to Nashville in 1987, where she continued collaborating with them and other leading US players like Mark O'Connor, Jerry Douglas, Edgar Meyer and Russ Barenberg.

Her first solo album **Western Highway** (1988) proved a major Irish hit while the second, **Just In Time** (1988), produced by Fleck, featured most of the above musicians, as well as guest vocals from Nanci Griffith, and offered a beguiling introduction to her evolving country-folk style. Its success saw her signed to Warner Bros for her next three albums, the Grammy-nominated **Helpless Heart** (1989), **A Real Life Story** (1991) and **Blue Is the Colour of Hope** (1992), through which she steadily broadened her vocal and stylistic compass to take in blues, soul, jazz, and pop shadings, covering songs by writers as diverse as Richard Thompson, Mary Chapin Carpenter and John Wesley Harding. She featured on both the mega-selling **A Woman's Heart** (1992) and **A Woman's Heart 2** (1994) albums and tours, resuming her own career with the alluringly multitextured **Stories** (1995), before revisiting her Irish roots in **Wandering Home** (1997), featuring some boldly individual takes on traditional and contemporary material, recorded in the company of Arty McGlynn, Dónal Lunny and Altan's Ciarán Tourish.

⊙ Wandering Home　　　　　　　　　　　　　　　　Rykodisc, 1997

Highlights include a reworking of "Do You Love An Apple" (as Irish blues) and an exquisitely poignant version of "Teddy O'Neill".

Robbie O'Connell

Waterford-born singer-guitarist, **Robbie O'Connell** was brought up in Carrick-on-Suir, Co. Tipperary, home to his uncles, **The Clancy Brothers**. His parents ran a hotel which featured a weekly folk club, a boon to an aspiring musician and Robbie became a regular performer there in his teens. After trying his hand on the English folk circuit, he took a degree at University College Dublin, using the vacations to establish his musical reputation in the

US. This led, in 1977, to his joining The Clancy Brothers and appearing on three of their albums. His own debut album, **Close to the Bone**, appeared in 1982, and shortly afterwards, he began working as a trio with **Mick Moloney** and accordionist **Jimmy Keane**, resulting in 1985's excellent **There Were Roses** album (featuring a splendid version of the Tommy Sands-penned title track) and 1987's **Kilkelly** (see p.387). Another notable 1980s collaboration was his liaison with Seamus Egan and Eileen Ivers in *The Green Fields of America* tour. Increasingly writing his own material, Robbie released **Love of the Land** (1989) and the superb **Never Learned to Dance** (1992), the latter featuring his maturing voice and a droll parody of Irish pub singers in "The Singer". By then, Robbie was back with the Clancys, featuring on **Older But No Wiser**, and joined Liam and Dónal Clancy for two further albums as Clancy, O'Connell, Clancy. His own latest album, **Humorous Songs**, is fair craic first time round, but does not endure repeated listening.

⊙ **Never Learned to Dance**   Green Linnet, 1992

O'Connell's finest album still contains one of the century's direst rhymes – "Dear Mr Galileo, please forgive the long delay-o."

Seoirse Ó Dochartaigh

Singer-guitarist **Seoirse Ó Dochartaigh** was born in Belfast and learned his first songs from his mother, Bride Doherty. It was not until he attended art college, however, that his interest in traditional music and culture was fully awakened and he began learning the Irish language. This led to a spell at the language school in Rann na Feirste where he started collecting Donegal songs. He has been based in the county since 1977 and developed a fine reputation as a painter while sporadically releasing albums on his own Errigal label. These include **Slán agus Beannacht** (1990), **Bláth Buí** (1992) and, the most experimental to date, **Oíche go Maidin** (1994). Using a sparse, echoic background and multitracking, Ó Dochartaigh's production blends non-traditional instruments (such as the recorder, cello and acoustic bass) and elements from both traditional and classical music to accompany his velvet-toned voice. Singing local and self-penned songs in Irish, English and the macaronic variety, the overall effect has – surprisingly enough – an almost Andalucian quality and makes perfect listening for a bright summer's morning.

⊙ Oíche go Maidin   Errigal, 1994

Stark, yet startlingly beautiful in places, this is Seoirse's most compelling work so far.

Lillis Ó Laoire

One of Donegal's foremost contemporary sean-nós singers is Lillis Ó Laoire from Gortahork, twice winner of the Corn Uí Riada in the 1990s and now director of The Song Centre in the Irish World Music Centre at the University of Limerick. Noted for his collecting of songs, particularly from Southwest Donegal and Tory Island, Lillis sings with a voice of velvet, sometimes producing sudden wonderful octave leaps in pitch. His only album, **Bláth Gach Géag dá dTíg** is a wonderfully warm collection drawn from Donegal's deep heritage. Highlights include "Sliabh a' Liag", a paean to the massive sea-cliffs written by a local Kilcar man as part of a poetic challenge with a bard from Ardara, and "A Phaidí A Ghrá", sung with Teresa Mc Clafferty and Eamonn Mac Ruairi in the unison style of their native Tory Island.

⊙ **Bláth Gach Géag dá dTíg**   Cló Iar-Chonnachta, 1992

Ó Laoire's vocal tour of Donegal is an indispensable survey of the strengths of the county's sean-nós tradition.

Iarla Ó Lionáird

Iarla Ó Lionáird has taken sean-nós singing to heights and places that few (including himself) dreamed possible. Indeed, in the early 1990s he took a two-year break from singing, feeling that no one shared his musical vision. Fortunately, Tony MacMahon persuaded him to sing at a festival in South Armagh, revitalizing Iarla's enthusiasm for his art and leading to his participation in the button accordionist's tremendous 1993 album with Noel Hill, **Aislingí Ceoil**. Seeking a record company which might equally value his

Jak Kilby

voice, Iarla wrote to Real World and found himself participating in one of the label's recording weeks. Also present was Simon Emmerson who was working on the first Afro Celt Sound System album and, on hearing Iarla sing, immediately invited him to participate. The resultant success of **Volume 1: Sound Magic** (see p.138) and the subsequent tours saw Iarla's memorable voice become well known to audiences around the world.

This was all a long way from the West Cork Gaeltacht of Cúil Aodha where Iarla was born into a family of twelve children in 1964. A mighty musical region, noted also for its poets and storytellers, Cúil Aodha is renowned for its singers and Iarla's mother and grandparents all sang in the sean-nós style, while his great-aunt was the late Elizabeth Cronin (see p.64). Iarla himself first performed at the age of five and first recorded for radio two years later, subsequently enhancing his reputation as a formidable singer by winning every competition he entered. Cúil Aodha's music reached many ears through Seán Ó Riada's formation of its local choir (Cóir Chúil Aodha) and Iarla was one of its members for many years until his early twenties, when he moved to Dublin to study literature at University College Dublin. Seán's son, Peadar, has remained a lasting influence on Ó Lionáird, who has described him as "the Brian Eno of Ireland...a sonic innovator". Iarla's growing reputation saw him appear at the Lorient Festival performance of Shaun Davey's **The Pilgrim** in 1983, featuring on the subsequent album and, by the end of the decade, he was presenting RTÉ's *The Pure Drop*. However, though his voice and teaching abilities were much in demand, he was becoming increasingly despondent about his music and the lack of comprehension of the essential elements of sean-nós: "They wanted to treat it as folk music, but sean-nós is darker, more passionate and ancient than that." Following his return, Iarla illustrated these qualities emphatically through his astonishing debut album, **The Seven Steps to Mercy – Seacht gCoiscéim na Trocaire** (1997) which includes a remarkably stark recording of him singing "Aisling Gheal" at the age of fourteen. Iarla's collaborator on the album was Michael Brook whose tape loops create an awesome ambience for the singer's exploration of the dark antiquity of sean-nós through spine-tingling renditions of songs such as "An Buachaill Caol Dubh". Iarla later took the album on tour, singing to a backdrop of computer-generated imagery and the accompaniment of Brook's tapes.

While continuing to tour and record with the Afro Celts, Iarla's next release was the soundtrack to Nichola Bruce's extraordinary film, **I Could Read the Sky** (2000), blending back-beats, samples and tape loops to depict the fragmented memory of an elderly Irish migrant labourer confronting the past in his London bedsit. Iarla's soundscapes match the subject's shifting reminiscences, whether of rural bliss in Co. Clare or the nightmares of urban existence. His singing is as atmospheric as ever and there are cameos for Martin Hayes and Noel Hill alongside a couple of chilling vocals from Sinéad O'Connor (undoubtedly, the finest she has ever recorded).

⊙ **The Seven Steps to Mercy**   Real World, 1997

Drenched in emotion, Ó Lionáird's elemental voice soars across space and time – a true musical voyager.

Melanie O'Reilly

Brian O'Nolan (aka Flann O'Brien/Myles na Gopaleen) once noted that it was no wonder the Irish had never taken to jazz as two of the word's letters didn't even appear in the Irish language, but then **Melanie O'Reilly** was no more than a tot when the great novelist and humorist died in 1966. Melanie is a complete original, drawing her influences from characters as far afield as the jazz divas Billie Holiday and Sarah Vaughan, Seán Ó Riada, Horslips and Joe Heaney to produce a unique and powerful Irish fusion of jazz and traditional music. Add to this Melanie's magical voice and you have a concoction as powerful as it is innovative. Her outstanding qualities first surfaced on 1995's **Trá na Mara/The Sea Kingdom**, but effervesced into full maturity on the astonishing **House of the Dolphins**. Melanie's songs, often co-written by pianist Frank Murray, are inspired by sources such as The Wren Boys' tradition (see p.533), on the wonderfully rhythmic "Chugat an Púca", and Celtic forms of prayer, on the soulful "A Chara". But the album's crowning glory is "Annie Moore", a contemporary classic about the first Irishwoman to enter the US via the infamous Ellis Island immigration centre.

⊙ **House of the Dolphins**   Mistletoe Music, 1999

Spellbinding, uplifting music from a true innovator.

Finola Ó Siochrú

Arguably, there is no sound more beautiful than the sean-nós singing of the Corca Dhuibhne Gaeltacht of West Kerry where songs of love, loss and longing dominate a musical landscape as breathtaking as the scenery. Though she was brought up in Dublin, Finola Ó Siochrú's father came from Ventry, west of Dingle, and she spent childhood summers there before returning herself in the 1980s and beginning to sing in local sessions, most notably with piper/low whistler Eoin Duignan. Now based in Kinvara, Co. Galway, Finola released an immaculate collection of West Kerry songs, **Searc Mo**

Chléib/Love of My Heart in 1999. Delivered with a voice rich with purity and passion, virtually all are love songs, including a stunning version of "Cáit Bhán agus í Marbh" (the original source for "I am Stretched on Your Grave"), with the exception of "Amhrán an tSagairt", an impudent ditty about a mischievous priest. Purists may quibble about her addition of music to five of the songs, which Finola sees more as interludes than new interpretations, and it's hard to argue when the musicians include Brendan Begley, Máire Breatnach and Steve Cooney.

⊙ Searc Mo Chléib   own label, 1999

Gorgeous, impassioned singing of some of West Kerry's "big" songs.

Niamh Parsons

Dubliner **Niamh Parsons** was one of the most startling vocal talents to emerge in the 1990s. From a family of singers on her father's side and Clare fiddlers on her mother's, Niamh regularly sang at Dublin's Brazen Head pub where she was spotted by **Gerry "Banjo" O'Connor** and subsequently spent two years in his band Killera. Meeting Belfast bass player Dee Moore saw changes in love and life and the formation of **The Loose Connections**, a powerful unit featuring John and Paul McSherry (pipes/whistles and guitar, respectively), Eddie Friel (piano) and the renowned, now deceased, drummer, Dave Early. As the line-up suggests, the band was a versatile blend of rock and traditional elements (and could throw in a little light jazz too) which admirably matched the powerful range of Niamh's soulful voice. The album **Loosely Connected** (1992) demonstrated her ability to sing in virtually any

HEIDI PEARSON

style, whether unaccompanied on a chilling "Lover's Ghost" or rocking away on "Little Big Time". A stint in **Arcady** ensued, including her magical rendition of "The Rocks of Bawn" on the band's **Many Happy Returns**, before The Loose Connections were reconvened for 1997's **Loosen Up**. Niamh's version of the Tom Waits song "The Briar and Rose" transformed the old growler's delicate love song into a traditional classic. However, even better was to come. Her 1999 album **Blackbirds and Thrushes** was one of the outstanding achievements of the decade. Traditional in content, it firmly established Niamh as a great singer of big songs, such as the unaccompanied "The Banks of the Nile". Other highlights included "Sally Sits Weeping", harmonized to wondrous effect with sister Anne, and "The Wounded Hussar" sung to a sparse accompaniment from Josephine Marsh's accordion. The following year's **In My Prime** was essentially more in the same vein: another powerful duet with Anne on the drone-backed title track, an unaccompanied but luscious rendition of "Annan Waters" and an atmospheric version of "Bold Doherty" culminating in a jig with the combined talents of Jo Marsh, fiddler Siobhán Peoples and Paul Kelly on mandolin.

⊙ **Loosely Connected**   Greentrax Records, 1992

One of the best debut albums of the last ten years.

⊙ **Blackbirds and Thrushes**   Green Linnet, 1999

An astonishingly sensual album from one of Ireland's great singers.

Rebel Songs

According to one school of thought, all traditional song is an inherently political medium, representing as it does the autonomous self-expression of those rendered otherwise voiceless or powerless. When you add to this Ireland's centuries-long history of political, economic and cultural oppression, and its even older history of music-making – in particular the ancient Celtic clan system of employing professional bards as chroniclers of the events of the day – it's hardly surprising that songs articulating some form of protest should figure so largely.

By the same token, distinguishing between what is and isn't a political or rebel song is frequently no simple matter. Sometimes it's a question of language, as with "Róisín Dubh", for instance, one of the best known Gaelic songs in the entire repertoire, dating back at least to the seventeenth century: it remains debatable whether it's written in subversive code, with the woman it describes symbolizing Ireland beset by political misfortune, or whether it's just a singularly eloquent love song. Muddying the waters further are the quantities of songs that have arisen from times of struggle against the machinations of self-serving authority (whether in the shape of an unjust landlord or the British government itself) as well as from the country's numerous outbreaks of actual armed conflict. References to taxation and unemployment in songs like "The Green Fields of America", as much as in explicit broadsides like "Wheels of the World", reveal a clear understanding among ordinary people of the larger forces at work behind their individual plight.

Emigration, particularly to the US, has also been a factor in both extending and altering the currency of songs which refer specifically to such events as the rebellion of 1798, the Fenians' campaigns, Easter 1916 and the Civil War, by simultaneously divesting them of immediate or concrete relevance, while investing them with totemic emotional importance. At the same time, until recent decades, these songs had to a large extent become absorbed into the wider ballad stock, regarded as items of orally transmitted history rather than political ammunition. Hence the fact that the **Clancy Brothers and Tommy Makem**, a key force in Irish music's return to popular respectability, could release **The Rising of the Moon: Irish Songs of Rebellion** (1959) as their debut LP without frightening the horses. The album contains many of the all-time classic rebel ballads, with the title song, "The Croppy Boy" and "Boulavogue" among those commemorating 1798, "The Foggy Dew" from 1916 and "Kevin Barr" from the Civil War.

Since the onset of the Northern Ireland Troubles in 1969, such songs have taken on a much more loaded significance, with a new chapter of Nationalist or Republican compositions also being opened, although its authors were often banned from the airwaves.

The **Moving Hearts** single "The Time has Come", evoking a mother's last goodbye to her hunger-striking son in the Maze, got past the censors in 1983, but **The Pogues'** "Birmingham Six" fell foul of freshly-reinforced restrictions a few years later.

One of the most thoughtful recent collections exploring the Irish rebel-song heritage is the double CD set **1798–1998: Irish Songs of Rebellion, Resistance and Reconciliation** (1998), compiled by **Ron Kavana** and performed by his twelve-piece Alias Acoustic Band, comprising mostly traditional material with a few contributions from the likes of W.B. Yeats, **Dominic Behan** and Kavana himself. From both a historical and a musicological perspective, **Frank Harte** and Dónal Lunny's **1798: The First Year of Liberty** (see p.76) vividly illuminates an iconic but often misrepresented episode, while for the full potent force – often as bitter as it's rousing – of the republican tradition, seek out Dominic Behan's **Easter Week and After** (see p.55), which recounts the history of the IRA from 1916 to Behan's own day.

⊙ 1798–1998: Irish Songs of Rebellion, Resistance and Reconciliation   Proper Records, 1998

From "Boolavogue" to "Skibbereen" and "James Connolly", Tommy Makem's "Four Green Fields" to Behan's "The Patriot Game", virtually all the traditional essentials are present.

Róise na nAmhrán

One of the queens of the Donegal sean-nós song tradition was **Róise Bean Mhic Grianna** (1879–1964), variously known as Róise Rua (Redhaired Rose) or, most commonly, **Róise na nAmhrán** (Rose of the Songs) who, though born on the mainland, lived most of her life on Arranmore Island. Róise's repertoire was fertilized by spells spent first when she was hired out to work in the area of East Donegal, Derry and Tyrone known as The Lagan and later in Scotland. She was recorded by Radio Éireann in 1953, singing around fifty songs, and though then in her seventies, still sang with passion and vigour. Twenty-five of these appear on **Songs of a Donegal Woman** and include popular Donegal songs such as "An Spealadóir" and "Má Théann Tú Chun Aonaigh".

Róise na nAmhrán

Songs of a Donegal Woman

⊙ Songs of a Donegal Woman	RTÉ, 1953

An estimable collection, including several otherwise unrecorded songs plus lyrics and song notes in a 52-page booklet.

Eleanor Shanley

Fresh-voiced singer, **Eleanor Shanley**, was working in an office in Dublin's Baggot Street and occasionally singing in sessions when she received the call to audition for **De Dannan**, thanks to a self-produced tape falling into the hands of Frankie Gavin. Replacing Dolores Keane, Eleanor stayed with the band until 1993 and can be heard in fine form on the **½ Set in Harlem** album. Her solo career was launched with 1995's eponymous album, a patchy release which revealed an eclectic taste in songs (from "Raglan Road" to Elvis Presley's "In the Ghetto"). 1997's **Desert Heart** is far superior, if still mainstream with Eleanor demonstrating that her voice is suited to ballads such as

"Sunday Morning, Holloway Road" and "Flame". Impeccably performed and produced, with stunning musicianship it is still a tad vacuous.

⊙ **Desert Heart** Grapevine, 1997

MOR Irish folk-rock, but, still, what a voice!

John Spillane

The Cork-based singer-guitarist who produced many a barnstorming performance with **Nomos** embarked on a solo career after the success of his 1997 self-penned solo album, **The Wells of the World**, produced by Declan Sinnott. There's a fine burr to Spillane's light tenor as he ranges across twelve self-penned songs of love, despair and deliverance (all in English apart from "Seachtain"). The opening "Johnny Don't Go to Ballincollig" is a cracker, the aforementioned "Seachtain" sees him applying sean-nós adornments in harmony with Mick Daly and Áine Whelan, while "The Bank of Ireland Sean-Nós Blues" is John's Irish take on the blues. He also provides some tasteful guitar playing (with the odd touch of concertina) and receives grand support from musicians including former Nomos colleagues Milne and Torpey and uilleann piper Brendan Ring.

⊙ **The Wells of the World** Hummingbird, 1997

One of the best of Ireland's new clutch of songwriters produces a magnetic debut.

Dáithí Sproule

A seminal figure in modern traditional music, singer and guitarist **Dáithí Sproule** (b. 1950) hails from Derry but spent most of his adolescent summers in the Rosses village of Rann na Feirste in the Donegal Gaeltacht. It was here that he first encountered the Ó Domhnaill family (Maighréad, Tríona and Mícheál), which in turn led to the formation of **Skara Brae**. In Dublin in the 1970s he made contact with many musicians including fiddler James Kelly and accordionist Paddy (Offaly) O'Brien with whom he formed **Bowhand** and recorded two albums. The band toured the US in 1979 and, subsequently, all three members settled there with Dáithí basing himself in Minnesota. Since then he's featured as accompanist on many albums (notably for Tommy Peoples on **Iron Man**), recorded two with **Trian** and maintained the Donegal connection through his long-time friendship with Maighréad Ní Mhaonaigh and membership of **Altan** (first appearing on record on their **Island Angel** album). The delicate finger-picked guitar style Dáithí first developed with Skara Brae is well to the fore on his own solo album **A Heart Made of Glass**, co-produced with his wife Patty Bronson. Dáithí's keen tenor voice has never lost its Northern edge and his diction is always precise. He delivers dandy versions of Ulster ballads such as "The Bold Belfast Shoemaker", while the harmonies on the Donegal emigration song "Gleanntáin Ghlas' Ghaoth Dobhair" (sung to the tune of "Paddy's Green Shamrock Shore") harken back to his Skara Brae days.

⊙ A Heart Made of Glass   Green Linnet, 1993

A mellow, relaxed gem from one of Derry's finest with Liz Carroll and Peter Ostroushko (fiddle and mandolin) appearing as guests.

Nioclás Tóibín

Some would argue that **Nioclás Tóibín** (1928–94) was not only the greatest singer from the Waterford Gaeltacht of Na Déise, but one of the most majestic voices Ireland has ever produced. From Rinn Ò gCuanach (Ring), Nioclás learned his songs from his parents who, in turn, had learned from their own forebears and it is almost impossible to describe the sheer beauty and power of his singing in words. His vocal control was staggering and allowed him to create the subtlest of inflections in his singing without ever detracting from a song's essential melodic line. Champion at the Oireachtas major singing competition (now Corn Uí Riada) for a unique three consecutive years (1961–63), his repertoire encompassed over three hundred songs, including those from local poets, but also many others from around the country. There is one song, in particular, with which he will always be associated. "Na Connerys", one of the "big" songs in the tradition, recalls the sufferings of three brothers transported from Waterford to New South Wales in the first half of the nineteenth century as a consequence of disputes over land rights. It's included on the definitive **Rinn na Gael**, an outstanding compilation of Tóibin's singing from the radio archives, which also features a quite extraordinary version of "Róisín Dubh", where his voice gives the impression of being just about to crack under the stress of emotion without ever quite doing so.

⊙ **Rinn na Gael**   Cló Iar-Chonnachta, 1970s–80s

Glorious singing from Nioclás Tóibín, one of the finest of all Irish singers.

Paddy Tunney

I n the forest of Castle Caldwell, Co. Fermanagh, there's a monument to a local musician, Denis McCabe, in the form of a stone fiddle bearing the letters DDD (taken by many to mean "Denis Died Drunk" on the day he fell from a barge and drowned in the lake). *The*

Stone Fiddle is also the autobiography of Paddy Tunney, one of the most colourful characters in traditional music and one of its finest unaccompanied singers. Paddy was born in Glasgow in 1921, though the Tunneys soon moved back to the Co. Donegal townland of Rusheen, a few miles west of Pettigo. Here he learned his first songs from his mother, Brigid, a notable singer herself, and began a process of collecting which has spanned eighty years. In his youth he was jailed for four years for IRA activities, using the time to exchange jigs and reels with fellow inmates by tapping on the water pipes. While inside he also studied and on his release moved to Dublin to train as a public health officer. When qualifed he took up his first post in Kerry in 1950, working the Dingle peninsula and taking the opportunity to learn new songs. He subsequently moved back to Donegal and, in 1952, was recorded (with his mother and Uncle Mick) by Radio Éireann singing a number of songs, including "The Flower of Sweet Strabane" and "The Enniskilling Dragoon" now available as **The Mountain Streams**.

Paddy continued his song collecting, meeting famed singers such as Geordie Hanna and Robert Cinnamond, while also writing his own, often witty material, such as "The Rodent Rebellion". In 1958, he and his brother Joe, a fine accordionist, performed at London's Royal Festival Hall as part of an international folk concert. Paddy sang two songs he helped to popularize, "The Mountain Streams Where the Moorcocks Crow" and "Lough Erne Shore" and was subsequently recorded for the English Folk Dance and Song Society's library. Always true to his roots, Tunney was vehemently critical of the ballad boom, memorably writing to the *Irish Press* in 1965 to pardon Ireland's young people for mistaking "the bellowing of bearded balladeers or the juggling and jingling of guitar-propped jokers for the genuine article". In the 1960s and 1970s he recorded a number of classic albums for the Topic label, including **The Irish Edge** (1967) and **The Flowery Vale** (1976). By the time of the latter, Paddy had moved to Galway – partly to see and meet some of the Connemara sean-nós greats – and shortly afterwards made his first American appearance. Publication of his autobiography was complemented by the release of **The Stone Fiddle** album, a classic collection of songs from the Fermanagh area sung, as ever, in Paddy's rich warm tones. Still thriving, Paddy's tales of his travels, *Where Songs Do Thunder* is a highly illuminating and often humorous account of the role of song in people's lives and includes many song lyrics.

📼 **The Mountain Streams**   Folktrax, 1952

Field recordings, including two of Paddy's most familiar songs, "Murlough Mary" and "The Rollicking Boys around Tandaragee".

📼 **The Stone Fiddle**   Green Linnet, 1982

Masterful interpretations of songs from Fermanagh adorned by Tunney's subtle vocal variations.

Pierce Turner

There is no one in the whole wide world of music quite like **Pierce Turner**; a unique visionary, the owner of a voice that drips emotion, a consummate lyricist and the creator of tunes which are both complex and accessible. Born and raised in Wexford town, Pierce's musical journey began as a boy soprano in his school choir and regularly sang in the local festival, an experience he describes as "like living inside a Catholic version of **Pet Sounds**" (the Beach Boys classic album). Plainsong was a formative influence, but the young Turner was developing his love of song through Emmet Spiceland and Tír na nÓg, while never losing his affection for the tunes of Carolan and the work of Seán Ó Riada. He was also learning the clarinet and piano and listening to the Beatles, Dylan and Pink Floyd. Spells in various beat groups, showbands and folk rock groups ensued before he and long-time friend (and future Black 47 singer/guitarist) **Larry Kirwan** set off for New York "just to escape the restrictions of Ireland and my own self-inflicted restrictions". They had a minor radio hit as a duo before forming new-wave band **The Major Thinkers** and nearly made it with a song called "Avenue B is the Place to Be".

Tiring of the scene, Pierce began composing instrumentals for modern dance and became friends with avant-garde composer Philip Glass. They headed for London and secured a record deal resulting in the album **It's Only a Long Way Across** (1986), co-produced by Glass, which included the classic "Wicklow Hills" (covered by Christy Moore) and Turner's droll account of Wexford gossip, "Musha God Help Her". Pierce next began collaborating with trombonist, **Fred Parcells** (later to join Black 47), resulting in a new depth to his sound, some astonishing live performances and 1989's stunning **The Sky and the Ground**. Even this, however, was surpassed by **Now is Heaven**, an album ridiculously overlooked by both critics and punters, and containing Turner's best-ever song, "All Messed Up", an exploration of personal confusion which draws on the flute of Seamus Egan to enhance the melody's traditional roots (the song "Seán Ó Duíbhir an Ghleanne"). Since then Pierce has released just two further albums, 1996's live **Manaña in Manhattan**, and the following year's superb **Angelic Language**. Record companies and record stores have problems categorizing Pierce (one Irish shop currently stocks his releases in the sean-nós section!), but the man's talent is unstoppable and deserves a far wider audience. Fortunately, he continues to write and play (the EP **Action** appeared in 1999), and the high points of his career have been collected on the comprehensive **The Compilation**.

⊙ **The Compilation**   Beggars Banquet, 1998

Just buy, listen and marvel.

Seán Tyrrell

In *Notes from the Heart* PJ Curtis described **Seán Tyrrell** as "the most intensely moving, soulful and talented singer of ballads and traditional songs in Ireland today". Born in 1943 in Galway city into a musical family Seán learnt the four-string banjo in his twenties and was regularly playing at the Folk Castle club, often as part of **Freedom Folk**. After a spell teaching in Belfast, Seán spent six years in the US, playing clubs and bars in New York and San Francisco and recording an album as part of the group **Apples in Winter**. Back in Ireland, living in The Burren, Seán continued writing and composing and in the late 1970s began playing a regular session in Kilfenora with Tommy Peoples at which, in later years, Davy Spillane often participated. His reputation as a singer grew, and his crowning achievement was to set eighteenth-century poet Brian Merriman's epic 1206-line poem *The Midnight Court* to traditional music. Launched at the 1992 Galway Arts Festival to enormous acclaim, it ran at the Druid Theatre for three weeks before an equally successful national tour.

Seán had appeared on Davy Spillane's 1989 **Shadow Hunter** album, but it was another five years before the release of his own first recording, the staggering **Cry of a Dreamer**. However, even this was surpassed by 1998's **The Orchard** where Seán packs almost 40 years of experience into a series of exquisitely performed songs, accompanied by musicians of the highest calibre (including co-producer Davy

Spillane, Josephine Marsh and fiddler John Kelly) plus his own sensitive playing of a variety of stringed instruments. Few would dare to open an album with "The Rising of the Moon" – irrevocably associated with The Clancy Brothers – but Seán's soulful tenor transforms the song from a battlecry to a tender message of hope. Elsewhere, there's a dramatic rendition of Liam Weldon's "Dark Horse on the Wind" and a witty "Curse on Casey". A brilliant singer at his brilliant best!

⊙ **The Orchard**   Longwalk Music, 1998

Staggering in concept, breathtaking in achievement.

Áine Uí Cheallaigh

Two times winner in the 1990s of the major sean-nós prize, Corn Uí Riada, **Áine Uí Cheallaigh** (née McPartland) was born in Belfast in 1959. Both parents were singers (her mother Póilín was from Ring in the Waterford Gaeltacht) although it was hearing a record by Nioclás Tóibín which inspired Áine to learn her first song in Irish. She studied music and Irish at University College Dublin, married husband Paddy and moved to Ring to teach. Once there, she began to immerse herself in the area's traditions, making a name for herself as an unaccompanied singer. Her reputation grew through winning the women's singing competition at the Ennis Oireachtas in 1990 and the prestigious Corn Uí Riada that same year and again in 1992. Her one solo album **Idir Dhá Chomhairle** (In Two Minds) is a treat for anyone who enjoys great singing. Áine's rich, powerful voice is equally at home with songs from the Ulster tradition, such as "Peace in Erin" (written by the Antrim schoolmaster Hugh McWilliams c.1783) and "Out of the Window", associated with Paddy Tunney. While songs from the Ring tradition include "A

Chumaraigh Aoibhinn Ó", where her backing band is nonpareil (Liam O'Flynn, Niall Vallely, Steve Cooney and the cello of Neil Martin). No subsequent albums have appeared, though Áine has sung in *Riverdance* and with **Anúna** and appears on **Who Fears to Speak**, the 1798 Bicentenary commemorative album, backed by the Irish Philharmonic Orchestra.

⊙ **Idir Dhá Chomhairle**   Gael-Linn, 1992

A magical album of solo and accompanied songs reveals Áine's incomparable ability to handle a variety of styles and emotions.

Ulster Singers

That the song tradition of the island's most northerly province, Ulster, developed predominantly within the English language is almost entirely due to the Plantation of settlers from lowland Scotland which began in the sixteenth century. With the notable exception of Co. Donegal, which remained relatively untouched by either British rule or settlement, the strength of Irish as a living language waned much more rapidly in Ulster than in most other parts of Ireland, and, by the time of Partition in 1921, English was the first language of almost the entire population of the six counties which constituted the new Northern Ireland.

However, singing in those six counties, in both neighbouring Monaghan and in the north of Louth (in Leinster province), continued to demonstrate its Irish origins and developed almost entirely separately to the folk-song traditions across the water. Estimates have suggested that roughly three-quarters of the songs in the Ulster tradition are of local origin, some indeed derived from poetry in Gaelic, while the remainder are of English or Scottish origin.

In a sense, unaccompanied singing in Ulster bears similarities to sean-nós, especially in that the tradition is as much about the singer as the song. Obviously, language difference creates its own variations, and singing in Ulster has been described in some quarters as "syllabic". However, there is considerable personal and regional variation. Fortunately, collectors were tirelessly active in the latter half of the twentieth century and some notable material has been recorded, though, sadly, almost in parallel to the gradual decline of the tradition. These include two collections sponsored by the Arts Council of Northern Ireland, Seán Corcoran's **Here's a Health** (1986), focusing on the singers of Co. Fermanagh, and Len Graham's **It's of My Rambles** (1993), concentrating on West Tyrone. Other major work has been undertaken by Robin Morton, through his book *Folk Songs of Ulster* and production of many records; Hugh Shields, whose *Shamrock, Rose and Thistle* examined the singing of North Derry, and, still flying the flag, John Moulden, editor of the Sam Henry collection of Ulster songs and disseminator of much material through his own Ulstersongs resource (see p.589).

Some of the key figures in Ulster song, such as **Len Graham**, **Pádraigín Ní Uallacháin**, **Paddy Tunney**, **Sarah Makem** and **Kevin Mitchell**, are described elsewhere. A huge influence was **Eddie Butcher** (1900–80), a labourer from Magilligan, Co. Derry, a rich area for song, well represented by singers in his own family. Eddie was one of the main subjects of Hugh Shields' research and, in consequence, became widely-known through broadcasts of his singing. His large repertoire consisted of local traditional songs, some of which he had learned as fragments and completed himself, and self-penned narrative ballads, all sung in a warm, leisurely and unelaborate style typical of both the area and the man himself. Reportedly, he was also fond of singing sentimental ballads such as "It's Only a Step from Killarney to Heaven". In the latter years of his life, he was visited by many singers (including Len Graham and Andy Irvine), eager to listen and learn. Eddie's few recordings include **Shamrock, Rose and Thistle**, which draws from the spectrum of his 200 or so songs.

Another notable singer was **Robert Cinnamond** (1884–1968) from Ballinderry, near Glenavy, Co. Antrim. A farm labourer, and later basket-maker, who also played the fiddle, Cinnamond possessed a unique repertoire and was much recorded in the 1950s and 1960s. Though a Protestant, he was equally at home singing songs from both sides of the political divide. However, Robert sang about many other subjects too and some of his material dated back to the early part of the nineteenth century. His singing style was deliberately high-pitched, but nonetheless effective, and can be heard on **You Rambling Boys of Pleasure**.

Joe Holmes (1906–78) was another Co. Antrim singer, but a much more active musician than Cinnamond, travelling around the county on his motorbike with his fiddle strapped to his back. The Holmes house in Killyrammer, near Ballymoney, was a popular calling point for musicians and Joe was heavily in demand as a player at dances. Though he stopped singing in the 1940s, an encounter with **Len Graham** (then a mere nineteen) in 1963 led to the pair forming a musical partnership based on unison singing which only ended on Joe's death. While Joe himself can be heard on various recordings, the pair recorded two grand albums, **Chaste Muses, Bards and Sages** (1975) and **After Dawning** (1978).

Geordie Hanna (1915–87) and his sister **Sarah Anne O'Neill** (b.1919) represent another aspect of the Ulster tradition. From Derrytresk, on Lough Neagh's Tyrone shore, Geordie possessed a voice aptly described by Ron Kavana as "most gentle and seductive" and demonstrated by the sheer beauty of his songs, such as "The Blackbird of Sweet Avondale". He and Sarah Anne shared and influenced each other's repertoire, while the latter's home was an important musical rendezvous in the 1960s where she often sang in her bright, eloquent style. The pair recorded the essential **On the Shores of Lough Neagh** in 1981. Though now in her eighties, Sarah Anne continues to sing in public.

Cathal McConnell and **Gabriel McArdle** have helped to maintain the Fermanagh song tradition while two other current singers worthy of attention are **Roisín White** (from Kilkeel, Co. Down) and **Patricia Flynn** (from Drumintee, South Armagh). Roisín's album **The First of My Rambles: Folk Songs from Ulster** (1992) includes songs from Joe Holmes delivered powerfully and lyrically while Patricia's **Stray Leaves** (1993) reveals a sweet voice with a remarkable tremulous edge.

◉ Shamrock, Rose and Thistle   Leader, 1971

Ballads, songs of courtship and labour, from the legendary Magilligan singer, Eddie Butcher.

▦ You Rambling Boys of Pleasure   Ossian Publications, 1950s–60s

Includes "Van Diemen's Land", the song most associated with Robert Cinnamond.

◉ On The Shores of Lough Neagh   Topic, 1981

A wonderful album from Geordie Hanna and Sarah Anne O'Neill, featuring Geordie's inimitable "On Yonder Hill There Sits a Hare".

⊙ Roisín White - The First of My Rambles   Veteran, 1992

Powerful unaccompanied songs from one of the North's most accomplished singers.

Liam Weldon

Agritty and majestic singer, **Liam Weldon** (b. The Liberties, Dublin, 1933) was one of the most popular figures in traditional music until his early death in 1995. His father bred greyhounds and worked as a bookie's runner and Liam learned much of his early music from travellers who found space for their caravans in his grand-mother's back yard. As a result, he retained a lifetime's fondness for the slow airs he first heard played by pipers, though his own early song collection was augmented by the dwindling breed of street singers and ballad-sheet sellers. When his father died in 1947, the fourteen-year-old Liam had to leave school to supplement the family's income, first as a bank messenger and later as a labourer in England. Returning in 1955, he worked at a variety of trades throughout the rest of his life, while honing his skills as a singer in Dublin's traditional clubs and pubs. He always preferred singing unaccompanied or to the sound of his own bodhrán, but also worked in a number of combina-tions: from 1966 with piper Paddy Keenan as **The Pavees** and, in the early 1970s, with Tommy Peoples and Matt Molloy as the short-lived 1691. In the subsequent decade he teamed up with Breton flute play-er **Pol Huellou**, releasing a jointly self-titled album for the French Goasco label in 1990. He also found time to run, with his wife Nellie, the Pavees Club throughout the 1970s, as well as other regular singers' clubs and sessions elsewhere. Much respected as a song collector, Liam's own songwriting skills were equally esteemed and reflected his lifelong and uncompromising support for the rights of the oppressed and underprivileged, especially the travelling people who had first inspired his own musical interests. His only solo recording, **Dark Horse on the Wind** (pronounced "wined"), released in 1976, is a glowing testimony to the man's passions. His own compositions include the title song (an awesome attack on political hypocrisy), "The Blue Tar Road" (defending the rights of travellers against the government) and "Jimmy Joe" (concern for the destiny of children). While traditional songs range from "The Well Below the Valley" to "Smuggling the Tin". All are sung unaccompanied or with just his own drum, bar an evocative accordion part for Paddy "Offaly" O'Brien on "James Connolly" and a couple of fine contributions from Dónal Lunny on guitar and bouzouki.

⊙ **Dark Horse on the Wind**   Mulligan, 1976

As marvellously passionate on record as in life, this is still an album of unrivalled power and eloquence.

Freddie White

Cobh-born singer **Freddie White** is both one of the more marginal and, conversely, influential figures working on the borderline of folk and rock. Releasing a mere five solo albums (including two live) in a career spanning more than 25 years, he has a well-earned reputation as one of the best interpreters of other's material and introduced the work of many international singers to Irish ears. His 1981 album **Do You Do**, for instance, included songs by writers as diverse as Jackson Browne, Frank Zappa and Randy Newman. His latest album, **My Country** is a paean to the poetry of his late brother-in-law, Don O'Sullivan, with verses adapted by Freddie and his sister Ann (Don's widow) and arranged in musical settings by the singer. It's an inspirational combination and provides ready fodder for White's emotionally-charged voice, whether exploring the quandaries of relationships in "The Devil and the Deep Blue Sea" or dealing humorously with the fate of the kidnapped racehorse Shergar in "The Last Supper".

⊙ **Do You Do**   Mulligan, 1981

A classic album by a classy singer.

⊙ **My Country**   Little Don Records, 1999

Wit and wisdom delivered perfectly packaged.

Gay and Terry Woods

One of the most important figures in the folk tradition since the mid-1960s, Dubliner **Terry Woods** began playing the banjo at the age of fourteen (moving on to guitar, cittern and concertina), before forming his first band, **The Apprentice Folk** with his girlfriend and future wife **Gay Corcoran**. In 1967 Terry replaced Joe Dolan in **Sweeney's Men**, recording the group's eponymous debut album as a trio and the ensuing **Tracks of Sweeney** as a duo with **Johnny Moynihan** after Andy Irvine had departed to travel around Eastern Europe. A spell then ensued with the loosely-knit collective **Orphanage** whose members included future Thin Lizzy stalwarts Phil Lynott and Brian Downey. Moving to England, Gay and Terry encountered Fairport Convention's former bass player Ashley Hutchings and formed a new folk-rock band with another folk duo, Tim Hart and Maddy Prior. This initial incarnation of **Steeleye Span** produced one album, 1970's **Hark! The Village Wait** before splitting. While Gay and Terry were forming **The Woodsband** (aka **Woods Band** and other variants), Steeleye Span reformed without them. Working first as a genuine band, but later reverting to their own names for tours and recordings with session musicians, the pair released a mixed bag of five albums between 1971 and 1978 playing, as one critic put it, "rock music with a lyrical, rustic flavour".

In 1980 the pair divorced and Gay formed the Dublin-based new-wave band **Auto da Fe** with keyboard player Trevor Knight. Noted for their vivacious theatrical performances, an eye-opener for those who had witnessed Gay perched on a stool, delicately strumming her autoharp, the band released a few singles, but failed to attract a major label and eventually folded. Meanwhile Terry Woods remarried, moved to the country and, apart from releasing a single ("Tennessee Stud") in 1981, took a musical backseat for almost 5 years until unexpectedly invited to join **The Pogues** in 1985 with whom he remained until 1993. He then formed **The Bucks** with **Ron Kavana** with whom he had previously co-written "Young Ned of the Hill" (on The Pogues' **Peace and Love** album), releasing **Dancin' to the Ceili Band** in 1994, and featuring the pipes of Paddy Keenan on the exotically titled "Psycho Ceili in Claremorris". Kavana departed after this album, but Terry still occasionally plays under the band's name. Meanwhile, in a surprising turnabout, Gay Woods rejoined Steeleye Span in 1994 and replaced Maddy Prior as its lead vocalist three years later.

⊙ **Dancin' to the Ceili Band**   WEA, 1994

A Bucks' album that is worth acquiring for the exotic "Psycho Ceili in Claremorris" alone.

Groups

E nsemble-playing is now the norm in Ireland and most musicians rarely play solo and unaccompanied in public, except in competitions or concerts. Apart from family-based bands, such as Na Casaidigh or Clannad, virtually every group has emerged from a session and its individual members will continue to play in other sessions too. Unlike the rock world, where "musical differences" are the hackneyed cause of personnel changes or disbandment, members of Irish traditional groups share the same music. Though people do fall out with each other, members leave for a variety of reasons: changes in employment, family commitments or simple relocation; a chance meeting and desire to further a new musical acquaintance; an offer of full-time paid musical employment, etc.

Band names tend to come in a limited range of varieties, nearly all are derived from either tune titles (Upstairs in a Tent, Toss the Feathers, The Moving Cloud); mythology (Danú, Oisín, De Dannan); place names or geographical features (Altan, North Cregg, The Dubliners); Irish patriots (The Wolfe Tones, Emmet Spiceland); or the Irish language (Anam, Solas, Déanta).

Aengus

I nfluential, though short-lived, **Aengus** consisted of Galwegian brothers **Jackie** (uilleann pipes, whistle and mandolin) and **Tony Small** (vocals, guitar) with **Garry Ó Briain** on mandocello.

Augmented by fiddler **Maurice Lennon** (Stockton's Wing), their only album, 1978's **Aengus**, is one of the decade's lost masterpieces. Immaculate ensemble playing characterizes the album from the opening set of double jigs, "Jackson's Morning Brush/Moloney's Wife", where Jackie's pipes blaze a powerful trail, via songs like the raunchy "The Card Game" to a closing set of now-familiar reels (the veritable "The Bucks of Oranmore" coming last of all). Jackie Small is nowadays better known as a broadcaster, archivist and music collector while Tony is still singing and writing songs ("The Welcome" features on Sliabh Notes' **Gleanntán**). Singer Robbie O'Connell and piano-accordionist Jimmy Keane recently revived the name Aengus for their own US-based quartet.

⊙ Aengus   Tara, 1978

A lost classic from the 1970s by four of the major figures in traditional music.

Afro Celt Sound System

Brought together by Grammy-nominated London producer Simon Emmerson, **Afro Celt Sound System**, an evolving collective of (mostly) Irish and African musicians, has achieved arguably the most successful synthesis to date of roots music and contemporary club culture. Their groundbreaking debut album **Volume 1: Sound Magic**, interweaving traditional instrumentation and vocals with techno, ambient and drum'n'bass soundscapes, was initially conceived as a one-off studio venture, but the ensuing enthusiasm among both band and audiences prompted longer-term ambitions. Apart from the African rhythms, the key to the Afro Celt sound is the use of uilleann pipes, with Ronan Browne and Davy Spillane featuring strongly on the first album. Founding Senegalese members **Kauwding Cissokho** and **Masamba Diop** were replaced by **N'Faly Kouyate** and **Moussa Sissokho**, on kora and percussion, joining Emmerson, whistle/bodhrán player **James McNally** (The Pogues/Marxman), sean-nós singer **Iarla Ó Lionáird** and Breton harpist **Myrdhin** from the original line-up. Their second album **Volume 2: Release** (1999) substituted some of its predecessor's shock-of-the-new edge for a more smoothly integrated sound, and featured a guest appearance from Sinéad O'Connor, among others, and had Mike McGoldrick replacing Spillane as second piper. Piping duties were subsequently the sole preserve of Emer Maycock.

| ⊙ Volume 1: Sound Magic | Real World, 1996 |

More erratic than its successor, perhaps, but positively crackling with the excitement of a trail being blazed.

Altan

The Donegal Gaeltacht of Gaoth Dobhair (Gweedore) is home to singer and fiddler **Mairéad Ní Mhaonaigh**, co-founder with the late **Frankie Kennedy** of **Altan**, the most successful traditional group of the last two decades. Their visionary approach drew its strength from a simple love for Donegal's musical traditions, whether the Irish songs Mairéad had learned from childhood or the region's Scottish influenced dance music – spiced with an occasional dash of Cape Breton. Their charismatic playing of fiddle and flute attracted some of Ireland's most talented musicians and Altan have deservedly become massively successful, though always retaining their integrity by refusing to adapt their sound to suit commercial pressures or international audiences.

Mairéad's father, Proinsías Ó Maonaigh, a renowned fiddler and teacher, has been one of the driving forces behind the enduring strength of Gweedore's musical tradition. His mother, Rósie Bheag Rósie Móire often played the melodeon in duets with Turlough Mac Suibhne, the Píobaire Mór, and some of the piper's dance tunes entered Proinsías's repertoire and reached Mairéad when she studied with him as a child. Like her sister Áine, Mairéad's first love was singing, but under her father's tuition she developed rapidly as a fiddler. Visitors to the house included fiddle teacher Dinny McLaughlin and, on occasions his pupil **Ciarán Tourish**. She also met John Doherty several times, while James Byrne, Danny O'Donnell and Tommy Peoples have remained lasting inspirations.

By her mid-teens Mairéad had become one of Donegal's most talented fiddlers with a distinctive style. Her hand grips the bow almost a third of the way up the shaft and seems to encroach even further as she bows with a dynamic rapidity, sometimes deliberately slurring and at others producing triplets of astonishing clarity. One man to be impressed was **Frankie Kennedy** from Anderstown in West Belfast whose affection for Donegal and affinity with its music inspired him to learn the flute. The pair's friendship blossomed while they trained as primary schoolteachers, and they continued to play together, making their recording debut in 1979 backing Belfast singer **Albert Fry**. Qualifying in 1981, they married and began teaching in Dublin. With **Dónal O'Hanlon** on bouzouki and Mairéad's brother **Gearóid** on guitar, the couple formed **Ragairne** ("revelry"), recording for RTÉ and playing the 1983 Belfast Folk Festival. By then, Frankie and Mairéad had begun work on the awesome **Ceol Aduaidh** ("Northern Music"), which on its release delighted audiences, thanks to the effervescent, fluid music which was to become Altan's hallmark. Alongside Gearóid, the album featured bouzouki player Fintan McManus and **Ciarán Curran** (from Kinawley, Co. Fermanagh) on cittern, while the version of the Munster love song "An Clár Bog Déil", included a young **Enya** on synthesizer. Subsequently, Mairéad, Frankie and Ciarán (switching to bouzouki) began to work as a trio, soon joined by Dublin-born guitarist **Mark Kelly**, though four years passed before their next studio venture, **Altan** (1987) which featured Mairéad's sister, Áine, on backing vocals. Recruiting fiddler **Paul O'Shaughnessy** Altan became a fully-fledged touring band and this line-up released three further albums, **Horse with a Heart** (1989), **The Red Crow** (1990) and **Harvest Storm** (1992). While still demonstrating their traditional roots, these display increasing imagination with the developing maturity of the band's sound captured in **Harvest Storm**'s wondrous Rathlin Island wedding song, "Dónal agus Morag", and Frankie's silvery rendition of "Drowsy Maggie".

Tragically, in 1991, Frankie was diagnosed with cancer, but he continued to play and tour despite increasing debilitation. In 1993 he appeared on Clannad's **Banba,** but his never-to-be-forgotten swan song was the consummate Altan album, the incomparable **Island Angel**. This marked the recording debut of another astounding Donegal fiddler, **Ciarán Tourish**, while another addition was longtime friend, guitarist **Dáithí Sproule** who had regularly participated in Altan's American tours. Launching Altan onto the world stage, **Island**

Angel is thoroughly gorgeous, whether it be the frenetic reels, such as "Tommy Peoples", the dynamic "Fermanagh Highlands" or the song about the efficacy of Donegal seaweed, "Dúlamán". Sadly, Frankie's condition deteriorated and he died the following year. A warm, kindly, but above all, spirited man, his life is commemorated by an annual winter school (see p.578) in Ghaoth Dobhair.

Featuring new recruit, button accordionist **Dermot Byrne**, Altan's first Virgin album, **Blackwater** (1996), naturally closed with "A Tune for Frankie", and together with the follow-up **Runaway Sunday** (1997), saw a period of consolidation and gathering international recognition. Personal change was also in the offing, and, in October, 1999, Mairéad and Dermot were married, an occasion celebrated at both church and subsequent party by a host of their friends from the music world.

Soon after came the release of **Another Sky**, an album of infinite grace and no little danger. While Mairéad's blithe voice has always been associated with songs in Irish (and there were three here), other material included a sensitive rendition of "Green Grow the Rushes", and, surprisingly, Bob Dylan's "Girl from the North Country". Unlike **Island Angel**, the album's overall mood is reminiscent of a relaxed Sunday morning rather than the fervour of the night before's session. Nevertheless, repeated playing reveals all the magnificence of the light on the Donegal skyline.

⊙ **Ceol Aduaidh**   Gael-Linn, 1983

An astonishingly strong debut album, establishing the template for Altan's subsequent success.

⊙ **Island Angel**   Green Linnet, 1993

Utterly peerless, the Irish album of the 1990s and most other decades too!

Anam

More by accident than design, **Anam** (Irish for "soul") have evolved over the years from an all-Irish college combo to that highly marketable commodity, the "pan-Celtic" band. Formed in 1992 by singer, songwriter, guitarist and bodhrán player **Brian Ó hEadhra**, they underwent various line-up changes before teaming up with Orcadian singer **Aimée Leonard** in 1994. After two independently-released albums, **Anam** (1994) and **Saoirse** (1995), and now slimmed down to a trio, completed by Dublin accordionist **Treasa Harkin**, they signed to Japan-based giant JVC and embarked on a hectic global touring schedule, between times recording their next two releases, the second introducing Cornish bouzouki/mandolin player **Neil Davey**. **First Footing** (1997) and **Riptide** (1998) saw Anam perfecting their deceptively delicate, thoughtfully crafted blend of traditional material and original folk-pop, with strong vocal contributions from Leonard and Ó hEadhra in both English and Irish. Following Leonard's replacement in 1998 by two more Scots, fiddler **Anne-Wendy Stevenson** and Gaelic singer/songwriter **Fiona MacKenzie**, **Tine Gheal** (2000) pointed to a continued, confident broadening of their musical palette. Treasa Harkin left Anam in 2000.

⊙ **Riptide**   Linn, 1998

Graceful, spacious song arrangements and sparkling instrumental work combine to produce Anam's most fully realized album.

Arcady

Formed in 1987 by **Johnny McDonagh** after leaving De Dannan, membership of **Arcady** has always been a moveable feast. The original line-up included singer/flute player **Seán Keane**, **Sharon Shannon** and **Cathal Hayden**, though, by the time of their 1993 album, **After the Ball**, new recruits included **Jackie Daly**, **Frances Black**, pianist **Patsy Broderick**, fiddler **Brendan Larrissey** and a Breton influence from guitarist **Nicholas Quemener**. Though reminiscent of De Dannan in both sound and style, the album's title track (an old music-hall favourite) became an unlikely hit single, though this and other country-tinged efforts failed to appeal to purists. Far more effective was 1996's **Many Happy Returns** which features some stunning vocals by **Niamh Parsons**, especially the Joe Heaney favourite, "The Rocks of Bawn" and an a capella version of "The Rambling Irishman" (with The Voice Squad guesting), together with taut instrumental playing from an almost unchanged line-up with the exception of **Conor Keane** for Daly.

⊙ **Many Happy Returns** Dara, 1996

Niamh Parsons' glorious singing could banish rainclouds and the band's playing is as tight as a glutton's belt.

Beginish

Taking their name from one of the Blasket Islands off the Kerry coast (beag inis means "little island"), the quartet **Beginish** play at a measured pace and with a delicacy unfashionable in this age of high velocity speed merchants. **Breandán Begley** (accordion), **Paul McGrattan** (flute) and **Paul O'Shaughnessy** (fiddle) are all well-known while fourth member, Mayo man **Noel O'Grady** (bouzouki) was a member of Liam O'Flynn's Given Note Band and has backed Matt Molloy and the Ní Dhomhnaill sisters. There are strong Donegal and Kerry flavours present in **Beginish**, the band's only album to date, with, for example, a couple of Pádraig O'Keeffe's slides leading into "Thadelo's" (learned from Johnny O'Leary), all played with a flowing and unfussed precision. Breandán's voice is in fine fettle on "The Rose of Aranmore" (associated with Seán Tyrrell) while Paul O'Shaughnessy shines in the true spirit of John Doherty on the march and subsequent reels "Kitty in the Lane/The Hawk/The Templeglentaun Reel". Guests include Arty McGlynn, Colm Murphy and, of course, the Ní Dhomhnaills!

⊙ Beginish   Tara, 1998

The wildness of the Kerry and Donegal styles combine to glorious effect.

Black 47

Larry Kirwan emigrated to the US with fellow Wexford man Pierce Turner in the early 1980s, first working as a duo before forming new-wave band The Major Thinkers. Following their break-up, he achieved success as a theatre director and playwright before forming **Black 47** (named after the worst year of the Great Famine) with uilleann piper, and then New York policeman, **Chris Byrne** (who also plays whistle and bodhrán and sings).

145

The pair devised a unique innovative sound, based on Byrne's traditional background and Kirwan's eclectic, sometimes industrial use of guitars, keyboards and programming and narrative song technique. A seven-year residency at Paddy Reilly's in Manhattan followed and the first of six albums came with a self-produced release, followed by major label signings by EMI America and then Mercury. By the time of 2000's **Trouble in the Land** the line-up included former Pierce Turner collaborator **Fred Parcells** (trombone, whistle), **Andrew Goodsight** (bass), **Thomas Hamlin** (drums, percussion) and original Dexy's Midnight Runners member **Geoff Blythe** (saxophones). The album reflects Black 47's reputation as one of the most innovative outfits around, blending influences as wide-ranging as traditional music, rock, rap, reggae and ska, while Kirwan delivers declamatory lyrics variously covering bigotry (the title track), lost love and goatskins ("Bodhráns on the Brain") and heroes ("Bobby Kennedy").

⊙ **Trouble in the Land**   Shanachie, 2000

Astonishingly powerful composite from a band ploughing its own furrow.

The Bothy Band

When it comes to making both a first and a lasting impression, The Bothy Band remain Irish music's unrivalled exemplars. More than a quarter-century later, their inaugural public performance – on February 2nd, 1975 in the Exam Hall of Trinity College, Dublin – is still talked of in awed, reverential tones, while their influence on successive generations of musicians continues to this day. Originally assembled for a one-off performance in 1974 by accordionist **Tony**

MacMahon, the prototype line-up – at first named Seachtar ("seven") – also featured **Paddy Glackin** (fiddle), **Matt Molloy** (flute, whistle), **Paddy Keenan** (uilleann pipes, whistle), **Dónal Lunny** (bouzouki, bodhrán), plus singers **Mícheál Ó Domhnaill** (guitar) and his sister **Tríona** (harpsichord, clavinet). Their immediate musical rapport, carrying over into subsequent sessions around Dublin, created its own irresistible momentum, and though MacMahon's day-job precluded his further involvement, the others rechristened themselves as a fully-fledged band. At the same time, where Planxty had borrowed from a rock-band format in their arrangement of instru-

ments within a band, the Bothys went a stage further and harnessed the power of rock'n'roll rhythms to traditional material and acoustic instrumentation.

Following that debut performance, offers of gigs began flooding in from around the fast-expanding Irish and international circuit, at which point Glackin moved on and was replaced by Donegal's **Tommy Peoples**. The similarly seismic impact of the band's self-titled first album (sometimes known as **1975**) soon prompted the move to a professional footing, launched with another legendary appearance at London's Hammersmith Town Hall.

Although The Bothy Band's concerts and recordings both contained their share of vocal highlights, often drawn from the vast store of Neillí Ní Dhomhnaill – the singers' aunt – they're remembered most vividly for their instrumental firepower, in an all-traditional repertoire of Irish and some Scottish tunes. The magnificent wildness and ferocity of Paddy Keenan's piping, the fiery verve of Peoples' fiddle, and Molloy's supple, muscular flute meshed triumphantly with compellingly forceful yet fleet-footed rhythm work, in which Lunny's self-styled "hacksaw" bouzouki technique, fusing rhythmic attack with elements of harmony and counterpoint to generate extra lift, played a crucial role. The six-strong line-up gave their sound unprecedented scale and depth for a traditional outfit, while providing abundant scope for variety within and between arrangements, even where, as on the first album, the material consists of virtually wall-to-wall jigs and reels.

Its successor, **Old Hag You Have Killed Me** (1976), aimed for rather greater diversity, making resonant use of multivocal harmonies on the otherworldly "Fionnghuala", a nonsensical piece of Scots Gaelic mouth-music, and another Caledonian borrowing, the sweetly mournful "Calum Sgaire", while also including three further songs among the twelve tracks, and even a couple of slower instrumentals. By this time, too, Kevin Burke had taken over from Peoples on fiddle, his highly ornamented, Sligo-derived style lending a marginally softer, more melodious edge to the overall sound. With the introduction of synthesizer and electric piano on **Out of the Wind, Into the Sun** (1977), the results were more polished yet, though still packing an explosive punch at full throttle.

After three albums in as many years, however, the pressures of sustaining such intense collective creativity alongside a full-time touring career were beginning to take their toll, with the band's members increasingly seeking other outlets in individual projects. There were to be no more studio recordings, although the concert album fans had been clamoring for, **After Hours – Live in Paris** (1979), stands as a fittingly incandescent valediction. The Bothy Band's last performance took place later that same year, but two BBC recordings of concerts in Paris in 1976 and London in 1978 (the former featuring Peter Browne in place of Keenan on pipes), released as **The Bothy Band – Live In Concert**, subsequently provided a last thrilling flourish to a brief but glorious career.

⊙ **Old Hag You Have Killed Me**   Mulligan, 1976

Combining their unsurpassed early drive and spirit of adventure with an assured broadening of their repertoire.

Bowhand

Amongst all the recent CD reissues – from the mainstream to the obscure – one band's name is remarkable by its absence. **Bowhand** were a vital trio consisting of fiddler **James Kelly**, button accordionist **Paddy O'Brien** (the younger one) and guitarist **Dáithí Sproule**. Though friends already, they only became a fully-fledged band through Shanachie's desire to record James who brought in Paddy and Dáithí for the session. This led to a successful tour, the album **Is It Yourself?** and the eventual settling of all three in the States. **Is It Yourself?** is a tremendous achievement, carefree in nature from the opening studio instruction "OK, lads" and featuring three musicians just out for wholehearted fun. Tunes don't so much trickle from fingers and bow as burst from the speakers, not least on Paddy's own composition, the reel "The Small Hills of Offaly" and a fine rendition of "The Rights of Man" hornpipe. Bowhand continued, on and off, until 1982 and released a second album, but this is the one to hunt out.

⊙ **Is It Yourself?** Shanachie, 1979

Captivating music from three of the best.

Boys of the Lough

Long before the concept of inter-Celtic kinship became the voguish selling point it is today, **The Boys of the Lough** brought together two Irishmen and two Scotsmen, with a view to exploring the connections and contrasts between their respective traditions. The very earliest sighting of the band, however, was as the all-Irish trio of singer/fiddler **Tommy Gunn**, singer and flute/whistle player **Cathal McConnell** – both from Co. Fermanagh – and Portadown singer, concertina and bodhrán player **Robin Morton**, who used the name for a 1967 TV appearance. After Gunn bowed out, McConnell and Morton continued as a duo, hooking up periodically with the Scottish pairing of Shetland fiddler **Aly Bain** and singer-guitarist **Mike Whellans**. They eventually formalized the arrangement following a well-received joint appearance at the 1971 Newcastle Folk Festival, resurrecting the name Boys of the Lough as it was one of the first tunes Bain and McConnell discovered they had in common.

It was also the tune that opened their eponymous debut album of 1972, by which time Whellans had left to go solo, replaced by Edinburgh singer-guitarist **Dick Gaughan**. That calling-card release introduced them as not-too-distant cousins of The Chieftains in terms of their sensitive ensemble arrangements and concentration on bringing out the instruments' natural colours – the application of such refined technique to traditional tunes then still being a notably innovative tactic. From the first, however, the Boys' repertoire also included songs, among the inaugural batch being Gaughan's quietly majestic "Andrew Lammie" a classic Scots ballad, and "In Praise of John Magee" – commemorating the nineteenth-century practice of wife-selling – sung unaccompanied in unison, Northern-style, by McConnell and Morton. A broad northern bias was another of the band's early signature traits, tracing an organic connection through the two Irishmen's body of songs and tunes, the Scots-influenced Donegal material provided by friends (like fiddler Tommy Peoples), and the many similarities between that region's renowned fiddle tradition and Bain's driving Shetland style – this last, too, consistently providing a vibrant counterweight to the arrangements' statelier tendencies.

"Music that tastes of itself" is the Boys' own summing-up of their methodology, one that has remained essentially unchanged through a career now spanning three decades and several personnel reshuffles. Gaughan's replacement in 1973 by Northumbrian multistringed instrumentalist **Dave Richardson** – author of the famous jig "Calliope House" – added another regional flavour to the pot, and completed the line-up that saw out most of the 1970s. Their recorded highlights included **Live At Passim** (1975), vividly capturing the convivial warmth of their concerts, and **Good Friends, Good Music** (1977), expanding the "Celtic-connections" theme via collaborations with top Scottish, American and Canadian guests. When Morton left in 1979, Richardson's brother **Tich** stepped in on guitar, his swing-accented style strongly influenced by the legendary Shetland player Willie Johnson, as introduced on **Regrouped** (1980). After a due pause following Tich's death in a car-crash in 1983, the band brought in uilleann piper and singer **Christy O'Leary** (from Kerry), and pianist/guitarist **John Coakley** (from Cork) who added a new southern slant to the overall sound, on albums such as **Welcoming Paddy Home** (1985) and **Farewell and Remember Me** (1987).

English guitarist **Chris Newman** took over briefly from Coakley during the mid-1990s, before he and O'Leary both left in 1997. Besides McConnell, Bain and Richardson, the Boys now include renowned Kerry singer/accordionist **Breandán Begley**, and young Scottish guitarist and bouzouki player **Malcolm Stitt**, a balance of continuity and freshness that's given the band yet another new lease of life, as highlighted on their latest release **The West Of Ireland** (1999). Memorable vocal performances from both McConnell and Begley combine with characteristically crisp and sparkling instrumental work, the latter further enlivened by contributions from guest pipers Kathryn Tickell (on Northumbrian pipes) and Mick O'Brien.

⊙ **Live At Passim**   Philo, 1975

A rich variety of material from Irish, Scottish and Shetland tunes to a traditional "cant" – the ancient Irish progenitor of talking blues.

⊙ **The Day Dawn**   Lough, 1994

A beautifully evocative semi-concept album featuring songs and tunes associated with northern midwinter traditions.

Bumblebees

Old friends **Colette O'Leary** (piano accordion and occasional cello), **Laoise Kelly** (harp and fiddle) and **Mary Shannon** (banjo, mandolin, mandola and fiddle) met up again in Galway in 1992 and started playing informally together. Invited by Mary's sister, Sharon, to join her in a series of gigs, the name **Bumblebees** was selected for their first appearance and promptly stuck like honey.

Their first, self-titled, album followed and they became a fully-fledged quartet in 1997 with the addition of Laoise's friend **Liz Doherty** on

fiddle, though she was to leave in early 2000. Criticized by backwoodsmen for "not being Irish enough", their latest album **Buzzin'**, co-produced with Lúnasa's Trevor Hutchinson, is a tour de force – at times more effervescent than a barrelful of sherbet, at others as dulcet as a nightingale. Yes, there are tunes from around the world, but, after all, Con Cassidy used to play "La Marseillaise" and it would be no surprise if a reel like "De Saint Paul à Terrebonne" ended up being played in bars from Cushendall to Cahirciveen.

⊙ **Buzzin'**   Beehive, 1999

An album which captures Bumblebees at their incomparable, eclectic best.

Buttons and Bows

Springing onto the scene in the early 1980s with flamboyant brio, came **Buttons and Bows**, a trio consisting of button accordionist **Jackie Daly** and the fiddlers, **Manus** and **Séamus McGuire** who had come together in regular sessions in Kinvara, Co. Galway. **Buttons and Bows** was originally the title of their 1984 debut album (referring to the members' instruments and not the Jane Russell song from the film *Paleface*!) but eventually attached itself to the band. Accompanied on record by **Garry Ó Briain**'s mandocello and **Charlie Lennon**'s piano, B&B took a global view from the outset, and the excellent **The First Month of Summer** saw sources such as French-speaking Canada for "Îles de la Madeleine" and "The Joyous Waltz", the Shetlands for "Margaret's Waltz" and Northumbria for the pipe tune "Sir Sydney Smith", while the outstanding track was Daly's vivacious version of the German-American J.J. Kimmel's "Fitzmaurice's Polka". Seemingly simple, but founded on massive collective experience, the band's music sparkled with a joie de vivre reminiscent of the dance band era. B&B reconvened with Ó Briain as a full member in 1994 for the equally animated **Grace Notes**.

⊙ **The First Month of Summer**   Green Linnet, 1987

Arguably the more influential of B&B's two early albums, thanks to Manus McGuire's penchant for French-Canadian material.

Calico

Voted best newcomers in *Irish Music* magazine's 1999 poll, Cork-based quartet **Calico** have actually been around for quite a while. Though released in 1998, their startling debut album **Celanova Square** was recorded between 1995 and 1996. The album showcased the brilliant interplay between the uilleann pipes and whistles of **Díarmaid Moynihan** (ex-Craobh Rua) and the fiddle of **Tola Custy** (brother of Mary), supported by the innovative accompaniment of **Donncha Moynihan** on guitar and **Pat Marsh** (brother of Josephine) on bouzouki. **Deirdre Moynihan** had joined by the follow-up **Songdogs** (2000), adding sparkling vocals to a collection which again highlighted the subtlety of Calico's arrangements and elegance of Díarmaid's instrumental compositions, not least on the cracking opener "The Red and the Gold" and the Galician-influenced "Santa Maria", while fiddles fly on Tola's invigorating "Up Downey". As on **Celanova Square**, clear Breton influences are apparent, but Calico's brilliance lies in their refreshing ability to absorb rather than replicate and **Songdogs** will surely enhance an already glowing reputation.

⊙ **Songdogs**   Black Hat Music, 2000

Crisp and discriminating music from a band who prove that there is no such thing as a "difficult" second album.

Na Casaidigh

F amilies play a formidable role in the continued vitality of traditional music in Ireland and there is no better example than **Na Casaidigh** (The Cassidys) from Gaoth Dobhair (Gweedore) in Donegal. This Gaeltacht area has produced an astonishing array of singers and musicians (Altan and Clannad being the most illustrious examples) and the Ó Casaide family is no exception. Singing and making music have been fundamental to Na Casaidigh's lives since childhood – their father is still choirmaster at the local church – and the original group of five brothers, **Aongus**, **Feargus**, **Fionntán**, **Odhran**, **Seathrún**, and their sister, **Caitríona** (replaced later by another brother, **Ciarán**), first drew widespread attention when the late tenor Frank Patterson invited them to appear on a recording. The 1980s saw the release of their first, self-titled album and recognition for their talents was reinforced by a live TV broadcast from Dublin

Castle, where the Irish government was hosting a banquet for Ronald Reagan. Whether Ronnie hummed along (or asked which band member was Hopalong) is unknown, but it set Na Casaidigh off on a busy international touring schedule which has taken in most of the world's continents and seen them memorably performing at a concert celebrating the signing of the Lómé convention in Togoland. Reprising their presidential engagements, they also played at the Belfast concert honouring Bill Clinton's involvement in the North's peace process.

Na Casaidigh have released several albums as staging posts throughout their travels. 1984 saw the grand **Féad an Iolair/Cry of the Eagle**, but the two to look out for are **1691** and **Óró Na Casaidigh**. The former is their

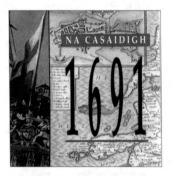

distinguished commemoration of the 300th anniversary of the Treaty of Limerick, the final act of the 1689–91 Williamite war. Concept albums are a rarity in traditional music (and succeed no more frequently than in other genres), but this is an astonishing achievement, capturing the course of the war's ending through a variety of moods from martial to melancholic. In contrast, **Óró** is Na Casaidigh's "heritage" album, a rousing re-creation of the songs and music learned in childhood. Some of it has a rock setting (with just a tad too much histrionic electric guitar) but otherwise the arrangements have an exquisite subtlety and are beautifully sung and played throughout. Among the very best unison singers around (they harmonize wonderfully too), the family's standard of musicianship never drops below the highest level.

⊙ **1691**   Gael-Linn, 1992

Forget Horslips, this is simply the best traditional concept album ever issued.

⊙ **Óró Na Casaidigh**   Sliced Bread Records, 1997

The original RTÉ release repackaged and reordered for the US market, but still as true in its translation as the day it was issued.

The Céilí Bandits

F amiliar figures around Clare since their formation in the mid-1990s, **The Céilí Bandits** original line-up consisted of singer, guitarist and bodhrán player, **Mick Casey**, fiddler (and no relation) **Yvonne Casey**, banjo player **Kevin Griffin** and bouzouki player **Eoin O'Neill**. This line-up graced many a session and recorded an eponymous debut album in 1998. By the time of the following year's **Hangin' at the Crossroads**, the Bandits were down to a core trio with mandolin and didgeridoo player **Quentin Cooper** replacing Mick and Kevin acquiring "honorary" membership. Yvonne is from Corofin (and a former pupil of Frank Custy) and has been sessioning since she was 13, while Eoin (originally from Dublin but based in Clare for many years) has graced many an album, most notably in recent years the outstanding Gerdie Commane/Joe Ryan collaboration. Quentin (also from Dublin) was inspired to learn mandolin by listening to Led Zeppelin! Fortunately, "Stairway to Heaven" does not feature on the latest album, an entirely instrumental venture on which the light blend of bouzouki and mandolin provides the perfect base for Yvonne's floating bow, resulting in a splendid, carefree set of tunes.

⊙ **Hangin' at the Crossroads** own label, 1999

A vagabond album in both name and nature.

Céilí Bands

Céilí bands can be seen as the phoenix that arose from the ashes of the old house-dance and crossroads dance traditions, after the 1920s craze for "modern" dances (waltzes, foxtrots, quicksteps, etc) finally saw the Catholic Church's age-old hostility towards dancing of any kind translated into draconian state action. Under the 1935 Public Dance Halls Act, all public dancing required a licence, thus shifting the locus of these social gatherings, based on "set" or formation dances (see pp.10–11) from domestic or outdoor settings to parochial halls (under the control of the priesthood) and private commercial venues. The old set and country dances were deemed unacceptable and figure dances (such as the four- and eight-hand reels) were now deliberately favoured, though illegal dance gatherings struggled on in some parts of the country. Musicians were forced to adapt to the new conditions (ie the extra volume required to play in bigger halls) as well as to competition from "modern" bands, by organizing themselves into groups, typically including fiddle, flute, accordion, piano and drums, although bass, banjo, uilleann pipes and even saxophone sometimes featured.

This new style of dance music was quickly popularized via radio broadcasts and by recordings of céilí bands (such as the **Moate** and **Aughrim Slopes**), and by its 1950s–60s heyday there were literally hundreds of bands in existence throughout Ireland, from ad hoc "scratch" outfits to fully-fledged professional acts, the latter, often decked out in suits and bow ties, touring internationally and playing to crowds of thousands at home and abroad. Despite purists' disdain for their non-traditional instrumentation and necessarily regimented rhythmic approach – Sean Ó Riada dismissed céilí bands as bearing "as much relation to music as the buzzing of a bluebottle in an upturned jam-jar" – many celebrated traditional players, including Tommy Peoples, Junior Crehan and more recently Martin Hayes have served their time in such line-ups. The advent of the showband era, and the rise of concert band acts like The Chieftains and Planxty, prompted a steady decline in céilí dancing from the mid-1960s on, although longstanding and close-knit acts like the **Tulla** and **Kilfenora** (both from Co. Clare) survived to welcome the renewed explosion in traditional dance's popularity during the 1980s and 90s.

Currently the tradition is being maintained by bands such as three-in-a-row All-Ireland champions, **The Táin Céilí Band**, based in Dundalk, while probably the most prolific recording band is the **Shaskeen**, formed in London in 1970, whose five-piece line-up includes two original members, Limerick banjo player Tom Cussen and percussionist Benny O'Connor from Co. Galway. The 1990s also saw the emergence of groups such as **Moving Cloud** (see p.211) and **Swallow's Tail Céilí Band**, sometimes described as "listening" céilí bands whose music deliberately harkens back to the Irish-American dance bands of the 1920s and 1930s.

⊙ **Tulla Céilí Band: A Celebration of 50 Years**   Green Linnet, 1996

P. J. Hayes still heads this legendary Clare outfit, whose unhurried style marries rock-steady timing with abundant frisky lift.

⊙ **Kilfenora Céilí Band – Set On Stone**   Torc, 1996

Even older than its Clare neighbour the Tulla, the Kilfenora today boasts a distinctively dynamic, pulsating style.

⊙ **Shaskeen – 25th Silver Jubilee Collection**   Own label, 1995

The latest album from the long-serving band now based in the West of Ireland is an ample demonstration of their lively, no-frills approach.

⊙ **Swallow's Tail Céilí Band**
– Hell for Leather   Sound Records, 1990s

A spirited, perky brew from the Sligo-based band, featuring accordionist PJ Hernon.

Celtus

Pat and **John McManus** were teenage prodigies, winning the All-Ireland championships on fiddle and tin whistle respectively before jettisoning their roots to form Mama's Boys (with their brother **Tommy** on drums), the hardest-rocking band ever to emerge from Co. Fermanagh – or the entire North, for that matter. They played with this line-up for most of the 1980s before re-emerging in the late 1990s as **Celtus** with an album, **Moonchild**, dedicated to Tommy who had died of leukaemia. Joined by **Jonathan Czerwik** on keyboards, their rich, multilayered sound (especially on the opening track "Strange Day in the Country") puts the "ether" in "ethereal" and steps boldly into Clannad's "Celtic Hush" territory. 1999's disappointing follow-up, **Portrait**, saw them regressing towards the stadium anthems of their previous incarnation, but is probably more internationally user-friendly, as a result. Czerwik was later replaced by **Dan Axtell**.

⊙ **Moonchild**   Soho Sony[2], 1997

You either love this music or search for the bin bags, whatever the case, there's no doubting the McManus brothers' ability.

Cherish the Ladies

Since their emergence in 1987, the Irish-American women's band **Cherish the Ladies** has been winning a deserved international reputation as one of the best traditional outfits around. Taking their name from the well-known jig, the band was formed following a series of New York concerts, organized by Mick Moloney, aimed at drawing attention to the growing numbers of Irish-American women playing traditional music in the US. The successful gigs led to the album, **Cherish the Ladies: Irish Traditional Musicians in America**, featuring performances by fiddlers **Liz Carroll** and **Eileen Ivers** and flute/whistle player **Joanie Madden**. While Ivers was an early member of the subsequent band which emerged, Madden and **Mary Coogan** (guitar, banjo, mandolin, bouzouki) have remained at its core throughout a significant number of changes.

Over the years the band's membership has included accordionist/flute player **Maureen Doherty Macken** (daughter of melodeon player Tom Doherty), fiddler **Win Horan**, singer **Cathy Ryan** and step-dancer **Eileen Golden** (whose dancing feet were a focal point of their stage act). However, by the time of their third studio album, **New Day Dawning**, the band's line-up had settled to include **Aoife Clancy** (vocals, guitar), **Siobhán Egan** (fiddle, bodhrán), **Donna Long** (piano, fiddle) and **Mary Rafferty** (accordion, concertina, whistle) – all born in the US, except for Aoife who is from "Clancyland", Co. Tipperary. The excellent **Threads of Time** followed, hotly pursued by their crowning glory, **At Home** (1999). The title celebrates the band's heritage and guests include Aoife's uncle Liam, Joanie Madden's father Joe, Siobhan's siblings Roryann and Seamus Egan and three generations of the Long family. As ever, CTL draw their material from a broad range of sources, often familial, and play with a light breezy style, underpinned by Long's stylish piano. Highlights include Aoife, plus assorted Clancys, singing on "John of Dreams", and a set of reels commencing with "Harvest Moon" (from Paddy "Tipperary" O'Brien). CTL's membership has subsequently changed again, with *Riverdance* fiddler **Liz Knowles** and singer **Deirdre Connolly** replacing Clancy and Egan. Aoife's own solo album, **It's About Time** (1994) is also well worth hunting down.

⊙ At Home	BMG/RCA, 1999

They say familiarity breeds contempt, but not in this grand romp from CTL and their kin.

The Chieftains

Without question, **The Chieftains** have done more than any other band to popularize Irish traditional music around the world. Their importance as role models, in pioneering musical methods and approaches which later became common practice, is simply incalculable. And with the band now approaching its fortieth anniversary, this trailblazing influence has derived not least from their resourcefully inventive handling of such a remarkably extended career trajectory.

Most of the original Chieftains – Dubliners **Paddy Moloney** (uilleann pipes, tin whistle), **Martin Fay** (fiddle) and **Séan Potts** (tin whistle), plus **Michael Tubridy** (flute, concertina) from Clare – first came together formally as members of Seán Ó Riada's Ceoltóirí Chualann during the early 1960s. In 1963, Guinness heir Garech Browne invited Moloney to make a one-off instrumental album for his fledgling Claddagh Records label (for whom The Chieftains were to record until the mid-1980s). With the aforesaid quartet joined by bodhrán player **Davey Fallon**, this Irish musical milestone was laid down over five nights (to accommodate the musicians' day-jobs) at Dublin's Peter Hunt Studios. In the context of the ballad boom – headed by the Clancys and The Dubliners – the spirited immediacy and stripped-down authenticity of **The Chieftains** (1964) was little short of revelatory. Moloney's arrangements of traditional airs and dance tunes were strongly influenced by Ó Riada's technique of spotlighting different instruments within a group format, as well as his use of harmony, eschewing pop inflections to focus on the tunes' inherent vitality and beauty.

This, in essence, was the approach that underpinned The Chieftains' musical evolution over the next two decades. **Chieftains 2** (1969) revealed their growing ensemble assurance, also marking the addition of young Dublin fiddler **Seán Keane**, and the elderly Fallon's replacement by yet another Dubliner, **Peadar Mercier**. The slight treading-water feel of **Chieftains 3** (1971) was forcefully dispelled by **Chieftains 4** (1973), which announced the arrival of Belfast harper Derek Bell. Besides enriching the subtle classical dimension of the band's sound, Bell also brought a new degree of lyricism and depth, consolidating Moloney's vision of how traditional music could be brought to a wider audience.

The potential extent of that audience was highlighted by a sell-out St Patrick's Day concert at London's Royal Albert Hall in 1975, after which the Chieftains embarked on a full-time career, signing internationally to Island Records in time for **Chieftains 5** (1975) and featuring on the soundtrack of Stanley Kubrick's Oscar-winning *Barry Lyndon* the same year. Heavy US radio airplay for their arrangement, taken from the film, of Ó Riada's "Mná na hÉireann" ("Women of Ireland") underwrote the success of their first full-scale American tour, while 1975 also saw the Chieftains named as *Melody Maker* Group of the Year. Peadar Mercier left after **Chieftains 5**, with bodhrán duties taken over by Kevin Conneff, whose singing talents were also subsequently incorporated into the band's performances.

There followed what's generally regarded as their most fertile period, with albums appearing thick and fast to satisfy their proliferating fan-base, from **Chieftains 6: Bonaparte's Retreat** (1976) to **Chieftains 9: Boil the Breakfast Early** (1980). The departure of Tubridy and Potts in 1979, and the addition of ex-Bothy Band founder and Planxty member **Matt Molloy** completed the line-up that remains today.

Folk-fusion projects may be ten-a-penny nowadays, but it was The Chieftains who paved the way, starting as early as **Bonaparte's Retreat**, with Moloney's extended, musical collage evoking the role of Irish exiles in the Napoleonic Wars. After **Chieftains 10** (1981) – itself containing a French carol and a set of Manx tunes – the '80s and '90s saw their development taking an increasingly international-ist, genre-spanning turn. The soundtrack projects, **Year of the French** (1982) and **Ballad of the Irish Horse** (1986), were notable for their technical ambition and imaginative orchestration, but it was **The Chieftains In China** (1985) which most strikingly signalled their broadening horizons, featuring traditional Chinese music alongside Irish material and some unexpected mergers between the two. With **A Celtic Wedding** (1987) it was Breton music's turn, after which the band promoted themselves into a different echelon of musical com-pany (not to mention marketability) altogether, accompanying Van

Van Morrison and the Chieftains, 1988

Morrison's renditions of traditional songs on the celebrated **Irish Heartbeat** (1988).

Throughout the late '80s and early '90s collaborations with star guest artists (including James Galway, Jackson Browne, Elvis Costello, Marianne Faithfull and Nanci Griffith), became the norm, although the results were often disappointingly bland. Having revisited their traditional heartland (and completed the Grammy hat-trick) with **The Celtic Harp: A Tribute to Edward Bunting** (1993), the Chieftains reached the acme of this glad-handing period with **The Long Black Veil** (1995). Contributions from the Rolling Stones, Van Morrison, Ry Cooder, Tom Jones, Sinéad O'Connor and Sting helped them towards their first US gold disc, a fourth Grammy, and *Time* magazine's vote for Album of the Year.

Switching tack yet again, the band headed for the "undiscovered" Spanish Celtic region of Galicia/Asturias, hooking up with the gifted young Galician piper Carlos Nunez and other local musicians (plus Ry Cooder and Linda Ronstadt) to explore the inter-Celtic and transatlantic musical links between Ireland, Spain and South America, in the rich musical tapestry of **Santiago** (1996). This was followed by **Tears of Stone** (1999), a stirring collection of mostly traditional songs themed around women and love, performed by female vocalists including Joni Mitchell, Bonnie Raitt and The Corrs. For their latest trick, The Chieftains returned to the source once more with **Water From the Well** (2000), assembling an array of luminaries to join in on their first all-traditional album in nearly a decade, testifying yet again to their unique – and seemingly inexhaustible – capacity for self-reinvention.

⊙ **The Chieftains**   Claddagh, 1964

The album that kick-started the modern evolution of Irish instrumental music.

⊙ **Chieftains 9: Boil the Breakfast Early**   Claddagh, 1980

The first recording from today's line-up, introducing Matt Molloy's distinctively powerful flute style and Kevin Conneff's singing.

Cían

The flute-concertina combination is a surprising rarity in Irish music, but maybe not for long after the success of **Cían**'s astounding debut album **Three Shouts from a Hill**. The unison playing of **Brian Duke** (flute) and **Padraig Rynne** (concertina) is almost peerless and the sparks really begin to fly when they crank up a gear on reels such as "The New Policeman". Meanwhile, bodhrán/percussion maestro **Damien Quinn** and ex-Danú man **Tim Murray** (guitar) generate rhythms of awesome complexity. Tim's in fine voice too on songs such as "Who Are You" and "Unquiet Grave". The band's repertoire covers many unfamiliar tunes, but it's worth seeking out their follow-up single "Paddy's Green Shamrock Shore" for their take on a more common song and, especially, for the two live tracks which demonstrate their equal brilliance in the flesh. Cían's name, by the way, comes from a character in Irish mythology and the album's title refers to a task set as part of a blood-fine to avenge his death. Padraig's earlier band, the then teenaged Turas, produced an effervescent recording, **Irish Traditional Music** (1996) which is also worth searching for.

⊙ **Three Shouts from a Hill**   own label, 1999

Duke and Rynne form a dazzling alliance on this energetic recording.

The Clancy Brothers and Tommy Makem

The Clancy Brothers tend to be viewed nowadays as a rather cozy institution, the granddaddies or elder statesmen of contemporary Irish music, whose trademark Aran sweaters have become the folk scene's most persistent sartorial stereotype. It's important to remember, however, that in the late-1950s and early-1960s heyday the Clancys were about as hip as they come, both in their adopted US, where they first emerged as the darlings of the burgeoning folk movement, playing the top Greenwich Village clubs and hobnobbing with the likes of Bob Dylan, Pete Seeger and the Reverend Gary Davis, and back in Ireland, where they were welcomed home as conquering heroes.

The Clancy fraternity – **Tom**, **Pat** and **Liam** – were born, between 1923 and 1932, into a well-known singing family in Carrick-on-Suir, Co. Tipperary. Tom and Pat, both aspiring actors, emigrated to Canada in 1947, moving on to Cleveland, Ohio, a year later, then to New York in 1950, where they began staging plays at the Cherry Lane Theater in Greenwich Village. Despite some successful productions, notably of *Othello* and O'Casey's *The Plough and the Stars*, money was always tight, so they hit on the idea of midnight folk concerts to help pay the rent on the venue, with Tom and Pat singing Irish songs alongside contributions from leading US performers including Seeger, Burl Ives, Jean Ritchie and Oscar Brand. These quickly proved a much bigger draw than the plays, and after Liam emigrated to join his brothers in 1955, together with his friend **Tommy Makem**, the four officially became **The Clancy Brothers and Tommy Makem**, as surprised as anyone else by their spiralling popularity, but figuring they might as well strike while the iron was hot.

America's new-found musical appetite for all things authentic also prompted Pat to set up his own Tradition Records label, which recorded other folk stars like Odetta, Lightnin' Hopkins and Mary O'Hara as well as the Clancys themselves, who released their first album, a collection of Irish rebel songs entitled **The Rising of the Moon**, in 1959, followed later the same year by **Come Fill Your Glass With Us – "Irish Songs of Drinking and Blackguarding"**. Songs like "The Croppy Boy", "The Foggy Dew", "Finnegan's Wake" and "Bold Thady Quill", were then largely unknown across the Pond, the Clancys' renditions being eagerly received as an antidote to the clichéd excesses of stage Oirishry. The group brought a potent combination of earthy vigour, honest sentiment and skilled stage technique to their performances, each taking turns on lead vocal, backed up with hearty choral harmonies and rudimentary instrumentation, on guitar, whistle, harmonica, drums and five-string banjo.

Their use of accompaniment, largely foreign to the Irish song tradition, reflected the influence of American folk outfits like The Weavers and The Kingston Trio, in turn being widely adopted by groups back in Ireland during the subsequent ballad boom. The natural exuberance and informality of the Clancys' performances, incorporating plenty of banter and backchat, also added to their appeal. A young Bob Dylan was regularly among the in-crowd thronging to the clubs, coffee houses and folk festivals, notably Newport, where the Clancys played, and incorporated several of their songs into his early repertoire, including his adaptation of Dominic Behan's "The Patriot Game" into "With God On Our Side".

By 1961, the year they released their third, self-titled album on Tradition (as well as their first on Columbia, **A Spontaneous Performance**), the Clancys were appearing at New York's biggest nightclub, the Blue Angel, where they were spotted by a scout for *The Ed Sullivan Show*. Their appearance on the show catapulted them to nationwide fame: within a year, they'd played Carnegie Hall, and in 1963 performed for President Kennedy at the White House. Back in Ireland, meanwhile, the collector and broadcaster Ciarán MacMathúna, who'd encountered the Clancys' records on an American field-trip, had brought some home and begun playing them on Radió Éireann and the group was taken swiftly to the nation's heart.

Arriving pre-endorsed by American celebrity, the Clancys were more or less guaranteed a rapturous reception for their first Irish tour in 1963 – during one sold-out concert, at Dublin's Olympia Theatre, they sang a number from an open window for the ticketless crowds outside. By turning old Irish songs into polished and enormously popular entertainment, without compromising their spirit, the Clancys played a crucial role in restoring Ireland's pride in its musical traditions, paving the way for the scores of ballad groups, including The Dubliners, that flourished during the 1960s.

Recording mainly for Columbia, the Clancys averaged at least an album a year throughout the decade. As the 1970s approached, however, the folk-song boom was running out of steam, and Makem's departure for a solo career in 1969, followed by Liam's in 1973 – the two subsequently playing as a duo for several years – signalled the beginning of the end of the Clancys as a full-time outfit, though they have continued to tour and record in various family permutations. In 1977 a fourth brother, **Bobby**, joined Tom and Pat in the line-up, along with nephew **Robbie O'Connell**, and a full reunion tour, with accompanying album, took place in 1984. Following Tom's death in 1990, Liam rejoined the group, which recorded **Older But No Wiser** in 1995, featuring versions of "Lili Marlene" and Dylan's "When the Ship Comes In", as well as traditional tracks like "Let No Man Steal Your Thyme" and "Curragh of Kildare". Liam, O'Connell and Liam's son **Dónal** then regrouped as **Clancy, O'Connell and Clancy**. Paddy Clancy, after retiring back to Carrick-on-Suir to raise Charolais cattle, died in 1998. Bobby currently performs in a trio with his son **Finbarr** and Massachusetts singer-songwriter **Eddie Dillon**, while his daughter **Aoife**, also continued the proud family tradition, singing with the Irish-American band **Cherish the Ladies**.

⊙ **The Clancy Brothers and Tommy Makem**   Tradition, 1961

The most assured of their early albums, includes "The Jug of Punch" and the tender love-lament "Ballinderry".

Clannad

F ew Irish bands surpass **Clannad**'s longevity or their capacity for reinvention, and their musical development has had a lasting impact on Irish music worldwide. Since its formation in 1970, the core of the band has remained the related Ó Braonáin (Brennan) and Ó Dúgáin (Duggan) families from the Donegal Gaeltacht of Gaoth Dobhair (Gweedore). **Leo Ó Braonáin** played accordion in his parents' band (featuring his mother on drums) which later developed into The Slieve Foy Band, offering a popular dance-hall blend of céilí and Glenn Miller tunes with Leo now on clarinet, saxophone and vocals and his wife Máire (known as Baba) on piano. The band proved successful, especially in Glasgow, in the 1950s and early 1960s and the couple's eldest daughter, **Máire**, recalls singing on stage the pop-ska song "My Boy Lollipop", dressed in her step-dancing outfit.

Leo and Baba eventually had nine children and the family pub in Meenaleck became a focus for their musical activity with the children regularly winning prizes at local feiseanna. While Máire was sent to a convent school in Sligo (partly in order to learn the harp), her younger brother **Ciarán** (guitar, double bass) began working on local Irish songs learned from his grandparents and sending them to Máire and brother **Pól** (flute, guitar, bongos) to learn at school. The three would get together to play in the holidays, often with their slightly older uncles, twin brothers **Noel** and **Pádraig Ó Dúgáin** on guitar/harmonium and guitar/mandola respectively. Persuaded to enter the 1970 Letterkenny Folk Festival, they lacked a name and so opted for the descriptive Clann as Dobhair (family from Dobhair), which in, abbreviated form, became Clannad. The competition's prize was a recording contract

REDFERNS/VAL WILMER

with the Philips label, though the company took three years to release the album on the grounds that songs in Irish were uncommercial.

Philips were finally convinced of the band's potential by their 1973 victory in the National Song Contest with the Mick Hanly song "An Phairc". By then, Máire was studying harp at the Royal Irish Academy of Music and the twins were training to be ships' radio officers, though the band had often appeared on TV on Irish language shows. The self-titled debut album had little impact, though it's dulcet marriage of Máire's still maturing voice and slightly jazzy arrangements reflected a delicacy then popular in the UK and Northern Europe through the work of Pentangle and John Martyn. Nevertheless, a Gael-Linn contract followed, producing **Clannad 2** (1974) and **Dúlamán** two years later. Following a successful tour of Germany in 1976 the band went full-time and remained a popular European draw, developing a relaxed fluidity best heard on their live album, **Clannad in Concert** (1978). A further change of labels the same year saw their most experimental album to date, **Crann Ull** with the track "Lá Coimhthíoch fan dtuath" (A Strange Day in the Countryside) blending haunting acoustic instrumentation and lush harmonies. The producer was Nicky Ryan, later to work regularly with Máire's younger sister, **Eithne Ní Bhraonáin** aka **Enya**, who had joined the band on keyboards and vocals for **Fuaim** (1982). The same year also witnessed the astonishing success of the band's single "Theme from 'Harry's Game'" – written for a UK TV drama about British espionage in Northern Ireland – which reached #5 in the UK singles charts and effectively "broke" the band in the US as the opening track of their album **Magical Ring** (1983) – though by then Enya's departure meant that Clannad was once again a quintet.

The rest of the decade saw the band increase its success, first through the **Legend** soundtrack (1984) and then through the huge-selling **Macalla** (1985). Augmented by sax, electric guitars and synthesizers, this is still the ultimate Clannad popular album. Gone are the old Donegal songs, replaced instead by English lyrics, both clichéd and obscure, and walls of ethereal sound, characterized by Máire's hit duet with U2's Bono on "In a Lifetime". Cynics noted that the sleeve art, depicting Máire with hands raised to ears in receipt of an echo (macalla in Irish) bore a striking resemblance to Edvard Munch's *The Scream*. Question marks about the band's own musical input were substantiated by the dreadful follow-up album **Sirius** (1987), which spawned the hit "White Fool" but featured a host of US rock sessioneers and a consequent soft-rock feel. Whatever the case, the band took heed and, since another soundtrack album, **The Angel and the Soldier Boy** (1989) have inhabited a territory known in some quarters as "Celtic hush" music, and, in others, as the aural equivalent of swimming in custard. It's a cozy world, defined by one-word album titles – **Anam**, **Banba**, **Lore** and, most recently, **Landmarks** (1998) – whispered vocals and instrumental doodling, in which the overwhelming presence is producer and writer Ciarán Ó Braonáin.

Pól Ó Braonáin left in 1990 in search of new musical directions which led to him producing the Chinese Guo Brothers' album **Yuan** and collaborating with the flute-playing brother Guo Yue and Japanese percussionist Joji Hirota on the self-titled **Trísan** (1992) – an odd East–West conjunction which has its moments. Máire, meanwhile, remains in the band but has guested on many others' albums and has developed her own solo career, producing three releases to date, the latest being **Whisper to the Wild Water** (2000).

⊙ Clannad 2   Gael-Linn, 1974

Best of the early albums and dig those hats!

⊙ **Macalla**   RCA, 1985

Still the ultimate "Celtic hush" album.

Cran

The powerhouse trio **Cran** emerged in the mid-1990s with a tremendous debut album, **The Crooked Stair**. Stunning vocal arrangements and immaculate musicianship established a formidable presence harnessing individual talents to generate sounds of astonishing depth and unstoppable force. The original line-up drew upon the strengths of celebrated singer, song collector and bouzouki player **Seán Corcoran**, the sublime flute of **Desi Wilkinson** (adept on clarinet, whistles, highland pipes as well as an expert lilter and singer) and the uilleann piper, **Neil Martin**, well-known also for his cello and keyboards work. **The Crooked Stair** established a successful blueprint which was reinforced by the subsequent **Black Black Black**, surprisingly produced by American rock legend Shel Talmy. By now piper **Ronan Browne** was on board for Neil Martin and this 1998 album also saw guest appearances by fiddler Kevin Glackin, the clavinet of Tríona Ní Dhomhnaill and the massed voices of Anúna. **Black Black Black** featured brilliant songs such as the infectious "Staimpí", the meditative "Coleraine Town" (with its remarkable descending flute and pipes motif from Desi and Ronan) and a storming unaccompanied trio rendition of "Willie Taylor", while tunes such as the closing set of jigs (kicked off by "The Humours of Ballyloughlin") were played with unstoppable vivacity.

It seemed impossible to top, but 2000 saw an even more remarkable album, **Lover's Ghost**. By this time Cran had become renowned for their live performances (even becoming stars in the Netherlands) and

Lover's Ghost saw them assuming the production reins to deliver a classic album firmly rooted in the tradition. Seán's song selection spread its wings to encompass a magical "Erin, Grá Mo Chro", a ploughing song ("Hó Bó"), an awesome prison song ("Sé Oakum Mo Phriosúin") and, the crowning glory, a version of "Stolen Bride" containing harmonies so warm they could toast bread. Again, the standard of musicianship set new highs with the slow reel, "The Killarney Boys of Pleasure", and the set dance, "The Ace and Deuce of Pipering", showing just what can be achieved when played with reverence and charm.

⊙ **Black Black Black**　　　　　　　　　　Claddagh, 1998

Sheer, unadulterated bliss!

⊙ **Lover's Ghost**　　　　　　　Black Rose Records, 2000

Buy this album or risk leading a poorer life.

Craobh Rua

Formed in the mid-1980s, the Belfast-based quartet take their name from The Red ("rua") Branch ("craobh") Knights of Ulster. The band's line-up has changed over the years, but original member and lynchpin **Brian Connolly** (banjo and mandolin) and fiddler **Michael Cassidy**, who joined in 1986, are still there. Though constantly progressing over five increasingly impressive albums, their sound is very redolent of the early Planxty or Bothy Band, though none the worse for that. **Craobh Rua** draw on Belfast argot for their album titles and the latest example is their most recent release, **If Ida Been Here, Ida Been There**. The sound of Connolly's banjo characterizes much of their relaxed unison playing and the album sees some classy arrangements of familiar tunes. These include the hornpipes "O'Connor's Favourite/The Lass on the Strand", with some understated piping from new member **Patrick Davey** (who elsewhere plays whistles and flute). Another recent recruit, the Edinburgh-based singer-guitarist and cittern player Aaron Jones, provides a fine rendition of "Cúil Tiubh Na bPéarli", a Donegal song learned from Dáithí Sproule. Past members have included the Calico piper **Díarmaid Moynihan** and the fabulous young Lurgan flute player **Barry Kerr** who joined for a recent US tour.

⊙ **If Ida Been Here, Ida Been There**   Lochshore, 2000

Belfast's most enduring band shows it can still cut the mustard.

Damp in the Attic

A Clare-based quartet with a mighty pedigree, **Damp in the Attic** was formed in February, 1998, and released their debut album

"I was... flyin' it" the following year. Founded on the bedrock of the bouzouki of **Cyril O'Donoghue** (ex-Fisherstreet) and the bodhrán of **Colm Murphy**, Damp in the Attic's instrumental leads are ex-Chatterbox and occasional Chieftain **Martin Murray** (fiddle, viola, mandolin) and Tulla Céilí Band member **P.J. King** (accordion). Their choice of tunes is hard to fault (and includes several from the playing of fiddler Siobhán Peoples). There's a set of French-Canadian reels first heard on a cassette player in the kitchen of Cherish the Ladies' Donna Long while Cyril's songs (from a range of traditions) provide a well-honed contrast to the energetic dance music.

⊙ **"I was... flyin' it"**   Magnetic Music, 1999

Luxurious, impeccable music from a well-seasoned quartet.

Danú

Currently the hottest young band in traditional music, **Danú** (named after the goddess of prosperity associated with the land) combine youthful vitality with a thorough respect for the music to create some of the most astonishing sounds around. The band's origins lie in Co. Waterford where friends **Benny McCarthy** (button accordion), **Donnchadh Gough** (bodhrán and uilleann pipes), fiddler **Daire Bracken** and guitarist **Dónal Clancy** (son of Liam) joined forces to perform at the Inter-Celtic Festival in Lorient, France. There they encountered brothers **Eamon** (bouzouki, mandola) and **Tom Doorley** (flute, low whistle) and, with the addition of guitarist **Tim Murray** replacing Dónal, became the fully-fledged Danú when invited back to Lorient the following year. Together they released their highly-regarded self-titled debut album in 1997, instantly bringing their distinctive brand of energetic, yet tasteful music to a wider audience. Expertly-played, and with an intelligent choice of tunes, the inclusion of the sean-nós singer **Cárthach Mac Craith** revealed a band unwilling to pad out their performances or records with sub-standard cover versions. Changes were afoot, however: Tim Murray left to form Cían and was replaced by **Noel Ryan**; Donna Long's son **Jesse Smith** came in for Daire Bracken; and another, even better, singer, **Ciarán Ó Gealbháin** stepped into Cárthach's shoes. Successful appearances at festivals in Spain, Maryland and, most notably, Cambridge saw the band signed by Shanachie and the

release of the gob-smacking **Think Before You Think** (2000), its title apparently based on advice once given to Donnchadh. It is an album as close to perfection as a stoat to an ermine, characterized once again by glorious ensemble playing that resists the temptation to press down on the accelerator pedal, as on the gorgeous reel "The Old Ruined Cottage" and a spell-binding rendition of "The Butlers of Glen Avenue", and singing from Ciarán which could uplift every hair on your body. The essence of Danú should be bottled and available in all reputable public bars!

⊙ **Think Before You Think**   Shanachie, 2000

As good as it gets and then some!

De Dannan

There's many a bar-room decision swiftly reached and slowly repented, but not in the case of **De Dannan**, formed one 1974 night by the members of a regular session at Hughes' Pub, Spiddal, Co. Galway. The original line-up consisted of then 18-year-old **Frankie Gavin** (fiddle, flute, whistle and piano), bouzouki-player **Alec Finn**, accordionist and banjo player **Charlie Piggott** and **Johnny "Ringo" McDonagh** on bodhrán and bones, while **Dolores Keane** was subsequently invited to provide vocals. While Gavin and Finn have remained at the band's core (and McDonagh lasted a mere nine albums), De Dannan's changing membership reads like a traditional music hall of fame. In addition to Keane, the De Dannan singers' club has included **Mary Black, Tommy Fleming, Andy Irvine, Tim Lyons, Jimmy MacCarthy, Maura O'Connell** and **Eleanor Shanley** while the latest recruit is young vocalist **Andrew Murray** from Inishbofin. **Aidan Coffey, Jackie Daly** and **Mairtín O'Connor** are all members of the accordionists' brigade, while other notable collaborators include Mary Bergin, John Carty, Johnny Moynihan, whistler Seán Ryan and, bizarrely, the hard-boiled American actor Harry Dean Stanton.

As a consequence, though they've suffered more than most through the fickleness of record companies, De Dannan has produced some of the best and certainly the most innovative Irish music over the last few decades. Although they've alarmed purists with adaptations of "Hey Jude" and "Bohemian Rhapsody", played with gospel choirs and the Andy Statman Klesmer Orchestra, given Handel the Galway treatment and revived music-hall songs from the 1920s, Finn and Gavin are, above all, consummate traditional musicians. The two share a marvelous musical understanding and an ability to achieve what most others even fail to imagine, and have carved for themselves an otherwise unfillable niche as originators of "The Galway Sound".

The spirit of De Dannan was captured on their 25th anniversary double CD **How the West Was Won** (1999) which draws deeply from their enormous back catalogue and includes seven previously unissued live tracks. Elsewhere, their self-titled 1975 debut LP is long out-of-print but worth seeking out for a grasp of the fresh-faced lads' initial esprit and Dolores' singing of "Rambling Irishman". 1980's **The Mist Covered Mountain** was the first to include Jackie Daly and featured songs by local singers Seán Ó Conaire, singing the Connemara Gaeltacht favourite "Máire Mhór" (Tall Maura), and 85-year-old Tom Pháidín Tom (from the Spiddal area) performing the old United Irishman ballad "Henry Joy McCracken" just a few months before his death. **Anthem** (1985) is the best sample from the Mary Black period and also includes Máirtín O'Connor's witty conversion of an old Eastern European tune into Irish, "Connie from Constantinople". The band's most recent regular release was **Hibernian Rhapsody** (1996) which saw a return to their sprightly best and some fine vocals from Tommy Fleming, a new young accordionist in **Derek Hickey** (ex-Skellig) and **Colm Murphy** in excellent form on the bodhrán. In 2000 Alec Finn's rock dabblings reached their apogee (or arguably their nadir) with **Welcome to the Hotel Connemara** on which the De Dannan treatment was applied to a host of classics, and included an alarming segue of "The Rocks of Bawn" and The Eagles' "Take it to the Limit".

⊙ How the West Was Won   Hummingbird, 1999

A truly great double-CD compilation which captures the essence of De Dannan.

⊙ **Anthem**   Dara, 1985

Mid-period treat, including both Mary Black and Dolores Keane
and featuring the fabulous "Ríl an Spidéal".

Déanta

Déanta, from Counties Antrim and Derry in Northern Ireland,
was one of the most innovative bands to emerge in the last
decade. Many saw close parallels in their music to Solas, not least
for the fact that in **Mary Dillon** Déanta possessed an equally pure-
voiced singer as Solas's Karan Casey. Such a comparison was
superficial, for Déanta's inspiration was drawn from their own roots
and, increasingly, from the Scottish folk tradition. Formed in the mid-
1980s, the band's increasing reputation attracted the interest of
Green Linnet who released their self-titled debut album, produced by
Steve Cooney, in 1993. At that time the line-up consisted of siblings
Eoghan (harp, guitar) and **Kate O'Brien** (fiddle, viola), **Paul Mullan**
(flute, whistles), **Clodagh Warnock** (bouzouki, fiddle, bodhrán) and
the aforementioned Mary Dillon. Mullan had left, however, by the time
of **Ready for the Storm** to be replaced by **Deirdre Havlin** (flute and
whistles) and **Rosie Mulholland** (keyboards and fiddle). Though
bristling with confidence and displaying their characteristic blend of
energy and sensitivity, this was merely an excellent foretaste of
things to come. The new sextet's increasing musical maturity and
understanding reached its apogee with the awesome **Whisper of a
Secret** (1997), one of the albums of the 1990s. Dillon's singing on
"Willie and Mary" is both knowing and sprightly, while her "Lone
Shanakyle" (accompanied by sumptuous harp and understated fiddles) would soften Fionn Mac Cumhaill's heart. The band was rocking

too and their work-out on the "Scarta Glen Road" reels, gradually augmented by Richie Buckley's wailing sax, was a fine reflection of their live performances. Sadly, the album proved to be Déanta's swan song. Four of the band's members got married in quick succession and, though most of the sextet are still musically active, they have not played under the name Déanta – which, appropriately, means "complete" – since November, 1997.

⊙ **Whisper of a Secret**   Green Linnet, 1997

A stunning curtain closer from the glorious sextet.

Deiseal

Deiseal (rhymes with "special") means "following the direction of the sun" and the Dublin-based trio certainly produced some of the brightest work of the early 1990s. In exploring a fusion of traditional, jazz and even calypso influences, the band showcased the astonishingly versatile and ever-lyrical whistle-playing and singing of **Cormac Breatnach** (who still treads a similar path in his current solo work). The lively mood was enhanced by **Paul O'Driscoll**'s double and fretless basses, while **Niall Ó Callanain**'s vibrant bouzouki and guitar tossed up a series of jazz-shaped patterns. "Raindrops" on the band's first album, **The Long Long Note** (1993), exemplifies the band's approach. Muted harmonies evoke gathering rainclouds, O'Driscoll enters with a driving calypso beat and is joined by Niall, and the whole climaxes in a stunning, improvised solo from Cormac before switching to a reel, "The First of May". The Deiseal sound was enriched by the addition of saxophonist **Richie Buckley** for 1996's **Sunshine Day**, but the album never surpasses the sheer surprise and beauty of its predecessor.

⊙ **The Long Long Note**   Starc, 1993

A sumptuous feast of an album with courses to suit most tastes.

Dervish

On their day one of the only bands currently capable of toppling
Altan from the traditional throne, **Dervish** are based just down
the road in Sligo. Though often erroneously compared to The Bothy
Band, the band's reference point is more appropriately De Dannan
and they share the latter's aim of bringing the spirit of the session to
their performances rather than the former's more grandiose arrangements. The band's roots are firmly entrenched in the local music
scene and the Sligo tradition. **Liam Kelly** (flutes and whistles) and
Shane Mitchell (accordion) have been playing together since their
teens, forming traditional band Poitín and later the rock band Who
Says What, in which they were joined by **Michael Holmes** (guitar,
bouzouki). At sessions in Sligo they regularly encountered man-
dola/mandolin-player **Brian McDonagh** who had been a founder
member of Oisín when he was a mere sixteen.

In 1988 the foursome (with the addition of Raphoe, Co. Donegal fiddler **Martin McGinley**) were asked by locally-based Sound Records to
make an album of session tunes. **The Boys of Sligo** ensued and the
name "Dervish" chosen in positive avoidance of self-consciously Irish
names (like Oisín or Poitín!). Booking enquiries followed the album's
release and the quintet became a sextet with the recruitment of
Longford-born singer and bodhrán/bones player **Cathy Jordan**. Soon
afterwards McGinley opted for a career in broadcasting and was
replaced on fiddle by **Shane McAleer**. The fruits of this liaison can be
heard on the staggering album, **Harmony Hill** (1993). Years of hard

touring had honed the bands' instrumental skills to the cutting edge, and yet it was Jordan's extraordinary range which caught the ear – as sweet as a plum on "Bellaghy Fair" and as earthy as a ploughed field on a ribald rereading of "The Fair Maid" (featured on Tríona Ní Dhomhnaill's **Triona** album). The plaudits followed and Dervish set off on a worldwide journey which

Cathy Jordan of Dervish

has seen the band play in countries as diverse as Bolivia and Japan and release another four high-quality albums. Touring can take its toll, however, and, by the time of 1999's **Midsummer's Night**, McAleer had been replaced by **Tom Morrow**, and **Séamus O'Dowd** had joined on guitar, fiddle and harmonicas. As ever the album features immaculate ensemble playing founded on the Mitchell–Kelly axis (with the "Tenpenny Bit" jigs an outstanding example) while Jordan is in impressive form throughout and continuing her quest for rare material has unearthed the splendid Roscommon tale of temptation "The Banks of Viledee". All Dervish's albums, except the instrumental debut appear on their own Whirling Discs label.

⊙ **Harmony Hill** Whirling Discs, 1993

A cracking album from the first sextet set the benchmark for others to follow.

⊙ **Midsummer's Night** Whirling Discs, 1999

As polished as an antique Chippendale table.

Dordán

The traditional and baroque band Dordán originated when tin whistler **Mary Bergin**, harper **Kathleen Loughnane** and fiddler **Dearbhaill Standún** came together to play a one-off concert at St Nicholas Cathedral in Galway in 1990. A successful performance prompted them to continue the arrangement and they've been going strong ever since. Two albums followed for Gael-Linn before their manager and publicist **Martina Goggin** joined on vocals, percussion and guitar. Dordán subsequently signed to Narada and their second album for the label, produced by Stephen Cooney, **Celtic Aire** (1999) encapsulates all the qualities of their unique sound. The band's name means "drone" or "buzz", but a better name might have been Mil (Irish for "honey") as there's a delicate sweetness permeating their amalgamation of the Irish traditional and classical heritages. Their arrangement of Carolan's "Sir Arthur Shaen" is impeccable while musical interplay adds new dimensions to familiar reels such as "Boys of the Lough". Finally, Stephen Cooney adds arrestingly stylish guitar to Martina's graceful rendition of "Mo Bhacghaillín Donn", additionally embellished by Mary's flute solo.

⊙ **Celtic Aire** Narada, 1999

A peach of an album from an outstanding quartet.

The Dubliners

The reaction of folksinger-turned-comedian Billy Connolly to his first encounter with **The Dubliners**, in Glasgow during the 1960s, vividly captures the impact of their arrival on the folk scene: "I sat mesmerised in the stalls being completely blown away. I had never seen such a collection of hairy people in my life. I had never seen such energy as **Luke Kelly**'s. I had never heard a voice as extraordinary as **Ronnie Drew**'s. I had never heard banjo playing as amazing as **Barney McKenna**'s. **Ciarán Bourke** looked like the gypsy from one of his own songs who was quite likely to run off with your girlfriend if you didn't keep a close eye on him."

If the Clancy Brothers represented the respectably well-scrubbed face of the 1960s Irish ballad boom, The Dubliners were its defiantly unsanitized bare-knuckle, hirsute champions. Formed in 1962 out of backroom sessions in O'Donoghue's bar, they brought a hard urban edge, a carousing irreverence and, increasingly, a robust political dimension to their ever-expanding store of traditional and contemporary songs. They were also one of the first groups to perform instrumental sets alongside vocal material. It was a combination that saw them rocket to mass popularity first in Ireland, then the UK, and subsequently throughout the world.

Originally known as the **Ronnie Drew Folk Group**, they changed their name in time for their first recording, although as the title of **The Dubliners with Luke Kelly** (1964) suggests, their second lead singer wasn't yet a fully-fledged member, being briefly replaced by **Bobby Lynch** for their second, live album, **The Dubliners In Concert** (1965). He returned to the fold, however, in time for their third, **Finnegan Wakes** (1966), while multi-instrumentalist **John Sheahan** (fiddle, tin whistle, mandolin, concertina, guitar and vocals) was brought in during his absence, mainly to share the lead with McKenna (tenor banjo, mandolin and melodeon) in the tunes.

Those first three albums – selectively compiled on **The Definitive Transatlantic Collection** – opened the bidding with a good many future Dubs' staples, including "The Wild Rover", "Tramps and Hawkers", "I'll Tell Me Ma", "The Rocky Road to Dublin", "The Patriot Game" and "The Leaving of Liverpool", as well as McKenna's party-piece reel, "My Love Is In America". They also introduced an unsuspecting world to the band's unique vocal attack which was jointly led by Kelly and Drew – the former with his fiercely impassioned bellow, the latter with a voice famously likened to "coke being crushed under a door" (a reference to the solid fuel rather than the white powdery stuff).

It was 1967, though, that was to prove their real annus mirabilis. Their recording of a popular Child ballad, entitled "Seven Drunken Nights", was banned by RTÉ for its bawdy content – but picked up by pirate station Radio Caroline, who gave it heavy rotation alongside the likes of The Beatles, Jimi Hendrix and The Kinks, sending it to #5 in the UK pop charts. The Dubliners' famous debut on *Top of the Pops* effectively launched their career as an international touring act

Hearteningly, it was The Dubliners' very authenticity that made them such a hit with audiences everywhere. Certainly they showed no inclination for tailoring their style to the whims of the pop scene, as John Sheahan later recalled: "Our attitude was, 'Here we are, take it or leave it'." At the same time, they took to the rock'n'roll lifestyle like ducks to water, generating a bacchanalian on-the-road mythology that did their credibility no harm at all.

The chart success of **A Drop of the Hard Stuff** (1967; renamed as **Seven Drunken Nights**), followed by that of **More of the Hard Stuff** (1967), **Drinkin' and Courtin'** (1968) and **At It Again** (1968; renamed

STEVE GILLETT

Seven Deadly Sins) proved The Dubliners to be more than one-hit wonders. Their initial novelty-band aspects were underpinned by first-rate musicianship, together with a stylistic repertoire considerably more sophisticated than it first appeared, including Irish-language songs, Scottish songs, Carolan tunes, and compositions by leading contemporary songwriters like Ewan MacColl and Dominic Behan, the last's frequent political content lending a serious side to their work that is sometimes overlooked.

The band's heady upward progress was abruptly interrupted during the '70s: Ronnie Drew left for a few years to pursue a solo career, returning in 1979, and the band lost first Bourke, then Kelly to illness (the latter dying in 1984). The refashioned line-up that emerged from these travails saw **Seán Cannon** taking over from Kelly, with **Eamonn Campbell** restoring the line-up to five in 1987 – the same year he engineered a timely shot in the arm for the band by teaming them up with The Pogues to record "The Irish

Rover". This resulted in another *Top of the Pops* appearance, twenty years on from their first, introducing them to a new generation of fans while underlining their elder-statesmen status.

Further collaborations featured on their excellent anniversary album **Thirty Years A-Greying** (1992), with guests including Hothouse Flowers, Rory Gallagher and The Pogues. Although rumours of their retirement have periodically circulated, after more than three decades in the business they were even able to weather the final departure of Drew who went on to release two solo albums, **Dirty Rotten Shame** (1995) and **The Humour is on Me Now** (1999). Having drafted in vocalist **Paddy Reilly**, The Dubliners remain a perennially popular draw around the concert and festival circuit. Both the content and the title of their latest release, **Alive Alive-O** (1997), recorded during a sellout German tour, encapsulate their continued determination to defy the passing years, with the odds on their making it to a fortieth-birthday album narrowing by the day.

⊙ **The Complete**　　　　　　Castle Communications, 1967–68
Transatlantic Collection

Capturing the freshness and heady excitement of their earliest years and first three recordings, including several live tracks.

⊙ **Seven Drunken Nights**　　　　　　Major Minor, 1967

Features the breakthrough single that remains their best-known signature tune, as well as other classics.

Fife and drum bands

Originating from military practice, fife and drum bands used to be a common sight in nineteenth-century Ireland and were usually associated with political organizations. As time went on, the fife was sometimes replaced by small flutes and piccolos, but overall the tradition had dwindled by the 1930s. In the Republic, flute bands now exist only on a small-scale competitive level in certain pockets of the country (eg Co. Donegal), though the marching-band tradition has maintained its political significance in the North, particularly through the parades associated with the Orange Order and Loyalist marches in general. Such bands can be distinguished between those focusing on the flute and the more obvious drum-heavy "No Surrender" style bands. The sound of the Lambeg drum (an enormous bass drum made from nanny-goat skin) is the most commonly heard at Loyalist parades (and also those of the Nationalist Ancient Order of Hibernians), but more recently the art of drumming has been revived in its own right and Lambeg drummers compete in competitions run by five county associations. **Lambeg Drums with Fife and Rattly** contains some of the prize-winning performances – "rattly", by the way, is a local name for the snare drum.

⊙ **Lambeg Drums with Fife and Rattly**   Outlet, 1996

For serious drummers only.

Na Filí

The Cork-based trio **Na Filí** ("The Bards"), one of the biggest names in traditional circles and popular on the folk-festival circuit in the 1970s, released six albums on a variety of labels before disbanding in 1979. The band consisted of uilleann piper, singer and composer **Tomas Ó Canainn**, fiddler **Matt Cranitch** and **Tom Barry** on whistle. Drawing on Matt and Tom's southwestern roots, and with Tomas (originally from Derry) supplying tunes and songs from the Ulster tradition, their combined style captured all the warmth of a fireside session. The result was a captivating contrast to the trails being blazed by contemporaries like The Bothy Band and Planxty. **Na Filí 3** is the best of the few reissues available with "Caitlín Triall" (a famous air from Bunting's 1796 collection) providing the most characteristic example of the trio's sound: Matt bows a sprightly reel before Tom joins in, then the drones announce the introduction of a solo piped air before all three reconvene, ending with the air's melody played over the reel. Ó Canainn's song selection is always interesting and among the treats is the lament "Caoineadh na dTrí Muire", a dialogue between Mary and the apostle Peter during the crucifixion.

⊙ **Na Filí 3**   Outlet, 1974

Three craftsmen at work, generating music of the highest quality.

Flook

O ne of the most original bands around, **Flook** caused a storm at the 1996 Sidmouth Folk Festival with the interplay between their then three flute and whistle players, **Brian Finnegan** (from Armagh and formerly of Upstairs in a Tent), **Sarah Allen** (from St Albans, England and one-time stalwart of The Barely Works and Bigjig) and **Mike McGoldrick**, backed by the doughty DADGAD-strung guitar of **Ed Boyd** (from Bath, England). Fortunately, their performance was recorded on the excellent **Live!**. McGoldrick subsequently departed and the band took the bold step of replacing him with a bodhrán player, although such a simple description fails to do justice to the extraordinary percussive powers of **John Joe Kelly** (born in Manchester to Irish parents) whose stage solo performance is gob-smacking. Finnegan and Allen have since developed into a great combination. The former is an inspired improviser whose influences include not just his traditional roots (as exemplified on his hard-to-find **Acoustic Radio** CD), but the Breton flute-player Jean-Michel Veillon and the Indian player Dipak Ram. Meanwhile, Sarah's flute playing creates the subtlest of harmonies (and she also contributes some formidable piano accordion). A second live album, **The Four of Us** (1999) was available in the US, but the one to look out for is **Flatfish** whose beautiful case reflects the glories within – no frills, no studio gloss, just simple unadorned pleasure from start to finish.

⊙ Flatfish   Flatfish Records, 1999

A sensational live act, this album places Flook securely in the front-rank of the innovators.

Four Men and a Dog

One of the 1990s' most exciting live acts, **Four Men and a Dog** also recorded four excellent albums – two outstanding – yet never quite fulfilled the major-league potential of their unique Irish/Americana blend. Their debut **Barking Mad** (1991), voted Album of the Year by *Folk Roots* magazine, combined driving yet tasteful instrumentals with well-chosen contemporary songs, including a poignant cover of Richard Thompson's "Waltzing's for Dreamers" and the infamous "Wrap It Up", an Irish rap delivered by extrovert outsize percussionist **Gino Lupari**. Originally a five-piece, the line-up eventually settled as Lupari, demon Tyrone fiddler **Cathal Hayden**, singer/songwriter **Kevin Doherty** and banjo player/fiddler **Gerry O'Connor**. From **Shifting Gravel** (1993) onwards, Doherty's country-rock tastes came increasingly to influence their sound, their last two albums – the brilliantly eclectic **Doctor A's Secret Remedies** (1995) and the blues-tinged **Long Roads** (1996) – being recorded with

HEIDI PEARSON

Gino Lupari

members of The Band at their Woodstock studio. With record-company wrangles repeatedly stalling their career plans, the band dispersed amicably towards various solo projects in 1998 (though they still meet up for occasional gigs).

⊙ **Doctor A's Secret Remedies**   Transatlantic/Castle, 1995

A headily restorative tonic concocted from extracts of folk, country, Latin and R&B, plus a band having one hell of a good time.

The Fureys

The **Furey** clan boasts one of the more sprawling histories in modern Irish music, its key players having evolved from groundbreaking 1960s firebrands into fondly-regarded veterans of the international expat circuit, via their commercial heyday as MOR folk-pop balladeers. The four Furey brothers – **Eddie**, **Finbar**, **Paul** and **George**, singers and multi-instrumentalists all – were born between 1944 and 1951 in Dublin, the progeny of a musical travelling family. By the late 1950s, Eddie and Finbar were joining their father, a fiddler and piper, at sessions in O'Donoghue's bar, going on to win numerous competition prizes before moving to Edinburgh in 1967. Labouring jobs soon gave way to concert and broadcasting appearances throughout Britain and Europe: Finbar playing uilleann pipes (then still a novelty to most non-Irish audiences) and whistles, with Eddie on vocals and guitar – the duo achieving worldwide renown after supporting The Clancy Brothers on their 1969 American tour. The rugged majesty and unforced virtuosity of their early Transatlantic recordings, **Finbar and Eddie Furey** and **The Lonesome Boatman** (1968 and 1969) together with Finbar's solo debut **Traditional Irish Pipe Music** (1969) remain instantly striking, on such classics and future signature tunes as "The Spanish Cloak", "The Curragh of Kildare", "Rakish Paddy" and "The Lonesome Boatman". Their next release, **The Dawning of the Day** (1972) signalled an expansion of their palette, with its inclusion of Gerry Rafferty's "Her Father Didn't Like Me Anyway", as well as featuring Finbar on vocals.

This shift in direction eventually saw all four brothers teaming up with Scottish singer-instrumentalist **Davey Arthur** (who with Paul and George had previously performed as **The Buskers**) and recording the winsome ballad "When You Were Sweet Sixteen", which made the UK Top 20 in 1981, relaunching The Fureys as a pop-inclined ballad group. They've continued essentially in this vein ever since, sustaining a solid international fan-base, although **Claddagh**

HEIDI PEARSON

Road (1994), following Arthur's departure, struck a somewhat grittier note. Though often decried for their later work's more crowd-pleasing aspects, their influence as traditional popularizers is undeniably significant, while Finbar (who went solo in the early 1990s) is recognized as one of the great contemporary pipers as well as one of the fastest. And in the same year as they released their twenty-first anniversary album (1999), their music was unexpectedly brought to an entirely new audience when the French DJ Shadow Blacque released a track featuring a remixed version of "When You Were Sweet Sixteen".

⦿ **Finbar and Eddie Furey/The Lonesome Boatman**   Transatlantic, 1968 and 1969

Featuring the two elder brothers at the peak of their early form.

⊙ **The Fureys Finest**   Castle, 1987

A Fureys compilation, containing the best of their 1980s hits, including "Sweet Sixteen" and "The Lonesome Boatman".

Goats Don't Shave

Between 1988 and 1995 the semi-electric band **Goats Don't Shave** from Dungloe, Co. Donegal were one of the most exciting outfits around. **Pat Gallagher** was their powerful singer (and eloquent lyricist) while their traditional credentials were underlined by the presence of fiddler **Jason Philbin** – grandson of the great Neillidh Boyle.

Initial Irish success with the single "Let the World Keep on Turning" was followed by the remarkable album **The Rusty Razor** (1992) which included their raucous take on the local Mary from Dungloe festival, "Mary Mary", the equally witty "Las Vegas (In the Hills of Donegal)" and, probably still Gallagher's greatest song, "The Evictions", a haunting testament to the tenants  cleared from nearby Derryveagh in 1861. 1994's follow-up, **Out in the Open**, included the fine love song, "Rose Street" (featuring excellent whistling from Declan Quinn) and the band's eulogy to "Arranmore". By this time, the Goats' punishing tour schedule (including Glastonbury and Cambridge Festivals plus the Finsbury Park Fleadh) had begun to take its toll and they announced a sabbatical in 1995. Pat returned to Donegal, playing a few local gigs, and writing the songs for his debut album **Tór** (1998), recorded in a house high in the hills above Crolly. Part-credited to GDS, though few of the band actually feature, the album revealed a mellowing Gallagher singing a straight pop song for his daughter, on "Sarah", an attack on the evils of drink in "You're Killing Me" and a song about coming home in "The Returning Islander".

⊙ **The Rusty Razor**   Cooking Vinyl, 1992

The Goats' humungous debut is still a tough one to top.

Horslips

Formed in Dublin in 1970, this trailblazing five-piece staked out a similarly sprawling art-rock and folk-rock territory to that explored by the likes of Jethro Tull and Fairport Convention, but sought to locate it within a distinctively Irish sensibility, drawing on both traditional music and Celtic mythology as key elements of their sound. Although reviled as much as celebrated, the project was a genuinely motivated one, involving a conscious decision to remain based in Ireland – the first successful Irish rock band to do so – and the aim, according to band member **Jim Lockhart,** of "using traditional music as an influence to develop a new idiom of rock'n'roll that would have some relevance to our own experience." To a large extent, their albums, all originally released on their own Oats label, now sound like typically tripped-out products of the later psychedelic era, but at their best – as on their debut release **Happy To Meet, Sorry To Part** (1972), its concept-album successor, **The Tain** (1973)

GEMS/REDFERNS

or the "Celtic symphony", **The Book of Invasions** (1977) – the five-way ferment of ideas and experimentation remains both exhilarating and intriguing.

Compared to most of their folk-rock contemporaries, **Horslips'** approach was an ambitiously organic one, with traditional material and instrumentation – including fiddle, uilleann pipes, whistles, mandolin, concertina and banjo – woven into their own wide-ranging compositions. Their ten-year career saw the band, comprising Lockhart, **Charles O'Connor**, **Barry Devlin**, **Eamon Carr** and **John Fean**, achieving major popularity with young audiences at home, and to a lesser extent in the UK and US. Their latter albums' shift towards a more straightforward rock sound signalled their ultimate creative exhaustion, and they split to pursue solo projects in 1980. A 1999 legal victory over back-catalogue rights was followed by the remastered CD reissue of their first four releases, with the rest to follow, but while the band have been recording again in O'Connor's Yorkshire studio, talk of a live reunion has yet to progress beyond rumour.

⊙ **The Book of Invasions**   Edsel, 1977

Horslips' "Celtic Symphony" garbs an ancient Irish myth in contemporary musical language.

The Irish Tradition

In 1975 accordionist **Billy McComiskey**, fiddler **Brendan Mulvihill** and guitarist **Andy O'Brien** (from Co. Kerry) came together for a week-long gig at the Dubliner, in Washington, DC. Instant popularity saw the week develop into a three-year residency and **The Irish Tradition** becoming key players in the Irish-American musical revival of the 1970s. Thanks to the band many dormant musicians were brought back into the fold and The Irish Tradition's reputation was enhanced by three fine albums, **Catchin' the Tune**, **The Corner House** and, finally, the aptly-titled **The Times We've Had**. Their success relied on the interplay of McComiskey's box and Mulvihill's fiddle and there's no better example than the last album's set of reels "Lad O'Beirne's/The Small Hills of Offaly", played in a characteristically lively composite of their respective Galway and Limerick roots. O'Brien provides understated rhythmic accompaniment and proves himself no mean singer too, especially on Scotsman Archie Fisher's "The Shipyard Apprentice".

⊙ **The Times We've Had**   Green Linnet, 1985

Hugely influential at the time and well deserving of their own mini-revival.

The Johnstons

Though now consigned to relative obscurity within Irish musical annals, thanks to their mid-career makeover from a folk band into a pop group, **The Johnstons**' early traditional recordings rank among the choicest fruits of the 1960s ballad boom. They started out as the sibling trio of **Adrienne**, **Luci** and **Michael Johnston**, from Slane, Co. Meath, performing a mix of traditional ballads and contemporary folk songs. Arriving on the thriving Dublin folk-club circuit, they shot to fame when their first-ever single, a cover of Ewan MacColl's "The Travelling People", went straight to #1 in Ireland. With the addition of **Mick Moloney** (vocals, guitar, banjo, mandolin) in 1966, and Michael's replacement by **Paul Brady** (vocals, guitar), they moved more decisively into a traditional vein, now equipped with four equally strong singers as well as two accomplished instrumentalists. Signing to London's Transatlantic records, they released their self-titled debut for the label in 1968, followed a year later by another traditional collection, **The Barley Corn**. In their choice of material, their outstanding individual and close-harmony singing, and their niftily picked instrumental arrangements, these two albums have more than stood the test of time. The release of **The Barley Corn**, however, was accompanied by that of **Give A Damn** (1969), comprising heavily orchestrated pop arrangements of exclusively modern material, including covers of Joni Mitchell, Leonard Cohen and Jacques Brel songs (nowadays sounding, ironically, almost quaintly dated), as record-company heads sought to reposition the group as the next Seekers. Although Luci left the group when they moved to London in 1969, the remaining trio enjoyed substantial international success over the next few years, with albums including **Bitter Green** (1969) and **Colours of the Dawn** (1971). As pop stylings came to dominate their sound, however,

Moloney grew increasingly unhappy with their musical direction and departed in 1971 leaving Brady and Adrienne to record one further album together before they, too, went their separate ways.

⊙ **The Johnstons/The Barley Corn**   Transatlantic,1968 and 1969

Chock-full o'treats, from rousing chorus songs to classic love laments.

Kíla

Formed as long ago as 1987, it's been a long time coming for **Kíla**, but, thanks to their astonishing live performances, the Irish

Jak Kilby

acoustic septet seem set to be the next big thing on the world music scene. At the band's heart is the awesome **Rónan Ó Snodaigh**, a dervish on stage with a unique "talking" bodhrán style, matched by his own distinctive percussive vocal chants in Irish. Meanwhile the rest of the band – Ronan's brothers, **Rossa** and **Colm**, **Dee Armstrong**, **Eoin Dillon**, **Brian** and **Lance Hogan** – take Irish traditional music to the bounds of

Rónan Ó Snodaigh

possibility, blending frenetic uilleann piping with township backbeats and mandolins strummed in fingernail-tearing frenzy. Their first album, **Handel's Fantasy**, appeared in 1993, followed two years later by **Mind the Gap** on which Kíla's virtuosity was demonstrated by "5.30", a bludgeoning guitar riff (reminiscent of Horslips) breaking into a sax-led 2-Tone freak out. The title track samples the infamous London Underground platform announcement and features a wild whistle solo from Rossa. 1997's **Tóg é go Bog é** enhanced their reputation further, but was a mere foretaste for the tremendous **Lemonade & Buns** (2000). As rhythmically driven as ever, this is the album where Kíla proved that it's not all hell for step-dancing leather in their cosmic ballroom: amidst all the furore, they take a breather on the stately "Listerine Waltz" and "Turlough's", a leisurely tribute to the legendary Donegal piper Turlough Mac Suibhne.

⊙ **Lemonade & Buns** Kíla Records, 2000

Kíla's masterpiece – a superb, monumental album.

Lá Lugh

Having already recorded a well-received duo album, **Cosa gan Bhróga** (1987) with flute player Desi Wilkinson, Dundalk-based husband-and-wife team **Gerry O'Connor** (fiddle) and **Eithne Ní Uallacháin** (vocals, flute, whistle) – he a co-founder with Len Graham (see p.71) of the influential group Skylark, she the sister of renowned Co. Louth singer Padraigín Ní Uallacháin – formed **Lá Lugh** in 1991. Their self-titled debut album (1991) was immediately acclaimed for the combination of O'Connor's gutsy, stylish playing and, especially, Ní Uallacháin's hauntingly pure, delicate voice, as well as their mining of the oft-neglected South Ulster tradition. Their follow-up **Brighid's**

Kiss (1996), further reflected their interest in the region's rich local culture and mythology, also featuring some original compositions, and was voted album of the year by readers of *Irish Music Magazine*. After their major-label signing for **Senex Puer** (1998), featuring traditional material artfully interwoven with everything from a tenth-century hymn to contemporary pop tinges, this fast-blossoming career was cut tragically short by Ní Uallacháin's untimely death in 1999.

⊙ **Lá Lugh**   Claddagh, 1991

Less ambitious or wide-ranging than its successors but bewitching in its combination of instrumental flair and exquisite vocal work.

Lia Luachra

This perky young quartet have nothing to do with the Cork–Kerry polka-land of Sliabh Luachra, but take their name from Celtic mythology – **Lia Luachra** being Fionn Mac Cumhaill's foster mother. Their 1998 eponymous debut album, a grand selection of traditional and self-penned tunes, was quickly recorded in the wake of their success at the Lorient festival that year. Ex-Big Geranium, Englishman **Jon Hicks** (guitar, vocals, shaker, keyboard) taps a left-field vein of material including Hoyt Axton's "The Gypsy Moth" (popularized by Freddie White) and "See It Come Down", associated with English socialist singer Roy Bailey. Rock bands always have problems with "that difficult second album", but not Lia Luachra. Now defining themselves as an acoustic rather than traditional group (though still drawing strengths from the latter tradition), 2000's **Traffic** sees Hicks and Tyrone man **Declan Corey** (mandolin, bouzouki) lay down an intricate finely-picked sonic carpet for the flights of fancy navigated by fiddler, **Tricia Hutton** (from Carlow), and the concertina of Dubliner **Shane Bracken**. This tight ensemble playing is the undoubted high point and **Traffic** opens with a stunning reel, "Changing Silver", written by Declan. Elsewhere, Hicks supplies a moody instrumental, "Traffic", and four of his own songs, including a guest spot for Niamh Parsons on "Sleeping at the Wheel". The best of the other tunes is the reel, "Francy Quinn's", while the juxtaposition of Scots and Greek melodies on "Morticia and the Greek" forms an eerie closing piece. Be warned, however, for this is possibly the first "traditional" album to feature not just one hidden track – some wistful solo fiddling from Tricia – but a second in the form of a weird disco break-out!

⊙ Traffic	Malgamú Music, 2000

Sparky, pert and bright – don't miss them live!

The London Lasses
and Pete Quinn

T hough the number of venues has declined in England's capital over the last decade, Irish music continues to thrive, thanks in part to the efforts of **The London Lasses**. Taking their name from the familiar reel, the Lasses were formed for a US tour in 1997 and have since developed into a powerful combination producing some of the liveliest music around. Fiddlers **Elaine Conwell** and **Karen Ryan**, both pupils of the late Tommy Maguire from Leitrim, have been playing together since childhood and, unsurprisingly, possess an almost symbiotic musical understanding. **Sharon Whelton** on flute is an astonishingly able player, equally adept in any key, while **Bernie Conneely** (now resident in Dublin) maintains the fine London banjo tradition. Their outstanding debut album saw the Lasses link up with pianist **Pete Quinn** (potentially the Charlie Lennon of the twenty-first century) and singer **Sue Cullen** to produce one of the most remarkable releases of 2000. Hitting a groove straight away with a set of reels propelled by booming chords from Quinn, the Lasses demonstrate impressive virtuosity across the spectrum of melodic forms – exemplified by Sharon's gorgeous rendition of the "Tenpenny Bit" jig. In contrast, Sue's songs tend towards the melancholic, none more so than the lost lover's "Johnny, Lovely Johnny".

⦿ The London Lasses and Pete Quinn	Lo La Records, 2000

Not so much promising as inevitable – a fabulously vibrant debut!

Lúnasa

The success of **Lúnasa**'s self-produced and self-titled debut album spawned a contract with Green Linnet and the resulting fabulous **Otherworld** (1999). Long known for the power of their public performance, this album captures all the group's spirit with higher production values ensuring a wonderful clarity. Lúnasa's sound is a unique composite of wind and string. **Sean Smyth**'s whistles and fiddle and **Kevin Crawford**'s flute and whistles soar and dip purposefully against a sonorous backdrop laid down by ex-Waterboy **Trevor Hutchinson**'s double bass or cello, while **Donagh Hennessy**'s guitar reinforces the rhythm or picks its own intricate melodies. If there was a single better track released in 1999 than "The Butlers of Glen Avenue/ Sliabh Russell/Cathal McConnell's" – on which the quartet are augmented by former member **Mike McGoldrick**'s uilleann pipes and whistle – then I've not heard it. Adding further nourishment to the album is another ex-member, piper **John McSherry** and a rare appearance by a flügelhorn (courtesy of Stephen McDonald). On the band's 2000 US tour the piping role went to **Cillian Vallely**, of the famous Armagh family. Sean Smyth's own solo album, **Blue Fiddle** (1993), is also

well worth tracking down, though punning sleeve notes about the fiddler's medical background (he is a qualified doctor) don't bear repeated reading!

⊙ **Otherworld**   Green Linnet, 1999

Awesome playing by a band described by one critic as "The hottest Irish acoustic group on the planet" and, possibly, the coolest too.

Macalla

The history of Irish traditional music is very much an account of "his story" and, for an assertion of women's place in that tradition, we should be eternally thankful for the existence of **Macalla**. Though relatively short-lived, the idea of bringing together the best women musicians in Ireland had a lasting impact and resulted in enduring recognition for many of the singers and players who toured with the ensemble and featured on their two albums. The list of all those involved would be too long to itemize, but included **Máire Breatnach**, **Mairéad and Áine Ní Mhaonaigh**, **Mary Mac Namara**, **Pearl O'Shaughnessy**, **Máirín Fahy**, **Joan McDermott**, **Catherine McEvoy**, **Mary Corcoran** and many others. Sadly, neither album has reappeared on compact disc, though cassettes may still be found. **Macalla 2**, produced by Paddy Glackin, is probably the most coherent of the two and features a mini-orchestra of seven fiddlers (heard to best effect on the waltz "An Roisín Dearg") while the best ensemble singing occurs on the Arranmore singer Róise na nAmhrán's "Casadh Cam na Feadamaí".

| Macalla 2 | Gael-Linn, 1987 |

As exciting as ever, this innovative recording surely deserves to be reissued.

Midnight Court

This isn't Martin Hayes's and Dennis Cahill's legendary Chicago trad-rock band though, coincidentally, this Berlin-based trio kicked off in the year following its namesake's demise. Berliner **Bernd Lüdtke** (fiddle, bouzouki, bodhrán, five-string banjo, vocals) has been leading the band since its formation and is currently aided by accordionist **Noel Minogue** from Co. Tipperary, former Junior and Senior All-Ireland Champion, and Belfast-born singer and guitarist **Aaron Shirlow**. The band's elegantly-packaged second album **Ear to the Ground** merits repeated listening and must be one of the few to include the actual notation of the tunes in the sleeve notes. There's a jolly swing to their step in the playing of the "Cape Breton Set" of jigs while other notable features include Aaron's fine voice and the revival of songs from the Northern tradition, such as the emigration song "Carrowclare". Other albums include the self-produced **Half Moon** and the recent release **Courting the Cat**.

⊙ **Ear to the Ground**   Magnetic Music, 1998

Strong singing and playing from a rapidly progressing trio.

Midnight Well

Still regarded with fond affection two decades on, **Midnight Well's** blend of country-rock and traditional music proved a popular draw in the late 1970s and provided a launching pad for the careers of three of its members. Californian singer **Thom Moore** composed all ten tracks on their only album, the self-titled **Midnight Well** (1977) which also featured American vocalist **Janie Cribbs** and guitarist **Gerry O'Beirne** (future Sharon Shannon band member) who laid down the basics for the accordion of **Máirtín O'Connor**. Moore's ability to pen catchy tunes is no better illustrated than the opening track "Still Believing", featuring infectious fiddle from guest Kevin Burke (others appearing include Dónal Lunny, Shaun Davey and Clannad's Ciarán Ó Braonain). Moore's songs bear the marks of Townes Van Zandt and carry the same emotional scars, and indeed his and Janie's delivery (as on "Soldier On" and "Wheel of Fortune") share Van Zandt's relaxed style. Moore still writes and regularly records, most notably the excellent **Gorgeous and Bright** (1994) while Janie Cribbs, now living on an island off the coast of Washington State, has just released her own solo album.

⊙ **Midnight Well**   Mulligan, 1977

"Still Believing" is one of the best openers ever recorded – a classic of its kind.

Moher

Clare band **Moher**'s roots are as rock solid as the famed cliffs from which their name derives and no fewer than five of the sextet come from the county. **Michael Queally** (fiddle) and **Noel O'Donoghue** (flute) have been duetting for more than a decade (co-founding the Gold Ring Céilí Band) and it shows to admirable effect on the band's second and latest album, **Over the Edge**. Nearly all the selections are local tunes, played in the exuberant Doolin style, and singer-guitarist **Liam Murphy** (who played with Eileen Ivers and Martin Hayes during an American sojourn) adds the elegant "Bonnie Irish Maid" and "Dónal Óg". Other Clare denizens of the band are **Pat Marsh** (bouzouki, guitar), **John Moloney** (bodhrán) and double-bass player **Paul O'Driscoll**, while fiddler Siobhán Peoples is a regular guest.

⊙ **Over the Edge**   Lochshore, 1998

Queally and O'Donoghue make a purposeful pairing and this is a thoroughly well-honed album.

Morning Star

Stalwarts of the New York Irish music scene since the 1980s, **Morning Star** are nowadays a quartet consisting of Kerry-born **Mary Courtney** (vocals, guitar, bodhrán), **Margie Mulvihill** (cousin of Martin) on tin whistle and flute, **John Nolan** (button accordion) and **John Reynolds** (fiddle, viola, mandolin). A great draw live, their third and latest release **Grá** ("love" or "sweetheart") showcases Mary's rich, warm voice on songs such as "Green Grow the Laurel" (a paean to Irish-American involvement in the Mexican-American war of

1845–47) and "The Queen of All Argyll" (by Scotsman Andy M. Stewart), although at times her guitar is a little too prominent in the mix. All-Ireland Champion Nolan (a guest at the time of recording) is on fine form throughout and there's excellent ensemble playing on a set of hornpipes, including "Off to California". Margie's whistle is brisk and lively, though there's not enough of her fine flute-playing, while John's fiddle is ever tasteful. *www.morningstar.iuma.com*

⊙ **Grá**   own label, 1999

Forceful, melodic playing from one of New York's finest bands.

The Moving Cloud

S et-dancing's popularity boomed in Clare in the late 1980s and there was no better group of musicians to supply the music than the band **Moving Cloud**. Sharing an affection for the dance-bands' golden era, and adopting the name of a popular reel, the original line-up consisted of **Paul Brock** (accordion, melodeon), fiddlers **Maeve Donnelly** and **Manus McGuire**, **Christy Dunne** (banjo) and **Carl Hession** (piano). Christy left after four years in 1993 and was replaced by **Kevin Crawford** (flute). Their self-titled debut album appeared a year later and, more recently, they've released the exuberantly infectious **Foxglove**. Maeve Donnelly's fiddle has never sounded better than on "Paddy Fahy's Reel" and when Manus joins for "The Ewe Reel" it's time to place your order for dancing shoes. Elsewhere, Brock supplies a virtuosic performance in the French musette style on "Swing Waltz" and Crawford offers a splendid solo rendition of "Knocknagoshel" then harmonizes with himself on "Ryan's" (thanks to double-tracking) before the band goes full tilt on "Come West Along the Road" – all three popular Kerry polkas.

⊙ Foxglove   Green Linnet, 1998

If this doesn't send you to set-dancing classes, then nothing else ever will.

Moving Hearts

After Planxty and The Bothy Band, came the third in the pioneering triumvirate of great Irish bands, **Moving Hearts**. Put on any of their four albums today, and the level of their achievement, in the space of four short years, is immediately apparent. Where most other folk-rock acts of the 1970s or 80s sound irretrievably dated, the Hearts, for the most part, might have been in the studio last month, the boldness of their musical vision abundantly matched by their individual and collective musical prowess.

The band was originally the brainchild of **Dónal Lunny** (bouzouki, synthesizer) and **Christy Moore** (vocals, guitar, bodhrán), both then members of the reformed Planxty, but finding that line-up increasingly constraining in terms of their individual musical development. Lunny was interested in furthering his exploration of traditional music's rhythmic dimension by combining folk material with rock instrumentation, while Moore wanted more opportunity to sing contemporary as well as traditional material. Leaving Planxty in 1981, they teamed up first with guitarist **Declan Sinnott**, and soon afterwards with the Hearts' other four founding members: **Davy Spillane** (uilleann pipes, whistles), **Eoghan O'Neill** (bass), **Brian Calnan** (drums, percussion) and **Keith Donald** (sax). Their self-titled debut album (1981) went straight to the top of the Irish charts, the power of instant-classic songs like "Hiroshima Nagasaki Russian Roulette", "Irish Ways and Irish Laws" and Jackson Browne's "Before the Deluge" vying for impact with dazzlingly adventurous instrumental arrangements, the latter a blend of trad, rock and jazz stylings driven by sophisticated, fleet-footed rhythm work and fronted by the radical partnering of uilleann pipes with saxophone.

Almost instantaneously, Moving Hearts acquired a huge and fervent following in Ireland, soon swelled further by their electrifying live performances, with appearances at Lisdoonvarna and their residency at Dublin's Baggott Inn still the stuff of legend to this day. Their second album, the slightly more pop-tinged **Dark End of the Street** (1982), which saw Calnan replaced by Matt Kelleghan, lacks some of its predecessor's edge in the songs – perhaps reflecting Moore's growing discomfort within a band format; he was to go solo for good later that year – though this is counterweighed by blazing instrumentals like "Downtown". Their upfront political convictions, however, remain well to the fore, in tracks like "Remember the Brave

Ones" and "Allende". Following Moore's replacement by singer-songwriter **Mick Hanly**, **Live Hearts** (1983), recorded at London's Dominion Theatre, served up a barnstorming taster of that unforgettable live atmosphere, after which they added a second piper, **Declan Masterson**, and swapped Kellaghan for **Noel Eccles**. The band were run as a collective and, despite a burgeoning international reputation, the logistics and punishing economics of maintaining such a large line-up were beginning to take their toll. **Flo McSweeney** took Hanly's place in 1984, but never recorded with the band, who succumbed to the inevitable later that year, after a farewell concert at Dublin's National Stadium. Their landmark "posthumous" release, **The Storm** (1985), six majestically extended all-instrumental sets, remains one of the finest musical sign-offs in history, as well as offering a broad and tantalizing hint as to how the band might have continued to evolve. Since disbanding, they have reformed for occasional one-off gigs, while wisely resisting the temptation to cash in any further on the enduring influence of their brief but brilliant career.

⊙ **Moving Hearts**   WEA, 1981

Maintains a high level of innovation and accomplishment throughout.

⊙ **The Storm**   Tara, 1985

An album of unsurpassed style which leaves you wanting more.

Nomos

Probably the only Irish band with a Greek name, **Nomos** means "melody" – a term used by Seán Ó Riada for some of his own compositions. The band, formed in Cork city in the early 1990s, comprised concertina-player **Niall Vallely**, fiddler **Liz Doherty**, **Frank Torpey** (bodhrán), **Gerry McKee** on mandocello and singer, guitarist, bassist, **John Spillane**. The line-up soon became known for its rous-

ing performances, especially the interplay between Niall and Liz, and Spillane's exquisite delivery of his own songs, and led to the splendid debut album, **I Won't Be Afraid Any More**. The demands of Doherty's academic career saw her leave the band in March, 1995 and her Donegal/Cape Breton influence was replaced by former Bone

set you free

Idol member **Vince Milne** whose playing combines his native West Cork style with his father's Sligo roots. Now signed to Grapevine, the new Nomos produced the matchless **Set You Free** which included two of John's best songs, "I'm Going to Set You Free" and "When You and I Were True", plus the tour de force traditional "Bean Dubh an Ghleanna", while the band's tremendous musicianship is displayed throughout, notably on "Brendan's Reels". Spillane subsequently left to follow his own solo path and the latest recruit is the young Cork-born singer **Eoin Coughlan**.

⊙ Set You Free   Grapevine, 1997

Honest, adventurous, peerless playing coupled with one of the best singers around, make this a required purchase.

North Cregg

The Valley connection continues (see overleaf) with **Caoimhín Vallely**, Armagh-born fiddler with another remarkable Cork-formed band, **North Cregg** who take their name from a Sliabh Luachra townland. The band originated from sessions in Cork's Gables and Lobby bars, featuring accordionist **Christy Leahy** and singer-guitarist **John Neville** who were subsequently joined by pianist **Ciarán Coughlan**, snare-drummer **Martin Leahy** and Caoimhín. A glance at the group's unique instrumental line-up indicates their special qualities, demonstrated to massive acclaim at successive Cork Folk Festivals in the late 1990s. A German tour in 1998 led to their signing by Magnetic Music and the release of their debut, **. . . And They Danced All Night**, on which they are augmented by subsequent full-time member, banjo player **Paul Meehan**. North Cregg's unusual rhythm section of swing piano, snare drum and driving guitar underpins energetic accordion and fiddle on fast-paced reels like "The Mullbrae" (from the Shetlands) and Sliabh Luachra polkas (learned from Séamus Creagh). The pace is broken up by Neville's own songs – the best of which is the laconic "The Wobbling Man", while "The Long Road", unfortunately, sounds like a Toss the Feathers out-take. Whatever your fancy, try to catch North Cregg in the flesh!

⊙ **...And They Danced All Night**   Magnetic Music, 1999

The title says it all – see North Cregg and you just might!

Óige

Óige means "youth" and the quartet from Dungiven, Co. Derry, was originally formed in 1990 by teenagers **Cara Dillon** (vocals, fiddle, bodhrán) and brothers **Murrough** (flute and whistles) and **Ruadhrai O'Neill** (fiddle and bodhrán) along with **Paul McLoughlin** (guitar) from Limavady who had married Cara's older sister, Mary of Déanta fame. Cara's voice is almost as sweet as her sister's and the youthful élan of the quartet's music is best heard on their debut live CD. Cara left to join English band The Equation in 1995 and was replaced by an old schoolfriend, **Maranna McCloskey**, who also plays concert flute. The band's

instrumental skills had progressed by the time of their follow-up album **Bang On**, on which Maranna's rich voice is at its best on "The Maid of Culmore" and "Bonnie Blue Eyed Lassie".

⊙ **Live**   Klub, 1994

Cara's in splendid form on "The Flowers of Magherally-o" and the band cook up a storm in these highlights of a 1993 Scottish tour.

Oisín

Like many other Irish groups, **Oisín** enjoyed critical acclaim at home but found commercial success abroad. Formed in Dublin in the mid-1970s, the band's overall sound was light and mellow thanks to the presence of the brothers **Brian** and **Tom McDonagh**

(mandolin and bouzouki respectively) and **Séamus MacGowan** (guitar, vocals) while attention usually focused on the fiddle of **Mick Davis** and the voice of Séamus's partner, **Geraldine MacGowan**. Paul Brady produced and played on their first two albums, 1976's self-titled debut and **Bealoideas**, both of which now sound curiously dated in comparison to the breakneck pace of many current bands. The third album, 1980's **Over the Moor to Maggie** saw the addition of **Gerry Phelan** on flute and whistles while fiddler **Paddy Glackin**'s production reflected the band's harder edge acquired through regular European touring. Glackin himself joins in on the lively "The Flogging Reel" while Geraldine's outstanding vocal track is the moving "The Bonny Light Horseman". Both Phelan and Brian McDonagh (who later formed Dervish) left after the album and the 1980s saw the McGowans and new accordionist **Ann Conroy** the only constant members through a swirl of changes: **Steve Cooney**, harper **Nóirín O'Donoghue**, pipers **Davy Spillane** and **Mick O'Brien** and fiddler **Gerry O'Connor** (plus several others) all played with the band before its demise in the late 1980s. Their last two albums, **The Jeannie C** and **Winds of Change**, are compiled on Ossian's **Celtic Dreams**. The McGowans and Mick Davis headed for Germany – Geraldine to begin a successful solo career and Mick to form Bachelor's Walk.

⊙ Over the Moor to Maggie   Ossian, 1980

A fine testimony to a tight-knit band often unjustly overlooked in retrospectives.

Osna

Mayo is long associated with migration. Even nowadays the percentage of youngsters leaving Co. Mayo to study in tertiary education elsewhere is higher than any other county. So it's great when a young homegrown quartet like **Osna** comes along. Three of the band – **Treasa Lavin** (vocals, whistle, keyboards, piano), brother **Padraic** (uilleann pipes, low whistle) and singer/guitarist **Daragh O'Reilly** – hail from the Lacken-Ballina area while button accordionist Johnny Towey comes from Kilkelly. The band's name means "sigh" and is associated with the desolate mood of Inis Ge and other, now uninhabited, islands off the county's northwest coast. Osna's self-titled debut album was three years in the making, but there's no sign of discontinuity as the band produces a set both spirited and sensitive, marked by Padraic's sublime low whistle on the air "Inis Ge" and racy ensemble playing on reels such as "The Hunter's Purse/Cameronian/The Gravel Walks".

⊙ **Osna**   Celtic Note, 1999

Enthusiastic playing that augurs well for the future.

Patrick Street

One of the first Irish traditional acts to attract the "supergroup" tag, **Patrick Street** came together out of a 1986 US touring package, "Legends of Irish Music", featuring the three remaining founder members – fiddler **Kevin Burke** (ex-Bothy Band), accordionist **Jackie Daly** (ex-De Dannan) and singer/multi-instrumentalist **Andy Irvine** (ex-Sweeney's Men, Planxty). Guitar wizard **Arty McGlynn** completed the original line-up. Despite operating in tandem with the membership's other projects, the band have sustained a steady recorded output, with their self-titled debut release (1986) establishing the musical hallmarks that still distinguish their sound today: tight, crisp, yet airily spacious arrangements of reels, jigs, slides, polkas and hornpipes, vibrantly foregrounding tone, texture and melodic nuance, together with a varied, authoritatively delivered selection of traditional and contemporary songs.

Their second album, **No.2** (1988) declined to tamper with a winning formula but their third, **Irish Times** (1990) sought a broader canvas, bringing in singer-guitarist **Gerry O'Beirne**, uilleann piper **Declan Masterson**, fiddler **James Kelly** and **Bill Whelan** on keyboards. The bigger arrangements, however, made for a weaker, less focused album, especially on the song front, although it did inaugurate the now-ubiquitous Penguin Café Orchestra tune, "Music For A Found Harmonium", into the contemporary Irish repertoire. **All In Good Time** (1993) saw the founding foursome augmented only by Whelan, whose presence and production occasionally obtrude in unwelcome pop tinges, but overall the band's clean, keen edge and sparkling finesse are firmly back to the fore. Following McGlynn's departure in 1996, Northumbrian guitarist and piper **Ged Foley** was introduced on **Cornerboys** (1996), with his nimble picking and inventive rhythms slotting neatly into the mix, and his smallpipes embellishing the vocal/instrumental hunting medley, "Pity the Poor Hare". **Made in Cork** (1997) further consolidated the band's benchmark reputation for unflashy excellence, while **Live From Patrick Street** (1999) commandingly captured the extra kick of their concert performances.

| ⊙ Patrick Street | Green Linnet, 1986 |

Echoes of Planxty in the song arrangements mesh impeccably with Burke's highly ornamented style and Daly's vivacity.

Planxty

From **Andy Irvine** and **Dónal Lunny**'s silvery opening cascade of mandolin and bouzouki, ushering in **Christy Moore**'s low, huskily charged voice on "The Raggle Taggle Gypsy", right until the last, briefly lingering note of **Liam O'Flynn**'s uilleann pipes four-and-a-half minutes later, it's still instantly, resoundingly clear just how vital an Irish musical landmark was established with **Planxty**'s self-titled debut album in 1972. The ensemble deployment of instruments (including the then new-fangled Irish bouzouki), based more on a rock'n'roll template than accepted traditional modes; the intricate, multilayered accompaniment to a traditional ballad; the triumphant segue from song to tune – virtually all of Planxty's key musical coinages are encapsulated within the space of that very first track. Even as they broke new ground, though, Planxty – named after a type of tune composed in praise of an individual – also adhered to certain time-honoured virtues, primarily in the calibre of their musicianship, combined with Moore's and Irvine's vocal facility for getting expressively and rhythmically inside the skin of a song.

The subsequent careers of all four original members provide eloquent testimony as to the once-in-a-lifetime concurrence of talent that took place in Dowling's bar, in the Co. Kildare village of Prosperous, where they first played together in sessions. Their inaugural studio collaboration was on Moore's second solo album, also called **Prosperous** (1972), the craic during recording being such that it seemed only logical to continue the party. The timing of Planxty's formation was also fortuitous, taking place amidst a burgeoning of economic and cultural confidence in Ireland, while the new aura of cool they brought to traditional music helped them win mass popularity among the youngest population in Europe.

As well as their innovative blend of instruments (also including guitar, bodhrán, whistle and, latterly, synthesizer) the line-up's respective musical backgrounds each contributed some distinctive flavour to the mix. None apart from O'Flynn, a former pupil of piping legend

Leo Rowsome, had been raised in the tradition; Moore, Lunny and Irvine were all early rock'n'roll or skiffle fans, discovering traditional music through the folk revival of the 1960s, their passion for unearthing and arranging old songs and tunes thus being fired with a converts' zeal. In addition Irvine, an ex-member of Sweeney's Men, having spent eighteen months busking around Bulgaria, Romania and Yugoslavia, brought not only the bouzouki but an extensive knowledge of East European music to the band's repertoire, besides emerging as a gifted songwriter.

The first two albums – that revelatory debut, commonly known as "The Black Album", being swiftly followed by **The Well Below the Valley** (1973) – remain the ultimate classics, each replete with definitive Planxty material including "The West Coast of Clare", "The Jolly Beggar", "The Blacksmith", "Cúnla", "As I Roved Out" and many more. Together with **Cold Blow and the Rainy Night** (1974), which contained perhaps their best-known track, "The Lakes of Pontchartrain", and saw Lunny replaced on bouzouki by **Johnny Moynihan** (though still featuring heavily as a guest), these form the basis of **The Planxty Collection** (1976), released following the band's initial break-up in 1975. Prior to that split, **Paul Brady** had stepped into the vocal slot vacated by Moore in 1974, although he never recorded with the band.

After a spell spent developing his solo career, it was Moore who instigated the founding quartet's reformation in 1978, together with flute player Matt Molloy, going on to record three more albums – **After the Break** (1979), **The Woman I Loved So Well** (1980) and **Words and Music** (1983) – featuring a variety of new members and guests, including **Nollaig Casey**, **James Kelly**, **Noel Hill**, **Tony Linnane** and **Bill Whelan**. Though the first two of these releases, at least, are frequently outstanding by any other standards, they couldn't quite match the musical heights scaled during Planxty's original incarnation, and following Lunny and Moore's departure to form **Moving Hearts**, the band split for good in 1983. In their pioneering approach to both instrumentation and song arrangements, however, and in setting new benchmark standards of musicianship – not to mention launching four of Irish music's most influential careers – they bequeathed a permanently enduring legacy.

⊙ Planxty   Shanachie, 1972

"The Black Album" sounds every bit as fresh as when it heralded the dawn of a new musical era almost 30 years ago.

⊙ The Well Below the Valley   Shanachie, 1973

Includes Christy Moore's first recording of "The Well Below the Valley" and Andy Irvine's seminal rendering of "As I Roved Out".

The Pogues & Shane MacGowan

Impelled by the slewed genius of singer and chief songwriter **Shane MacGowan**, **The Pogues** didn't so much push the envelope of Irish musical tradition as rip it to pieces and pogo on the remains. In doing so, however, they forged a sound that not only resonated afresh with the wild extremes of celebration and desolation the Irish have always distilled into their songs and tunes, but gave vent to those emotions in a defiantly fractured, hybrid voice at once vividly redolent of its time and place – Thatcher's Britain, as seen by the emigrant Irish – and (when at their soul-searing best) magnificently timeless.

With all due respect to his long-suffering colleagues, too often portrayed as mere props to his talent, it is MacGowan's story that shamelessly upstages the larger Pogues narrative. Born in Kent on Christmas Day, 1957, he spent his first few years in rural Tipperary, doing party pieces at family singing sessions and listening to the early ballad groups on the radio. Uprooted to London in 1964, he

was left with a profound sense of alienation that saw him gravitating naturally as a teenager into the thick of the burgeoning London punk scene. After the collapse of his first band, psychobilly/punk combo The Nips (originally The Nipple Erectors), he hooked up with whistle player **Spider Stacy**, drafting in former Nip guitarist **Jim Fearnley** to back their furiously souped-up versions of Irish rebel songs. The addition of **Jem Finer** (banjo and guitar), **Andy Ranken** (drums) and **Cait O'Riordan** (bass) saw the band emerge as Pogue Mahone (Irish for "kiss my

Shane MacGowan

arse") around 1983, shortening their name the following year.

Their debut album, **Red Roses for Me** (1984) was essentially a snapshot of their early live shows – raw, chaotic, seething with equal parts vitriol and black humour, with compositions like "Dark Streets of London" and "Streams of Whiskey" introducing MacGowan as a songwriter to watch. It was with **Rum, Sodomy and the Lash** (1985), produced by Elvis Costello (who The Pogues had supported on tour), that their full potency began to be felt, with classic MacGowan originals including "A Pair of Brown Eyes" and "The Old Main Drag", plus superbly scabrous covers of Ewan MacColl's "Dirty Old Town" and Eric Bogle's "And the Band Played Waltzing Matilda". The band now included guitarist **Philip Chevron**, and the sizeable cult profile they had attained in both Britain and America was already being fuelled by tales of MacGowan's prodigious consumption of drink and drugs. After a couple more personnel changes – O'Riordan was replaced by **Darryl Hunt**, and **Terry Woods** (banjo and concertina) joined the line-up – they signed to Island and released their biggest-selling album **If I Should Fall From Grace With God** (1988), popularly memorable for its hit Christmas single "Fairytale of New York", featuring guest vocalist Kirsty MacColl. Other standout tracks include the frenetically madcap "Fiesta", and the fiercely moving emigration anthem "Thousands Are Sailing", written by Chevron.

This was to prove the peak of The Pogues' career trajectory, with MacGowan's relentless bodily abuse increasingly taking its toll on the rest of the band. The dubiously-received stylistic mishmash of **Peace and Love** (1989), featuring just six MacGowan compositions, mirrored these internal tensions, and by the time **Hell's Ditch** (1990) appeared, Stacy and Finer were singing most of the songs. Despite a warmer critical reception, the album sold poorly, not least because MacGowan's erratic behaviour made proper promotion impossible, and he was asked to leave the band in 1991. Ex-Clash singer **Joe Strummer** stepped in briefly and unconvincingly, as frontman, before Stacy took over vocal duties, but despite the more chart-friendly aspirations of **Waiting For Herb** (1993), it was clear that the guts were gone from the band, who finally bowed to the inevitable in 1996.

After a few years in the wilderness, punctuated by the odd inebriated live appearance, MacGowan re-emerged, Lazarus-like, with his new band **The Popes**. Their first release **The Snake** (1994) contained ample of the old Shane magic to give would-be obituarists pause, although the follow-up, **The Crock of Gold**, was dismissed by many critics as simply a crock. With The Popes performing without him as much as with him, MacGowan's next move awaits to be seen – although the mere fact that he's shambling around the planet continues to lend his persona a compelling patina of myth, if not miracle.

⊙ **Rum, Sodomy and the Lash**   Stiff, 1985

Still the favourite of the cognoscenti, thanks to its compelling combination of untrammelled spleen and dark lyrical beauty.

Providence

Formed only in 1999, **Providence** take Irish music back to its roots, allowing the inherent rhythms to flow and the music to speak its own subtleties. It's a refreshing, albeit unfashionable agenda, founded on expert musicianship and ex-Fallen Angel **Joan McDermott**'s blithe voice. Bouzouki/guitar player **Paul Doyle** (an early Arcady member who pops up on many records) lays down the foundations for the melodies of **Mícheál Ó Raghallaigh**'s concertina and accordion, **John Wynne**'s flute and whistle and **Clodagh Boylan**'s fiddle. Their self-titled debut album (which included Clodagh's predecessor **Méabh O'Hare** on fiddle) includes much unfamiliar material, including the rare song "Seven Gypsies" (a variant of "The Raggle Taggle Gypsy") though Joan's best song is probably the melancholy "Óchón Ochón Mo Challín" learned via Liam Weldon. Tunes flow easily too, such as the stylish jig "The Dooney Rock".

⊙ **Providence**   Rolling River, 1999

Relaxed and refreshing – the simple pleasures rediscovered.

Reeltime

C entred primarily on the double partnership – in music and in life – of traditional fiddler and lead vocalist **Máirín Fahy**, and ex-rock guitarist **Chris Kelly**, this Galway-based outfit has frequently had to share its personnel with *Riverdance* – Fahy and the band's two current accordionists, **Éilís Egan** and **Luke Daniels**, have all performed extensively with the show. **Reeltime** – whose original line-up also included **Benny Hayes** on keyboards (later replaced by **John Flatley**), and now features Fahy's sister Yvonne on percussion – have nonetheless found time to record two well-received albums, their eponymous debut (1995) and **Live It Up** (1998). Each winningly high-lights their squeaky-clean technical finesse, brightly polished delivery and mix'n'match musical approach: their core Irish repertoire being deftly spiced with everything from ragtime to Pachelbel, Western swing to French musette. Cloyingly soft-focus song arrangements, however, are a less winning trait, while their sound overall would ben-efit from more meat on its bones and some dirt under its fingernails.

⊙ **Reeltime**   Green Linnet, 1995

The songs might set your teeth on edge, but agile, impishly effervescent instrumental work offers ample compensation.

Rig the Jig

Five-piece **Rig the Jig** have rapidly acquired a justifiable reputation as one of the most exciting session bands in the West of Ireland, and have almost singlehandedly reinstated Roscommon town on the country's musical map. Formed in the local pub that gave their boisterous first album it's title, **One Night in Harlow's**, the band consists of **Michael Banahan** (vocals, guitar, bodhrán), **Jimmy Flanagan** (vocals, guitar, banjo, harmonica), **Brendan Doyle** (accordion, guitar), **Noel Carberry** (pipes, whistle, bodhrán) and **Johnnie Duffy** (vocals, guitar, banjo). Their first studio excursion was 1999's **Finding the Gold**, a generally fine brew of traditional music, revealing occasional bluegrass influences and a liking for the songs of John Prine. The only stumer is the inclusion of a "joke" version of Luka Bloom's "An Irishman in Chinatown" which might work well after a few pints but sounds simply crass on disc. Still – one to watch for the future!

⊙ Finding the Gold   Anew, 1999

Grand playing throughout, but programme your player to skip track 10.

Scullion

Evolving around the creative nucleus of **Philip King** (vocals, hamonica) and ex-Tír na nÓg founder **Sonny Condell** (vocals, guitar), **Scullion** were one of Ireland's most inventive and least classifiable bands. The original line-up, formed in 1975, also featured guitarist **Greg Boland** (replaced in 1986 by Robbie **Overson**) and piper **Jimmy O'Brien-Moran**. Their sound comprised a shifting and sometimes eccentric blend of folk, pop, jazz, reggae, blues and rock, their influences ranging from Frank Zappa to John Martyn. Though they attracted a considerable fan-base, not least for their exceptional live shows, and released several well-received albums, including **Scullion** (1979), **Balance and Control** (1980) and **Spin** (1985), their approach ultimately owed more to the freely experimental days of the 1970s than the punk and new-wave era that followed, and by the late 1980s they were in semi-retirement. King subsequently became a highly successful TV producer, while Condell continues to perform and record as a solo artist.

⊙ **Eyelids Into Snow**   Hummingbird, 2000

Combining back-catalogue cuts with live material, this 18-track compilation offers a wide-ranging career overview.

Shantalla

Belgium is famous for fruit-flavoured beers, chocolates and – inaccurately – for its dearth of famous people. It's an unlikely base for an Irish traditional band, but that's exactly where **Shantalla** can be found. Taking their name from an old metaphor for Ireland (Sean Talamh – the old ground), the band has been cooking up a storm in Northern Europe – selling out their gigs well in advance – and its 1998 self-titled debut album was picked up by Green Linnet for US and Asian release. The band's origins are diverse – guitarist **Joe Hennon** is from Dublin, while **Michael Horgan** (uilleann pipes, flute, whistles), **Kieran Fahy** (fiddle, viola) and **Gerry Murray** (accordion, bouzouki, mandolin, low whistles) are, respectively, from Down, Galway and Monaghan. The blend's last ingredient is supplied by the voice and bodhrán of singer **Helen Flaherty** from East Kilbride,

Scotland. Though they can hammer out the reels if they so wish, Shantalla's strengths lie in their subtle arrangements, particularly of songs such as "Fine Flowers in the Valley" where Kieran's fiddle adds a mournful closure and the show-stopper, "The Blantyre Explosion", a Scots song learned from Dick Gaughan.

⊙ **Shantalla**   Wild Boar Music/Green Linnet, 1998

A grand song selection marks a more than promising debut.

Sín É

When Downpatrick teenager **Steáfán Hannigan** attended his first ever gig (by Planxty) it set him on a musical course he'd not previously envisaged, acquiring multi-instrumental skills (uilleann pipes, flute, whistles, bodhrán) along the way. Moving across the water to England he played in various bands, wrote a bodhrán tutor and recorded a solo album of variable quality, **Natural Selection** (1991), before forming London-based **Sín É** (literally "That's It") with **Mike Cosgrave** (keyboards, guitar), **Taz Alexander** (vocals, fiddle, guitar), **Anuman Biswas** (tablas, congas and assorted percussion), **Teresa Heanue** (fiddle, whistle) and former All-Ireland champion uilleann piper **James O'Grady**. Their initial self-titled album gave little indication of the invention that was to follow, other than a tendency to incorporate Biswas's Indian rhythms into traditional melodies and a penchant for punning titles (eg "The Houmous of Green Lanes"). However, the increasing rhythmic experimentation and offbeat arrangements apparent in the follow-up, **It's About Time** (described by one critic as "Clannad meets Massive Attack"), came to a head with their 1999 major label outing **Deep Water Drop Off**. By this time Heanue and Biswas had been replaced by **Gerry Diver** (guitar, fiddle, pipes) and **Ben Clark** (tablas, percussion) and traditional tunes had made way for self-penned trance experimentation and a misguided cover of the classic "Sankofa" by US jazz diva Cassandra Wilson. Here's a snippet from the sleeve notes re "The Streets of Derry": "Being a traditional song we have used the appropriate accompaniment of 72 layered berimbaus and brass clusters". Irony or navel-gazing? The choice is yours.

⊙ **It's About Time**   Rhiannon Records, 1997

The best of the "Celtic" trance fusion albums which you can interpret as you wish.

Skara Brae

One of the most beautiful records ever made was recorded in just one afternoon in 1970 by a youthful quartet, **Skara Brae**. Named after an archeological site in the Orkney Islands, the quartet's origins lay in the Donegal Gaeltacht village of Rann na Feirste (Rannafast) where **Dáithí Sproule** spent his summers learning Irish and becoming friends with **Tríona** and **Maighread Ní Dhomhnaill** and their brother **Mícheál**. Musical affinity was found through songs learned from the siblings' father Aodh and his sister Neilí, a shared love of Beatles songs and afternoons spent jamming with Ciarán and Pól Brennan (soon to form Clannad). By the late 1960s Dáithí, Mícheál and Tríona were all studying at University College Dublin. The ensuing two years saw them playing around Dublin, developing a repertoire which drew upon the Donegal tradition and the open-tuned guitar interplay of Bert Jansch and John Renbourn and featured harmonized vocals and Tríona's distinctive clavinet. Maighread became a regular member of the band while still at school.

The album **Skara Brae** has a unique ambience, no matter whether songs are lively, such as "Cad é sin don té sin?", or dignified, in the case of the unaccompanied "Báncnnoic Éireann Ó". All the group sing, and their voices blend and mesh to delightful effect; Dáithí and Mícheál's guitars and Tríona's clavinet are rarely obtrusive and the over-all product is a glorious confection of mellow harmonies and subtle backing. Sadly, there was no follow-up and, indeed, Skara Brae's sound was already evolving, with instruments (even the clavinet) becoming amplified and a bass guitarist being added. They went their separate ways in 1972, though reuniting 25 years later for a one-off (and, by all accounts, magical) gig as part of the Frankie Kennedy Winter School. By then, of course, all four had become major figures in Irish music.

⊙ Skara Brae   Gael-Linn, 1971

Uplifting, soul-inspiring and tender as a baby's skin – absolutely essential.

Sliabh Notes

Y ou know that you're in for a treat from the opening moments of Sliabh Notes' second album **Gleanntán** as accordionist **Dónal Murphy** delicately wraps his fingers around the sway of Pádraig O'Keeffe's "Annaghbeg Polka" before **Tommy O'Sullivan**'s guitar drops into the background. Dónal then slides into "Pete Bradley's Polka" and finally **Matt Cranitch**'s fiddle picks up the melody as the three of them ease into the "Gleanntán Polka". Like these three tunes, much of the album draws upon the group's shared interest in the music of Sliabh Luachra where polkas predominate (Gleanntán was the birthplace of Pádraig O'Keeffe), though Tommy has a fine eye for a song as he demonstrates with Tony Small's "The Welcome" and Jimmy MacCarthy's "The People of West Cork and Kerry". Cranitch had been a member of Na Filí and Any Old Time and both he and Tommy had spent spells in London while Dónal Murphy (whose father was a box player and mother a noted step-dancer) had been an early member of Four Men and a Dog. Though the trio had been friends for some time, it was not until a hugely enjoyable impromptu session in Dingle in 1992 that they entertained the idea of playing together on a more permanent basis, resulting in their 1995 album **Sliabh Notes** – the source of the band's name.

⊙ **Gleanntán**   Ossian, 1999

A gorgeous album, replete with outstanding musicianship and tasteful interpretations of classic material.

Solas

The most talented ensemble to emerge in the second half of the 1990s, the Irish-American group **Solas** (Irish for "light") draws upon the multiple skills of its members to produce a sound in which dynamism and tenderness are compellingly balanced. At the heart of Solas since its formation until recent times have been the multitalented **Seamus Egan**, New York-born classically-trained fiddler and champion step-dancer **Winifred Horan** and the guitarist, Dubliner **John Doyle**, while one of the key elements of the band's sound, the honeyed tones of Co. Waterford singer **Karan Casey**, provided a vital ingredient until her departure in 1999. Their self-titled 1996 debut album proved a solid start while the following year's **Sunny Spells and Scattered Showers** opened with Casey's butter-melting rendition of "The Wind that Shakes the Barley" and still sounds as fresh as the day it was released. Original accordion/concertina player,

John Williams, left after this album, being replaced by Co. Kilkenny's **Mick McAuley** (same instruments plus low whistle) in time for the stupendous **The Words That Remain** (1998), an album containing some of the most glorious ensemble playing ever committed to tape. Highlights include Karan's luxuriant version of Woody Guthrie's "Pastures of Plenty", while the band explodes into action on the successive tracks, "The Stride Set" and "The Waking Up Set", producing music of furious complexity with a technical superiority that is simply mind-boggling.

LIVING TRADITION

Win Horan

After Casey's departure, **Deirdre Scanlan** joined Solas for their performance as house band for Jean Butler's *Dancing on Dangerous Ground* (music written by one S. Egan) when it opened in London. The limpid purity of her voice, evident on her own, largely unaccompanied, album **Speak Softly** (1999), was almost certainly the main reason she was selected to replace Karan Casey. However, the Solas sound was now becoming increasingly aggressive and percussive, as revealed in **The Hour Before Dawn** (2000), an album which captures all the verve of their thrilling live performances. There are some superb vocals from Deirdre on "Bonny Man" and Mick on "A Miner's Life", plus a set of reels – sparked by "New Custom House" – which showcases playing of breathtaking finesse from Seamus, Win and Mick, driven along by John's frenzied guitar. Subsequently, John Doyle left the band and has been replaced by Dónal Clancy.

⊙ **Sunny Spells and Scattered Showers**   Shanachie, 1997

Contains Karan Casey's magical "The Wind the Shakes the Barley" and a host of excellent tunes.

⊙ **The Words that Remain**   Shanachie, 1998

Simply breathtaking – an astounding amalgam of vocal and musical virtuosity.

Stockton's Wing

Throughout a career that's lasted more than twenty years, **Stockton's Wing** have stepped back and forth across the line dividing folk music from pop, frequently keeping one foot either side. Their founding line-up in 1977 included four All-Ireland champions – Leitrim fiddler **Maurice Lennon**, West Limerick's **Tommy Hayes** on bodhrán and Jew's harp, **Kieran Hanrahan** and **Paul Roche**, both from Clare, on banjo and flute – plus Galway singer-guitarist **Tony Callanan**. Their eponymous debut album (1978), a predominantly traditional collection of freshly-arranged instrumentals interspersed with three songs, combined high-calibre musicianship with sparkling youthful vitality. Callanan's replacement in 1979 by **Mike Hanrahan**, Kieran's singer/songwriter brother, introduced original material into their sound and began their extended flirtation with the pop world, these influences coming increasingly to the fore over their next two albums, **Take a Chance** (1980) and **Light in the Western Sky** (1982). The latter featured new member **Steve Cooney** (see p.376) on bass and digeridoo – the earliest instance of the Australian instrument's use in Irish music.

Despite the generally anodyne nature of their vocal material, the third album spawned two hit singles, "Beautiful Affair" and "Walk Away", contributing to the Wing's escalating international popularity. After Hayes' departure in 1983, the addition of drums and keyboards created their most fully-fledged folk-rock incarnation, with the band subsequently enjoying substantial commercial success in America. The 1990s, however, saw them reverting to a largely traditional, acoustic approach (minus bass and drums) while banjo/mandolin player **Davey McNevin** joined up in place of Kieran Hanrahan. The resulting back-to-basics album **The Crooked Rose** (1992) shows off their sweetly spliced melody playing in accomplished instrumental sets like "Aaron's Key" and "The Prince's Feather", but Hanrahan's songs continue to strike a saccharine note, a tendency exacerbated further by his subsequent replacement **Eamon McElholm** on the band's most recent release, **Letting Go** (1995).

⊙ The Crooked Rose   Tara, 1992

Ignore the soupy ballads and relish the vibrantly layered, crisply delivered instrumental work.

Sweeney's Men

The trio known as **Sweeney's Men** was one of the most influential bands of the 1960s Irish folk revival. Formed in 1966, it's original all-singing line-up consisted of guitarist **Joe Dolan** (not the MOR singer of the same name), **Andy Irvine** (mandolin, guitar, harmonica) and **Johnny Moynihan** who had previously worked with the English folk-singer Ann Briggs and was responsible for introducing the bouzouki into Irish music. Heavily influenced by Old Timey American musicians from the 1920s and 1930s, the group also drew its material from the Irish, Scots and English traditions and had an early Irish hit single with "The Old Maid in the Garrett". After this, Dolan returned to painting and songwriting (Christy Moore covers two of his songs on **The Iron Behind the Velvet**) and was replaced by guitarist, five-string banjo and concertina player **Terry Woods**. The band recorded another couple of singles before laying down the tracks which formed their debut album **Sweeney's Men** (1968). The bouzouki-mandolin interplay featured on its opening track, "Rattlin' Roarin' Willy" would later become a prominent element on Planxty's music, and this and the remaining cuts saw Sweeney's Men pushing back the boundaries of folk and traditional song through distinctive arrangements of ballads such as "Willie O'Winsbury" or a wonderful a capella version of Dominic Behan's "Dicey Riley".

Andy Irvine left soon afterwards to travel around Eastern Europe and Moynihan and Woods soldiered on as a duo with the help of guitarist **Henry McCullough** for their last release, **The Tracks of Sweeney** (1969), a largely blues-tinged album bar the eerie closing "Hall of Mirrors". Terry Woods went on to join Steeleye Span with his wife Gay Corcoran, later enjoying success with The Pogues, while Johnny Moynihan – truly one of Ireland's great singers – had spells with De Dannan, Planxty and, during the 1980s, his own band, The Fleadh Cowboys. He continues to sing and play regularly on the Dublin scene.

⊙ Sweeney's Men/The Tracks of Sweeney   Castle Communications, 1968–69

Both original transatlantic albums, plus the single "Old Woman In Cotton" on one excellent-value CD.

Tír na nÓg

The partnership of **Sonny Condell** and **Leo O'Kelly** left an indelible stamp on folk music both in Ireland and across the water. Formed in 1969, their original five-year career produced three idiosyncratic albums which explored the same margins of folk and rock as their UK contemporaries Nick Drake, John Martyn and Bridget St. John. Both Leo and Sonny played acoustic guitar and wrote prolifically, often with a quirky edge to lyrics or melody and sometimes both. Their 1971 self-titled debut is the lightest of the three, and includes the lively audience favourite, "Aberdeen Angus". Subsequent albums, **A Tear and a Smile** and **Strong in the Sun**, saw them moving closer towards rock, with the latter produced by former Procol Harum keyboards player Matthew Fisher and featuring their best-known song, "Free Ride". Noted for their constant touring (they seemed to support everyone in the early 1970s), the duo split in 1974 but have occasionally reunited with some success, including the recent **Live at the Hibernian** release. Condell went on to form Scullion and both he and O'Kelly are still regular performers on the Dublin scene.

⊙ **Strong in the Sun**   Demon, 1973

Strong singing, sensitive guitars and some of the duo's best songs, including the anthemic "Free Ride" and the melodic title track.

Trian

The acclaimed Irish-American trio **Trian** (Irish for "third"), consisting of fiddler **Liz Carroll**, button accordionist **Billy McComiskey** and guitarist/singer **Dáithí Sproule**, released their debut album for

Flying Fish in 1992. The follow-up **Trian II** (1995), a grand collection of self-penned tunes and others acquired along the way, also features the playing and arrangements of guitarist **Ciarán Curran** (Altan) and Sproule's erstwhile collaborator in Skara Brae **Tríona Ní Dhomnaill**. Dáithí's guitar-playing is as economical as ever while his songs include the splendid "The Lurgy Streams", learned from fellow Derry-man Kevin Mitchell. Liz and Billy play together with a natural refinement, especially on the familiar reel "The Humours of Ballyconnell" while Liz's playing of her own slow air, "The Air Tune", is close to perfection.

| ⊙ Trian II | Green Linnet, 1995 |

Three mighty talents produce a scorcher of an album.

The Voice Squad

Fran McPhail, **Gerry Callen** and **Phil Callery** are the Irish masters of unaccompanied harmony singing. With each well-known as a fine solo singer, as **The Voice Squad** they grafted the ensemble method onto Irish song, particularly drawing on the strengths of the Northern tradition. Their 1987 album **Many's the Foolish Youth** was an astounding debut, refreshing for its apparent simplicity, and included a benchmark rendition of one of the big Ulster songs, "The Banks of the Bann". **Hollywood** (1992), recorded in St Kevin's Church, Hollywood, Co. Wicklow, was even better, with the venue's acoustics enriching the trio's perfect harmonies. There's a tremendous version of "A Stór Mo Chroí", but the real high spot is their remarkable rendition of "Sarah Jane", learned from the singing of Eddie Butcher. Phil Callery's own solo album, **From the Edge of Memory** was one of the superior releases of 1999, worth acquiring simply for his vibrant version of "Westlin Winds" (a Robert Burns poem learned via Len Graham) on which Frankie Lane's dobro and Mick Kinsella's harmonica embellish the low-key backing with remarkable subtlety. Much in demand as vocal accompanists, The Voice Squad have featured on many recordings, including Arcady and Rita Connolly.

⊙ **Hollywood**   Hummingbird, 1992

The reverberant acoustics enhance the atmosphere on this outstanding recording.

⊙ **From the Edge of Memory**   Tara, 1999

Phil Callery's solo venture was a highlight of 1999.

The Waterboys

Given that the sole constant in **The Waterboys'** mercurial career has been the presence of Scottish singer, songwriter and guitarist **Mike Scott**, their inclusion here might seem anomalous. But it was their extended flirtation with Irish music that saw the band attaining their peak of popularity. This so-called "raggle-taggle" phase of their career began at a point when they seemed poised for stadium-rock stardom, after three increasingly successful albums' worth of anthemic, wide-screen "big music". Irish fiddler **Steve Wickham** (of In Tua Nua), who had guested on the third album **This Is The Sea** (1985), now joined the line-up (keyboards player Karl Wallinger and saxophonist **Anthony Thistlethwaite**) full-time and invited Scott over to Dublin in early 1986. This became the start of a five-and-a-half-year Irish sojourn for the frontman, with recordings for the band's next album stretching over nearly half that period. Immersing himself with zeal in Irish and American folk music, Scott invited double-bass player

Trevor Hutchinson to join the band, and presided over the recording of literally scores of tracks, many featuring leading traditional Irish players, although of these only a few, including accordionist **Máirtín O'Connor** and De Dannan's **Alec Finn**, appeared on the finished product. The final studio sessions took place in Spiddal, Co. Galway, where Scott had rented a cottage from fiddler Charlie Lennon, and **Fisherman's Blues** eventually appeared in autumn 1988. With its acoustic-based, traditionally-flavoured sound, even weaving in a few instrumental jigs and reels among the songs, the album became their biggest-selling release, its highlights including the buoyant country/folk title track, a winsome cover of Van Morrison's "Sweet Thing" and the setting of W.B. Yeats' poem "The Stolen Child".

The follow-up **Room to Roam** (1990), also recorded in Ireland, continued the traditional theme – abetted by the presence of **Sharon Shannon** on accordion – with instrumentals such as "The Trip to Broadford" and the song "The Raggle Taggle Gypsy". Within days of its release, Wickham quit the band following a disagreement, prompting another abrupt musical volte-face back towards a harder, rock-oriented approach. Hutchinson left the following year to join Shannon's touring band, after which Scott moved to New York, subsequently pursuing a solo career before launching a new Waterboys line-up with **Rock In the Weary Land** (2000). Combining elements from Scott's solo spiritual meanderings with echoes of the band's early majesty, the album fell decidedly short of a triumphant comeback, but talk of issuing material from the extensive horde of unreleased **Fisherman's Blues** recordings raises a rather more tantalizing prospect.

⊙ Fisherman's Blues   Ensign, 1988

Scott's seemingly artless convert's enthusiasm creates an album of considerable and enduring charm.

The Wolfe Tones

Now approaching their fortieth anniversary as a professional touring act, **The Wolfe Tones** combine staunchly Republican politics with an old-fashioned ballad-group style. It's a formula which has remained essentially unchanged throughout their career, and has tended to find more favour abroad – especially in the US – than at home. As their records were being banned in Ireland during the late 1960s, Los Angeles was awarding them the keys to the city, an honour it had last bestowed on The Beatles. As the *Irish Independent* once put it, "the Wolfe Tones have the roar, the thunder and the simplicity our American cousins require, in contrast to the quieter cadences that battle-weary natives at least sometimes want to hear."

The band was formed in 1963 by Dublin-born **Warfield** brothers, **Derek** (mandolin, vocals) and **Brian** (guitar, banjo, harp, bodhrán, vocals) along with their friend **Noel Nagle** (uilleann pipes, whistle). Naming themselves after Wolfe Tone, one of the leaders of the doomed 1798 Rebellion, they enlisted lead singer and guitarist **Tommy Byrne** the following year, turning professional soon afterwards. With the ballad boom in full swing, they established themselves first on the UK and home folk circuit, making their first trip Stateside in 1966. Radio and TV appearances helped boost sales of their early albums, and in 1968 they were voted Ireland's second most popular group. They were courting controversy from an early stage, too, with their single "James Connolly" being banned in 1966. Another contentious hit was "The Helicopter Song", mischievously commemorating the escape of three IRA prisoners from Mountjoy prison, which went to #1 in 1973. Although best known for their Republican material – much of it composed by Brian Warfield – they have always denied any sectarian agenda, and from the beginning their repertoire also included traditional and popular ballads, street songs, emigration songs, historical anthems and instrumental sets. Though now widely regarded by traditionalists as little more than a nostalgia act, they still command a loyal core audience in Ireland and the UK, and continue to draw large crowds on their annual US tours.

⊙ **25th Anniversary**   Celtic Connections, 1989

A double CD collection with many favourites, including "James Connolly", "The Helicopter Song" and "Rock on Rockall".

Families

A s the saying goes, the family that plays together, stays together and lineage plays an integral role in the continuation of Ireland's musical traditions. Songs are learned from the cradle onwards and instrumental skills are handed down the moment a child reveals an aptitude. Certain families are revered for their abilities and the multifaceted skills of their members. Most are included in this section, although you will find those connected to a specific instrument in the appropriate part of the musicians directory (eg the Dorans under uilleann piping, the Lennons under fiddle, etc).

The Begleys

S ong and dance are strong in the West Kerry Gaeltacht and the **Begleys** (nine brothers and sisters) from Baile na bPoc, have been at the heart of the tradition for many years. Their grandfather, **Mickey Begley**, once ran a speakeasy in New York, but, returning home, took up the reins of the local pub and later converted his other business, a fish-curing shed, into a dance hall in the 1930s. This proved a popular venture, though not with the local priesthood, and provided a musical education for the grandchildren, especially when it was redesigned as a ballroom in the 1950s. Both their parents sang and all the children have inherited the talent. House parties were a regular event and often featured their father's melodeon – an instrument which all the children would eventually try. The eldest, **Máire**, moved on to the piano accordion at fourteen and learned her craft playing for the sets and for the old-time waltzes and quicksteps. These feature on her only solo release to date, **Siar ar Bhóithrin na Smaointe** (1993).

Séamus too is a fine singer, but his prowess as a stupendous button accordionist received broader recognition with the release of **Meiteal** recorded with guitarist **Steve Cooney**. The pair had already combined in 1992's **Bringing It All Back Home Tour**, but few could have expected the impact of **Meiteal**, a record at times so infectious it could fill a casualty ward with dance victims. Some claimed the album incorporated rock rhythms, but anyone who's seen Séamus's mighty forearms powering a box knows that he needs no such assistance. As he once remarked, "I don't see much point in playing music unless there's somebody dancing to it" and the invitation is impossible to resist on this magical recording.

Seosaimhín Ní Bheaglaoich is well known as a journalist with Raidió na Gaeltachta, before that she was a founding member of the all-woman band **Macalla** in 1984, and featured on its two albums. A noted dancer and concertina player her solo album, **Taobh na Gréine/Under the Sun** (1994), produced by Dónal Lunny, showcases her voice on a selection of songs from the region. Sister **Eilín** returned after 20 years in Australia to record another fine album of local songs, **Míle Dath/A Cloak of Many Colours**. The youngest of the nine is **Breandán**, singer, accordion and melodeon player, well-known through his membership of **Boys of the Lough** and **Beginish** and through recordings with The Chieftains. Though Breandán always wanted to be a fiddler, he's a master accompanist for dancing, as can be heard in his contribution to **Set Dances of Ireland** and on his second solo album **We Won't Go Home 'Til Morning** (1997). Despite its rhythmic qualities there's an inherent wild loneliness in the sound of Breandán's accordion, especially heard in the slow air "Dónal Óg". His marvellous voice is also given a grand airing on songs such as "Cailín na Gruaige" and "The Kerry Hills".

⊙ Meiteal	Hummingbird, 1992

Irresistible and uplifting music and song from the box and guitar duo of Séamus Begley and Steve Cooney.

⊙ We Won't Go Home 'Til Morning	Kells Music, 1997

A sumptuous album from the brilliant Breandán Begley.

The Blacks

Thanks primarily to the efforts of its female progeny, the Black family name is one of today's best-selling Irish musical brands. **Mary Black**, followed increasingly closely by her younger sister **Frances**, has scaled the heights of adult-contemporary, folk-pop success on either side of the Atlantic, their popularity having increased the further they've moved away from their traditional roots. Both, in fact, exemplify a now well-established tendency among Irish female vocalists to use a traditional or folk background as a springboard into a more mainstream, pop-oriented style – a trend significantly catalysed by the two mega-selling **A Woman's Heart** albums released in the early 1990s.

In the beginning, though, music was very much a family affair. Encouraged by their parents – Mum sang, Dad played fiddle – Mary, Frances and their brothers, **Michael**, **Shay** and **Martin**, cut their performing teeth together singing in Dublin folk clubs. Mary joined the traditional band **General Humbert** in 1977, going on to record two albums with them, before her eponymous solo debut (1983) fetchingly showcased her limpidly soulful, delicately nuanced voice in a blend of traditional and contemporary material, reaching #4 in the Irish album charts. She sang with **De Dannan** for three years, appearing on their **Song For Ireland** and **Anthem** albums, meanwhile teaming up with producer/guitarist **Declan Sinnott** for her own second release **Without the Fanfare** (1985), a distinctly poppier foreshadowing of her future musical direction.

Mary Black

The **Black Family** continued performing periodically during this time, having won a sizeable following for their close-harmony renditions of ballads and sea shanties. Their first album, simply entitled **The Black Family** (1986), featured all five siblings, but Mary's escalating solo commitments cut down her involvement with its follow-up, **Time for Touching Home** (1989), although she and Frances contributed harmony vocals to the three brothers' **What A Time** (1995), which also included their mother, Patty, enjoying herself on "Now I Have to Call Him".

After the second family album, Frances joined the group **Arcady**, whose debut LP, **After the Ball** (1991), and its winsome title track both made the Irish Top Ten. Their traditional/contemporary mix of instrumentals and songs was also making inroads in the US, but the pressures of touring prompted Frances' departure in 1992. The gathering plaudits for her subsequent duo with Co. Down singer-songwriter **Kieran Goss**, and their self-titled joint recording (1992), were soon eclipsed by **A Woman's Heart** (1992), the all-female compilation which features Frances on two tracks and Mary on three. Following this mass exposure, her first solo single, the Christy Hennessy-penned "All the Lies That You Told Me", charted at #3, while its parent album, **Talk To Me** (1994), containing four previously unrecorded Nanci Griffith compositions, spent several weeks at #1. It was swiftly followed by the release of **A Woman's Heart 2** (1994), **The Sky Road** (1995) and, two years later, **The Smile On Your Face**. On each album Frances' warm, silvery vocals – a shade lighter and brighter than her big sister's – steer deftly between folk, country, pop and jazz-lite stylings, albeit with lapses into the excessively mannered, soft-focus preciousness that's increasingly beset her recent work, including her latest CD **Don't Get Me Wrong** (1998).

A similarly creeping MOR blandness has latterly cost Mary Black many of her earlier fans, though they're amply outweighed by new ones. Mary is now officially the biggest solo female artist in Ireland, with several platinum-selling albums to her credit. Her breakthrough recordings, **No Frontiers** (1989) and **Babes in the Wood** (1991), which marked her arrival in the US market, have their cloying moments, but are redeemed overall by her silkily expressive singing, especially on ballads like the former's title track, or the latter's "Thorn Upon the Rose". Like many of her albums, before and since, they draw heavily on the work of contemporary Irish songwriters such as Jimmy MacCarthy, Mick Hanly and Noel Brazil. Her next three releases, however – **The Holy Ground** (1993), **Circus** (1995) and **Shine**

(1997) – combine largely insipid material with cloyingly smooth production, although **Speaking With the Angel** (1999), partly produced by Dónal Lunny, marks a welcome return to a leaner, rootsier approach and is her most characterful release in years.

⊙ **The Black Family**   Dara, 1986

A sense of innocence pervades this family debut, together with a wealth of sparsely accompanied five-part harmonies.

⊙ **Talk To Me**   Dara, 1994

Strong material, including previously unrecorded Nanci Griffith compositions, underlines the charm of Frances's early style.

⊙ **Mary Black**   Dara, 1983

This, by far Mary's most folk-oriented album, highlights her honeyed sweetness and lyrical fluency.

The Coens

Jack (b. 1928) and **Charlie** (b. 1934) Coen come from Woodford in East Galway, but have each been based in the US for more than 40 years. Their father, Mike, was an expert on the concertina, playing at local dances and parties, and it was from him that the brothers acquired their early repertoire. Both began on the tin whistle and progressed to the wooden flute in their teens, though Charlie later turned to the concertina. The brothers have been part of New York's Irish music scene for many years, Charlie moving there after being ordained as a priest, and have made a number of recordings, of which the best is **The Branch Line**, originally released by Topic in 1977. The brothers still play in their father's simple, steady style, as in "Mike Coen's Polka", where the measured pace was ideal for dancers. Unusually, jigs dominate the recording and are played in unison with a confident, unelaborate ease, but still with many shades of subtlety, as on another of their father's tunes "Have a Drink on Me" which changes into "The Blarney Pilgrim" – learned from Jack's long-time friend, the late fiddler Larry Redican.

⊙ **The Branch Line**   Green Linnet, 1977

Two New York stalwarts provide a musical treat in the East Galway style.

The Flanagan Brothers

The three Flanagan Brothers, **Joe**, **Louis** and **Mike**, were one of the most popular and prolific Irish acts playing and recording in the US during the 1920s and 1930s. All were born in the last decade of the nineteenth century and moved with their parents to Albany, New York State when the family emigrated from Waterford city in 1911. The brothers moved to New York around 1920 and began playing the dance-hall circuit, fronting dance bands whose size varied according to the venue. Over the next fifteen years they released an astonishing 160 sides for a variety of labels, often accompanied by **Ed Geoghegan** on piano. Joe was the lead singer while Louis provided a bedrock of driving rhythms on either banjo or a rare twin-necked guitar, but the key to their sound was Joe's accordion playing in unison with Mike's banjo or mandolin. A grand selection of the Brothers' records has been remastered by Harry Bradshaw on **The Tunes We Like to Play on Paddy's Day**, including popular songs such as "The Grand Hotel in Castlebar" and "Maloney Puts His Name Above the Bar", alongside a number of the jigs and reels which kept dancers in a frenzy for hours on end. Their most well-known song, "My Irish Molly-O", was revived by De Dannan in 1981 while Van Morrison gave a notable performance of the Brothers' "Tura Lura Lura" on The Band's **The Last Waltz** album. Both Joe and Louis died in the late 1930s, but Mike lived on until 1990.

⊙ **The Tunes We Like to Play on Paddy's Day**   Viva Voce, 1920s/30s

Another superb remastered compilation from Viva Voce that includes all the Brothers' most familiar songs.

▭▭ **An Irish Delight**   Ossian, 1920s/30s

Cassette reissue of the 1979 Topic compilation, complete with needle hiss, provides a rawer alternative.

The Hernons

The **Hernons** hail from Roisin na Manach, Carna in the Connemara heartland, though **P.J. Hernon** (button accordion & melodeon) now lives in Co. Sligo. His mother was a noted dancer (as is his sister, Máirín) and her uncle was the celebrated melodeon player **Peaitín Phádraig Mháirtín** (Connolly) from Feenish Island. The Hernon household was where Séamus Ennis (see p.404) stayed when collecting for the Irish Folklore Commission in the 1940s. Introduced to the accordion by his father, there's always been a touch of Paddy (Tipperary) O'Brien in P.J.'s own playing but his style, especially on the melodeon, still retains that unique Connemara friskiness. By the time P.J. won the All-Ireland Senior solo accordion prize in 1973 (when he was 22) he was already two years into a five-year stint as a member of the céilí band **Shaskeen**. Most of his recordings since then are now only available on cassette, apart from his superb self-titled 1978 album for Gael-Linn. Playing melodeon and a two-

row B/C accordion, Hernon gives a virtuoso, largely unaccompanied performance, with a stand-out version of "The Collier's Reel", a favourite of uilleann pipers. P.J. has also recorded two fine albums with his brother Marcus (see below). A music teacher since the early 1980s, P.J. can now be regularly heard and seen in the Sligo-based **Swallow's Tail Ceili Band**.

P.J. Hernon's younger brother **Marcus** is one of the most gifted and prestigious flute players to have emerged from Connemara in the last few decades. He lived and worked in London for a while before joining up with his elder brother to produce 1989's memorable **Béal a' Mhurlaigh**, a puckish brew of sprightly local dance tunes (and more) on which he really shines. Marcus is also a prolific composer, albeit one with an ornithological bent – his latest album with P.J., **The Grouse in the Heather**, consists of twenty-three tunes all bearing the name of a bird (eg "The Peeping Plover" and "The Invisible Corncrake"). If you were none the wiser, you might not realize that these are original offerings for the tunes connect to the traditional landscape the Hernons inhabit, and they feel and sound like the tunes they grew up with. There is also a céilí band feel to some of the music, thanks to the drumming of Paddy Higgins, but he and the other contributors (Charlie Lennon, Steve Cooney and harper Laoise Kelly) primarily serve to enhance the melodic power of the Hernons' partnership. Their younger brother, Seán, a lively tin whistler (in the Mary Bergin style) and banjo player, released the stylish **An Nóra Bheag** in 1997.

⊙ **P.J. Hernon**   Gael-Linn, 1978

Dashing and melodious music from the Connemara box man.

⊙ **The Grouse in the Heather**   Feenish Sound, 2000

Old skills and new tunes combine as one to provide a seamless package.

The Keanes

T**he Keane family** from Caherlistrane, Co. Galway, is one of Ireland's most illustrious musical dynasties of whom the most famous and influential member is the singer and flute player, **Dolores**. Though the family's musical lineage can be traced back several generations, it was her aunts, **Rita** and **Sarah** who first won international acclaim. Though both skilled musicians (on accordion and fiddle respectively), it was their singing that attracted attention to their home in northeast Galway. Though steeped in the sean-nós tradition, the Keane sisters were unusual in that they sang together in unison, their voices combining with an almost plaintive delicacy. The album **Once I Loved**, recorded in the late 1960s, was remarkable for the emotional intensity they brought to their material, in particular a near-flawless account of "Sail Óg Rua" from Sarah. The sisters later featured on 1985's **The Keane Family** album, featuring ten members of the family, and on their own **At the Setting of the Sun** (1994).

Dolores (b. 1953), brought up at her grandmother's by her aunts, revealed such a precocious singing talent that Radio Éireann recorded her when she was five. Soon afterwards she began to enter competitions and enhanced a burgeoning reputation through winning All-Ireland titles singing in both Irish and English. In the 1970s BBC TV presenter **John Faulkner** came to Caherlistrane to record Rita and Sarah for a programme and while capturing both sisters on film also captured Dolores's heart. Soon afterwards she was invited to join the original line-up of **De Dannan** and featured on the group's self-titled debut album whose spin-off, the Irish #1 hit "Rambling Irishman", won her national attention. Her reputation was further enhanced by her appearance on the following year's **Bonaparte's Retreat** release by **The Chieftains**, by which time Dolores and John were living in London where she worked as music researcher. Married in 1977, the couple became well-known on the London folk scene and formed the band **Reel Union** whose line-up included the fiddler Ciarán Crehan and piper Eamonn Curran. The upshot was her 1978 album, **There was a Maid**, a record of extraordinary power and one of the most influential in recent Irish musical history. Dolores demonstrates all the glorious versatility of her voice and its astonishing range on the unaccompanied "Tá mo Chleamhnas Déanta" while her interpretation of "Seven Yellow Gypsies" is still replicated by today's singers. She also proved herself no mean flute player on "Lament for Owen Roe O'Neill". Two further albums, **Broken Hearted I'll Wander** and **Farewell to Eirinn** emerged from the London period but the best product of the Keane/Faulkner musical partnership, **Sail Óg Rua** (1983), came after her return to Ireland (by which time Reel Union had become **Kinvara**). Among the album's highpoints are a wonderful reading of the emigration song "Galway Bay" and the title song performed with her aunt Sarah.

The Keane Family's album came in 1985, by which time Dolores had rejoined De Dannan for two further releases (**Anthem** and **Ballroom**). 1988's self-titled second solo album marked a controversial change in direction as Dolores largely jettisoned traditional song in favour of soft-rock ballads like Anna McGarrigle's "Heart Like a Wheel" and a bizarre rendition of "Lili Marlene". 1989 saw another hit with John Faulkner's Nelson Mandela tribute "Lion in a Cage", while the album of the same name continued to show a preference for cover versions, though it did include a memorable duet with Mick Hanly on his epic "My Love is in America". By this time, Dolores and John's relationship was over, though the couple have continued to collaborate. The 1990s have seen Dolores featuring on **Bringing it All Back Home** and **A Woman's Heart**, guesting on numerous albums, collaborating with Norwegian singer **Rita Eriksen** and releasing two further solo albums **Solid Ground** (1993) and **Night Owl** (1997). Unfortunately, on the latter album, the deterioration in her voice, noted by many at live gigs towards the end of the decade, cannot be masked by Faulkner's production.

During the 1990s Dolores's brother, **Seán** developed his own substantial reputation both as a singer and a fine flute player. He began learning the flute around the age

Dolores Keane

255

of eight or nine, but it was his traditional singing which won him early acclaim and during his childhood and teens he amassed no fewer than thirteen All-Ireland titles. In the 1970s, Seán sang and played with the band **Shegui**, recording the album **Around the World for Sport**, before a stint with **Reel Union**. He was later involved in the early incarnation of Johnny McDonagh's band **Arcady** and recorded **Atlantic Breeze** with **Shaskeen**. Seán's reputation as a fine interpreter of songs, both traditional and contemporary, gathered pace with his own first album, 1993's **All Heart No Roses**, produced by John Faulkner and Arty McGlynn. The same team produced its successor, **Turn a Phrase** (1996), which included Dolores on harmony vocals and a storming unaccompanied version of "A Stór Mo Chroí". The album's next track, "Galway to Graceland", was to prove remarkably prophetic – the follow-up, **No Stranger** (1998) was recorded in both Galway city and Nashville, and has a country-tinged edge though the songs were drawn from sources as diverse as Mick Hanly and Sting. **The Man That I Am** (2000) includes backing vocals from Nanci Griffith and Kathy Mattea, and an even more intriguing collaboration with Sir George Martin (The Beatles' producer) who arranged the old McCartney classic, "Blackbird", for Seán. A song's lyrics must mean something to Seán if he is to "feel true to the song" as his evocative rendition of Brendan Graham's emigration song, "Isle of Hope, Isle of Tears", admirably reveals. Though he now rarely plays on record, Seán tours with his own band, still playing his flute and, on occasions, the uilleann pipes.

📷 **Once I Loved**   Claddagh, 1967

Fabulous, beautifully unadorned singing from Rita and Sarah Keane.

⊙ **There Was a Maid**   Claddagh, 1978

An undisputed classic recording, revealing all of Dolores's astounding vocal powers.

⊙ **Sail Óg Rua**   Gael-Linn, 1983

Dolores Keane and John Faulkner's best album features a glorious version of "Green Grow the Laurels".

⊙ **The Man That I Am**   Grapevine, 2000

Glossily-produced showcase for the unique voice of Seán Keane – his most musically mature album to date.

The McCarthys

The name of the late **Tommy McCarthy** (1930–2000) is synonymous with traditional music, both in his native Co. Clare and in London, where he lived for many years. Inspired by Wren Boys who came calling to the family home in Shyan, near Kilmihill, West Clare, he began playing a wooden whistle, later progressing to both fiddle and concertina and learning tunes from local players such as Stack Ryan and Solus Lillis. Tommy developed his skills on the concertina accompanying dances and playing at American wakes, before emigrating to London with his wife Kathleen in 1952 where he acquired a set of uilleann pipes and took lessons from Leo Rowsome. During the 1950s London was a mecca for Irish musicians and Tommy played with just about everybody, though especially fellow Clare exile, the fiddler, **Bobby Casey**. The McCarthy household, first in Kentish Town and later in Hornsey, became almost a secondary musical venue and all four of Kathleen and Tommy's children became adroit musicians. Tommy returned to Ireland for the inaugural meeting of Na Píobairí Uilleann in 1968, subsequently co-founding the London Pipers' Club in 1980. He took part in the inaugural CCÉ US tour in 1972, performed around Europe and in Australia and toured the UK's folk clubs with a group featuring his children. Though his recording credits are with artists as varied as Kate Bush and Horslips, Tommy must be the only Irish traditional musician to have played on a British chart-topping single, "The Lion Sleeps Tonight" by Tight Fit, which occupied the #1 slot for seven weeks in the 1980s. In London his music was heard accompanying notable ballet and theatrical productions, while the family group would sometimes play with The Chieftains at their many concerts in the city Indeed, it is the McCarthys' feet which can be heard dancing a Clare set on the **Bonaparte's Retreat** album. Tommy moved back to Co. Clare in 1991, settling in Miltown Malbay, and continued to play, recording his first album, the wonderful **Sporting Nell** in 1997. Displaying his versatility, highlights include a perky "The Pigeon on the Gate" on concertina, an eloquent and mournful Connemara air, "Anach Chuain", on whistle, and a piped "Cherish the Ladies" that simply breathes life into the familiar jig.

All of the McCarthy children have moved back to Ireland (except fiddler **Tommy junior** who runs a bar in New York) and **Jacqueline** (b. 1957) has a growing reputation as one of the best concertina players around. Taught by Tommy senior from the age of nine, she went on to play in the family group and is still a member of the band performing music for the Rambert Dance Company ballet "Sergeant Early's Dream". Married to uilleann piper, **Tommy Keane**, Jacqueline is now based in Galway, where she teaches music and also plays in the group **Maigh Se-la**, as well as raising a family and touring regularly with her husband. Her own album, **The Hidden Note**, takes its title from fiddler Tommy Potts' oft-quoted definition of the invigorating factor in traditional music, which, in Jacqueline's words "drives Irish music along". The force and vibrancy of her music is certainly evident in the album, which draws upon familial strengths (sisters **Marion** on uilleann pipes and **Bernadette** on fiddle and piano, plus the presence of all three Tommys) as well as Alec Finn's bouzouki to tremendous effect, not least on the spouses' powerful arrangement of the jig "Cheer Up, Old Hag".

⊙ **Sporting Nell**   Maree Music, 1997

Tommy McCarthy was a much-loved and highly-regarded artist. Listen to this and discover the reason why.

⊙ **The Hidden Note**   Maree Music, 2000

The quality continues in the next generation as proved by this outstanding album from Jacqueline McCarthy.

The McDonaghs

The recordings of Michael Coleman, Paddy Killoran and James Morrison had such an powerful impact on Ireland's musical consciousness that it can often be forgotten that some of their contemporaries were actually uninfluenced and continued to play in the old style, not least in their native South Sligo. One such family was the **McDonaghs** of Ballinafad, three bachelor brothers – **Paddy** (1902–85) who played flute and whistle, fiddler **Michael Joe** (1904–88) and **Larry** (1911–84) primarily a flute player but also a fine fiddler. Though the brothers' repertoire included tunes from the American 78s, it largely consisted of music played in a style characteristically described as "hearty" in which tunes were usually played individually rather than grouped together. The McDonaghs' house (with its portrait of Carolan over the kitchen fireplace) was a musical magnet and, fortunately, those visiting sometimes brought tape recorders. Recently remastered, these tapes form one of the integral components of Ireland's musical heritage, the stunning CD, **The McDonaghs of Ballinafad and Friends play Traditional Music of Sligo**, dating from the 1960s. Unfortunately, Paddy's poor health meant that he was no longer playing, so the bulk of the album's thirty-seven tracks feature Larry and Michael Joe. Fourteen also include their life-long friend, fiddler **Tommy Flynn** (1910–94) from Corrigeenroe while others include three men from over

the border in Roscommon: the late flute player **Michael Daly** (one-time Mayor of Worthing in England), bodhrán player **Tom Harte** and fiddler **Paddy Ryan** (Music Officer of CCÉ since 1985 and the driving force behind the album's release). One can only regret that, in Paddy's own words, this "lovely, merry, hearty old style of music making…has gone from us forever." If you need convincing, just listen to the McDonaghs' rendition of "Saddle the Pony" with Tommy Flynn.

⊙ The McDonaghs of Ballinafad and Friends
play Traditional Music of Sligo   CCÉ, 2000

Not just a landmark recording, but a complete redrawing of Ireland's musical map.

The McNamaras

There can be few more prodigiously talented families than the McNamaras from Aughavas in the south of Co. Leitrim. Long known for their unstinting support of traditional music, they brought their region's distinctive style to an international audience with the release of **Leitrim's Hidden Treasure**, seventy minutes of pure joy plus illuminating and meticulously researched sleeve notes. The breadth of music and strength of playing is staggering and includes old-style reels and a substantial number of hornpipes. Head of the clan is **Michael McNamara** whose children are fellow flute player **Ciarán**, uilleann pipers **Brian** and **Ray** (the latter also adding tin whistle), concertina player **Deirdre** and **Enda** on fiddle. South Leitrim is especially strong in flute and fife playing, producing a bright, short-phrased style often termed "lifty". Fiddle playing and piping traditions were both strong too, though the latter had seriously declined until revived by the McNamaras (both Brian and Ray are consummate players) in the late 1970s. Concertinas are unusual in the area, so it's intriguing to hear Deirdre apply her skills to the local style.

Former All-Ireland champion Brian MacNamara has subsequently released his own exceptional album, **A Piper's Dream** (2000), one of the finest statements of the piper's art to have been recorded in the last few decades. Brian's control of

Brian McNamara — A PIPER'S DREAM

tone and sense of purpose is matched by his mastery of the instrument and his playing of slow airs, especially "Ní ar Chnocht ná ar Ísleacht", is exquisite. Dance tunes, particularly the single jig, "Stoney Batter", are rendered at a measured pace which starkly demonstrates both the force of the melodic line and a musician utterly at one with the tradition.

⊙ **Leitrim's Hidden Treasure**   Drumlin Records, 1998

Add this gem to your collection for endless delight.

⊙ **A Piper's Dream**   Drumlin Records, 2000

Utterly magnetic piping from a true modern master, Brian McNamara.

The McPeakes

A household name during the 1960s, the scarcity of available recordings makes contemporary judgement of the **McPeake Family's** impact almost impossible. Albums from that decade such as **Irish Folk!** (1964) and **Welcome Home** (1967) are now highly sought-after collectors' items, and the only currently available release is the cassette reissue of their 1962 debut album for Topic. The McPeakes were effectively first one, then two trios founded upon a unique combination of voice, pipes and harp. The clan elder was **Francis** (born in Belfast in 1885, but of Derry stock) who first learned the flute before being lucky enough to study under the blind Galway piper, John O'Reilly (or Riley). He acquired his own set of pipes around 1906 and his progress was such that he won the 1909 Belfast feis and represented Ireland at the 1911 Pan-Celtic Congress in Brussels (performing with the Welsh harper John Page). Francis also caught the attention of **Captain O'Neill** (see p.13) and his photograph appears in

Irish Minstrels and Musicians where the great collector also describes the young McPeake as the only Irish piper he had ever encountered who was able to sing to his own accompaniment!

Family fame arrived with the formation of a trio, led by Francis with his sons **Francis junior**, known as **Frank** (b. 1917), and **James** (b. 1936) on pipes and harp respectively. Peter Kennedy recorded the family for the BBC in 1952 (thought to be the first ever recording of the Irish harp). They appeared at the Moscow World Youth Festival in 1957, won major prizes at the Llangollen International Eisteddfod in 1958, 1960 and 1962 and were regular performers on radio and television (often with a second trio consisting of Frank's children **Francis** and **Kathleen** and their cousin **Tommy McCrudden**. The McPeake Family cassette captures the essence of their style and unique sound, though the song most often associated with them "Will Ye Go Lassie Go" unfortunately appears elsewhere. Often introduced by Francis's narrative explanation, there are ballads and songs in Irish and English, (often with, what was then, a radical edge) interspersed with dance tunes and airs.

Irish Traditional Songs and Music	Ossian reissue, 1962

A classic album by the pioneering McPeakes, includes their versions of "The Lament of Aughrim" and "The Verdant Braes of Skreen".

The Ó Domhnaills

Maighread Ni Dhomhnaill, Tríona Ni Dhomhnaill and Mícheál Ó Domhnaill are three of the foremost figures in recent Irish musical history. Although the three were brought up in Kells, Co. Meath, their father, **Aodh**, came from the Donegal Gaeltacht of Rann na Feirste where the family subsequently spent their summers. A fine singer himself. Aodh also collected songs for the Irish Folklore Commission, not least from his own sister **Neillí Ní Dhomhnaill** (1907–84), renowned as one of Donegal's greatest singers. Neillí possessed a vast repertoire of songs (both in Irish and English), many of which she passed on to her nephew and nieces who also learned much from her relaxed, yet extremely subtle singing style.

Dáithí Sproule (see p.121), a young singer and guitarist from Derry, was another regular summer visitor to Rann na Feirste where he struck up an enduring friendship with the Ó Domhnaills. This eventually resulted in the formation of **Skara Brae** (see p.231) and the release of a startlingly beautiful album, recorded while Maighread was still a schoolgirl. Mícheál and Dáithí's often open-tuned guitars or Tríona's clavinet wove a subtle backcloth over which all four's voices blended with a gossamer delicacy. The group never recorded again and, indeed had already moved on musically by the time of the album's release in 1971.

After Skara Brae Mícheál teamed up with singer Mick Hanly to record the latter's **Celtic Folkweave** while Tríona joined the short-lived **1691** with Tommy Peoples, Peter Browne and Liam Weldon. The siblings soon met up again as members of **Seachtar**, a band originally assembled in 1974 for a one-off gig which soon transformed into **The Bothy Band**. Unsurprisingly, songs from Aunt Neillí's featured in the Bothys' repertoire and the next five years saw the band attain unprecedented heights of popularity, receiving plaudits for their unstoppable stage shows and four still hugely influential albums.

Following The Bothy Band's break-up in 1979, Mícheál recorded **Promenade** with Kevin Burke before emigrating to the US, settling finally in Portland where, almost a decade later, he and Burke would reconvene for the aptly-titled **Portland**. Another long-standing collaboration has been with fiddler Paddy Glackin, extracts of which would appear on Windham Hill's **Celtic Christmas** series, produced by Mícheál himself, in the 1990s. Rumours of a long-overdue album by the pair were rife at the time of writing.

Tríona's first album appeared in 1975. Brim-full with delights, it contained beautiful Irish songs such as "Na Gamhna Geala" and "Stór a Stór Ghrá", learned from her aunt Neillí, while Tríona's harpsichord added a Baroque touch to remarkable renditions of "When I Was a Fair Maid" and "The Wee Lass on the Brae". After The Bothys'

demise Tríona also moved to the US, trying her hand in Nashville before relocating to North Carolina, where she linked up with Claudine Langille (vocals, mandolin), Mark Roberts (five-string banjo) and Zan McLeod (guitar) to form **Touchstone**, a band blending Irish and bluegrass influences which released two albums for Green Linnet. Almost

simultaneously she and Mícheál, hooked up with the Scottish Cunningham brothers, John (fiddle, vocals) and Phil (accordion, whistles, synthesizer, vocals) – both at the time in **Silly Wizard** – to form **Relativity**. The better of the quartet's two albums, **Gathering Pace** (1987), effectively integrates overlapping traditions and contains Tríona's memorable singing of "Má Théid Tú ún Aonaigh". Back in the US, Mícheál had already commenced work on his next project, the decidedly ambient **Nightnoise** with violinist and keyboards player,

Billy Oskay. Tríona and flute-player Brian Dunning were both on board by the time of the second album, **Something of Time** (1987) and fiddler Johnny Cunningham later stepped in for Oskay. All told, the band released seven albums (and a retrospective) culminating in 1997's **The White Horse Sessions**, each comprising their own mood-enhancing, modern compositions and improvisational skills.

Meanwhile, through all this coming and going, Maighread has continued to live in Ireland. She released her own self-titled solo album in 1976, as well as making **Sailing into Walpole's Marsh** (with fiddler Maeve Donnelly, singer Séan Corcoran and harmonica player Eddie Clarke) following a successful CCÉ North American tour. Though she occasionally sang in Dublin's clubs, and notably supported The Chieftains in a major London concert in 1980, family life took precedence and it was not until the 1990s that she effectively made her comeback. This was marked by the release of the memorable **Gan Dhá Phingin Spré/No Dowry**, the start of her collaboration with Dónal Lunny, a distant cousin whose mother also hailed from Rann na Feirste. The lay-off seemed to have strengthened Maighread's voice and her singing is utterly mesmerizing and reaches untold heights on "An Cailín Gaelach" (a song collected from Tory Island by her father) and the unaccompanied "The Green Wood Laddie". Both Mícheál and Tríona feature on the album. Maighread's musical liaison with Lunny was to lead to her appearance with **Coolfin** and involvement in one of the most vital releases of the last decade. Skara Brae had reconvened in 1997 for a special 25th anniversary concert and both Mícheál and Tríona were now back living in Ireland. While the former worked on a new project with ex-Bothy colleague Paddy Glackin, the two sisters combined with Dónal to produce the star-studded **Idir an Dá Solais/Between the Two Lights** (or **Twilight** in Donegal Irish). Adorned by dazzling vocal solos and duets, unison

and harmony-singing, songs come from sources as varied as Frank
Harte, Róise na nAmhráin and Éilís Ní Shúilleabháin from Cúil Aodha.
Dónal Lunny's production is immaculate and his playing (and contributions from Mícheál, Laoise Kelly, John McSherry and others) is as
fresh and as tasteful as ever.

⊙ **Tríona**   Gael-Linn, 1975

Tríona Ní Dhomhnaill's remarkable debut announces itself with a
flourish and still sounds stupendous twenty-five years later.

⊙ **Gan Dhá Phingin Spré**   Gael-Linn, 1991

Powerful singing marked the charismatic Maighread's return to
the musical fold.

⊙ **The White Horse Sessions**   Windham Hill, 1997

The last and the best of the Nightnoise albums, all the fresher for
being recorded live.

⊙ **Idir an Dá Solais**   Hummingbird, 1999

Maighread and Tríona Ní Dhomhnaill with Dónal Lunny prove that,
thirty years after Skara Brae, none of the magic has disappeared.

The Russells

The village of Doolin became a mecca for Irish music connoisseurs in the 1970s and, as P.J. Curtis writes, "No visit to Doolin
was complete...without hearing one of the legendary **Russell** brothers, **Micho**, **Gus** or **Pakie**", usually found playing or talking about
music in O'Connor's pub. The brothers' parents were native Irish
speakers and they were brought up in the townland of Doonagore at
a time when house dances were thriving and the Doolin area was

abundant in storytellers. Most famous of the trio was Micho (1915–94), who was introduced to music by his mother **Annie** (a concertina player) and began playing a Clarke's tin whistle at eleven. A neighbour, Patrick Flanagan, (another concertina player) helped to widen the boy's repertory of tunes, and at fourteen – the year Micho left school to begin farm work – an uncle brought him a wooden flute from the US. Meanwhile younger brothers Pakie and Gussie also began learning the whistle (Pakie would also in time become a fine concertina player) and the trio would eventually play together at dances. Micho was also building up an extensive collection of songs in English and Irish, learned in part from his father, **Austin**, a seannós singer. When the house-dance scene waned, the brothers were

content to make music at home or for their neighbours, until – some years on – the local pubs opened their doors to musicians.

While his brothers were happy to stay at home, Micho's life changed when he went to Dublin in 1969, at Tony MacMahon's invitation, to play at Slattery's of Capel Street. The fresh, unadorned simplicity of his music immediately attracted interest, leading to return appearances and, consequently, regular trips to Dublin on one of which he encountered Breandán Breathnach. Enthralled by Micho's playing and extensive repertoire, Breathnach transcribed hundreds of the

Clare man's tunes, some of which are included in Volume II of his collection *Ceol Rince na hÉireann*. International engagements soon also followed: Micho played with The Johnstons in London in 1969 and made the first of many trips to continental Europe in 1972. In 1973 he won the All-Ireland whistle title and, three years later, made the first of five trips to play in the US.

The best of the early recordings, **The Russell Family of Doolin, County Clare**, reunites the brothers in O'Connor's for a grand mix of pure traditional music: embellishments are minimal, the settings are perfection and the whole session makes a fitting memorial to Pakie who died in 1977. Micho went on to make a number of solo recordings, often characterized by his foot-tapping on both down- and up-beat, the best of which is unquestionably **Ireland's Whistling Ambassador**. A selection of live concert and private recordings from his US visits in the 1990s, the album was produced by Bill Ochs who also issued an excellent live video cassette of the same name. The recording captures all the exuberance of Micho's whistling (he was not playing flute much at the time) with an accuracy that whisks you straight to North Clare. Unfortunately, Micho died soon afterwards, killed in a car crash in February, 1994, but Gussie continues to thrive and play in Doolin. A lifelong bachelor, Micho retained humility even in the limelight, commenting in 1992 "I'm still an old farmer someway or another. The more I'm getting publicity, 'tis back the other ways I'm going."

⊙ **The Russell Family of Doolin, County Clare**　　Green Linnet, 1975

The brothers' unambiguously joyful music is here in all its splendours.

⊙ **Ireland's Whistling Ambassador**　　The Pennywhistler's Press, 1995

Easily the best of Micho's various recordings and a solid reminder of the man's humour and humility.

The Sands Family

This multitalented clan from Co. Down have long been stalwarts of the Northern scene, first emerging as **The Sands Family** in the 1970s, whose all-singing line-up proved popular in Northern Europe and consisted of **Ann** (bodhrán), **Ben** (fiddle, sitar), **Colum** (guitar, concertina, fiddle), **Eugene** – known as Dino – (guitar, bouzouki, mandolin, whistle) and **Tommy** (guitar, five-string banjo). Sadly, Dino died in a road accident in Germany in 1975, but the band continued into the 1990s and still occasionally re-forms. Their early albums for EMI are now collectors' items, but fortunately their largely folk-based harmonies can be heard on the comprehensive **The Sands Family Collection**, spanning 1974 to 1993.

Tommy, who has the most incisive voice, is best known for his much-covered elegy to The Troubles, "There Were Roses", which appears on 1989's **Singing of the Times**. His last album for EMI, **The Heart's a Wonder** (1995), included fine duets with Pete Seeger and Dolores Keane with whom Tommy went on to record "Where Have All the Flowers Gone" for a Seeger tribute album of the same name in 1998. Tommy's most recent release is **Sarajevo – Belfast** (1999), a forceful collaboration with the Bosnian cellist **Vedran Smailovic,** famed for publicly playing his cello at 4pm each day in commemoration of 22 people killed by a shell when waiting in a bread line in Sarajevo. Colum also has been recording since the early 1980s and runs Spring Records from its studio base in Rostrevor. His light tenor voice is ideal for the narrative and often introspective songs that he writes. **The March Ditch** features his multi-instrumental talents and the excellent songs "The Marching Season" and "Lookin' the Loan of a Spade". 1996's **All My Winding Journeys** offers higher production values, an all-star cast (including piper Liam

O'Flynn) and a classic song in "The Night is Young". Finally, the mellowest voice of the three, Ben has issued a pair of albums, of which 1997's **Roots and Branches** best demonstrates his prowess.

⊙ **The Sands Family Collection**   Spring Records, 1994

Highlights from two decades packed into one superb album.

⊙ **The March Ditch**   Spring Records, 1990

Colum Sands' best album to date draws attention to his eloquent writing skills.

⊙ **Sarajevo – Belfast**   Appleseed Recordings, 1999

Vedran Smailovic and Tommy Sands in a compelling musical collaboration which makes a powerful cry for peace.

The Vallelys and The Armagh Pipers' Club

Many a CD cover bears the distinctive artwork of the prestigious painter **Brian Vallely** (b. 1943) but he is equally renowned for his establishment of **The Armagh Pipers' Club** which he still runs with his wife, the fiddler **Eithne Carey**. Brian himself is a whistle and flute player and was introduced to the uilleann pipes by Pat McNulty. He formed the club in the 1960s when an antagonistic reaction to a concert he had organized (featuring Séamus Ennis) caused him to resign as secretary of the local CCÉ branch in the belief that a new organization was required to maintain the piping tradition. Since its foundation the APC has been devoted to this aim and mounts an annual festival in honour of the pipe maker William Kennedy (see p.577). It has also played a major role in the continuation of traditional music in Armagh and the surrounding area through its Saturday morning music classes in a range of instruments. Thousands of pupils have enhanced their skills through attendance while an even greater number have benefited from the tutorial books which the Club began publishing in 1972. Flook's flute player, Brian Finnegan, was a successful student while the Vallelys' own children have become familiar faces on the traditional circuit – concertina player **Niall,** through his work with **Nomos** and his own superb solo album, fiddler **Caoimhín** who plays with **North Cregg** and piper **Cillian** who has recently worked with **Lúnasa**. Several of the tunes from the APC's popular graded whistle tutorial series appear on **Song of the Chanter**, commissioned as a consequence of the demand for an accompanying album. This features Brian and Eithne, alongside Niall on bodhrán, and long-time associates Paul Davis (flute, concertina, harmonica) and harper Patricia Daly who now runs a sister organization, the Armagh Harpers Association.

Brian's cousin **Fintan Vallely** (b. 1949) is also a highly regarded flute player and piper who has released two flute albums under his own name, plus another with singer **Tim Lyons** as the duo **Schitheridee**. He has also written *Timber*, the first traditional flute tutor, but is nowadays best known as a journalist (initially with *The Irish Times* and currently *The Sunday Tribune*) and writer on traditional music. With Charlie Piggott he co-wrote *Blooming Meadows* (see p.591) and single-handedly edited the mammoth *Companion to Irish Music* (see p.000) while his other credits include working as programme consultant for RTÉ's traditional music output.

⊙ **Song of the Chanter**　　　　　　　　　　Outlet, 1996

Intended as an aid to learning, this merits a hearing in its own right, thanks to the remarkable level of musicianship throughout.

Fiddlers

T he violin – in traditional music always referred to as the fiddle – arrived in Ireland in the late seventeenth century. Unlike most classical violin music, virtually all Irish dance tunes only require the fiddler to play in first (basic) position. Since this means that the non-bowing hand does not move up and down the finger board, there is no necessity to hold the fiddle against the neck (though nowadays most fiddlers do) and it is sometimes played pressed against the chest or the shoulder. There are also variations in the way the bow is held, some players, such as Altan's **Mairéad Ní Mhaonaigh**, gripping it a third of the way along. Most players prefer steel to gut strings and and some employ alternative tunings, such as AEAE (rather than the customary GDAE).

Fiddlers use a wide variety of techniques to embellish their playing, most commonly triplets and rolls (see p.28) and double-stopping (where two strings are fingered and bowed together). Some create a drone effect, redolent of the uilleann pipes, by having an open string constantly bowed while the melody is played on the adjacent (higher) string. The sound of the pipes is also suggested by the way two fiddlers playing together will often play the tune an octave apart. Vibrato hardly features in Irish fiddle playing although it seems to be on the increase in the playing of slow airs.

Surprisingly, considering the fiddle's supremacy as the most popular traditional instrument, there have been very few collections released or recorded with the noteworthy exceptions of specific compilations covering Donegal (see p.312) and Sliabh Luachra (see p.349). The 78s era is represented by Rounder's mighty **Milestone at**

Fiddle styles

In the days when people travelled no further than to the nearest market, there was widespread variety in local styles of playing, just as the Irish language had many different dialects and accents. Though still noticeably distinctive, regional differences in fiddle playing have been gradually eroded over the last century, although in recent years there has been a determined effort to preserve those which still exist. While the recordings of the Sligo fiddlers **Michael Coleman** and **James Morrison** established a dominant style and set standards across the whole of Ireland, the influence of migrants returning from England, Scotland and the US with new tunes and new ways of playing them was equally important. Radio, TV and the ready availability of a wealth of recordings also played an enormous role in dissemination of different ways of playing.

There are individual entries on the fiddle music of Donegal (see p.308) and the region around Sliabh Luachra (see p.346) on the borders of counties Cork, Kerry and Limerick. However, the best-known regional style is that of **South Sligo**. As the late Cree fiddler, **Patrick Kelly** once remarked, "the worst thing that ever happened to the West Clare style of fiddling was the appearance of Michael Coleman's records". Many musicians adopted Coleman's typically fast-paced, light and bouncy style, sometimes described as "lifty", which characterized his own

the Garden which collates famous players, such as **James Morrison**, **Paddy Killoran**, **Michael Coleman** and **Denis Murphy**, rare recordings by **Lad O'Beirne** and **Danny O'Donnell**, plus a **Paddy Canny** track from 1959. The quintessential collection is **From**

original locale. Coleman's contemporary, James Morrison, was also hugely influential while other notable South Sligo fiddlers include **Paddy Killoran** and **Fred Finn** (who played regularly as a duo with **Peter Horan**).

While not as driven as neighbouring Donegal, the music of counties **Leitrim and Fermanagh** is characterized by a jaunty, lyrical feel exemplified by fiddlers such as **Ben**, **Charlie** and **Maurice Lennon**, **Séamus Quinn** and **Tom Mulligan**. Uilleann piper, Dinny Delaney, was a major influence on **East Galway** fiddlers both through the quality of his piping and his collaboration with other musicians. As his pipes were pitched in B flat, this entailed many fiddlers, such as **Paddy Fahy**, relearning tunes in unusual keys and developing a "wistful", slower paced sound in their arrangements. The fiddle music of **East Clare**, best illustrated by **Paddy Canny**, **P.J. Hayes** and his son **Martin**, still carries some of the characteristic lonesome sound of neighbouring Galway, but it adopts a more lyrical approach as it gets further towards the western seaboard, most notably in the playing of the late **Junior Crehan** and **Bobby Casey**, and **Joe Ryan**.

Individual style is very much a matter of personal taste and some of the finest contemporary fiddlers, such as **Tommy Peoples** or **Frankie Gavin**, are instantly recognizable in their own right rather than being strictly representative of their respective counties, Donegal and Galway.

a Distant Shore, originally released as four separate albums, which brings together recordings from the Cork University Traditional Music Festivals, 1991–94. This comprises **Fiddlesticks**, devoted to the Donegal fiddle and featuring both **Tommy Peoples** and a rare duet between **Mairéad Ní Mhaonaigh** and her father **Proinsías**; **Traditional Music from Cape Breton Island**, representing both Irish and Scots traditions; **Dear Old Erin's Isle**, featuring US musicians, including several fiddlers, such as **Eileen Ivers**, **Liz Carroll** and **Séamus Connolly**; and the Anglo-Irish **Across the Waters**, which covers a range of instruments, but includes fiddlers **Brian Rooney**, **Brendan McGlinchey** and **Brendan Mulkere**. Lastly, **My Love is in America**, recorded at the 1990 Boston College Irish Fiddle Festival, has a host of fine tunes from leading lights, such as **Martin Hayes** and **Kevin Burke**, to less well-known émigrés like the **Cronin** brothers and the Chicago-born fiddler **Johnny McGreevy**.

⊙ **Milestone at the Garden**   Rounder, 1923–59

Twenty-five cuts from the era of 78s demonstrate the range and strengths of the fiddle tradition.

⊙ **From a Distant Shore**   Nimbus Records, 1991–94

An utterly essential, four-CD collection, highlights of which have been captured on the label's budget-priced **A Taste of Ireland**.

⊙ **My Love is in America**   Green Linnet, 1990

A collection which covers a variety of styles, including a rare appearance by the late Sligo fiddler, Martin Whynne.

Randal Bays

Despite having no Irish roots **Randal Bays**, from Seattle, is the genuine article, a real traditional fiddler whose skills are amply demonstrated on his last album, **Out of the Woods**. Already an accomplished guitarist, Bays was inspired to learn the fiddle by seeing Kevin Burke and Mícheál Ó Domhnaill play in Portland. Kevin sub-

sequently became a near neighbour, offering advice and encouragement and pointing Randal towards other great players, such as Paddy
Canny and P.J. Hayes. When **Martin Hayes** later arrived in Seattle,
the pair clicked immediately for, as Randal says, "I already had his
family repertoire in my brain." Bays provided tasteful guitar accompaniment on Martin's first two albums and an East Clare influence pervades **Out of the Woods**. Randal's choice of material draws both on
Clare and further afield and he employs multitracking in order to
accompany himself on several cuts, while his solo guitar work on
"Austin Tierney's Reel" is a formidable demonstration of its capablities
as a traditional instrument. An earlier album, **Pigtown Fling** (1996)
with harmonica-player **Joel Bernstein**, harkens back to another great
Clare fiddler, Joe Ryan and his partnership with Eddie Clarke.

⊙ **Out of the Woods**	Foxglove Records, 1997

Randal has drunk at the pool and savoured the waters on this
excellent album of Clare-inspired fiddling.

Neillidh Boyle

It's an oddity indicative of the Irish experience that one of the greatest Donegal fiddlers, **Neillidh Boyle** (1889–1961), sometimes
known as Neil O'Boyle, was born in Easton, Pennsylvania and died in
Glasgow, Scotland. His parents Pádraig (from Cruit Island) and Nancy
(from Keadue) arrived in the US in the 1880s and Neillidh spent his
first seven years there before the family returned to live in
Cronshallog, near Dungloe. Neillidh's background was intensely musical – his maternal grandfather, Pádraig Mac Suibhne, was a singer
and storyteller reputed to have the largest song collection in The
Rosses, while his mother was a renowned singer, regularly visited by

students and folklorists. Neillidh and his two brothers, Con and Charlie, all learned the fiddle early, and Neillidh would try to re-create the haunting quality of his mother's lilting through his transposition of tunes into minor keys. Another major influence was the Scottish classically-trained violinist William McKenzie Murdoch whom Neillidh saw during a visit to Glasgow when he was fifteen. As a consequence, he started playing in positions other than the basic first position (uncommon in traditional music) in the hope of becoming a concert performer. Though he first worked at farming, in 1925 he was recruited by a travelling cinema to accompany silent films for which his ability to play mood music and imitate animal sounds endeared him to audiences (his lion imitations were especially popular!).

In the 1930s Neillidh joined a jazz group, The Dungloe Quartet, though he had already begun to play his own traditional compositions in regular broadcasts on the national 2RN radio station and, later, for the BBC. In 1937 he married a local girl, Annie Sweeney and began making his first recordings for Regal Zonophone. One of these, featuring "The Pigeon on the Gate", learned from his mother's lilting, was to become one of the most influential recordings in Irish music. Neillidh never again recorded commercially, thanks to a dispute with the record company over distribution and royalties, but he was taped by Séamus Ennis for the Irish Folklore Commission in the 1940s and Peter Kennedy for the BBC in 1953, the latter later released as **The Moving Clouds**. Neillidh refused to record unless he could voice his opinions on the current state of music in Ireland in the form of a diatribe about jazz and a warning about the condition of traditional music. He then demonstrates his talents on a selection of tunes including two long associated with him, "The Moving Cloud" and "The Harvest Home". Though still played with typical verve and skill, Neillidh's playing had declined in comparison to the original 78 version of "A Harvest Home", an astoundingly rapid and ornamental rendition which appears on **From Galway to Dublin** (see p.41). Neillidh continued to broadcast in the 1950s, but eventually moved to Glasgow where he played solo and in small orchestras until his death.

▣▣ **The Moving Clouds**   Folktrax, 1953

Until someone reissues all his 78s together, this recording should be relished for its insights into a great player.

Paul Bradley

A mong the rising crop of talented young musicians to emerge recently from the North is fiddler **Paul Bradley** from Bessbrook, Co. Armagh. His brother Joe is also a skilled musician who, whenever possible, recorded the older players from South Armagh. These tapes had a marked influence on Paul's musical development, but he also learned from watching **Josephine Keegan** from Cullyhanna (a fiddler with a crisp, fluent style and a renowned piano accompanist) and from listening to records of fiddlers, especially Tommy Peoples. Living in Belfast brought contact with a wider circle of musicians and styles and, for a while, Paul played in the band **Trasna**. Now working as a fiddle-maker, Paul's debut album **Tuaim Ná Farraige/The Atlantic Roar** demonstrates just how much he's learned on the way. There's a marked Donegal edge to his fiddling, especially on "The Piping Jig", learned from Danny O'Donnell's playing, and a closing set of a highland and reels where the Peoples influence is readily apparent. But Paul is his own master too and proves it in a sparkling duet with piper John McSherry on the old charmer "Toss the Feathers". Paul is now part of Na Dórsa whose debut album, **The Wild Music of the Gael**, was released in November, 2000.

⊙ **Tuaim Ná Farraige**   Outlet, 1997

Armagh meets Donegal in Paul Bradley's promising debut album.

Máire Breatnach

A fiddler, viola player, keyboard player and occasional singer, **Máire Breatnach** was classically trained at Dublin School of Music, and later at University College, she also attended the all-Irish Scoil Mhuire, along with many other budding traditional players. After postgraduate study, she lectured in music for most of a decade, first testing the waters of a performing career with the group **Meristem** in the late 1980s, alongside flute player Cormac Breatnach and bouzouki player Niall Ó Callanáin. Since becoming a full-time musician in 1990, she has worked extensively as a session player (with Christy Moore, Sineád O'Connor and Sharon Shannon among others), a producer (albums by Sonny Condell, the Black Family and Padraigín Ní Uallacháin) and on film and TV soundtracks, including *In the Name of the Father* and *Rob Roy*. She was also the lead fiddler on the original **Riverdance** album of 1995.

In addition to her other projects, Máire has released three entirely self-penned solo albums – one of them twice. **Angels' Candles/Coinnle na nAingeal** first came out in 1993, winning a warm critical reception for its richly melodic compositions – many of them inspired by mythological stories and children's lore – and for her playing which combines classically-tinged lyricism with traditional sinew and fire. She took the unusual step of re-recording and re-releasing the album in 1999, and pulled off what might have been taken for a cynical sales ploy with more rave reviews, the intervening years reflected in the extra depth and contemplative subtlety of her delivery. Between times, she followed up her debut with **Voyage of Bran/Branohm** (1994), a loosely themed and abundantly diverse evocation of a legendary Celtic odyssey, and **Celtic Lovers** (1996), in honour of famed romances from Ireland's mythic past. Despite the frequent New Age gushiness of Breatnach's observations on the music, her actual playing is spare and unfussy with restrained arrangements often featuring long-time collaborators like accordionist Máirtín O'Connor, percussionist Tommy Hayes and her two Meristem colleagues.

⊙ Angels' Candles/Coinnle na nAingeal   Cala Music, 1999

An album rich in moods and colours, from the high jinks of "Beta/Carnival" to the beseeching title track.

Kevin Burke

Born in London, **Kevin Burke** began learning classical violin at age eight, but it was the recordings of Coleman, Morrison and Killoran that his Sligo-born parents played at home which would ultimately exert the greater influence. Once in his teens, he soon found his way into the midst of London's vibrant 1960s Irish music scene, encountering other regional fiddle styles, notably through the playing of Co. Clare's Bobby Casey, and Armagh's Brendan McGlinchey. By 1972, he was crossing paths with US folk singer Arlo Guthrie, who invited him to the US to perform on his **Last of the Brooklyn Cowboys** album, a trip which also led to Burke's first solo album, **Sweeney's Dream** (1973).

Burke then headed for Ireland to work with Christy Moore, before joining **The Bothy Band** in 1976, remaining a linchpin of that seminal line-up until its demise in 1979. His resulting friendship with

Míchéal Ó Domhnaill led to two warmly acclaimed duo albums, **Promenade** (1979) and **Portland** (1982), the latter named for Burke's by-then adopted US home in Oregon. His solo career continued with **If the Cap Fits**, on which, in his own words, he "tried to retain, as much as possible, the old traditional moods of Irish music, as it used to be played long ago in rural areas by small groups of musicians…as an expression and a relaxation". The stellar list of accompanists on this album – Gerry O'Beirne, Paul Brady, Peter Browne, Jackie Daly, Mícheál Ó Domhnaill and Dónal Lunny – gives an indication of Burke's standing within traditional music even so early in his career. **Up Close** (1984) served up another slice of Burke's elegant yet vigorous, earthy yet lyrical playing with varied accompaniment from accordionist Joe Burke, Matt Molloy on flute, the harmonica-playing Murphy family as well as the Americans Mark Graham (harmonica) and Paul Kotapish (cittern, mandolin).

The last two named were subsequently involved in **Open House**, Burke's deliberately quirky sideline from **Patrick Street**, the traditional "supergroup" he formed in 1986 with **Andy Irvine**, **Jackie Daly** and **Arty McGlynn**. Drawing on a mix of Irish, American, East European and jazz influences, together with Kotapish's original comic songs and the stunning percussive dancing of Sandy Silva, Open House released three critically-praised albums during the 1990s, but ultimately fell between too many stools, in audience terms, to remain viable. Another occasional side project is the **Celtic Fiddle Festival** – also with two albums to their credit – featuring Burke alongside Scottish fiddler Johnny Cunningham and Brittany's Christian LeMaître. His latest release **In Concert** (1999) sees him abandoning all safety-nets, playing live and largely unaccompanied, bar a few guest appearances by fiddler Martin Hayes and guitarist Aidan Brennan, in a recording that beautifully captures the pure-drop essence of his playing.

⊙ **In Concert**   Green Linnet, 1999

Ranging through Burke's entire back-catalogue, as well as introducing several new sets, this is the genuine less-is-more article.

James Byrne

Long-known both for the warmth of his personality and his awesome fiddle-playing, **James Byrne** from Mín 'a Croise (Meenacross) near Glencolmcille is a member of one of Co. Donegal's most renowned musical dynasties. The Byrnes were celebrated as exceptional players at a time when the Glen's house dances flourished and James's own father, John, was regarded as one of the best. Surrounded by fiddle playing and musical lore, James progressed rapidly, inheriting the local crisp, attacking style which has remained significantly uninfluenced by external factors thanks to the area's relative isolation (electricity didn't reach Glencolmcille until the 1950s). Though James rarely left the area, his reputation grew gradually, thanks to appearances at events in the county and occasional radio broadcasts. Increasing interest in Donegal fiddle music saw his recording debut on the classic **The Brass Fiddle** (see p.311) where his astonishing rendition of the reel "Biddy from Muckross" drew comparisons with John Doherty (James also cites Danny Meehan and Tommy Peoples as important influences).

James's only solo album to date is **The Road to Glenlough**, one of the mightiest recordings of the fiddler's art. Whether playing solo or doubling up with either fellow fiddler (and producer) **Dermot McLaughlin** or a young **Dermot Byrne** on accordion (both playing in the lower octave), Byrne's fiddling is inspirational – an unstoppable amalgam of dazzling vitality and sheer finesse – throughout and leaves the listener gasping for more. Sadly, there were no further recordings until his appearance on **The Fiddle Music of Donegal – Volume 2** (see p.311) where he mesmerically repeats and varies the melody several times in true house-dance fashion on a jig, "John Byrne's", learned from his father. Now in his mid-fifties, James continues to be active in Donegal music as a player, teacher and inspiration to others.

⊙ The Road to Glenlough   Claddagh, 1990

Donegal music at its very best, played by one of the all-time fiddle greats.

Paddy Canny

F ew musicians wait until their seventies to release their debut solo album and fewer still achieve the accolade of seeing that album voted best traditional album of the year by *The Irish Times*. The year was 1997 and the album was **Paddy Canny's Traditional Music from the Legendary East Clare Fiddler**. The year before Paddy had guested on Gearóid Ó hAllmhuráin's **Traditional Music from Clare and Beyond**, his first appearance on disc since 1959's **All Ireland Champions**. Yet despite the sparsity of his recordings, his influence has been extraordinary. Born in 1919 in Glendree, near Tulla, Paddy learned the fiddle from his father Pat, who had himself been taught by a blind fiddler, Paddy McNamara, who he put up every winter. As well as his own children, Pat taught many local youngsters, to the extent that the distinctive East Clare style can justifiably be said to have emanated from Glendree. Paddy Canny's lessons began at ten and he took to the instrument rapidly. Further lessons came from fiddler Martin Nugent, with Paddy comparing notes with his great friend and contemporary, Martin Rochford. By the 1930s he was a popular figure at house dances and co-founded the **Tulla Céilí Band** in 1946 remaining a member until 1967.

An All Ireland Champion in 1953, Paddy appeared solo at New York's Carnegie Hall three years later. His live fifteen-minute radio broadcasts gained him increasing fame and his version of "Trim the Velvet" became the theme tune for Ciarán Mac Mathúna's popular radio show. It wasn't over yet for the shy farmer (who still sometimes hid behind others while soloing for the Tulla). 78s were recorded for Gael-Linn, while the 1959 **Champions** album – made with his future brother-in-law **P.J. Hayes**, **Peadar O'Loughlin** and pianist **Bridie Lafferty** – cemented his reputation with appearances on TV helping viewers put a face to the music. After leaving the Tulla, however, and disliking playing in pubs, Paddy's music was largely reserved for family and friends until his 1997 album. His fiddling has often been described as having a characteristic "lonesome" touch, though he rarely played slow airs, and the CD consists entirely of jigs, reels and hornpipes played with an idiosyncratic, slightly slurred roughness in which notes slip and slide together to reach the goal of Paddy's acute vision. A master at work!

⊙ Traditional Music from the Legendary
East Clare Fiddler   Cló Iar-Chonnachta, 1997

Motivational music at its most inspired by a man who can justifiably be called a living legend.

Cape Breton Fiddlers

Cape Breton Island sits in the Atlantic Ocean to the south of Newfoundland in the Canadian province of Nova Scotia. Originally inhabited by Native Americans and later by French Acadians, the island saw an influx of Irish and Scottish settlers from the eighteenth century onwards and, through a process of physical and cultural isolation, evolved its own rich musical traditions. Descendants of Highland Scots still form the largest section of the population, but some thirty percent owe their origins to Ireland. While the music of the former has diverged from traditional music in Scotland, the Cape Breton Irish still reveal close connections with their roots, reinforced in the twentieth century by increased ties with Irish-Americans and Ireland itself. However, there has also been substantial cross-fertilization and nowadays musicians from each community will know and play a significant number of tunes from the other, while the influence of the Highland bagpipes is still an audible element of the music.

Two instruments, the fiddle and the piano, dominate the island's music. Pianists across Cape Breton play with a bouncy, florid exuberance which can surprise ears attuned to the restrained chordal accompaniment of their Irish equivalents. Thanks largely to the influence of the prolific **Winston "Scotty" Fitzgerald** (1914–87), fiddlers have generally adopted a style described as "clean", closely modulated to the piano's bright sound and focused on a "correct" rendition of the tune, without the scope for variation which exists within Ireland itself. Though individual styles vary, there is an overall confident swing to the fiddle's sound and, again unlike Ireland, mixed medleys of tunes and consequent acceleration are common. For instance, a fiddler may begin with a march, progress to a set of strathspeys and then change to a set of reels.

Another key figure was **Joe Confiant** (1899–1986) who maintained repertoires and his own settings of both Scottish and Irish tunes which he passed on to his nephew **Johnny Wilmot** (1916–93) whose own recordings of Co. Sligo-influenced music in the 1950s and 1960s are compiled on **Another Side of Cape Breton**. A fiddler with an intense, driving style, Wilmot would often play with the harmonica virtuoso, **Tommy Basker** (see p.529). Confiant's grandnephew is **Bobby Stubbert** (b. 1923), responsible for many of the Irish tunes in the current Cape Breton repertoire and father of **Brenda Stubbert**, a fine fiddler and composer whose album **House Sessions** (1992) is a remarkable, crisply-played journey around the local musical landscape.

Irish tunes have become far more apparent in the repertoires of musicians of Scottish origin in recent times and feature in the playing of internationally-known Cape Breton fiddlers such as **Natalie MacMaster** and **Ashley MacIsaac**. Sadly, one of the great modern fiddlers from the island, **John Morris Rankin** was killed in a car accident in 2000. Cape Breton has also attracted terrific fiddlers from the American continent, including **Jerry Holland** from Boston and **Paul**

Cranford from Toronto, both prolific composers whose store of tunes includes music drawn from across the communities. The annual Cape Breton Celtic Colours Festival, inaugurated in 1997, has become a major magnet for traditional musicians from Ireland, Scotland and around the world.

⊙ **Traditional Music from Cape Breton Island**   Nimbus Records, 1993

Part of **From a Distant Shore** (see p.276), this is the obvious starting point for an exploration of Cape Breton fiddling.

⊙ **Another Side of Cape Breton**   Breton Books & Music, 1950s/60s

Pulsating music from Johnny Wilmot, including a dazzling duet with Tommy Basker.

⊙ **House Sessions**   Cranford Publications, 1992

This CD reveals Brenda Stubbert in sparkling form and boasts some astonishing medleys of hornpipes and reels.

Liz Carroll

The doyenne of Irish-American fiddlers, **Liz Carroll** (b. 1956) was raised by her Irish parents on Chicago's Southside. She began learning music on her father's accordion, before switching to the fiddle at nine, taking classical-music lessons and picking up her traditional repertoire from tagging along with her father to sessions. Liz also began to write her own music, commencing at nine with a reel, and is now one of the most prolific traditional composers, writing more than 170 tunes. Carroll's reputation as a prodigious fiddling talent began with her All-Ireland Senior title in 1975. Her first album, **Kiss Me Kate**, recorded with button accordionist **Tommy Maguire**, appeared two years later, closely pursued by her first solo album proper, **A Friend Indeed** (1979), which included five of her own tunes, and still sounds abundant with energy. The opening notes of her own "The Monemohill Reel" are some of the most memorable in traditional musical history and announced the presence of an accomplished musician with a vision to match.

For much of the following decade she was content merely to play live and it was 1988 before she returned to the recording studio with guitarist **Dáithí Sproule** for her stupendous self-titled album. This is Liz at her majestic best, beginning with a magical gypsy flourish on the French-Canadian "Reel Beatrice" right through to the closing effervescent reel, "The Road to Recovery", and illustrates the robust, driving style she picked up from Joe Cooley and the Chicago fiddler, Johnny McGreevy. Liz and Dáithí subsequently formed **Trian** with box player **Billy McComiskey**, enjoying some success in the 1990s, a decade which also saw her appear on two live albums, including **My Love is in America** (see p.276), and Sproule's **Heart of Glass**. Finally, in 2000 came her long-awaited **Lost in the Loop** album, produced by

LIZ CARROLL

Seamus Egan and featuring himself and other Solas members alongside Zan McLeod and a returning Dáithí Sproule. Whether Carroll's many fans found it worth the wait is disputable as it's a mixed bag of an album with unfortunate soporific tendencies in places (especially the air "Lament of the First Generation"). There's undoubted fire and passion in her playing, but too often Liz seems to be fighting her accompanists for dominance in the mix and at others it's as if Solas have recruited a new fiddler. Still, listen to the hornpipe and reel "The Drunken Sailor/The Bag of Spuds" and marvel at a magician at work.

⊙ **Liz Carroll with Dáithí Sproule**　　　　　Green Linnet, 1988

Devastating, dashing, delightful and Dáithí too!

John Carty

Raised in London, fiddler, flute player and banjo virtuoso **John Carty** was fortunate to come under the wing of renowned teacher Brendan Mulkere from Co. Clare. Though he could already read music, it was the youngster's almost supernatural ear for a tune which enhanced his rapid development. He became a mainstay of the London Irish music scene in the 1980s and acquired a deserved name as a skilled teacher. Returning to Ireland in the early 1990s, he settled with his family in his father's home town of Boyle, Co. Roscommon and soon released his first album, **The Cat That Ate the Candle**, with **Brian McGrath**. This was John's banjo album as on virtually all the tracks he expertly plucks away to McGrath's relaxed piano accompaniment. However, it was his fiddle playing on "Sligo Maid" which caught not only the listener's ear but the attention of Shanachie who signed him for **Last Night's Fun** (1996). A gentle warm breeze of an album, thanks to Carty's fluent bowing and sensitive ornamentation, many of its tunes are drawn from the repertoires of the great Sligo fiddlers. Accompaniment comes mainly from Brian McGrath again and Garry Ó Briain's mandocello, while some of Carty's arrangements, such as the reel "The Glen of Aherlow", create subtle tonal shades through lowering the tune's key. John nowadays also leads **At the Racket,** a light-hearted combo, determinedly re-creating the sound of the 1930s dance bands, such as The Flanagan Brothers.

⊙ **Last Night's Fun**   Shanachie, 1996

After a great banjo album, came this superb feast of fiddling.

Bobby Casey

The death of **Bobby Casey**, aged 73, in 2000 saw the dwindling band of the great West Clare fiddlers lose yet another of its most illustrious members. Born in Annagh near Milton Malbay in 1926, Bobby's father John, known as Scully, was an esteemed musician, generally regarded in his day as the area's best fiddler and possessor of a wealth of tunes. Bobby would try to pick some out on his father's fiddle (while Scully was out of doors) and learned his first tune proper at the age of seven from Junior Crehan. In time he progressed to playing at house dances and American wakes, often with **Willie Clancy**. In 1952 he and Willie moved to Dublin to seek work in the building trade, but a slump in the city's house-building saw them soon move on to London. Clancy returned in 1957, but Bobby married in 1954 and stayed in the capital until 1992 when he and his wife, Ann, moved to Northampton. In London Bobby struck up a life-long friendship with another West Clare man, piper and concertina player **Tommy McCarthy**, and the pair became hugely influential figures in the Irish music scene.

Bobby can be heard on the excellent compilation **Paddy in the Smoke** (see p.358) playing solo and duetting with the fine Galway fiddler, **Lucy Farr**. The Caseys regularly returned to Clare each year and a visit in 1959 saw Bobby call in at Junior Crehan's house or, rather, cowshed since the Crehan's home was being renovated and the animals' quarters had been converted to temporary accommodation. Persuaded to play, Bobby was recorded on tapes which finally emerged as **Casey in the Cow House** in 1992. This is one of those recordings that simultaneously oozes magic and provokes awe, as the relaxed Casey, inspired by the company of friends, produces music to dance to until the cows come home (fortunately, they stayed in the field). Killoran's reel "My Love is Fair and Handsome" is astonishingly soulful while a duet with Tommy McCarthy on "Galway Reel/Ships Are Sailing" simply drips nostalgia. Though Bobby was to release further albums in the late 1970s, **Traditional Irish Music from Galway and Clare** and **Taking Flight**, and continued to produce music of an extraordinary quality, the Cow House tapes caught him at the very peak of his powers. His last recording was for **Bringing It All Back Home** (see p.46) whose producers brought Bobby and old friends such as flute-player Roger Sherlock and accordionist John Bowe together for a session at Roger's "home" pub, the White Hart in Fulham, London.

📷 Casey in the Cow House	Veteran, 1959

One of the outstanding fiddlers of his generation, a master of ornamentation captured at the zenith of his abilities.

Nollaig Casey

A classical training is often seen as a hindrance to a would-be traditional player, but **Nollaig Casey** is proof that the best of both worlds can be combined. The daughter of a well-known musical family from Cork (her sister is the harper Máire Ní Chathasaigh), was already playing piano, tin whistle and uilleann pipes by the time she started on the fiddle aged ten or eleven. After attending the Cork School of Music, she studied music at University College Cork, graduating at nineteen, meanwhile picking up several All-Ireland titles for both fiddle and traditional singing. She played with the RTÉ Symphony Orchestra for five years before turning freelance, after which offers of traditional work began gradually to supersede those from the classical side. She guested with Planxty for a while towards the end of their career, and has long been in demand as a session player, having recorded with Elvis Costello, Mary Black, Liam O'Flynn, Maura O'Connell and singer Seán Keane, among others. She was involved in both the major TV series *Bringing It All Back Home* and *A River of Sound*, a member of the in-house band on Dónal Lunny's all-star session show *Sult*, and more recently featured in the film soundtracks for *Dancing at Lughnasa* and the hit comedy *Waking Ned*. After *Sult* had run for two series, the house band hived off into Lunny's current ensemble project, **Coolfin**, in whose buoyant, groove-driven instrumental arrangements Casey's venturesome yet gracefully poised playing is always well to the fore.

Despite the widespread respect she commands among her peers, Casey has made only two albums under her own name, both in a duo with her guitarist husband **Arty McGlynn**; both illustrating the full, richly cosmopolitan extent of each player's skills, splicing together blues, country and rock with Irish, classical and pop strands. **Lead the Knave** (1989) won the *Belfast Telegraph* Entertainment Media and Arts Award for excellence in the field of folk music, but of the two it's perhaps **Causeway** (1995) that has the edge, the assertive, snake-hipped swagger of up-tempo tracks like "Jack Palance's Reel" contrasting artfully with the sweetly schmaltzy, classically-tinged air "Trá an Phéarla", the jazzy, suitably bittersweet "Rainy Summer" and the delicate lullaby "Seo Leo 'Thoil".

⊙ Causeway	Tara, 1995

The album includes three tracks of Casey's tenderly expressive singing, with Brendan Power's harmonica an added bonus.

Michael Coleman

More than one commentator has likened the impact that **Michael Coleman** (1891–1945) had on Irish traditional music to that of Elvis Presley on rock'n'roll. Although his historical importance was, in one sense, essentially the product of happenstance – the occurrence of a huge natural talent, in the right place at the right time – the fact remains that the style and repertoire of this one musician played a fundamental role in defining the form in which much traditional music exists today.

The first geographically fortuitous element in Coleman's story was his native turf of Killavil, Co. Sligo, then a remarkably rich pocket of fiddle talent even by the area's music-steeped standards. He was born there in 1891, the last of seven children, and grew up in a household well known locally as a musical one, his father being noted as both a flute player and a welcoming host. Coleman began learning the fiddle aged five or six, taught primarily by his elder brother James, and within a few years was exhibiting not only unusual promise, but an insatiable accompanying appetite for learning more. In this he was fortunate to live mere minutes' walk from the homes of several top local players – John O'Dowd, Mattie Killoran, Phil O'Beirne, Jack McHugh – although as he grew older he would also routinely tramp several miles to a house dance or session, thus encountering other Sligo greats like P.J. McDermott, James Gannon, Paddy Curley and Richard Brennan. Several of these would later be commemorated in the titles he gave to tunes when recording them in America.

Coleman crossed the Atlantic in 1914, finding well-paid work almost immediately – first touring the vaudeville circuit and then in the dance halls and saloons of New York. Better was to follow, though, after Manhattan music-shop owner Ellen O'Byrne de Witt struck a deal with the fledgling Columbia label, in 1916, to record some of the city's myriad immigrant Irish musicians, thus inaugurating the Irish traditional music recording industry. This new market rapidly flourished, with many 78s – including Coleman's – soon selling thousands upon thousands of copies, both to America's huge Irish community and in Ireland itself. It is one of the symbolic ironies of Irish music that, one of its greatest ever traditional musicians only achieved success by emigrating and exporting his music back home. There's even the sad symmetry of the fact that his brother James,

MICHAEL COLEMAN
1891-1945

CEOLTÓIR MÓRTHIONCHAIR
NA hAOISE

Ireland's most influential traditional
musician of the 20th century.

regarded by a good many contemporaries as the better player, remained in Co. Sligo to see out his days in impecunious obscurity.

After he made his first recordings in 1921, Coleman's star shifted firmly into the ascendant, to the extent that within a few years, on his occasional trips to perform in other cities, his arrival would be greeted by cheering crowds of banner-waving fans. The many US radio stations catering for Irish immigrants were also important in establishing his massive popularity. He was an immediate inspiration to other players, like Hugh Gillespie who he encouraged and, indeed, partnered after the latter's arrival in New York in 1927. Harder times ensued with the music industry's general contraction after the 1929 Crash, but by 1934 Coleman was back in the studio, continuing up to within a year of his death, although his very last recordings, made for radio in early 1944, have been lost. Some 80 "sides", however – usually pairs of tunes, enough to fill one side of a 78 – have survived, enough in our own time to fill a lovingly compiled, digitally remastered double album, **Michael Coleman 1891–1945**, on which the extraordinary verve, finesse and expressive power of his playing sing resoundingly down the decades, despite the generally execrable quality of his piano accompanists.

The Sligo style that Coleman inherited, with its fast, smoothly rhythmic bowing, buoyant lift and liberal decorative use of triplets and rolls, was invested by him with a rare and extravagant individual virtuosity. Elements of this included his unmistakeably bright, sweet tone, an inspired feel for the shape and scope of a melody, a singular capacity for absorbing and embellishing the best from other players, and his forceful yet marvellously fluent rhythmic drive. Among the supreme exemplars of these qualities are some of the recordings he made in the late 1920s, including "The Grey Goose", "The Green Fields of America", "The Swallows' Tail" and "Lord McDonald", as well as the reel that almost became his signature tune, "The Boys of the Lough". At the same time, although slow airs seem barely to have featured in his repertoire, the quicksilver vitality of his playing often overlaid a haunting deeper pathos, as in the reel "Farrel O'Gara", for instance, expressed through a quivering touch, or a delicate, fractional lingering on certain phrases.

The concurrence of such gifts with the birth of the record industry resulted in the Sligo style – now primarily identified with Coleman, although other emigrant fiddlers from the region, notably **James Morrison** and **Paddy Killoran**, also enjoyed wide popularity – being widely copied and then generally adopted throughout the home country. Even beyond the matter of style, this defining influence remains widely apparent throughout the instrumental repertoire, with many of Coleman's chosen tune combinations still played as standard sets. The fashionability of the new gramophone technology, coinciding too with a period of both particularly virulent antagonism from the Church towards live music-making and dancing, also abetted the displacement of other local styles. If this loss is to be debited against the Sligo fiddlers' account, however, the latter must also be substantially credited with rescuing Irish traditional music at a particularly precarious point in its fortunes.

The Coleman Irish Music Centre (see p.587) was established in 1991 to commemorate his achievement and to ensure the continuation of his legacy.

⊙ **Michael Coleman 1891–1945**   Viva Voce/Gael Linn, 1921–35

Forty-eight sides' worth of Coleman's genius, carefully cleaned up and with an account of his life and music by Harry Bradshaw.

Séamus Connolly

Fiddler **Séamus Connolly** (b.1944, Killaloe, Co. Clare) has been based in Massachusetts since 1976 where he is Head of Irish Music at Boston College. However, before his emigration Séamus had gained a reputation as one of Ireland's most prodigious fiddlers, thanks in part to a series of All-Ireland titles (he was the youngest ever Senior fiddle champion in 1961) and his legendary partnership with **Paddy "Nenagh" O'Brien** (the pair had first met when the seven-year-old Connolly's hurling ball had landed in Paddy's aunt's back yard). Séamus took up the fiddle at nine and, like many, was inspired by the influential 78s of Coleman, Killoran and Morrison, and later played with both the **Leitrim** and **Kilfenora Céilí Bands**. He also developed a liking for playing with accordionists, including the Tipperary box player **Paddy Ryan** and later **Paul Brock** before forming **Inis Cealtra** with O'Brien in the mid-1960s. The duo went on to record the celebrated **The Banks of the Shannon** (see p.503).

Since moving to the US, Séamus has enhanced his acclaim as an inspirational teacher and has also released three fine albums, showcasing his enviable skills on the fiddle, **Notes from My Mind** (1988), **Here and There** (1989) and **Warming Up** (1993), the last with accordionist Martin Mulhaire, flute player Jack Coen and Felix Dolan on piano. The first album probably best demonstrates the breadth of Connolly's playing through an elegiac, inspired version of the air "Blackbirds and Thrushes" and a, contrastingly, sprightly rendition of the set pieces "The Sprig of Shillelagh/Planxty Perry".

⊙ **Notes from My Mind** Green Linnet, 1988

Awesome, charismatic fiddling from a true modern classic.

Matt Cranitch

An exceptional musician and an authority on Irish fiddle-playing, Cork's **Matt Cranitch** has been a major force in Irish music since the early 1970s. His membership of three renowned trios (**Na Filí**, **Any Old Time** and **Sliabh Notes**) has taken his music to audiences all over the world, while his comprehensive understanding of the music of Sliabh Luachra is second to none. Add to this Matt's authorship of the definitive tutor, *The Irish Fiddle Book*, his readiness to teach and inspire others and you have one of the most dedicated musicians in the field.

Matt received his first fiddle as a Christmas present when he was five or six and his earliest teacher was his father, though he was soon attending lessons at Cork's School of Music. His musical development thus progressed along two parallel lines – formal classical training at the School and traditional music at home where Matt was soon part of a family band. His repertoire developed through watching and listening to fiddlers, in particular **Denis Murphy**, while playing with other musicians saw Matt develop both a meticulous, though relaxed technique and a superb control of rhythm. His two available solo albums are required listening, especially **Give it Schtick!** (1996) which reveals Cranitch's utter mastery of slow air playing, on "An Buachaill Caol Dubh" alongside vivacious slides, reels, jigs and polkas. Most tracks are unaccompanied, though elsewhere his sister Bríd provides piano and harpsichord accompaniment, and there's also stunning unison playing with Dave Hennessy on melodeon and Eoin Ó Riabhaigh's uilleann pipes. **Bríd Cranitch** herself features on a number of releases and especially noteworthy is **A Small Island** (1994) which she recorded with fiddler Vince Milne (now with Nomos) and box-player Pat Sullivan.

⊙ **Give it Schtick!**   Ossian Publications, 1996

Versatile, vibrant fiddling from the stylish Cranitch.

Séamus Creagh

It says much about Ireland and its music that for a couple of evenings on most weeks of the year you can find one of the best traditional fiddlers in the world tucked away in a snug in one of Cork's oldest bars, surrounded by musicians, and producing some of the most sublime sounds on the planet. Born in Killucan, Co. Westmeath, in 1946, **Séamus Creagh** has often wondered "…if I

wasn't a changeling – nobody in our house smoked, drank or made music." He began by picking out tunes on a tin whistle and attempted formal fiddle training in Mullingar but left in preference for the more rigid teaching style of neigh-bour Larry Ward. Larry's repertoire was largely non-traditional and Séamus aug-mented this through listening to the radio. However, by his late teens, he'd abandoned the fiddle and was hammering an electric guitar for a local showband, though a spell in Dublin and visits to O'Donoghue's revitalized his interest. After a stint in London as a builder and busker and a return to Dublin (where he joined a ballad group called The Dragoons) Séamus went to Baltimore, Co. Cork for a weekend and ended up staying, eventually becoming the postman on Sherkin Island where he started playing the fiddle again.

Soon afterwards Séamus met accordionist **Jackie Daly** at CCÉ's regular Friday session at Cork's Country Club Hotel, resulting in a musical partnership that endured throughout the 1970s and which was captured on one of the all-time classic recordings **Jackie Daly and Séamus Creagh**. The pair's playing for set dancers had created a symbiotic understanding of the polka and there are plenty here, together with a mighty solo slow air from Creagh ("An Gleann Faoi Dhraíocht") but sadly, just one song ("An Táilliúir Bán") from Séamus who has a fine voice. From 1988 to 1992, Séamus lived in Newfoundland, collecting tunes and songs and releasing another excellent album, **Came the Dawn**, and also a record with local band Tickle Harbour.

Returning to Cork, he subsequently formed another fabulous fiddle-accordion partnership with **Aidan Coffey**, their sessions at An Spailpín Fanach acquiring the status of legend. Posterity required a recording and gained satisfaction with another self-titled classic (see p.479), featuring impeccable and exhilarating playing by both partners on tunes from the length of Ireland, in particular their interweaving on the slides "The Ceanngulla/The Gleanntán Frolics" approaches perfection).

⊙ **Jackie Daly and Séamus Creagh**   Gael-Linn, 1977

Indisputably, one of the all-time classics of Irish music – a box and fiddle combination to die for!

Mary Custy

For almost forty years Frank Custy from Toonagh has been teaching music to Clare's young hopefuls and his pupils have included some of the county's most distinguished musicians. His own children have benefited too: Frances also teaches and runs a music shop in Ennis, while Cathy is an accomplished concertina player and Tola a skilful fiddler (and member of both The Bowhouse Quintet and Calico). However, thanks in part to her time in Doolin in the early 1990s, **Mary Custy** is the most well-known. Her stay in Doolin coincided with the village's peak years as a musical magnet, giving Mary a thorough traditional grounding and resulting in her recording two now hard-to-find albums, **With a Lot of Help From Our Friends** and **The Ways of the World**, with guitar and bouzouki player **Eoin O'Neill** (now of The Céilí Bandits).

Mary's musical influences have always been broad and in the mid-1990s she joined the jazz-rock band **Bushplant**, members of which appear on her own **The Mary Custy Band** album. Here her fiddling is energetic and lyrical, but the occasionally lumpen bass and some histrionic guitar echo the worst excesses of the 1970s electric folk-rock era. Thankfully, she returned to her roots with the assistance of guitarist **Stephen Flaherty** to release the excellent and moody **After 10.30**. Though known for the occasional wildness of her fiddling, this

DEREK SPEIRS/REPORT

is Mary's relaxed late-night album, exemplified by her gorgeously understated playing on the B minor reel constituting the first part of "The Woman of the House". That she can swing too is grandly evident on "The Road to Miltown", while Stephen Flaherty's own solo piece "After 10.30" is a gem.

⊙ **After 10.30**   own label, 1999

Custy's partnership with Stephen Flaherty makes for some relaxed and soulful music – a grand way to round off an evening.

The Dohertys

The influence of the **Doherty** family on the development of music in Donegal over the last two hundred years is simply incalculable. Interconnected by marriage to the Mac Sweeneys of Doe Castle (one of the most powerful families in northwest Donegal prior to their dispossession during the Ulster Plantation of the early seventeenth century), the Dohertys were travelling people and fiddlers, often working as tinsmiths. One branch of the family was headed by Mickey Mór Doherty, born in the middle of the nineteenth century, a fiddler himself, whose third, sixth and ninth children, **Simon**, **Mickey** and **John**, essentially cast the mould of the region's music during the following epoch. **Simon Doherty**, known as Sími (also, confusingly, the nickname for all the male Dohertys) was known as a confident player, especially popular at dances, and was recorded, along with John, by Ciarán Mac Mathúna for RTÉ in 1957. Unfortunately, the few examples of his solo playing remain in the archives and the only published recording available is on **The Donegal Fiddle** (see p.311) where, in a duet with his younger brother, Sími plays the upper octave on the reel "The Pigeon on the Gate" while John supplies the lower. Octave playing is sometimes known as reversing in Donegal and this is a literal reversal too, as their roles in duets were usually the other way around. Símí died in 1961 when his home burned down.

Mickey Doherty (1894–1970) is reckoned to have inherited both his father's fiddle style and tinsmithery skills. Married at nineteen to Mary Rua, a union which produced nine children, the family lived for a time in Glenfin, between Glenties and Ballybofey. The five boys all later emigrated on reaching adulthood, while the three surviving girls all went into service (as Caoimhín MacAoidh recounts, a picture exists of one daughter tending a young Paul Brady!). Mickey's beat included the isolated Irish-speaking area known as Na Cruacha (The Croaghs) in the glens of the Blue Stack Mountains. During the day he travelled from house to house making "pandies", household tinware, and would also buy and sell fiddles Indeed, he became known as a maker of tin fiddles, with a soldered tin body and whatever wood he could find for the neck. According to legend, he was so adept that he could start and finish one during an evening's card-playing session, which he would play for dancing at the games' end before subsequently raffling it!

In later life, Mickey and Mary Rua settled in Ballybofey before finally moving to nearby Stranorlar where Mickey took every opportunity to visit Hugh Gillespie who had recently returned from the US. Mickey was taped both privately and by public organizations over the years and the most extensive collection of his music is **The Gravel Walks**, a double cassette of recordings made for the Irish Folklore Commission at a house in the Blue Stacks in 1949. As Jackie Small remarks in the sleeve notes, this represents "a sort of 'Sunday Best' performance by the fiddler" since it draws less upon the local dance tunes and more on a later repertoire, largely favouring Paddy Killoran's recordings.

Nevertheless, it still reveals a remarkably talented musician, more legato in bow style than John, and favouring triplets, though equally confident in his use of rolls. The presence of piping tunes in the Doherty repertoire is explicitly evident in a version of the programme piece, "The Fox Chase", here called "The Hounds after the Hare" where he uses all his skills to emulate the sounds of the chase.

John Doherty (c.1895–1980) was undoubtedly the most illustrious scion of Mickey Mór and had already, by the 1920s, developed the lifestyle which characterized much of his adult existence. By then he was known as a fiddler of stunning genius whose playing and extensive knowledge of folklore made him a welcome guest on his travels. John's beat favoured rural Donegal, encompassing the villages and townlands between Ballybofey and Glencolmcille, where he would work as a tinsmith during the day, and taught tunes or played for dances in the evenings. Piping tunes figured in his repertoire, but he also absorbed many melodies from recordings, particularly those of the Scottish fiddler, James Scott Skinner, Paddy Killoran, and Neillidh Boyle from The Rosses.

John's own unique style drew upon his use of an

EAMONN O'DOHERTY

John Doherty

excitingly powerful staccato bowing style, while fingering rapid triplets, rolls in both directions and atmospheric use of double stopping, although his playing of airs involved much longer bowing to replicate the sound of the pipes. John's fame began to accrue as collectors visited the county in the 1940s and by the 1960s had increased to the extent that it was widely misconstrued that if Donegal's fiddle music did not sound like John Doherty, then it was not the authentic article. For a while he based himself in Carrick, effectively becoming a full-time musician, but after a brief spell in hospital, he moved into his sister-in-law's house in Stranorlar where he was often found in the company of another great fiddler, Danny O'Donnell, who lived across the bridge in Ballybofey. John Doherty died in 1980 and is buried in the family plot in Fintown. Many of the tunes associated with him, such as "The Black Mare of Fanad" (aka "The Nine Points of Roguery"), remain prominent in the repertoires of many contemporary fiddlers and his influence on fiddle playing will long survive his passing.

Apart from various archive collections, three commercially available recordings of John Doherty are available, though sadly not the album he recorded for CCÉ in 1974. **The Floating Bow** consists of 25 tracks selected from a huge number of recordings made by Alun Evans between 1968 and 1974 in the house of John's friend, Mickey Browne, in Glenconwell with John playing Evans's own eighteenth-century fiddle. Through the privacy of the setting, the full force of Doherty's playing and its extraordinary range of ornamentation imbues these wonderfully natural recordings. **Taisce – The Celebrated Recordings**, originally released on vinyl in 1978 and subsequently remastered, comes from an informal session in Glencolmcille in 1974. Finally, **Bundle and Go** was recorded "in the field" by Allen Feldman during his researches for *The Northern*

Fiddler (see p.590) and originally issued on vinyl in 1984. Doherty was about 83 at the time and leaves you goggling at what he must have been like at 33!

⊙ **The Floating Bow**   Claddagh, 1968–74

Astonishingly accomplished fiddling from John Doherty, sparked by the company of friends.

⊙ **Taisce –The Celebrated Recordings**   Gael-Linn, 1974

The full versatility of John Doherty's fiddling captured across a range of tune forms.

▦ **The Gravel Walks**   Comhairle Bhéaloideas Éireann, 1949

This double cassette of the much overshadowed Mickey Doherty reveals him to be a glorious fiddler in his own right.

Liz Doherty

L ike Altan's Ciarán Tourish, fiddler **Liz Doherty** is from Buncrana, Co. Donegal, and was similarly taught by the accomplished teacher, Dinny McLaughlin. Her interest was further inspired by sessions in Glencolmcille, featuring musicians such as Ciarán himself, Mairéad Ní Mhaonaigh, Frankie Kennedy and the Derry fiddler Dermot McLaughlin, while seeing James Byrne and Con Cassidy there in concert had a lasting impact. A graduate of Mícheál Ó Súilleabháin's traditional music course at University College Cork, she developed an interest in Cape Breton music and lived there for a time while undertaking her doctoral research. Back in Cork and now teaching music herself at University College, she was an early member of **Nomos** and subsequently joined **Bumblebees** in 1997, featuring on the **Buzzin'** album, while also playing with her own **Liz**

Doherty Band which she has continued to lead since leaving the Bumblebees. Liz's own solo album, **Last Orders**, is an eclectic mix of tunes from around Ireland, the Orkneys and Cape Breton played with her own inimitably exuberant style – though the Donegal touch is still evident. A younger Liz can be heard on the **Fiddlesticks** album (see p.275) while 2000 saw the release of her imaginative initiative **Racket at the Rectory** on which Liz leads a fifteen-strong band of traditional fiddlers, also confusingly called **Fiddlesticks**. Dauntless to the last, Liz is currently editing the complete O'Neill song collection.

⊙ **Last Orders**   Foot Stompin' Records, 1999

A selection reflecting the diversity of Liz's musical interests, all played with her customary panache.

Donegal Fiddlers

To ears accustomed to the predominant Sligo style of playing (see p.274), first hearing a Donegal fiddler can provoke rather a shock, albeit one of the exhilarating kind. The music seems piercing to some, yet grating to others, but all agree that the county's music in general is characterized by a captivatingly raw and driving vigour. However, there is not one simple Donegal style but a multiplicity of variants and it would take a book to distinguish them. Fortunately, **Caoimhín MacAoidh**, a fiddler himself and major figure in the maintenance of the tradition, has already written it and his *Between the Jigs and the Reels: The Donegal Fiddle Tradition* (see p.591) is an exemplary account of the music's history and differing styles around the county, together with biographies of many fiddlers and analyses of their techniques.

The origins of Donegal's individual sound are complex. The county has long held close ties with Scotland, thanks in part to common ancestry – major families like the Mac Suibhne clan actually originated from the Hebrides – but more to emigration and temporary migrant labour, to the extent that Glasgow is sometimes referred to as the county capital! This resulted in dances such as the highland and strathspey having a currency in Donegal unknown anywhere else in Ireland and tunes in these forms still regularly feature in sessions around the county, as does the German, a barndance and adaptation of the form known as a Schottische. There is also less instrumental variety in Donegal than perhaps any other county. Flute players are relatively rare and accordionists uncommon, though Altan's Dermot Byrne is a renowned exception. Far more influential on the predominant fiddle is the county's piping history, both through the uilleann pipes and the playing of the war pipes, the latter again reinforcing the Scottish link. The most famous piper (of both instruments) was **Turlough Mac Suibhne** (1818–1916), known as An Píobaire Mór, often described as the winner of the first, and only, World Piping Competition in Chicago, an event which almost certainly did not exist. What is more certain is that a significant number of piping tunes entered the fiddlers' repertoire as did various techniques, like the **Dohertys**' habit of retuning a fiddle to ADAD in order to provide a constant background drone. Certainly, the Donegal style is both loud and bright and features much staccato bowing with an emphasis on extremely crisp triplets, rather than the rolls of, say, Sligo, and sometimes features position playing (see p.273) almost certainly a Scottish import thanks to the local popularity of the recordings of the Scots fiddler Scott Skinner.

Currently, the most widely known Donegal fiddlers are **Mairéad Ní Mhaonaigh** and **Ciarán Tourish** of **Altan**, but the county has produced a wealth of other tremendous musicians. Several of the most prominent (**John** and **Mickey Doherty**, **Neillidh Boyle**, **Hugh**

The 'Ó Beirne Brothers – Mickey (left) and Francie

Gillespie, **Danny O'Donnell**, **Tommy Peoples** and **James Byrne**) have their own entries in this guide, along with the **Glackin** brothers whose origins lie in the county. Other influential figures include: the Teelin fiddlers, **Frank** and **Con Cassidy** and **Jimmy Lyons**; the brothers **Mickey Bán** and **Francie Dearg Ó Beirne** from nearby Kilcar; the **Campbell** family from the isolated Blue Stack Mountains, most notably **Vincent Campbell**; two eminent teachers, Mairéad's father, **Proinsías Ó Maonaigh**, from Gweedore, and **Dinny McLaughlin**, from Inishowen; and the long-time London resident, **Danny Meehan**, from Mountcharles.

There are a number of remarkable compilations, including **The Donegal Fiddle**, recorded for Radio Éireann by Séamus Ennis in 1949 and Ciarán Mac Mathúna in 1957 and recently remastered. This is a sumptuous record of some of the most astonishingly versatile fiddlers

EAMONN O'DOHERTY

to come from the county. Francie Dearg and Mickey Bán Ó Beirne are well-represented with thirteen field recordings and the former's playing on "The Donegal Castle Hornpipe" is lightning incarnate. Also featured are Jimmy Lyons, the Ardara trio of Paddy and John Gallagher and James McHugh, and the Dohertys – John, Mickey and the less familiar Simon. Add to this some extraordinarily informative sleeve notes, especially on tune origins, and voilà – the pure drop. The album that really opened Irish ears to the breadth of the Donegal tradition was **The Brass Fiddle** and, though some of the tunes (eg "Vincent Campbell's Mazurkas") may have entered the broader canon, there's still much here to excite and astound. Produced by fiddler Dermot McLaughlin, the album features solo playing by James Byrne, Vincent Campbell and the late Con Cassidy (recorded in the Highlands Hotel, Glenties, 1986) and an earlier 1983 home recording of Francie Beirne. If you've never heard one before, you'll marvel at Con Cassidy's vivacious "The Low Highland" and Vincent also provides a couple of rare dance tunes "The Marine" (only danced nowadays around Glenfin) and "The Lancers". Again, sleeve notes are hugely informative. **Fiddle Sticks: Irish Traditional Music from Donegal** taped live in Cork during the January, 1991 Fiddlesticks Festival, is tremendous stuff and includes a rare recording of Mairéad and Proinsías Ó Mhaonaigh duetting on two mazurkas. Lastly, **The Fiddle Music of Donegal** consists of three CDs recorded at the Donegal Fiddlers' Summer Schools at Glencolmcille in August, 1995 and 1999 and represents a marvellous and colourful insight into the various nuances of the area's fiddle tradition. Other fiddlers to look out for include Roisín McGrory and Damian Harrigan from Burnfoot, Inishowen, the mighty Martin McGinley, the Scotsman Stephen Campbell (long based in Donegal), Paula Doohan from Gweedore and the young, extraordinarily talented Stephen Gallagher from Kilcar.

> 🎞 **Ceol Na dTéad**   Cló Iar-Chonnachta, 1992

Astonishing interplay between brothers Francie Dearg and Mickey Bán Ó Beirne characterizes this stunning recording.

> ⊙ **The Brass Fiddle**   Gael-Linn, 1987

This brought the playing of Francie Ó Beirne, James Byrne, Vincent Campbell and Con Cassidy to a wider audience.

> ⊙ **The Fiddle Music of Donegal**   Cairdeas Recordings, 1995–1999
> **Vols 1/3**

Unaccompanied fiddlers, all playing with typical exuberance, recorded at the Glencolmcille Summer School.

Des and Dezi Donnelly

A dynamic fiddler whose range encompassed raw ferocity and tender subtlety, **Des Donnelly** from Lacca, near Fintona, Co. Tyrone, was a leading musical light in Northern England's Irish community until his tragically early death aged 40 in 1973. That very same year he had won the All-Britain Senior title for the second year running. Fortunately, we're still able to marvel at his ability on the album **Remember Des Donnelly** (originally released in 1979). Mainly unaccompanied – apart from his own stamping foot and occasional piano – Des coaxes his fiddle around "The Star" hornpipe with a witty chortle to his tone, while his playing on "Jackie Coleman's" reel exhibits all the vibrance and crisp vivacity characteristic of many players from Ulster.

Dezi, Des's nephew, has carried on the family tradition and was voted Ireland's Young Traditional Musician of the Year in 1999 (although had actually been around since the late 1980s). Born in Manchester in

1973, Dezi first came to prominence with the band **Toss the Feathers**. He subsequently worked as a duo both with Northern Irish guitarist **Skirm**, releasing 1995's excellent **Welcome**, and more regularly with **Mike McGoldrick** with whom he recorded the even better **Champions of the North**. He also played in an assortment of pop, punk and rock bands before, finally, releasing an album of his own. **Familiar Footsteps**, which appeared in 1998, reveals the extent to which Dezi has watched and listened to the great fiddlers, adding a touch of his own panache. Listen to the sweep of the bow on "Sean McGuire's" or the jollity of "The Spey in a Spate", both learned from tapes of Uncle Des, or the awesomely emotive rendition of John Doherty's "Paddy's Rambles through the Park" (all accompanied by Andy Jones on guitar) and you know there's a genius in the house.

⊙ **Remember Des Donnelly**   independent release, 1979

Vital playing from the influential Tyrone fiddler.

⊙ **Familiar Footsteps**   own label, 1998

Dezi's abilities are frightening, but he rarely substitutes sheer speed for grace on this corker of an album.

Ted Furey

Known as "The Chief", **Ted Furey** (father of the Furey brothers) was a fiddler with a ruggedly gregarious style as well as a singer and raconteur. A regular performer in Dublin's O'Donoghue's bar, he continued playing right up to his death in 1979. Though his recordings include **Irish Folk Music** for the Breton Artfolk label and **The Furey Family** for Germany's Intercord, his only currently available release is **Toss the Feathers** made on one of Ted's frequent trips to Belfast. Recorded in 1967, the master tape subsequently disappeared and was only rediscovered after a 1972 bomb blast! Ted is partnered by his regular bodhrán-playing accomplice, **Brendan Byrne** whose old-style drumming – he uses his knuckles on a bodhrán with tambourine-like jingles – may seem strange to ears attuned to "Ringo" McDonagh. With the exception of the air "The Coolin", Ted's style is largely unelaborate, allowing the simplicity of the mainly familiar jigs and reels to shine through.

⊙ **Toss the Feathers**   Outlet, 1972

Dodgy sound quality, but infectious playing by The Chief who personally introduces many tracks.

Frankie Gavin

Life isn't always fair. While most of us struggle with one instrument, there's **Frankie Gavin** mastering fiddle, flute, whistle, pipes, accordion and piano and supplying us with decades of great music through his partnership with **Alec Finn** in **De Dannan**. Frankie's household in Corundulla, Co. Galway, was staunchly musical – both parents were fiddlers and his mother also played the concertina – and after an early start on the whistle, Frankie turned to the fiddle at ten. Though subsequently teaching himself the other instruments, it's the fiddle with which Frankie will always be associated. No less than Yehudi Menuhin has described him as one of the best players in the world and Frankie always seems to play with a flair and zest no matter the tune nor the genre. Gavin has guested on too many albums to mention, though note should be made of his role in Charlie Lennon's **Island Wedding** and the 1986 Joe Cooley tribute album recorded with Paul Brock. While his solo albums **Croch Suas**

S. MOORES/REDFERNS

É (1983) and **Frankie Goes to Town** (1991) are fine in themselves, probably the most direct approach to the man's playing is through **The Best of Frankie Gavin**, a selection of tracks from various sources recorded between 1977 and 1995 (though the sleeve notes provide no details of when, where or with whom). Apart from a stunning performance on the De Dannan favourite "The Humours of Galway" there's astounding droned playing on the syncopated "Way too Jazzy". Frankie's colourful flute-playing should not be forgotten too and included here is his hallmark rendition of "Mná na hÉireann".

⊙ **The Best of Frankie Gavin**   Chart/RTÉ, 1977–95

Virtuoso fiddle and flute from the Galway master.

Hugh Gillespie

Though he was born and died in Co. Donegal, **Hugh Gillespie** (1906–86) spent more than 35 years in the US where he acquired a major reputation as a fiddler. Born at Drennan, near

Ballybofey, he began playing at the age of seven, influenced by his father and his uncle Johnnie who was reckoned to be one of the best fiddlers in the region. Hugh himself developed into a popular player at house dances but a disagreement over his sheep grazing on his father's cattle pasture led to the 21-year-old deciding to try his hand in the States. Within four days of arriving in New York he met **Michael Coleman** who, on hearing Hugh's fiddle, decided immediately that the pair should play together. Though working as an engineer for Consolidated Edison, Hugh broadcast almost daily with Coleman for several years on a variety of local radio stations, the two playing unaccompanied. Hugh also played in a variety of dance bands in New York, usually led by his cousin, Jim Gillespie, a button accordionist. One band, the **Four Provinces Orchestra**, often played a Polish club where there was much demand for dances such as the Varsovienne and mazurka, so it was no surprise that Gillespie's first recordings in 1937 included "The Irish Mazurka".

Unlike his Sligo contemporaries who usually had piano accompaniment, Hugh regularly recorded with guitarists, first with neighbour **Mark Callahan** and later **Jack McKenna**. The latter's choice of chords sometimes owed more to contemporary jazz guitarists like Charlie Christian, but his driving, percussive style laid the foundations for future work by Paul Brady, Dónal Lunny and Arty McGlynn. Hugh returned to live near Ballybofey in 1964 and, when he died in 1986, was buried with his fiddle. Fortunately, his musical legacy includes **Classic Recordings of Irish Traditional Music** containing sixteen of the twenty sides he recorded between 1937 and 1939. Hugh's style is markedly hybrid in form, blending his Donegal background with the Sligo style to produce a sound often described as "singing". He acquired technical devices from Coleman, such as "back trebling", but fluent bowing and slight flattening or sharpening of notes gave his music its own infectious edge whether on reels like "Paddy Finley's Fancy" or hornpipes such as "Mountain Stream".

⊙ **Classic Recordings of Irish Traditional Music**   Green Linnet, 1937–39

An essential purchase for those interested in the development of Irish fiddling.

The Glackins

The three Dublin-born **Glackin** brothers owe their musical heritage to their father **Tom Glackin** (1925–88) who, though born in Stirling, Scotland, was reared in Falmore, near Dungloe, Co. Donegal. Tom was a gifted fiddler and teacher, playing in the driving, rhythmic style of The Rosses, and helped to bring Donegal music to a wider audience following his move to Dublin to become a Garda in 1947. While on the beat a chance meeting with fiddler John Kelly, led to his introduction to Dublin's traditional network and, eventually, friendship with Breandán Breathnach. A consistent champion of Donegal music, it was Tom Glackin who arranged for Breathnach to record John and Mickey Doherty in 1965.

His eldest son, **Paddy**, was at the historic Dohertys recording in 1965 and soon became a committed traditional fiddler, while also pursuing classical training at Dublin's College of Music. Paddy made his session debut in a duet with the Sligo flute player, John Egan and became a sought-after player, often in company with Mary Bergin and accordionist John Regan. A member of the Ó Riada-inspired **Ceotóirí Laighean**, public prominence resulted from his role in **The Bothy Band**'s original line-up. Subsequently, Paddy developed an enduring collaboration with guitar and keyboard player **Mícheál Ó Domhnaill**, while also featuring on – and sometimes producing – a huge number of records. He has also worked in radio and TV, presenting *The Pure Drop*, and as the Irish Arts Council's first traditional music officer, but he is best celebrated as an outstandingly accomplished solo fiddler who has also generated some remarkable collaborations with uilleann pipers. Recordings of the latter include **Flags of Dublin** (with Mick O'Brien), **The Whirlwind** (with Robbie Hannan) and, best of all **Doublin'** (1978) in cahoots with Paddy Keenan. **Doublin'** is one of the outstanding recordings of the decade, where the two Paddys re-create the verve and warmth of their regular session duets. For Paddy's solo work, look no further than the vivacious **Rabharta Ceoil/In Full Spate** (1991), where he's joined by old friend Dónal Lunny.

Paddy's younger brothers, **Séamus** and **Kevin**, are also fine fiddlers. Kevin, with his demonstrative attacking style, is the better known player; a member of **Bakerswell**, he has worked as a duo with **Ronan Browne** (appearing on Cran's albums) as well as with Davy Spillane. The three brothers have rarely recorded together, an exception being their performance of "Glen Road to Carrick" on **Bringing It All Back Home** (see p.46), however, in 1989 Kevin and Séamus released the superb **Na Saighneáin/Northern Lights**. Featuring some marvellous unison fiddling, highlights include a spirited version of the John Doherty jig "King of the Pipers" and an ornate hornpipe from Andy McGann.

⊙ Rabharta Ceoil	Gael-Linn, 1991

"I set the outlines, Dónal fills in the colours" is how Paddy summarizes his partnership with Dónal Lunny.

⊙ Na Saighneáin	Gael-Linn, 1989

Kevin and Séamus Glackin are on barn-storming form throughout this finely-crafted album.

Vincent Griffin

Born in 1932 in the townland of Ayle, near Feakle, Co. Clare, Vincent Griffin comes from a family of musicians. Related to the songwriter Johnny Paterson (whose odes include "Goodbye Johnny" and "The Stone Outside Dan Murphy's Door"), Vincent's mother sang and played the concertina, while his father was a melodeon player who always fancied the fiddle and encouraged his children to take up the instrument. At seven, Vincent took a few lessons from the Tulla fiddler, Paddy Powell, and further encouragement came from his own elder brother Patrick. More was learned from listening to other local fiddlers and from the concertina player, Jim McNamara, who had a strong melodic style. Michael Coleman's records provided a further influence on Griffin's style and repertoire, but admiration did not become emulation as Vincent sought to follow his own path.

In the early 1950s Vincent joined the **Shamrock Céilí Band** (sometimes also playing with the Kilfenora) and played in London with the band in 1958. Liking the city, he returned to work there a year later and stayed until 1965, often playing sessions. Back in Clare, he worked as a joiner and ran a small farm, before taking a job as a music teacher with the Shannon Development Board, becoming so successful that his pupils won half a dozen awards at the 1976 Fleadh Cheoil. Runner-up in the senior fiddle competition in both 1956 and 1973, Vincent became the champion in 1974. His only album, **Traditional Fiddle Music from County Clare** (1977) includes a grand array from his repertoire, including several Coleman tunes, "The Trip to Sligo" jig, learned from neighbour Paddy Canny and a marvellous Mayo air popular with pipers, "Se Bhfarth Mo Bhfuartha". Vincent's fiddle has a resolute singing style thanks to fluent bowing and exceptionally neat slurring, heard to great effect on the reel "The Gatehouse Maid". Vincent is still playing and was recently seen in the environs of an Ennis recording studio, fiddle in hand.

⊙ **Traditional Fiddle Music from County Clare**   Topic, 1977

Well worth hunting down, this is a superb album of fiddling in the vibrant East Clare style.

Gerry Harrington

R egarded as one of the best modern exponents of the Sliabh Luachra style, **Gerry Harrington** hails from Kenmare, Co. Kerry, where an early influence was the erstwhile Boys of the Lough uilleann piper, Christy O'Leary. Others who played a role in his musical development include fiddlers Joe Thoma, Connie O'Connell and Denis McMahon. Gerry moved to the US in the 1980s, spending much time in Chicago, where he encountered the renowned fiddler Johnny McGreevy and notable musicians such as Liz Carroll and the one-time Solas accordionist, John Williams. Returning to Ireland in 1990, he settled in Co. Waterford and soon struck up a partnership with the accordionist **Eoghan O'Sullivan**, from Mitchelstown, Co. Cork, who shared Gerry's interests in Sliabh Luachra's music. Developing a rapport through regular sessions in Dungarvan, they released two fine albums, **Scéal Eige** and **The Smoky Chimney**. Preferentially, the latter gets the vote, largely because of the self-evident maturity of their partnership, their clear love of the music and the excellent accompaniment provided by Paul de Grae's guitar. The album's air of relaxed pleasure starts from the outset with a curvaceous version of the renowned Pádraig O'Keeffe/Denis Murphy duet, "I'd Rather Be Married Than Left", and takes listeners on a fun-packed itinerary which, while firmly rooted in Munster, draws in barndances from Pearl O'Shaughnessy and reels from her fellow fiddler, Josephine Keegan from Co. Armagh. Eoghan cites Jackie Daly as an influence, but he's his own man throughout and his combination playing with Gerry is simply sumptuous. Gerry has since forged a partnership with **Charlie Piggott**; their album, **The New Road**, is reviewed on p.508.

⊙ **The Smoky Chimney**   Fætain, 1996

As a friend once said, "This is the album I put my feet up to, but they soon start twitching!"

Cathal Hayden

Like a musical mirror-image of his **Four Men and a Dog** band-mate Gerry O'Connor, **Cathal Hayden** divides his talents between both fiddle and banjo, but is considerably better known as a fiddler. Born in Pomeroy, Co. Tyrone, he was taught first by his similarly bi-instrumental father, originally on the banjo, taking up the fiddle in his mid-teens and learning most of his music from older players in his home area. He won several All-Ireland titles on both instruments before recording his first album, **Handed Down** (1982), a sparkling collection of fiddle and banjo tunes, with accompaniment from **Arty McGlynn**, **Johnny "Ringo" McDonagh** and **Nollaig Casey**. As the title suggests, it pays celebratory homage to his various formative influences, among which he also cites De Dannan and The Bothy Band. Together with McDonagh, Hayden was a member of the original **Arcady** line-up in the late 1980s, but left after a couple of years to co-found Four Men and a Dog, his pyrotechnic fiddle workouts and inventive song accompaniment remaining a standout feature of their Irish/Americana blend throughout their ten years on the circuit. Since the band split (though they still get together for one-off shows), Hayden has released his long-awaited solo follow-up, simply entitled **Cathal Hayden** (1999). Comprising virtually wall-to-wall reels and jigs – aside from one set of slides, one hornpipe and one song, the last courtesy of Séamus Begley – and announcing his "rediscovery" of the banjo alongside the fiddle, the album is again anchored by Arty McGlynn on guitar, with further subtle touches of keyboards and percussion framing Hayden's gloriously ebullient, fierily virtuosic playing.

⊙ **Cathal Hayden**   Hook Records, 1999

Among the many highlights are several one-man fiddle/banjo duets – courtesy of multitracking.

Martin Hayes and Dennis Cahill

L ike the man said, it's a long, long way from Clare to here. "Here" for **Martin Hayes** being not only his adopted home town of Seattle, but also his unquestioned status as the most widely fêted and influential fiddler of his generation. Hayes' musical journey, however, has ultimately been a circular one, leading him right back to the heart of his native East Clare, into renewed communion with the spirit of predecessors and early mentors like Martin Rochford, his uncle Paddy Canny and his father P.J. – fiddler with the **Tulla Céilí Band** for the past fifty years.

Born in 1962, Hayes began playing aged seven, learning first from his father, then via the numerous sessions that took place in the family home, joining the Tulla himself at fourteen. After moving to the US in 1984, he teamed up with guitarist **Dennis Cahill**, the Chicago born son of Kerry parents, in the folk-rock band **Midnight Court**, only to find himself inexorably drawn back to his musical roots he thought he'd left behind. His self-titled first solo album (1993) introduced what were soon to become known as the hallmarks of his style – intense, unhurried lyricism, lavish yet delicate ornamentation, exquisite dynamic control – while his second, **Under the Moon** (1995) underlined his fast-growing reputation as a defining exponent of the tradition.

The subsequent revival of his partnership with Cahill further enriched his sound, thanks to the guitarist's subtly innovative, richly complementary picking style, distilled from folk, blues and classical influences, and to the uncanny near-telepathy between the duo. Their first joint recording, **The Lonesome Touch** (1997), is generally regarded as a contemporary classic, named for the bittersweet, otherworldly quality, characteristic of the East Clare tradition, which makes Hayes' playing so mesmeric. Intimately close-up production vividly captures the way each set of tunes seems to become, in Hayes' hands, a genuine and soul-searching journey, or exploration, running the full emotional gamut from profound, heartrending pathos to wild exultation, sympathetically shadowed by Cahill at every step, the most notable example in the extended five-tune track led off by "Paul Ha'penny". In concert, the duo will often play uninterrupted for half an hour or more, as revealed on their second release, **Live In Seattle** (1999), the centrepiece of which is a medley lasting almost 28 minutes, the journey in this case becoming an utterly spellbinding epic.

⊙ **The Lonesome Touch**   Green Linnet, 1997

Regarded as a contemporary classic, this spellbinding album highlights Hayes' rich musical chemistry with Cahill.

Eileen Ivers

Thanks to **Cherish the Ladies**, *Riverdance* and *River of Sound*, not to mention her trademark blue fiddle, **Eileen Ivers** is one of the best-known fiddlers in the Western world. Born in New York's Bronx in 1965 to parents who had emigrated from Co. Mayo in the 1950s, she progressed so rapidly under the tutelage of Martin Mulvihill that she won her first All-Ireland Junior title at the age of 11 and the senior title at 18. After a spell with Seamus Egan and Robbie O'Connell in the Green Fields of America tour, her first album, **Fresh Takes** was recorded with **John Whelan** in 1986. Subsequently. Eileen joined Cherish the Ladies in 1987, though by then she was already experimenting with differing musical forms and playing in a variety of

clubs and bands on the New York scene (including, in 1991, the white-boy soul group led by Hall and Oates). Though by this time she was exploring the potential of the electric fiddle, her 1994 self-titled solo album was still markedly traditional in nature. 1995 saw her starring role in *Riverdance* and since then she's never looked back.

The best introduction to her music is undoubtedly the **So Far** compilation which kicks off with the then fourteen-year-old playing in competitive style on "The Kerryman's Daughter" and includes her elegant duet with Win Horan on "Pachelbert's Frolics". **Wild Blue** (1996) is her most rounded release to date and features lightning dexterity on the opening "On Horseback" and her elegiacal solo rendition of "Lament for Staker Wallace". However, in "Blue Groove" she seemed to be edging ever closer to the wayward meandering sometimes favoured by Jerry Goodman (fiddler with jazz-rock fusionists The Mahavishnu Orchestra). This was confirmed by the release of her latest album **Crossing the Bridge** (1999), a turgid hotchpotch of tired jazz-funk clichés and African rhythms on which style masquerades as substance and the supporting cast even includes a turntableist (sic)!

⊙ **So Far**   Green Linnet, 1979–95

This really does include all the highlights of Eileen's career.

Seán Keane

Born in Drimnagh, Co. Dublin, in 1946, **Seán Keane** is a fiddler of international stature, thanks to his long-time membership of **The Chieftains** whom he joined in 1968. Both Seán's mother (from Co. Clare) and father (from Co. Longford) were traditional fiddlers, so it was no wonder when he followed suit, starting at the age of six, later being sent to Dublin's School of Music for classical training. Like his accordionist younger brother, James, Seán was a regular feature of Dublin's sessions and a member of the **Castle Céilí Band**. At seventeen, he was recruited by Ó Riada for **Ceoltóirí Chualann** and featured in a number of performances and recordings (where he is sometimes listed as Seán Ó Catháin). The life of a Chieftain can be a hectic international whirl but Seán has found time to appear on other recordings, including his brother James's **Sweeter as the Years Go By** (1999). He has also made several albums of his own including the powerful **Gusty's Frolics** (1978), on which the fiddle becomes a medium for piping tunes. 1985 saw him pair up with fellow Chieftain **Matt Molloy** for the eloquent **Contentment is Wealth**, and the two combined with piper **Liam O'Flynn**, seven years later, for **The Fire Aflame** a positive powerhouse of an album which includes an unusual G minor rendition of "The Drunken Sailor" and accompaniment to Brian Keenan's reading of his own poem "Night Fishing, 30th January 1972".

By then Seán had released his own second solo album, **Jig it in Style**, demonstrating the mesmeric power of his honey-toned fiddling in reels such as "Kiss the Maid Behind the Barrel" with accompaniment from Paul Brady. Keane's rendition of the slow air "Dark Lochnagar" is frankly mind-boggling in the way he uses rolls, staccato bowing and extended sliding notes to create music of intense passion. Elsewhere, Liam O'Flynn joins for "The Maids that Jig it in Style", there's a soupçon of bluegrass and, most startlingly of all, a virtuoso rendering of Elvis Presley's "Heartbreak Hotel" (thankfully, instrumental and not vocal!).

⊙ **Jig it in Style**   Claddagh, 1989

Eclectic and emphatic playing from the daredevil Keane – pure bliss.

The Kellys

One of the most important figures in the 1960s traditional revival was the fiddler and concertina player, **John Kelly** (1912–87) from Irish-speaking Rehy West in Co. Clare. Kelly's music shop on Dublin's Capel Street offered a warm welcome to musicians from the 1940s onwards and he was a key mover in many of the developments which followed. His family was highly musical, both his mother and an uncle were fine concertina players and John took up the instrument at the age of seven moving on to the fiddle a few years later. Taught by Patsy Geary, a travelling fiddler from Tipperary, John retained his teacher's simple approach while adding to his repertoire through his appreciation of other styles (notably, Sligo, Donegal and Scots). Kelly was a founder of **Ceoltóirí Chualann**, a member of the **Castle Céilí Band**, a regular performer at the Pipers', Church Street and Tradition clubs and for twenty years played with fellow Clare-exile and fiddler, **Joe Ryan**, in O'Donoghue's and the Four Seasons. Sadly, both his only solo album and others in which his playing features (such as **Seoda Cheoil**) have long been deleted, though he can be heard on both fiddle and concertina on the **Folk Music and Dances of Ireland** CD (see p.43). When he wasn't holding court in his shop or the Four Seasons pub next door, or helping to form CCÉ, Kelly still found time to collect 78s and tour the country taping musicians with one of the first portable recorders in Ireland.

Kelly's wife Frances was an expert accordionist and their children all played the fiddle. His sons **James** and **John,** the best known of his offspring, both inherited their father's style and recorded together on **Irish Traditional Fiddle Music** (1982). While John junior featured in **Bakerswell**, James is known for his roles in **Bowhand** (with Dáithí Sproule and Paddy "Offaly" O'Brien) and **Kinvara** (with Jackie Daly,

Dolores Keane and John Faulkner) and has also played with The Chieftains, Planxty and Patrick Street. His often skittishly playful style is best heard on **The Ring Sessions** (1995) recorded with Appalachian guitarist Zan McLeod. James is one of music's wittiest fiddlers – listen to the perkiness of the Cape Breton strathspey "Molly's Graduation" for evidence. His own innovative compositions include the "Mad Jig Set" which features another strathspey evolved via key changes to "The Dublin Reel", and "The Christchurch", a tune commemorating a regular visitor to the Kelly household, piper Johnny Doran.

⊙ **The Ring Sessions**   Fætain, 1995

Exquisite fiddle and guitar from James Kelly and Zan McLeod, plus some great skin-work from Johnny McDonagh.

Paddy Killoran

Paddy Killoran, the youngest member of the great triumvirate of Co. Sligo fiddlers, was born in Ballymote in 1904. Though the area is renowned for its fiddle and flute music, the Killorans were more musical than most. Paddy's father played the flute, his mother the concertina and all of his six brothers and sisters were accomplished musicians too. While influences on Paddy's own fiddling style were many, Lad O'Beirne's father, Phillip, is reckoned to have had a particular significance. Paddy arrived in the US in 1925, working first as an elevator operator and later running a bar in the Bronx. At a time when a decent musician could make a living playing Irish bars and dance halls and broadcasting on one of the many radio shows, a skilled fiddler, like Paddy, had no problem making a name for himself. He played in **The Pride of Erin Orchestra**, New York's most popular

Irish dance band, and also made regular recordings throughout the 1930s.

Oddly, unlike his illustrious elders, Coleman and Morrison, Paddy has been largely ignored by those involved in the remastering of 78s and a revival of his work is long overdue. Though a few sides do appear on collections such as **From Galway to Dublin** (see p.41), no single compilation of his own recordings exists bar the 1977 Shanachie LP **Back in Town**. Paddy recorded both as a duet, with fellow Sligo fiddler, **Paddy Sweeney**, as well as with a variety of accompanists, including Welsh guitarist Whitey Andrews and pianists Jim McGinn and Edmund Tucker. His playing, in which reels predominated, drew upon all the strengths required of a professional player for dances: so, in a reel such as "Roaring Mary", or a jig like "Geese in the Bog", the tempo is slightly quicker and there is substantially less ornamentation than you might hear on a Coleman recording. Paddy rarely rolled but he was fond of triplets – often slightly extending a note which was then curtailed by a subsequent triplet. Nevertheless, while grace notes might have been less prominent, there was both bounce and cunning in Killoran's playing and many of the tunes he recorded remain favourites to this day, many years after his death in 1965.

⊙ Paddy Killoran's Back in Town   Shanachie, 1930s

Classic dance music recorded by a master fiddler at the peak of his powers.

Brendan Larrissey

Brendan Larrissey learnt his earliest music as a child in his native Dundalk, starting on whistle at seven before plumping for the fiddle four years later. Competitions and sessions followed in his teens and his crowning achievement came with victory in the senior fiddle championship at the 1987 Listowel Fleadh Cheoil. A short stint with Dolores Keane and John Faulkner followed before he joined **Arcady**, subsequently touring widely with the band and featuring on both its albums. As most of Arcady lived in Galway, Brendan relocated to the county and has been based there ever since, playing and teaching. His auspicious debut, **A Flick of the Wrist** (1995), was followed by the even better **Up the Moy Road** which derived its title from his own address. Accompanied by old friend and neighbour, Mike Considine on bouzouki, Brendan's mellow but clearly articulated fiddle playing swoops across a range of dance tunes including a couple written for his daughters, the polka "Nessa the Mover" and the reel "Hat for Hannah". Slow airs usually separate the soarers from the scrapers, and Brendan places himself firmly in the first camp with the elegaic "Sliabh na mBan". Brendan also plays for the band **Callino**, along with piper Mick O'Brien and singer Niamh de Burca.

⊙ **Up the Moy Road**   own label, 2000

Committed and adept playing from Larrisey well supported by Mike Considine.

The Lennons

The **Lennon** family hails from Kiltyclogher in the northern lakeland of Co. Leitrim, an area famous for its fiddlers. **Ben Lennon** (b. 1928) is the eldest of four sons born to parents, Jim and Sally (née McGriskin). While his mother was a pianist who also sang, his father played fiddle (albeit with a limited repertoire) and was a tailor by trade. Ben himself first learned to play on a fiddle which had only three strings, acquiring a repertoire from the many musicians who would visit the household, both from Leitrim and from neighbouring Co. Fermanagh. In 1949, he moved to London to study the clothing trade but in his five-year sojourn, during which he met and married his wife, Patsy, he did not play at all. Returning to Ireland, the couple settled in Limerick but it was another ten years before Ben began to pick up the threads of his fiddling. Rediscovering his abilities from scratch, thanks in part to a developing friendship with fellow fiddler Séamus Connolly (who shared Ben's admiration for Michael Coleman), Ben began to play regularly again. In the mid-1960s, the family moved to Cork, at a time of one of the city's peak periods of traditional music. Ben formed a group called **Shaskeen** (not connected with the later band of the same name) with **Jackie Daly**, **Charlie Piggott** and **Gary Cronin** which made several TV broadcasts. He continued to session wherever he could before another move in 1972 took him to Rossinver, Co. Donegal, a mere four miles from Kiltyclogher. He has remained there ever since, while continuing to play sessions and venturing forth to annual events such as Willie Week (see p.573).

Ben's fiddle style has been described as "sweet, but irresistibly driving" and, to him, music must have that indefinable something which he calls the "nya". This first bore fruit for a wider audience on an album he recorded with younger brother **Charlie** in 1979, called **Lucky in Love**. Ten years later **Dog Big Dog Little** proved to be an even more treasured record. Named after two hills lying between Kiltyclogher and Derrygonnelly (in Co. Fermanagh), this was a spirited cross-border confection which neatly blended the closely-related styles of the two counties. The album featured Ben with fiddler, accordionist and pianist **Séamus Quinn** from Derrygonnelly along with concertina player and singer, **Gabriel McArdle**, and Altan's **Ciarán Curran** on cittern, both from Kinawley, Co. Fermanagh.

Containing some fine dance music from the region, not least "Mrs. Devlin's Polkas", from Fermanagh, the album was spiced by McArdle's luscious delivery of songs from the broader Fermanagh tradition and beyond. A gap of ten years ensued before Ben recorded under his own name again with **The Natural Bridge**, the bridge in question being that over the Kilcoo river linking Leitrim and Fermanagh. Their shared tradition produces a bouyant and infectious brand of music which, for added authenticity, was recorded live in Meehan's Cosy Corner Bar, Kiltyclogher. Ben's intricate fingering is best heard on the hornpipes "Maguire's Fiddle/O'Donnell's", associated with Killoran, but there's equally fine flute and viola-playing respectively from sons Brian and Maurice and brother Charlie on violin and piano, while once again the Fermanagh element was provided by friends Curran, Quinn and McArdle.

Brian Lennon began playing the flute at fourteen and has appeared on a number of albums, including the **Ceol Tigh Neachtain** Galway compilation and The Lennon Family's own excellent **Dúchas Cheoil** release from 1995. Nowadays, he is a doctor in Mayo, while brother **Maurice** embarked on a professional musical career after becoming the then youngest winner of the All-Ireland Senior Fiddle title in 1977. He appeared on Aengus's self-titled album the following year by which time he had already helped to form **Stockton's Wing**, remaining with the band for twenty years. After that he spent a year with the **Dublin City Ramblers** before applying his notable compositional skills to the creation of a conceptual album based on the Brian Ború legends (due for release at the time of writing). An offshoot from this project is the band **Kincora** which also features piper Mick O'Brien.

Yet another expert fiddler, Ben's youngest brother **Charlie** (b. 1938) is widely regarded as the most accomplished piano accompanist of his generation and, more recently, as a composer of innovative orchestral pieces. Charlie started learning both classical piano and traditional fiddle (the latter from Ben) at the age of seven and began his musical career aged twelve, playing in a local dance band, and going on to feature in a number of céilí bands, including five years touring professionally. For most of the 1960s he was based in Liverpool where he studied physics at the University (eventually attaining a PhD) while playing in the celebrated **Liverpool Céilí Band.** He also recorded a couple of albums, won two All-Ireland titles and played major concerts both sides of the Atlantic. In 1966 Charlie married sean-nós singer **Síle Ní Fhlaithearta** and the couple moved back to Ireland three years later basing themselves in Dublin until Charlie's retirement in 1998. At that point they returned to Síle's hometown of Spiddal, Co. Galway, and established a new recording studio, Cuan. Charlie's list of recording credits include Joe Burke, Séamus Tansey, Frankie Gavin, Liam O'Flynn, Steve Cooney and the celebrated **Banks of the Shannon** with Paddy O'Brien and Séamus O'Connor. A prolific composer of traditional-style tunes, some of which are included in his collection *Musical Memories*, he featured on The Waterboys' **Fisherman's Blues**, where he insinuated his own tune "River Road Reel" into the track "When Ye Go Away". However, Charlie is equally well-known for his orchestral compositions, which include **The Emigrant Suite** (1985) and **Flight from a Hungry Land** (1995). The most renowned is **Island Wedding** (1992) portraying life on the Aran Island of Inisheer and blending original traditional-style compositions with orchestral pieces performed by the RTÉ Concert Orchestra. More recently, Charlie has issued his first solo fiddle album since the 1970s, **Time for a Tune** (2000) which features some sparkling interaction with melodeon player Johnny Connolly amongst a host of guests, including his daughter Éilis.

| ⊙ The Natural Bridge | Cló Iar-Chonnachta, 1999 |

Linger a while in Co. Leitrim with this effervescent brew from Ben Lennon and friends.

| ⊙ Island Wedding | RTÉ, 1992 |

The most accomplished of Charlie Lennon's orchestral recordings, equally evocative and inventive.

Séan Maguire

As musical birthplaces go, Co. Cavan may lack the instant kudos of Clare, Kerry or Sligo, but it nonetheless boasts its own distinctive tradition of fiddle playing, in particular, clear elements of which can be heard in the playing of **Séan Maguire**, one of Ireland's most individual and immediately distinctive traditional stylists. Though he was actually born in Belfast, in 1927, his first musical influence was that of his father, Johnnie, a Cavan man from Mullahoran, who played fiddle, concert flute, piccolo and whistle, and had himself been strongly influenced by one of the county's best-known musicians of the time, fiddler James McInerney. The Cavan hallmarks of clean, crisp, strongly accented rhythm, liberal use of bow-length and a penchant for tricksy tunes are as much foundation-stones of Maguire's playing as the rock-solid timing honed by years of playing in céilí bands, even if these more prosaic aspects tend to be overshadowed by his more pyrotechnic attributes. His two other early teachers were Professor George Vincent, to whom he attributes his fingering method, and "Madame" May Nesbitt, a rigorous disciplinarian in the matter of bowing technique, backed up by an extensive armoury of exercises.

As a traditional player, Maguire performed on BBC Overseas Radio aged fifteen and won the Oireachtas gold medal at 22. This grounding in both traditional and classical music, combined with the frequent exposure to Scottish music that came of growing up in Belfast, provided the ingredients for a style Maguire himself has labelled "progressive traditional", and that has caused many others to label him, in turn, "the Stephane Grappelli of Irish music". As the latter suggests, there's a substantial and gleefully extravagant improvisational dimension to Maguire's playing, too, though how much is down to his own rococo imagination and how much to the jazz he must have encountered on his tours of America from the 1950s on, is hard to discern. These further reaches of his style – also drawing on a level of classical prowess that saw him joining the ultraselect list of those invited to play the Stradivarius and Guarnerius violins held in trust by Wurlitzers of New York – have led some to question whether he can in fact be regarded as a traditional player. The testimony of many a satisfied céilí dancer, together with the long-time endorsement of such traditional icons as accordionist **Joe Burke**, with whom Maguire toured extensively in the UK and released a superb duo album, **Two Champions** (1971), would argue otherwise, however; his fiddling is surely best regarded as a genuine and marvellously fertile fusion of disparate elements. Highlights of a long and illustrious career include his concert at Carnegie Hall in 1952, followed by appearances on the Ed Sullivan and Arthur Godfrey shows, the 1987 Fiddlers' Green Hall of Fame Award, and a Lifetime Achievement Award from Comhaltas Ceoltóirí Éireann. His 1990 album **Portráid**, made with guitarists Steve Cooney and Pat Conroy, and Shetland pianist Eileen Hunter, marked his return to the studio after a long period of illness; seven years later his 70th birthday concert in Dublin's National Concert Hall, featured various friends and admirers including Joe and Anne Conroy Burke, Frankie Gavin and piper Ronan Browne.

⊙ **Portráid** Celtic Music, 1990

Maguire's mature style in all its glory, from gypsy-jazz style hornpipes to his capricious rendition of the "Boys of the Lough".

Andy McGann

Though himself born in New York (in 1928), **Andy McGann**'s parents both came from Co. Sligo. Neither was musical, so when the seven-year-old Andy began showing an interest in the fiddle, they had to find a teacher. **Michael Coleman** was a family friend, but not fond of teaching beginners, so Andy first began lessons with Katherine Brennan, one of the master's own pupils. She was also studying classical violin, which may explain how Andy's characteristically Sligo style of playing is sometime coloured by the use of vibrato. He learned much too from Coleman's regular visits and from attending an informal club in the 1940s where another great Irish-American fiddler **Lad O'Beirne** regularly played, though Andy was also developing as an excellent solo and team dancer.

By the 1950s, McGann was playing regularly at weddings and céilís, for dancers and on TV and later also joined **The New York Céilí Band** which contained some of the best Irish musicians in the city. Together with the pianist **Felix Dolan**, and the accordionist **Joe Burke** Andy recorded the album **A Tribute to Michael Coleman** (1966), a classic homage which brought fame to all three musicians. He also frequently worked with fiddler **Paddy Reynolds** and recorded his first album with him in 1977. His own solo album, **It's a Hard Road to Travel**, followed two years later with Paul Brady on guitar. Its impact remains undiminished today as Andy, a reticent man, lets his fiddle not so much talk as give an aural lecture on Coleman's legacy. His tone is always sweet, especially on the Coleman reel "Paddy on the Turnpike", which leads into "A Hard Road to Travel", one of the few Irish tunes in the key of C. Touches of light vibrato and slides up to – and sometimes beyond – the note give some of the tunes a melancholic air which belies the overall joyfulness of his playing and the album ends on laughter when he almost indetectably blows the closing bars of "The Millstone".

⊙ **It's a Hard Road to Travel** Shanachie, 1979

The spirit of the great Sligo fiddlers lives on in McGann's stylish playing.

Manus and Séamus McGuire

The twin fiddles of brothers **Manus** and **Séamus McGuire** have been among the most influential in modern Ireland. While each has a firm grasp of his traditional roots, inheriting the native Sligo style from their father, Paddy, the McGuires developed a natural rapport from years of playing together and share an affinity for the fiddle music of other countries (not least Canada where they spent some time at the end of the 1970s). Mainstays of the band **Buttons and Bows**, the brothers recorded their own **Carousel** album, supported by guitarist Dáithí Sproule, in 1985. Drawing from the fiddle music of Scotland, Scandinavia and French-Canada, the pair generate a truly magical musical dialogue. Manus relocated to East Clare that same year, becoming a founder member of **Moving Cloud** and also featuring on Paul Brock's **Mo Chairdín** album, before releasing his own solo album, **Saffron and Blue** (2000). Despite taking its title from his adopted county's colours, this is an eclectic album drawing heavily on Manus's own compositions and a strong component of Scots musicians and tunes. More to the point, it's also exceptional fun!

Meanwhile, Séamus has produced two contrasting albums, **The Missing Reel** (1990) and **The Wishing Tree** (1994). The former is a delightful collaboration with South Leitrim flute player **John Lee**, drawing substantially from John's collection of music from the Aughavas and Cloone area. Many of the tunes, such as the reel "Old Mickey McKernan's" or the jig from John's father "Peter Lee's", had not been recorded before and the playing throughout neatly combines Lee's typically lively flute with McGuire's exuberant fiddle. True to form, Séamus sneaks in a grand Swedish wedding dance and a Scottish air. **The Wishing Tree** shares the title of a Séamus Heaney poem and features McGuire's own compositions which, sadly, wander dangerously close to ambient mood music for comfort, though, as ever his playing is elegant and the support impeccable.

⊙ Carousel   Gael-Linn, 1985

Fabulous interplay by the McGuires with ever-sensitive support from Dáithí Sproule.

⊙ The Missing Reel   Gael-Linn, 1990

Séamus McGuire and John Lee provide a vivid demonstration of the delicious sound of South Leitrim.

Jim McKillop

As a relative latecomer to traditional music, fiddler **Jim McKillop** (b. 1946 in Cushendall in the Glens of Antrim) is somewhat of a rarity. Though his father played the banjo and was a noted mouth-whistler, McKillop's interest in traditional music wasn't fully awakened until his twenties when he was working as a ship's engineer and heard notable players such as **Seán Maguire** on the radio. Inspired to learn the fiddle, he discovered previously untapped abilities and progressed so rapidly that within four years he had won the All-Ireland Senior Championship. While his interest in the fiddle expanded to the extent that he is now one of Ireland's best-known instrument makers and repairers, his own musical talents have been recorded infrequently. Elements of Maguire's flamboyant style are echoed in McKillop's playing on **Irish Traditional Music** (accompanied by the redoubtable **Josephine Keegan** on piano) and his expressive warmth does much to overcome the generally poor quality of the recording. More recently, on **To Hell With the Begrudgers** – playing one of his own fiddles, alongside flute-player Séamus Tansey – he shows that he is equally at home on Antrim versions of jigs (such as "Frieze Britches") and slower pieces such as the Carolan air "Blind Mary".

⊙ **To Hell with the Begrudgers**   Sound Records, 1998

Jim likes audiences to listen to his music (rather than chat over it) and his immaculate fiddling should leave listeners speechless

James Morrison

The names of Michael Coleman and **James Morrison** (1893–1947) dominate any account of the extraordinary impact of the South Sligo style of fiddling on traditional music in the first half of the twentieth century. Their recordings left an indelible stamp, yet Morrison's reputation has always trailed in the wake of his more famous contemporary. Since the 1980s, however, a resurgence of interest has occurred; thanks in part to musicians such as Frankie Gavin and Charlie Lennon. His music is now commemorated by an annual festival in Riverstown (see p.574), and Morrison's devotees are still growing in numbers.

Born in the townland of Drumfin, near Riverstown, the second youngest of eleven children, Jim's maternal uncle, Charlie Dolan, was the local dancing master and it was while taking lessons at Charlie's house that he first met another young pupil, Michael Coleman from Killavil. Jim's musical potential was recognized by a local priest, Father Creehan, who taught him and his brothers to read and write music. Having already revealed his ability on his brother

2 CASSETTES   Recorded 1921-1936

JAMES MORRISON &THE& PROFESSOR

Tom's flute, he was given his first fiddle by his parents at thirteen. Four years later, Father Creehan, now an official in The Gaelic League, encouraged Jim to become involved in the League's new Irish language college at Tourmakeady and its 1911 prospectus duly lists one "Séamus Morrison of Drumfin, who teaches the best tradition of Irish dancing". Like his Uncle Charlie, Jim now became a full-time dancing master, advertising lessons in Sligo town as "Professor Morrison" while also learning Irish. This resulted in his employment by The Gaelic League as a travelling teacher in both language and dancing, based in Manorhamilton, Co. Leitrim. He held this position for two years, while regularly cycling over the mountains to spend weekends playing with the fiddler and flute player John Joe Gardiner of Corhubber at whose house he met Teresa Flynn – his future wife.

While living in Manorhamilton he gave his first public performance in 1913 and two years later won the senior fiddle competition at the Sligo Feis Cheoil. The prize of ten shillings helped pay his fare to the US and later that year he sailed for Boston where five of his siblings already lived; two of whom, Tom and John, ran their own band. However, with Teresa's arrival in New York in 1918, Jim moved to be near her, making an immediate musical impact by winning the city's Feis. The two were married in 1919 and Jim had a variety of day jobs while doing the usual round of Irish bars, dance halls and radio shows and giving fiddle lessons in his spare time. His recording career began in 1921 and continued until 1936, producing a total of eighty-four sides, including some of the most influential releases in the history of traditional music. He recorded solo and in a variety of combinations, including duets with the Chicago-born uilleann piper **Tom Ennis**, accordionists **Tom Carmody** from Kerry and **P.J. Conlon** from Galway and with the Leitrim flute player **John McKenna** with whom he duetted on tin whistle – the only occasion when he was recorded without his fiddle. He also played professionally, including as a notable duo with one of his pupils, co-fiddler, **Paddy Killoran**, but it was **The James Morrison Band**, a quartet formed in 1929 with Tom Carmody, that cemented his fame. Despite the Wall Street Crash of that year, Morrison continued to record, the breadth of the Band's repertoire illustrating that Jim was in touch with the times and capable of playing any form of dance music. Strangely, despite their proximity and shared background, Morrison and Coleman never recorded together, though they are known to have played together privately.

Jim's career reached its peak at the same time as his marriage hit the rocks, he and Teresa (now mother to five children) separating in the mid-1930s. He carried on teaching music while, at the same time, taking various state examinations just, it seems, out of interest, for he never took up any of the employment his success might have secured. However, news of his academic achievements brought other students to his door seeking assistance and led to the revival of his old assumed title, "The Professor". He continued to make occasional public appearances, but derived most of his income from teaching, though increasing alcohol dependency meant that he would sometimes disappear. The resulting debilitation eventually led to his death in 1947 and, in one final twist of fate, he was buried in the same cemetery as Coleman, St. Raymond's in The Bronx.

The sheer exuberance of Morrison's glorious, driving and always tasteful fiddle style, with its masterful floating bow, is demonstrated on three impressive selections from his recordings. The first of these, **The Pure Genius of James Morrison**, appeared in 1978 and includes his classic versions of "The Tailor's Thimble" reel and the intricately bowed hornpipe, "Flowers of Ballymote". Some solo recordings and others made with Tom Ennis are compiled on **James Morrison and Tom Ennis**, released in 1983, including their renditions of "New Steamboat" and "The Bucks of Oranmore". Undoubtedly, however, the finest selection is Viva Voce's **The Professor**, two cassettes covering some thirty of his recordings, superbly remastered by Harry Bradshaw who also supplies an exemplary biographical account of Morrison's life and music. Not only does this span his entire musical career, but equally demonstrates the extensive range of Morrison's material, from reels, jigs and hornpipes via waltzes and two-steps to the strange "descriptive" travelogue, "Rambles Through Ireland", from which Morrison later dissociated himself. Unfortunately, no CDs of Morrison have yet appeared.

📼 **The Professor**   Viva Voce, 1921–1936

This double cassette is an indispensable record of one of traditional music's greatest fiddlers.

Martin and Brendan Mulvihill

There's many an Irish-American fiddler who owes their success to the late West Limerick man **Martin Mulvihill** (b.1919 in Ballygoughlin) who arrived in the US in 1965 after a long stint in England. He established his own School of Irish Music in New York in 1970 and many pupils subsequently crossed the Atlantic to compete successfully in competitions. Apart from his *First Collection of Traditional Irish Music*, containing 513 tunes and published in 1986, he also recorded one LP, **Traditional Irish Fiddling from County Limerick**, accompanied by Mick Moloney. It's a first-rate collection, characterized by the slightly mournful tone of Martin's fiddle, best heard on "Limerick is Beautiful" (an alternative title for "Dawning of the Day", the air more commonly known as the setting for "Raglan Road").

One of Martin's most assiduous pupils was his son **Brendan** (born in Northampton, England) who inherited his father's sound, combining it with a technical expertise that is second to none. For evidence, listen to the CD he recorded in 1992 with Cherish the Ladies' future pianist **Donna Long**, **The Morning Dew**. The pair had been duetting for ten years by the time of this release and, whether together on an exuberant quartet of jigs (often played by Martin) or on several homages to Carolan, they reveal an understanding so close as to be symbiotic.

🎵 Traditional Irish Fiddling from County Limerick   Green Linnet, 1978

In partnership with Mick Moloney, the acclaimed teacher proves he was a substantial fiddler in his own right.

⊙ **The Morning Dew**   Green Linnet, 1992

Superb fiddling by Brendan with exemplary piano accompaniment
from Donna Long.

Connie O'Connell

The Sliabh Luachra area lies to the northwest of Cill na Martra in the
Múscraí Gaeltacht, Co. Cork, where the well-known fiddler
Connie O'Connell was born. Múscraí (Muskerry) has its own strong traditions – Connie's mother played the melodeon at house dances – but
Sliabh Luachra's music has proved to be an enduring influence. Now a
member of the traditional music teaching staff at the Music Department
of University College Cork, Connie has frequently performed on radio
and TV since the 1970s and his stylish fiddle can be heard on **Ceol Cill
na Martra – Music from Cill na Martra** along with his daughter **Áine Ní
Chonaill** (fiddle), **Eibhlín de Paor** (flute) and an array of quality backing
musicians. Highlights are the almost lazy intricacy which Connie
employs on the reels "Dan Cronin's/Fire in Clann Rátha" followed
instantly by a couple of bouncy slides, "Follow Me Down to
Carlow/Padraig O'Keeffe's" – the former learned from Johnny O'Leary.

⊙ **Ceol Cill na Martra**   Shanachie, 2000

Immaculate playing of slides and slip jigs and a wonderfully
evocative slow air, "The Cill na Martra Exile".

Danny O'Donnell

The celebrated Donegal fiddler, **Danny O'Donnell**, is one of the
last-remaining connections to a bygone age. Born in 1910 in

Meenbannad in the Upper Rosses, he began playing in his teens, being particularly influenced in his development by his uncle, Jimmy Doherty from Cruit Island – now a host of holiday cottages, but in those days a hotbed of dancing and music. Like his idol and friend the great Rosses fiddler, Neillidh Boyle, Danny recorded 78s in the 1930s but did not record again until **The Donegal Fiddler** LP appeared in 1973. By this time Danny was living in Ballybofey, after long spells in the US and Scotland, and was spending much of his time with the legendary John Doherty. After the latter's death in 1979, Danny rarely played in public, but he was cajoled out of retirement at the age of 87 to record for Raidió na Gaeltachta and the results can be heard on the stunning **Ón tSean-Am Anall**. All his accumulated knowledge is packed into these marvellous tunes, which are played with his customary precise, though relaxed style, featuring his characteristic "slurred triplets", as on the marvelous reel "Seán sa Cheo".

⊙ **Ón tSean-Am Anall**   Raidió na Gaeltachta, 2000

Glorious, carefree fiddling and a fitting tribute to a seminal figure in the history of Co. Donegal's music.

Máire O'Keeffe

Tralee-born **Máire O'Keeffe**'s first major musical influence was the Castleisland fiddler Nicky McAuliffe, but after moving to Dublin in the late 1970s her interests expanded to encompass Donegal, Scots and Shetland styles. Later she was to develop an interest in Cape Breton's music and her only solo album to date, **Cóisir/House Party** (1994) was recorded in a private house on the island. Much of the release features a trio consisting of Máire, pianist Ryan MacNeill and Paul MacDonald on guitar, with additional assistance from her sister **Siobhán** on flute, the great fiddle master **Jerry Holland** and Cape Breton's most well-known harmonica player, **Tommy Basker**. Máire's playing is always crisp, exuberant and infectious and tunes are drawn not just from the island's heritage, but include sources as various as John Doherty, Charlie Lennon and her illustrious namesake Pádraig. More recently Máire's playing featured on **The County Bounds** (see p.349) including a duet with Jackie Daly that makes essential listening.

⊙ **Cóisir**   Gael-Linn, 1994

An Irish-Cape Breton hybrid draws life from both traditions.

Pádraig O'Keeffe and the Music of Sliabh Luachra

One of the most distinctive styles of traditional Irish music emanates from the area on the borders of Cork, Kerry and Limerick associated with Sliabh Luachra, "the rushy mountain". The fiddle and the accordion are the ruling instruments of the Sliabh Luachra style and, despite a strong literary tradition, it is unusual in having virtually no songs of local origin. Dance music reigns in Sliabh Luachra and rarer forms too, such as the slide and the polka which are often played by duetting fiddlers, one of whom might "bass" the melody by playing in a lower octave.

The central figure in the music's development during the twentieth century was **Pádraig O'Keeffe** (1887–1963), sometimes known as "The Last of the Fiddle Masters", from Gleanntán, near Castleisland. After a brief career as a schoolteacher, Pádraig became an itinerant music tutor, employing his own alternative means of notation using the numbers 0 to 4 to represent the left-hand's fingers and the four spaces in between the lines to symbolize the appropriate string. He was a massive retainer of melodies, reckoned to have learned all 1001 in O'Neill's collection. Despite the popularity of dancing, Pádraig preferred what he termed "listening music" a concept he instilled in his pupils. Indeed, he was sometimes known to break a string deliberately when tiring of playing for dancers. Pádraig roved the lanes between the houses of his pupils for more than 40 years, bequeathing both a legend and a legacy. He was not recorded until he was almost 60 and the only available release consisting entirely of his own playing, **The Sliabh Luachra Fiddle Master** dates from 1949. Though there are plenty of the dance tunes, including the definitive slide "The Gleanntán Frolics", Pádraig's playing on the slow airs is astonishingly emotive, in particular "The Old Man Rocking the Cradle" a piece he used to play with a large metal door key in his mouth, using it to mute the fiddle and imitate a baby's cries!

Pádraig's best-known pupils were the sister and brother **Julia Clifford** (1914–97) and **Denis Murphy** (1910–74) from Lisheen, Gneeveguilla, Co. Kerry. All three can be heard on the excellent **Kerry Fiddles**, recorded for the BBC in 1952 by Séamus Ennis in Charlie Horan's Bar, Castleisland while the siblings appear alone on the equally classic **The Star Above the Garter**. Julia married piano accordionist **John Clifford** and spent much of her long life in London, recording several LPs for Topic and playing pub residencies and dance halls as **The Star of Munster Trio** with son **Billy** on flute. Despite distance, the family retained contact with Kerry, and Julia's influence on local playing remained strong and she became a role model for generations of women fiddlers.

Like his sister, **Denis Murphy** spent part of his life out of the country, emigrating to America with his wife (also called Julia) in 1949 and spending ten years there in three separate spells before returning for good in 1965. While in New York he played in sessions with many of the great fiddlers (including Lad O'Beirne, Paddy Killoran, Andy McGann) and recorded both solo and with the **Ballinamore Céilí Band**. Back in Lisheen he became close friends with Seán Ó Riada (who made a film about him) and once memorably took time off from the Sunday session at Dan O'Connell's pub in Knocknagree to go on a week-long journey through Ireland with Séamus Ennis, Johnny Cronin and the poet Dylan Thomas. His talents can also be heard on **Music from Sliabh Luachra**, recorded at various sessions between 1948 and 1969, which includes duets with O'Keeffe, McGann and accordionist **Johnny O'Leary** (with whom Denis played for 37 years) and as a trio with his sister Julia plus **Séamus Ennis** on pipes.

Other notable Sliabh Luachra fiddlers include the aforementioned **Johnny Cronin** and his brother **Paddy** also from Gneevguilla, Co.

DENIS MURPHY

Music from Sliabh Luachra

Kerry, both of whom emigrated to the US in the 1940s. Johnny recorded an album **Cronin and Burke** with the banjo player **Joe Burke** for Shanachie in 1978, while Paddy had been earlier recorded by the BBC and released **Music in the Glen** in the 1950s and **Rakish Paddy** (1975). Both appear on **My Love is in America** (see p.276).

The modern Sliabh Luachra tradition has been maintained by local musicians, such as fiddler **Noeleen O'Connor** and her brother, accordionist, **Paudie**, while others from outside the area, like Matt Cranitch, Séamus Creagh, Johnny McCarthy, Máire O'Keeffe and Gerry Harrington have all taken to the music as their own.

⊙ **The Sliabh Luachra Fiddle Master**   RTÉ, 1949

Utterly essential recordings of Pádraig O'Keeffe, one of Ireland's most influential and impassioned fiddlers.

⊙ **Kerry Fiddles**   Ossian Publications, 1952

O'Keeffe joined forces with Julia Clifford and Denis Murphy for a superb demonstration of fiddling expertise.

⊙ **The County Bounds**   Ossian Publications, 1999

A stunning album of modern musicians from Sliabh Luachra, neighbouring Mhúscraí and their friends.

Peadar O'Loughlin

A major presence in the music of his native Co. Clare for more than half a century, **Peadar** (sometimes Peter) **O'Loughlin** (b. 1929) hails from the Cullen townland, near Kilmaley. Peadar's status in traditional music is due in part to his appearance on the near legendary 1959 **All-Ireland Champions** LP he recorded with fellow fiddlers (and long-time friends), Paddy Canny and P.J. Hayes and pianist Bridie Lafferty. Before this he had developed a significant reputation playing with the **Fiach Rua Céilí Band** and as a duo with concertina player **Paddy Murphy**. Peadar also often played in Touhey's Bar, Ennis, with another great friend, the accordionist, **Joe Cooley**, most notably at Cooley's American Wake in 1954. His own earliest influence was his father, who played concertina, fiddle and flute – passing his gifts on the latter two instruments onto his son. Peadar was also introduced to the uilleann pipes by Seán Reid, leader of the **Tulla Céilí Band** (with whom Peadar also played), who later gave him a set as a wedding present. Peadar's only subsequent album release is the sumptuous **South West Wind** with piper **Ronan Browne** (see p.398 for review), though he continues to play regularly with his long-time friend **Paddy Canny** and is a popular teacher at the Willie Clancy summer school.

Paul O'Shaughnessy

One of the most welcome releases of 1999 was **Stay Another While** by fiddler **Paul O'Shaughnessy** and **Frankie Lane**. Though the latter provides adept accompaniment (on guitar, dobro, mandolin and bass) and co-produced the album, it's effectively a long overdue debut from the former **Altan** fiddler O'Shaughnessy. Born in Dublin's Northside, Paul learned his earliest music from his mother, **Pearl McBride** (herself a fine fiddler and a former member of Macalla), and took lessons from Cavan fiddler Antóin Mac Gabhain, while the Sligo flute player John Egan was another formative influence. Paul began visiting Donegal in his late teens, learning from and playing with fiddle masters such as Con Cassidy and James Byrne and hearing John Doherty in Carrick's Cellar Bar. Paul acquired a "natural" Donegal edge to his playing which led to his membership of Altan and appearance on three of the group's albums. Since then he has worked regularly with flute-player **Paul McGrattan**, recording **Within a Mile of Dublin** (1995) before both joined **Beginish**. There's a vibrant dash to Paul's playing on **Stay Another While** (reminiscent of the young Tommy Peoples), and though he's certainly one of the loudest fiddlers around, there's no lack of subtlety as he demonstrates on the intricate swing of "Low Highland" and elsewhere on tunes learned from Francie Dearg Ó Beirne and Frankie Kennedy.

⊙ **Stay Another While**   own label, 1999

It's been a long time coming, but the wait proved worthwhile!

Tommy Peoples

Unquestionably, the most influential Irish fiddler of the last fifty years, **Tommy Peoples** is a master magician, his music a startling combination of brilliant technique, improbable invention and true soul. Born in 1948 into a noted musical family based around the village of St. Johnston, Co. Donegal, Tommy learnt his first tunes from his father Tom, before beginning to take formal lessons at the age of seven from his elder cousin, **Joe Cassidy**, himself an inspired fiddler. Joe passed on his own strict staccato bowing style and also taught Tommy to read music. His own experiences were broadened when he began to attend Comhaltas sessions in Letterkenny and came into contact with other young fiddlers, including Vincent Campbell and Frank Kelly. He began to experiment with his own bowing style, eventually developing his characteristically crisp way of playing triplets. After leaving school, Tommy headed for Dublin where he soon began to play in sessions and made contact with many other musicians, forming **The Green Linnet Céilí Band** (which also included whistler Mary Bergin) and making his first professional appearances with **Matt Molloy** as the warm-up artists before the then popular ballad groups took the stage. After a short spell in the Gardaí, which took him via Bray to Limerick, in 1969 Tommy married Marie Linnane, daughter of Kitty, leader of the **Kilfenora Ceili Band**, with whom he was later to play.

After a start with the short-lived **1691** band, Tommy replaced Paddy Glackin in the hugely influential **Bothy Band**, taking his music to an ever-growing audience with albums such as **1975**. He remained with the band for a year before leaving in 1976 to resume a solo

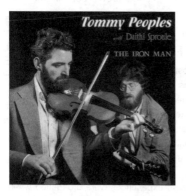

career which encompassed some of the most glorious recordings of traditional music ever caught on tape (see below). However, increasing dissatisfaction with the music industry saw him turn his back on the hectic world of tours and recording and for much of the last twenty-five years Tommy has been content to remain at home in Clare (though he moved back to Donegal in 2000), playing sessions with musicians of the calibre of **Davy Spillane** and **Seán Tyrrell**. Though the urgency of his younger playing style may have mellowed, it has been more than adequately compensated by the inventive melodies of his own compositions and Tommy has proved himself a tremendous teacher, his most notable successes including his daughters **Siobhán** and **Gráinne** and his nephew, the Donegal fiddler, **Séamus Gibson**.

Though he's guested on many albums, Tommy's own discography is remarkably sparse for a performer of such stature. The earliest dated album available is 1976's **The High Part of the Road** recorded with **Paul Brady** on guitar. All of Tommy's peerless skill is encapsulated in "The Nine Points of Roguery" where his triplets are as crisp as a cracker. The following year saw the pair record **Molloy/Brady/Peoples** with the addition of Tommy's old Bothy Band chum **Matt Molloy**. Flute and fiddle intertwine with infinite charm to produce consummate renditions of reels like "Speed the Plough" while Brady's one song is the peerless "Shamrock Shore". A gap then ensued before Tommy's next album, **The Iron Man** (1985), with another fine guitarist, **Dáithí Sproule**, which, despite the title (actually a gentle strathspey) demonstrated an increasing tempering of tone. That album marked the end of Tommy's involvement with record companies and his increasing cult following had to endure thirteen barren years until **The Quiet Glen/An Gleann Ciúin** emerged on his own label in 1998. The opening notes of the very first track, "Jocelyn's Waltz", are instantly captivating and Tommy, conspiring with another ace guitar accompanist, **Alph Duggan**, goes on to produce an album with more majesty than the entire crowned heads of Europe. "Hector the Hero" is revived from his Bothy Band days with incomparable guile, "Kitty Come Down to Limerick" is pure authentic Peoples while his own compositions "The Mouse in the Attic/The Fat Cat" are just plain fun. Peoples completists should also be aware of other recordings from the 1970s. Sadly, his self-titled album for CCÉ has never re-emerged on CD, but Ovation has issued the undated **Master Irish Fiddler** which, despite sounding as though it was recorded in a gymnasium with an out-of-tune guitarist, is still tremendous.

⊙ **Molloy/Brady/Peoples**   Green Linnet, 1977

More superlatives, please!

⊙ **The Quiet Glen**   own label, 1998

Passionate, powerful and evocative, this glorious album is simply one of the best ever recorded.

Tommy Potts

Tommy Potts was one of the most significant figures in traditional Irish music and, more than a decade since his death in 1988, continues to generate unparalleled degrees of debate. To some, Potts was a mere "soul" fiddler who undermined the tradition's strengths through improvisation and by incorporating classical and jazz influences into his playing. However others, notably his great champion, **Mícheál Ó Súilleabháin** (who wrote his doctoral thesis on Potts), believe that the fiddler deliberately set himself on the periphery "by choosing the path of innovation". Tommy was born in Dublin in 1912, his father being **John Potts**, a notable uilleann piper and flute player from Co. Wexford to whom Breandán Breathnach dedicated the first volume of *Ceol Rince na hÉireann* (no fewer than 56 of its 214 dance tunes were collected from John and Tommy). The Potts household in The Coombe was a popular musical meeting place and Tommy, by his own account, began playing fiddle at the age of fifteen while admitting that, even then, he "was not satisfied fully with sheer precision and stereotyped settings". However, it was probably not until the 1950s that he really began to unleash his urge for innovation. Unlike Ó Riada, whose work with Ceoltóirí Chualann in the 1960s involved deliberate experimentation and restructuring, Potts's creations came from within himself, though often stimulated by others. His oft-quoted reference to "the hidden note" describes the way a musician may hear a tune and learn it before, in time, discarding it, having wearied of its repetition. Then comes a time when the player hears another musician play the same tune, but with a subtle altering of a note or two which suddenly suggests new possibilities to the listener's imagination.

Considering the tradition's implicit conservatism, it is not surprising that Potts only recorded one album, 1972's remarkable **The**

Liffey Banks. He did, however, also make a considerable number of home tapes, and, unusually, notated his music, which Ó Súilleabháin has used to analyse variations and developments in Tommy's playing. Few musicians were capable of playing along with Tommy Potts, simply because they couldn't keep up with his flights of fancy. Tommy's renditions are clearly rooted in their original sources, but evolve new directions through his imaginative powers. Listen to his version of the reel "Rakish Paddy", on which Potts adopts a variation he heard in one of Liszt's Hungarian Rhapsodies, or "My Love is in America", in Tommy's hands an epic of improvisation. Potts's influence could never be compared to, say, Michael Coleman, but elements of his style can be heard in the playing of many contemporary musicians, especially Martin Hayes and the flute player Niall Keegan.

⊙ **The Liffey Banks** - Claddagh, 1972

The definitive statement of the power of Tommy's imaginative response to the tradition.

Jimmy Power and the Irish in London

While the power of the tradition waned so dramatically in Ireland in the 1940s and '50s that some despaired for its survival, the focus of Irish music shifted to London. Many Irish men and women migrated to England's capital and other industrial cities (such as Birmingham, Coventry and Manchester), attracted by better work opportunities. Many came from Ireland's western counties to assist in London's postwar building boom or to work in the Midlands' car factories and in their evenings made music, initially with some difficulty.

As the Waterford-born fiddler, **Jimmy Power** once remarked, "In them days you'd be hit over the head with a bottle, if you tried to play a tune in a pub". Gradually, the pubs of Camden Town and nearby Kentish Town, such as The Black Cap or The Bedford Arms (where **Margaret Barry** and **Michael Gorman** held court) became the centre for music-making. In the 1950s, as more migrants arrived, the trend spread to other areas of London. In 1957 the Galtymore Ballroom opened in Cricklewood with its own resident céilí band, and in the same year the first London branch of CCÉ was established in Fulham. The list of those who lived (or spent lengthy visits) in London during these years is a staggering roll-call of traditional music greats. There were fiddlers like Bobby Casey, Danny Meehan, Martin Byrnes, Joe Ryan, Seán Maguire, Lucy Farr and Julia Clifford; flute players of the calibre of Paddy Taylor and Roger Sherlock; great accordionists such as John Clifford, Raymond Roland and John Bowe; the concertina maestro and piper Tommy McCarthy and even Willie Clancy was there for a spell. Céilí bands flourished, more ballrooms opened and the music continued to prosper in the 1960s.

Labels such as Topic and Leader were now amassing a huge archive of recordings and, though many musicians returned home, many married and settled in London with their families. From the late 1960s to the mid-1980s The Favourite, a pub at the bottom of Hornsey Road became the pre-eminent venue and it was here that **Jimmy Power** held court on Sunday lunchtimes with his trusty piano accompanist, **Reg Hall** and accordionist **Tony Ledwith**. Born in 1918 into a labouring family in Ballyduff, Co. Waterford. Jimmy was a virtually self-taught fiddler who acquired his early repertoire listening to Coleman, Gillespie and Killoran on records and the radio. Getting into some trouble in his teens, he was ordered to leave home by the parish priest and enlisted in the Royal Irish Fusiliers, playing pipes in its band. However, Jimmy and military life did not mix and he deserted on the eve of the regiment's departure for Malta, just prior to the outbreak of World War II. Fetching up in Glasgow, he met and wed Kathleen O'Connor, moving to London in 1947 and working in the building trade as a self-taught carpenter. He played in pubs and for

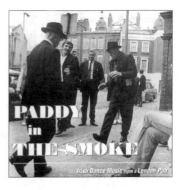

London County Council dance classes from the 1950s and, though never a fiddler of the quality of say Bobby Casey or Danny Meehan, became something of a cult figure thanks to his appearance at a major concert with The Dubliners and on the compilation album **Paddy in the Smoke**, recorded in The Favourite. The pub's proximity to the Underground made it easily accessible and many musicians passed through its doors and were invited onto its rudimentary stage. While licensing laws then decreed that closing time was 2pm, the music would continue until brought to an end by Jimmy's regular announcement "Now, go home to your dinners" or variants thereof. Jimmy died in 1985, the pub (where The Popes' banjo player Tommy MacManamon was raised) changed hands and things were never the same again. However, though the number of venues may have declined, great musicians such as Brian Rooney and John Carty continue to play and the hugely influential teacher Brendan Mulkere (who for a time ran his own Inchecronin label in the 1970s) has ensured that many have continued London's own tradition.

⊙ **Paddy in the Smoke** Topic, 1968

The Favourite's great days, featuring Jimmy Power, Con Curtin, Bobby Casey, Lucy Farr and many others.

⊙ **Martin Byrnes with Reg Hall** Leader, 1969

The effusive fiddler from Ballinasloe, Co. Galway, was a regular feature of the London scene.

▭ **Irish Fiddle Player** Ossian, 1976

Jimmy Power and Reg Hall on fine and evocative form.

Ed Reavy

E d Reavy's name (in a variety of spellings) is often seen listed in the writing credits of album sleeve notes, for the fiddler from Maudabawn, Co. Cavan, was one of the twentieth century's most prolific composers of traditional music. Born in 1898, he was only fourteen when he emigrated to the US, eventually settling in Philadelphia where he lived until his death in 1988. During the 1920s, Reavy recorded several solo 78s for RCA Victor – a couple of tunes appear on **Farewell to Ireland** (see p.41) – and several others as a member of Tommy Caulfield's **Erin's Pride Orchestra**. However, the vast bulk of his recordings were made at home on six-inch 78 rpm discs. Many of his compositions have been collected and it's reckoned that every day of the year someone somewhere is almost certainly playing his reel "The Hunter's House". In 1979 **Mick Moloney** co-ordinated the production of a tribute album on Rounder Records which is now available on cassette as **The Music of Ed Reavy**. The fiddler himself plays on six of the tracks and other musicians paying homage include **Liz Carroll** and **Brendan** and **Martin Mulvihill**.

🔲 **The Music of Ed Reavy** Cló Iar-Chonnachta/Ossian Publications, 1979

A fine tribute to a remarkable composer and fiddler.

Brian Rooney

If there's one modern fiddle album that everyone should own, it's **The Godfather**, the staggering debut CD by **Brian Rooney** which takes its title from the fiddler's nickname. Brian's roots lie in the North Leitrim townland of Derragoon, near Kiltyclogher, and, as Noel Hill notes, there's a characteristic "loneliness" in his music that is typical of the area. His father Jack was himself a fine fiddler and Brian later received lessons from the Fermanagh man John Timoney. For 30 years Brian has been a mainstay of the London Irish traditional scene, influencing many who heard his mellow-toned fiddle and astonishing all with his effortless technical ability. Fortunately for us he was finally persuaded to record **The Godfather** with long-time friend John Carty behind the controls. There's an elegant simplicity to much of the album where Rooney's floating bow swoops and soars over the discreet

piano of **Brian McGrath**, especially on the fiddler's own compositions "M and M" and his fantastic reel "Brian Rooney's". He's happy

fronting larger ensembles too and Frankie Gavin, Alec Finn and Carty himself provide buoyant and expert accompaniment.

⊙ **The Godfather**   Racket Records, 1999

Already regarded as a modern classic and justifiably so.

Joe Ryan

One of the last surviving members of the great era of West Clare fiddling, **Joe Ryan** was born near Inagh in 1928. His father was a fine singer whose lilting skills were often demanded for house dances. Joe first taught himself the tin whistle while walking to school, before trying his hand at a fiddle which hung in a shop in Ennistymon around the age of 18. A wheelwright by trade, he spent some of his spare time in the **Fiach Rua Céilí Band** before moving to Dublin in 1951 where he met – and was greatly impressed by – legendary fiddler Tommy Potts. Joe soon moved on to London where he spent a decade working as a carpenter and playing with notable musicians such as Bobby Casey, Martin Byrnes and Roger Sherlock. Returning to Dublin in 1962, he was invited by accordionist **Tony MacMahon** to play as a regular duo in O'Donoghue's. However, when Tony's commitments made him unable to continue, Joe in turn invited fellow West Clare man **John Kelly** (fiddle, concertina) to join him, initiating a partnership which endured for 20 years (the last eight in the Four Seasons, North King Street). Joe also played regularly with piper **Liam O'Flynn**, winning Oireachtas duet competitions three years running between 1968 and 1970. He repeated this feat in 1972 with harmonica player **Eddie Clarke**, a unique and magical pairing which produced the stunning album **Crossroads** in 1981.

Joe later moved back to Co. Clare and released the excellent **An Buachaill Dreoite** with guitarist **Jim McArdle** in 1995, but 2000 saw the arrival of one of the great albums of traditional music, **Two Gentlemen of Clare Music**. The second fellow was concertina player **Gerdie Commane** from Kilnamona, making his first ever recording at he age of 82 and at whose house it was taped. Accompanied by **Eoin O'Neill**'s trusty bouzouki, the pair produce a lasting testimony to the enduring strength of Clare's music. The gentle pace and the subtle mastery of the players is ever easy on the ear while the beautiful tone and rolling grace of Joe's fiddle on his own set of jigs ("Joe Ryan's") cannot be beaten.

⊙ Two Gentlemen of Clare Music   Clachán Music, 2000

Wonderful, magical, life-enhancing music with added atmosphere provided by Gerdie's reminiscences and a howling gale outside!

Harpers

F ollowing the defeat of the old Gaelic Order in the seventeenth century (see p.7) the bardic harping tradition went into a period of terminal decline which saw the eventual disappearance of its itinerant exponents in the early part of the nineteenth century. The harp disappeared into the drawing rooms of polite society where its strings, now made of gut, were plucked and strummed (very much in the Welsh harping style) to accompany songs.

With the notable exception of Belfast's **McPeake Family** (see p.262), the harp had little connection with traditional music until the 1970s. Before then the instrument featured strongly in tourist cabarets, such as Bunratty Castle, where simple chords accompanied precisely enunciated voices. Though not a cabaret performer herself, **Mary O'Hara** is the most well-known singing harper in this style while the major figure in the revival of the wire-strung harp and in the understanding of the old oral tradition was **Gráinne Yeats**. Though still rarely seen at sessions, the harp's role as a traditional instrument was first pioneered by **Máire Ní Chathasaigh** whose astonishing technique for playing dance music has influenced a modern generation of harpers, such as **Laoise Kelly** and **Micheál Ó Ruanaigh**, most of whom play lightweight nylon-strung harps manufactured in Japan and the US.

All the best-known harpers are included here, but other notable players are **Antoinette McKenna** (see p.414) who usually plays as a duo or in groups with her husband, uilleann piper, Joe; the innovative **Ursula Burns**; former Déanta man **Eoghan O'Brien**; and **Nóirín O'Donoghue** (who used to play with Fisherstreet).

Derek Bell

In 1974, Belfast-born **Derek Bell**, then lead harper with the BBC Northern Ireland Orchestra, was told by his boss, "if you really feel you want to run around with a tatty folk group, you'll have to resign". That "tatty folk group" was **The Chieftains**, and Bell has been running around with them ever since. A former child prodigy and prizewinning classical player, trained at London's Royal College of Music, Bell is also expert on the piano, oboe, cor anglais and hammer dulcimer. During his pre-Chieftains career he played with several leading European and US orchestras, including a spell as principal oboe, horn and piano player for the American Wind Symphony Orchestra; he has also composed a number of classical works. He didn't take up the harp until he was almost thirty, studying first with Sheila Larchet-Cuthbert and later Gwendolyn Mason, mastering both the classical and traditional versions of the instrument, and being appointed Professor of Harp and Irish Harp at Belfast's Academy of Music and Dramatic Art in 1970. His heavyweight credentials and extensive research into harping history, combined with The Chieftains' blossoming international fame by the mid-1970s, established him as the instrument's leading Irish exponent, laying much of the groundwork for its subsequent wider revival. Besides his recordings with the band, he has also released eight solo albums, starting with **Carolan's Receipt** (1975), the first-ever album dedicated entirely to the legendary harper's compositions, and still ranked among the most authoritative renderings of his work. Bell explores the full range of Carolan's music using both the harder-toned metal-strung harp, responsible for the harpsichord-like effects on "Sidh Beag agus Sidh Mhor" and the melancholic progression of "Carolan's Quarrel", as well as the better-known gut-strung version. There are further recordings in this vein – **Carolan's Favourite** (1978), featuring the New Irish Chamber Orchestra, and **Ancient Music for the Irish Harp** – while other albums include the mischievously-titled folk/light-classical selection **Derek Bell Plays With Himself** (1981), and the New Age-oriented **The Mystic Harp, Vols I & II** (1996 and 1999).

⊙ Carolan's Receipt   Claddagh, 1975

An expert exploration and celebration of Carolan's music, accompanied by other members of The Chieftains on several tracks.

⊙ Ancient Music for the Irish Harp   Claddagh, 1992

To his own interpretations of tunes played at the 1792 Belfast Harp Festival, Bell adds a couple of wild-card South American dances.

Patricia Daly

Patricia Daly has played a considerable role in the harp's revival in Ireland, not least in her native Armagh where she co-founded the Armagh Harpers Association (AHA) in 1995. She studied the piano from the age of seven and began learning the harp at fifteen, progressing through competitions and winning Slógadh and Oireachtas titles and the All-Ireland championship on more than one occasion. As a qualified traditional music teacher, Patricia organizes the AHA's teaching programme in both harp and song, and has played a part in the revival of door dancing where a step dance is performed on an ordinary wooden door on which a glass of stout or water has been placed at each corner – the aim being to execute the dance without spilling a drop! She has also been a key figure in establishing the annual Edward Bunting International Harp Festival (see p.572), and has recorded with the Armagh Pipers Club. Her own solo album, **Harping Daly** (1998), featuring her brother Martin on uilleann pipes, is a blend of adept renditions of Carolan pieces, such as "Fanny Power" and "Charles O'Connor", slow airs (including one by pupil Ailish McMahon who also features in a duet), reels and a clan march, "The Song of the Chanter" (from the Bunting collection). Songs are mainly drawn from the Ulster tradition and include a grand rendition of "On the Banks of a River Near Blackwatertown", learned from song collector Robin Morton.

⊙ **Harping Daly** own label, 1998

A well-balanced blend of harp and song from an influential figure.

Janet Harbison

Widely-known as a harper, teacher and composer, **Janet Harbison** (b. 1955, Dublin) has a musical pedigree of the highest quality. A classically trained pianist, she studied harp under Máirín Ní Shé whose previous students had included Mary O'Hara. Keen to play traditional music, Janet was one of the first to acquire a lightweight Japanese harp, considering it a more suitable form of the instrument for dance tunes. Janet turned professional in the late 1970s, touring the US and playing in cabaret at Bunratty and Knappoge castles. While studying music at Trinity, she worked as the resident pianist in the Shelborne Hotel and often played in jazz clubs. Her studies continued at University College Cork where she undertook postgraduate research into Edward Bunting. An All-Ireland Senior champion, she formed Cláirseoirí na hÉireann (The Harpers' Association) in 1987, while also working as Curator of Music at the Ulster Folk and Transport Museum in Cultra, Co. Down, a post she held until 1994. Janet organized the 1992 World Harp Festival in Belfast (commemorating the 200th anniversary of its famous predecessor) and now leads the Belfast Harp Orchestra (BHO). Her own releases include the 1985 cassette **O'Neill's Harper** and, more recently, **Dear Heart of My Country** (1997), a double album of Thomas Moore's compositions made with the tenor James W. Flaherty. However, her best-known recording is as leader of the BHO on The Chieftains' **The Celtic Harp** (1993) a tribute to Bunting that followed a successful concert in Belfast's Ulster Hall during the previous year's bicentenary celebrations. Two of the tracks on which the BHO features date from that concert (a great opening march and decorous "Planxty Bunting"), while the remaining pair were recorded live in London later in 1992 – a sprightly rendition of "Sonny Brogan's Mazurkas" and a splendidly stately version of "Carolan's Concerto" arranged by Paddy Moloney.

⊙ **The Celtic Harp**   RCA Victor, 1993

The Chieftains combine with the Belfast Harp Orchestra in a reverential salute to the great collector, Bunting.

Laoise Kelly

"Triplets made in heaven", Derek Bell of The Chieftains once remarked on hearing **Laoise Kelly**, not, of course, suggesting that Laoise had a couple of sisterly look-alikes, but simply describing the quality of her playing. Born in Westport, Co. Mayo, in 1973, Laoise studied music at Maynooth and University College Cork and has since become one of Ireland's foremost traditional harpers. Known in part through her membership of **Bumblebees**, Laoise's solo career has encompassed a large number of recordings, including releases by Dónal Lunny, Sharon Shannon and the Ní Dhomhnaill sisters. She has also become widely known to television audiences through appearances in *A River of Sound* and *Eurovision*, played in Bill Whelan's *Seville Suite* with the RTÉ Concert Orchestra and toured the US and Australia in performances of Charlie Lennon's *Famine Suite*. Building on the pioneer efforts of Máire Ní Chathasaigh, Laoise has redefined the harp's potential, moving it a step nearer its reinstatement as a traditional instrument. Through sheer talent and technical brilliance she has transformed it into a conduit for her remarkable interpretations of dance music. Her 1999 solo album, **Just Harp**, simply oozes flair and gaiety with sparkling melodic lines, resonant chords and a subtle use of the bass strings to create harmonic richness while maintaining an almost unstoppable rhythm. All of this is encapsulated in her extraordinary playing of the jigs "The Yellow Wattle/Trip to London/Trip to Brittany" where she plays a walking, syncopated bass line that some jazzers would die for.

⊙ **Just Harp**   own label, 1999

Stylish and stunning music from a truly original musician.

Kathleen Loughnane

Kathleen Loughnane, who plays with **Dordán**, is one of Ireland's leading harpers. Originally from Nenagh, Co. Tipperary (but based in Galway since 1982) Kathleen began playing the harp as a child and went on to study the instrument at the Royal Irish Academy of Music and the College of Music, Dublin. For some time her especial interests have focused both on compositions by the seventeenth- and eighteenth-century harpers, and traditional dance tunes and airs, a combination that has featured prominently in both her own work and Dordán's. She published her first collection of harp arrangements, *Harping On*, in 1995, followed two years later by a second volume, *Affairs of the Harp* – also the title of her first (and so far only) solo album. This showcased her deft and delightful playing on a varied selection of tunes drawn from across the centuries, from "Port Athol", attributed to the sixteenth-century composer Rúairí Dall Ó Cathain, to her own composition "The Open Road". The album also features a number of remarkable duets including a memorable reading of "The Drunken Sailor" hornpipe with Sharon Shannon, a gorgeous slow air (and variant of "The Blackbird") "Inion an Fhaoit ón nGleann" with whistler Seán Ryan, and a grand barn dance, "Kitty Sheáin's", with accordionist Mary Staunton. Alec Finn provides matchless guitar and bouzouki accompaniment on a number of tracks.

⊙ **Affairs of the Harp**   Reiskmore Music, 1998

A sublime album which confirmed Kathleen as one of Europe's leading harpers.

Máire Ní Chathasaigh

Máire Ní Chathasaigh is the great innovator of modern Irish harping, a player of outstanding technique and imagination who has significantly influenced the approach to traditional music of many other harpers. Born in Bandon, Co. Cork in 1956 to a well-known musical family (fiddler **Nollaig Casey** is her sister), she began playing harp at the age of eleven, progressing to win All-Ireland Junior and Senior championships and Pan-Celtic titles in the 1970s, participating in CCÉ international tours and albums during the same decade, and making many TV and radio appearances. For some time too, Máire played in a trio with Nollaig and the uilleann piper **Máire Ní Ghráda**. However, it was her love of the connecting sean-nós and piping traditions plus her desire to establish an authentic style of playing traditional music on the harp, which has made the most enduring impact. For evidence look no further than her revolutionary album, **The New-Strung Harp** (1985) and her staggering version of the reels "The Gander in the Pratie Hole/The Queen of the Rushes". Replete with startling rolls and triplets as crisp as a cracker,

JAK KILBY

augmented by use of a droning D note to suggest the uilleann pipes, Máire's playing simply set new parameters for what could be done with the instrument. Consummate arrangements abound, whether on John Doherty's "The Boys of Malin" or more "stereotypical" harp pieces, such as "Carolan's Farewell to Music", all characterized by astonishing dexterity and embellishments of great subtlety. The album's rapturous reception – not least amongst some of the doubters – encouraged many others to follow suit and her workshops at summer schools around the world are usually crammed with avid young harpers. Since 1987 Máire has been working as a duo with English guitarist, **Chris Newman,** and his often percussive style of accompaniment has proved a natural foil for Máire's flying fingers. The pair recorded the superb **The Living Wood** a year later and have released a number of tremendous albums since. These include two cassettes devoted to Carolan (now released together on one CD as **The Carolan Albums**) and most recently, **Live in the Highlands**, a stupendous demonstration of the pair's artistry revealing Máire's qualities as singer and Chris's ability to pick tremendous reels. Máire's book *The Irish Harper* contains many of her tune arrangements.

⊙ **The New-Strung Harp**   Temple Records, 1985

An earth-shattering re-evaluation of the harp's potential whose tremors still reverberate today.

⊙ **Live in the Highlands**   Old Bridge Music, 1995

With Chris Newman caught live in Scotland.

Mary O'Hara

Aharper and singer with an instantly recognizable, prim and pure soprano voice, **Mary O'Hara** achieved fame both sides of the Atlantic in the late 1950s and early 1960s. Born in Sligo town, she moved to Dublin at thirteen to be educated at Sion Hill school where she studied the harp under Máirín Ní Shé. Her singing drew the attention of Seán Óg Ó Taumdha of Radio Éireann, who taught her much of her repertoire. She made her first radio broadcast at sixteen, soon had her own show and appeared at the Edinburgh Festival and on British television. Singing in both Irish and English, she spent some time on the Hebridean island of South Uist, acquiring fluency in Scots Gaelic. She recorded two albums for the English Decca label before releasing her first American album, **Down by the Glenside:**

Songs of Ireland for Patrick Clancy's Tradition label. This essentially captures the spirit of the first phase of Mary's career, drawing together a huge range of material (from nursery rhymes and nonsense songs to lullabies and sean-nós) usually accompanied by harping consisting of simple chords or arpeggios resembling the Welsh tradition of playing. Mary's enunciation is always precise and songs are delivered in a jaunty, melancholic or quasi-operatic manner with the exception of a remarkable unaccompanied, "Sliabh na mBan" one of the "big" songs from Co. Waterford's Déise Gaeltacht. Further

international success ensued but it was abruptly curtailed by the tragic early death of her American husband, Richard Selig. In consequence, Mary sought retreat in a convent where she remained for twelve years, only returning to performance in 1974. Since then she has continued to tour internationally and has released a startling number of albums, many of which are compilations on budget labels. Of note are **At the Festival Hall** (1977) and **Live at Carnegie Hall** (1984). Both feature her now characteristic blend of hymns, Hebridean songs and middle-of-the road pop.

⊙ **Down by the Glenside: Songs of Ireland**   Tradition, 1960

Capturing Mary at the height of her fame, this demonstrates exactly why she became so popular.

Micheál Ó Ruanaigh

Highly proficient in many instruments, including concertina and flute, **Micheál Ó Ruanaigh** (from Scotstown, Co. Monaghan) is probably best known for his harping. A popular teacher and adjudicator too, Micheál is a member of the Belfast Harp Orchestra and graduated in Ethnomusicology and Celtic Studies from the city's Queen's University. His first album to date was **Ocras – Music from the Famine Remembrance**, originally performed in 1996 and consisting of his own compositions. On disc he is joined by the History Ireland Performance Company and the combination presents a successful interpretation of the composer's skills in melodic construction, especially on "Na Maithe Móra". Micheál has recently released **Traditional Music on Fiddle, Banjo and Harp** (2000) with Clare fiddler **Oisín Mac Diarmada** and Limerick banjo man **Brian Fitzgerald**, an enthralling combination whose imaginative choice of material includes a jig composed by Peadar Ó Riada, tunes associated with Willie Clancy and the Kerry fiddler Johnny Cronin, and several pieces from Micheál's own recent *Millennium Suite*, including an admirable pair of slip jigs "Tigh Rabhartaigh/Gort na Móna", named after local Monaghan townlands.

⊙ Traditional Music on Fiddle,   Cló Iar-Chonnachta, 2000
Banjo and Harp

Ó Ruanaigh, Mac Diarmada and Fitzgerald form a highly effective trio on this accomplished and enjoyable album.

Gráinne Yeats

Gráinne Yeats (b. 1925, Dublin) is a key figure in the twentieth-century revival of the Irish harp, both as a player and researcher. Raised in a bilingual household, she attended the Royal Irish Academy of Music, studying singing, piano and the harp, and subsequently developed an extensive repertoire of traditional songs and music through stays in Gaeltacht areas. A frequent broadcaster on both radio and television, Gráinne has toured internationally and opened many ears to the sound of a bygone era – the wire-strung harp, much sharper-toned than the now prevalent nylon or gut string varieties. Her ground-breaking 1983 LP **A Rogha Féin** (Her Personal Selection) was one of the first-ever professional recordings to feature the instrument and includes tunes as varied as "Carrickfergus", "The Blackbird" and "Gusty's Frolics" and songs in Irish. Naturally, the 200th anniversary of **The Belfast Harp Festival** was a significant event for anyone with an interest in harping, and Gráinne celebrated this with a stunning double album of music and songs. Immaculately played throughout, the first disc is devoted to pieces by Carolan while the second covers tunes from the repertoire of the harpers who attended the festival. Just how close Gráinne's playing is to the original harpers' sound is impossible to say: not just because the original tunes were filtered through the classically-trained ear of transposer Edward Bunting, but also because the instrument (and ways of playing it) has changed significantly over the years.

⊙ The Belfast Harp Festival: 1792–1992   Gael-Linn, 1992

A marvellous, reverent and evocative double CD from the wire-strung harp of Gráinne Yeats.

Other string players

Largely thanks to The Dubliners' **Barney McKenna**, the banjo became one of the key instruments of the 1960s folk revival. Barney's prowess on the instrument and his use of GDAE tuning were massively influential and many aspiring banjo players followed in his wake. Banjos come in a variety of sizes, but the most popular form in traditional music is the four-string tenor banjo which has either seventeen or nineteen frets and is usually played with a plectrum. Its crisp tone renders it ideal for picking out the melodies of dance tunes and adding embellishments, though it is less frequently used for accompaniment.

Similarly, the now ubiquitous six-string guitar played little part in Irish traditional music until the '60s when the popularity of the **Clancy Brothers** led to a host of imitators. The Clancys emerged from the folk-song revival in the US where singers used the instrument to provide simple chordal or finger-style accompaniment. Ireland's subsequent ballad boom was short-lived, but guitarists continued to experiment with accompaniments, exploring percussive rhythmic effects and the open tunings popularized by finger-style guitarists. **Paul Brady**, **Mícheál Ó Domhnaill** and **Dónal Lunny** were also taking up the mantle of Jack McKenna who accompanied fiddler Hugh Gillespie in the late 1930s and clearly drew much of his own style from jazz guitarists such as Charlie Christian. Brady's recordings set a standard for subsequent accompanists to follow, but the most significant recent influence has been the Australian, **Stephen Cooney** who employs the entire length of the fretboard and uses the bass strings and rapid strumming to produce a tidal wave of percussive sound. In contrast, the American **Dennis Cahill** (see p.322), one of the few guitarists to use the standard EADGBE tuning, has developed a restrained, pared-down style, in particular when partnering fiddler Martin Hayes. Another notable accompanist, **Arty McGlynn** has successfully demonstrated the instrument's potential as a melodic instrument, picking out jigs and reels with astonishing speed and clarity.

Second only to the guitar as an accompanist's instrument is the bouzouki. A Greek instrument resembling an enlarged mandolin with an elongated neck, the Irish adaptation of the bouzouki has four sets of double metal strings and is usually played in an open-tuning (GDAD or ADAD) with a plectrum. **Johnny Moynihan** is credited with introducing the instrument to Ireland in the 1960s, and it was subsequently adopted by his fellow member of Sweeney's Men, **Andy Irvine** who, with **Dónal Lunny**, considerably raised the instrument's profile. Other notable players include Altan's **Ciarán Curran** who is also highly regarded for his use of the cittern. This has a shorter neck than the bouzouki and sometimes has a fifth pair of strings, again usually open-tuned, producing a somewhat brighter sound.

The mandolin is rarely seen in sessions, thanks, in part, to it's lack of volume. Short-necked and squat with either a round- or flat-backed pear-shaped body, the mandolin again has four pairs of strings and is usually tuned like a fiddle in GDAE. Ideal for picking out melodies, two of its best contemporary players are **Paul Kelly** and **Martin Murray**. Larger versions of the mandolin family, graduating upwards in neck length, include the mandola and the mandocello, the latter associated with the well-known accompanist **Garry Ó Briain** and both with singer **Seán Tyrrell**.

A rare instrument in traditional music, the hammer dulcimer's most illustrious exponent was **John Rea**. The dulcimer is trapezoid in shape and has strings stretched across its width, divided by two bridges which create a variation in pitch. The player strikes the strings with a "hammer" held in each hand (in Rea's case two pieces of bent wire bound with darning wool), but is unable to prevent the strings from reverberating and producing a bright, echoic sound.

Stephen Cooney

If any one individual can be credited with popularizing the rapid-fire, high-tensile, percussive style of guitar accompaniment now embraced by most of Ireland's leading players, it's the Australian-born ex-rocker and dreadlocked free spirit **Stephen Cooney**. The son of a first-generation Irish professional guitarist, he was raised on an early diet of jazz, swing and gospel, discovering Irish music via a Mary O'Hara record. After playing with various antipodean rock bands, he left Australia to escape the Vietnam draft, arriving in Ireland in 1981. Shortly afterwards he joined the group **Stockton's Wing**, originally as a bass player, and stayed for ten years, becoming the first to introduce Australia's national instrument, the didgeridoo into Irish music. A noted songwriter, Cooney has since fought shy of protracted involvement with any one line-up, preferring the freshness and spontaneity of short-term projects, including albums by Sharon Shannon, Altan, Mary Black and umpteen more. The exception to this is his ongoing duo with his Co. Kerry neighbour, accordionist **Séamus Begley**. Affectionately known locally as "Brute and Nut", they were voted most popular traditional act of 1997 in the National Entertainment Awards, on the strength of their sole album to date, **Meiteal** (1997). The blend of influences in Cooney's background, including rock, classical, reggae, "Celtic" and Balkan music, together with his hyperactive rhythmic energy, are distilled into a uniquely dynamic but never overbearing style. As Begley describes it, "The way Steve plays behind you, it lifts you, even the most stupid tune that you'd be sick and tired of playing all your life – it's like putting a turbo on a Morris Minor." A fluent Irish speaker and passionate champion of traditional culture, Cooney is also involved in archiving the old music and songs of his adopted home area, and in 1998 arranged and performed the music for **Rabhlaí Rabhlaí**, a University of Limerick-sponsored CD of Irish-language nursery rhymes.

⊙ Meiteal	Hummingbird, 1997

A heaven-made marriage producing tight yet frisky slides, polkas, jigs and reels, plus three haunting songs from Begley.

Alec Finn

Instantly identifiable from his big shock of hair and companion bouzouki, **Alec Finn** (b. Yorkshire, England, 1944) has been one of the prime movers in traditional music since the early 1970s. Of Irish parentage, Alec began as a guitarist and his love of pop, rock and blues still occasionally infiltrates his work with **De Dannan**, the band he and **Frankie Gavin** have run since the 1970s, most recently on the album **Welcome to the Hotel Connemara** (2000). A musical visionary, Alec's arrangements and Frankie's endless capacity to

LIVING TRADITION

interpret them have generated a host of fine albums while Alec's own list of appearances on other artists' releases challenges the Galway *Yellow Pages* for length. So far the only release to bear Alec's name alone is the distinctly odd **Blue Shamrock,** though its subtitle, "Irish airs played on guitar and bouzouki", gives the game away. Alec picks out the melodies of ten largely familiar slow airs ("Seán Ó Duibhir an Ghleanna", "The Water is Wide", "Sally Gardens", etc.) in the company of fine players such as the whistlers Mary Bergin and Seán Ryan and piper Tommy Keane. The results, despite the participants' supreme competence, are both trite and monumentally dull. For a far better understanding of Finn's powers, seek out his playing on the Noel Hill and Tony Linnane album or his arrangement of "Hey Jude" and the subsequent flight of frenzy, "St Jude's Reel" collected on **How the West Was Won** (see p.181).

⊙ Blue Shamrock	Cross Border Media, 1994

Competently played but distinctly dull, despite the presence of Alec and a great supporting cast.

Kevin Griffin

O ne of the modern generation of musicians from Doolin, Co. Clare, **Kevin Griffin** took up the tenor banjo at the age of fourteen. Working at McGann's pub in the village, he was soon exposed to the wealth of talent, both local and from further afield, who frequented the regular sessions. The banjo playing of Mick Moloney and Kieran Hanrahan particularly struck a chord, and he cites De Dannan as a major musical inspiration. An honorary member of **The Ceili Bandits**, Kevin's own second solo album, **Traditional Irish Music from Doolin, Co. Clare**, appeared in 1997. Accompanied throughout by that fine guitarist Gerry O'Beirne, the assortment of adroitly plucked tunes spotlights Kevin's abilities while offering guest spots to Sharon Shannon, Tommy Hayes, Eoin O'Neill and Mary Custy among others. An earlier self-produced cassette, **Down in Doolin**, is now virtually impossible to find.

⊙ Traditional Irish Music from Doolin, Co. Clare	Ossian, 1997

Subtle plucking throughout, especially on his own "The Ballyvoe Hornpipes" and the ragtime tune "48 Dogs in a Meathouse".

Kieran Hanrahan

F ollowing firmly in Barney McKenna's masterful footsteps, Ennis man **Kieran Hanrahan** is one of Ireland's most-celebrated exponents of the tenor banjo. A relative late starter on the instrument (he didn't begin playing until he was fourteen), he made quick progress and was All-Ireland Senior champion five years later. Subsequently, he formed the short-lasting **Inchiquin** with Noel Hill, Tony Linnane and guitarist/vocalist Tony Callanan before founding **Stockton's Wing** in 1978 and playing with the group for a decade. After his departure he next formed **The Temple House Ceili Band** in 1988 and has been presenting *Céilí House* on RTÉ Radio 1 for more than ten years. He finally released his own debut solo album, **Kieran Hanrahan Plays the Irish Tenor Banjo** in 1997. Featuring a couple of great reels associated with Barney McKenna, "Colonel Frazier" and "The Mason's Apron", the album's guests include brother Mike on guitar, Tommy Hayes on percussion and concertina wizard Sonny Murray on a couple of selections.

⊙ **Kieran Hanrahan Plays the Irish Tenor Banjo**   own label, 1997

A master at work, still playing with refreshing zeal after all these years.

Paul Kelly

Nowadays the mandolin has a low profile in contemporary Irish music, but that may not remain the case thanks to the work of Martin Murray and **Paul Kelly**. The latter first caught the ear as a teenaged traditional fiddler, but moved onto bluegrass with **The Sackville String Band** and then a rock orientation with **The Fleadh Cowboys** and Mick Hanly's **Rusty Old Halo**. In the 1990s Paul went back to his roots, recording and touring as a member of Sharon Shannon's band. He now plays with guitarist **Seán Whelan** in the quartet **Faolán** and runs his own label, Malgamú Music, among whose initial releases was his own **A Mandolin Album**. It's a wholesale delight of an album, especially in the way that Kelly exploits the instrument's timbral properties (sometimes using damping) on a series of traditional tunes, including some of his own. Sources for the tunes include his late teacher, Des Carty, flute-player Emer Mayock, the French-Canadian band La Bottine Souriante as well as Paul's trips to Sweden. Paul has also recorded **Live at Hughes's** (1995) with dobro player **Frankie Lane**.

⊙ A Mandolin Album | Malgamú Music, 1998

Exquisitely played music and imaginative arrangements from the talented Kelly.

Frankie Lane

Former star of **The Fleadh Cowboys**, one of 1980s Dublin's hottest live acts, Meath-born Frankie Lane is a dab hand on the dobro, pedal steel guitar and five-string banjo – instruments not usually associated with Irish music. Much in demand as a session player, Frankie's own solo album **Dóbró** appeared in 1993. Whether the dobro's fundamental whimsicality is suited to traditional tunes is a matter of taste, but Frankie demonstrates all its possibilities, most notably on the neat

FRANKIE LANE

D ó b r ó

call-and-response duet with Ciarán Tourish on Tommy Peoples' "Jenny's Welcome to Charlie" and with Dermot Byrne on a couple of Bobby Gardiner tunes. Elsewhere Frankie's musical tastes are revealed in Hawaiian, Finnish and Mexican numbers together with a curious rendition of Chopin's "Nocturne in E♭". Other albums to look out for include his collaborations with Paul O'Shaughnessy and Paul Kelly.

⊙ **Dóbró**   Gael-Linn, 1993

A unique album, adroitly played but probably only for the suitably intrigued.

Dónal Lunny

In a poll to name the single living individual who has exerted the greatest influence over the modern development of Irish music, **Dónal Lunny** (b.Newbridge, Co. Kildare, 1947) would romp home. It's not just his plethora of job titles – guitarist, bouzouki pioneer, bodhrán player, composer, arranger, bandleader, producer, musical director – that sets him apart, but an appetite for innovation and discovery that has driven him ever since he began experimenting, during the 1960s, with unusual guitar chords at sessions in the Kildare village of Prosperous, ten miles from his Newbridge home.

It was through Prosperous, too, that Lunny's musical career took off in earnest, following a spell with the ballad band **Emmet Spiceland**, when his one-time schoolfriend and ex-duo partner **Christy Moore** came home from London to make his second album (1972), named after the local musical mecca. These recording sessions led directly to the formation of **Planxty**, marking the start of Lunny's involvement with all three of Ireland's definitive progressive folk bands – Planxty, **The Bothy Band** and **Moving Hearts** – during the 1970s and '80s.

Early on in this period, Lunny is credited with having invented the Irish bouzouki, adapting the round-backed Greek version to one with a flat back and a shorter neck, strung with unison rather than octave strings to produce a brighter, more silvery sound. In the Bothy Band, he began to develop the dynamic, percussive style that remains a hallmark, while Moving Hearts introduced him to working with a rock-style rhythm section. The challenge of augmenting traditional music's rhythmic dimension, without dead-ending down the folk-rock road, has been an enduring preoccupation. "If you take Irish music and then draw the components and the character from within the music itself," he's said, "then the music is actually generating the rhythms and the syncopation and the punctuation: that's what I've always been trying to do."

It's this organically sensitive approach that underlies the immense respect Lunny commands as a producer, now with well over 100 albums to his credit. Among the many traditional luminaries who've called on his skills are, Kevin Burke, Altan, Sharon Shannon and virtually all his former band colleagues, as well as rock and pop artists including Elvis Costello, Kate Bush and Rod Stewart. Since Moving Hearts disbanded, he's also been active in TV production, notably as musical director of the award-winning BBC/RTÉ series *Bringing It All Back Home* and the companion album (1992) and the acclaimed live-music magazine show *Sult* (1996).

A major live project during this period was the eight-piece band and suite of music, much of it original, which Lunny put together for the Sean Ó Riada Retrospective Concert in 1987. A recording of the performance, vividly conveying the occasion's heady atmosphere, became the first album released under his own name (1987). With its upfront rhythmic approach and its large-scale, tight yet spacious arrangements, this ensemble was a clear forerunner of Lunny's current **Coolfin** outfit, which emerged from the *Sult* house band, and includes fiddler **Nollaig Casey** and piper **John McSherry**, assertively backed with keyboards, bass, drums and percussion. Their self-titled debut album (1998) intersperses funky, groove-based instrumentals with a mixed bag of guest-vocal numbers, from Eddi Reader's eerie rendition of "The Lowlands of Holland", to Maighread Ní Dhomhnaill's rather over-ethereal "Siúl A Rúin".

Lunny's latest release is the best-of double album **Journey** (2000). While the nature of his career renders a representative cross-section well-nigh impossible, the collection revisits most of the essential high spots alongside a good many previously unreleased tracks, including striking vocal contributions from Christy Moore and Liam Ó Maonlaí, among others, closing with the ambitious if patchy "Millennium Suite", a pan-Celtic extravaganza commissioned for Dublin's millennial New Year's Eve festivities.

⊙ **Sult**   Hummingbird, 1996

A proto-Coolfin house band accompanies guest stars, including Sharon Shannon, Van Morrison and Paul Brady.

⊙ **Journey: The Best of Dónal Lunny**   Hummingbird/Grapevine, 2000

A thoughtfully potted and, for the most part, richly rewarding career history.

Arty McGlynn

While the idea of a traditional Irish guitar player may be an inherently problematic one, Co. Tyrone's **Arty McGlynn** has done more than any other player to flesh out the concept with both creative technique and critical respectability. His early influences, though, lay in the rock, jazz and blues fields, among them Barney Kessel, Wes Montgomery and Chuck Berry, and he cut his teeth in the 1960s touring more or less anonymously with various pop and rock outfits, whilst teaching himself the pedal steel guitar. The advent of Planxty and The Bothy Band in the mid-1970s reawakened his interest in Irish music (several of his family were traditional players), and towards the end of the decade he released his first solo album **McGlynn's Fancy** (1979). Generally considered *the* breakthrough album in Irish traditional guitar, it displays McGlynn's fleet-fingered melody picking and subtly sophisticated musical approach in such tunes as "Arthur Darley's Jig" and "The Floating Crowbar". Its enthusiastic reputation swiftly elevated McGlynn to most-wanted status among Irish guitarists, a reputation further underlined by his time with the bands **Four Men and A Dog** and **Patrick Street** during the 1980s and '90s. He married fiddler **Nollaig Casey** in 1984, and the couple have released two acclaimed duo albums, **Lead the Knave** (1989) and **Causeway** (1995), each exploring the range of McGlynn's skills on acoustic and electric instruments, from nimbly picked jigs and reels to muscular blues workouts. His combination of melodic sensitivity and rhythmic imagination have also seen him collaborating with such contemporaries as Van Morrison, Liam O'Flynn and Christy Moore, while recently he has been in demand as a producer, too, working on albums by singer Seán Keane, Maura O'Connell and Alan Kelly.

⊙ McGlynn's Fancy	Mint Records, 1979

This seminal guitar album is hard to track down but well worth the effort (available in the US as Celtic Airs).

Brian McGrath

Four-string banjo master and pianist **Brian McGrath** comes from Brookeborough, Co. Fermanagh where his parents ran a pub well-known in traditional music circles. Fiddler Jim McKillop came to play one night, bringing with him a selection of his handmade fiddles, and Cathal Hayden's father purchased one for his son. Cathal had been learning the banjo, but now left it behind with Brian and the young McGrath took up where his friend had left off. Later both were to be founder members of **Four Men and a Dog**, but Brian was never fond of touring and already settling down in Galway where he still lives. A man of broad musical tastes (from bluegrass to R&B), Brian has played with Dervish, Moving Cloud and Noel Hill amongst others and is a member of **At the Racket** (with whom he plays piano) and released the dynamic **Dreaming Up the Tunes** (see p.481) with fellow Seán Keane band member, accordionist **Johnny Óg Connolly**. Brian's piano accompaniment is a feature of John Carty's own excellent banjo album **The Cat That Ate the Candle** (see p.290).

Mick Moloney

Born in Limerick in 1944, the multitalented **Mick Moloney** played major roles in both the 1960s folk revival in Ireland and the following decade's resurgence of Irish music in the US: he continues to be a pivotal figure. A student at University College Dublin in the 1960s, Moloney's voice and tenor banjo (he also plays mandolin and guitar) were prominent features in Dublin's folk clubs, either performing solo or with groups such as **The Emmet Folk** or **The Rakish Paddies**. Fame came with his membership of **The Johnstons** with whom he recorded several albums before deciding to settle in the US in 1973. Since then Mick has combined successful careers as an academic, as researcher (he holds a PhD in folklore and folklife) and teacher, administrator and promoter, radio and TV performer, producer and presenter, and, of course, musician. His list of credits on others' albums is seemingly endless and he has been instrumental in encouraging the development of many other singers and musicians, not least through such enterprises as The Green Fields of America tours (featuring **Seamus Egan**, **Eileen Ivers** and **Robbie O'Connell** among others) and **Cherish the Ladies**. Mick has also ensured that many older musicians, such as **Martin Mulvihill** and the Derry fiddler **Eugene O'Donnell**, were recorded. His own credits are too numerous to list, but special attention should be drawn to the two albums he recorded with Robbie O'Connell and the piano accordionist **Jimmy Keane** in the 1980s, **There Were Roses** (whose title track is a sublime rendition of the classic Tommy Sands song) and the equally elegant **Kilkelly**. More recently, Moloney combined with Egan and O'Donnell for the splendid **3 Way Street** which includes Mick in fine voice on the old vaudeville favourite, "Uncle Dan McCann", while his banjo skills are to the fore on the reels "The Maid of Mount Kisco/Dowd's No. 9".

⊙ **Kilkelly**   Green Linnet, 1988

Includes The Green Fields of America, a sequence of songs and tunes recounting the Irish-American experience of the last 150 years.

⊙ **3 Way Street**   Green Linnet, 1993

Moloney plus Eugene O'Donnell and Seamus Egan make a powerful and engaging combination.

Martin Murray

Widely appreciated for his excellent fiddling, **Martin Murray** is also a superb practitioner of both mandolin and banjo. A founder member of **Damp in the Attic**, the man from Co.

Tipperary has featured on many albums, including releases by Garry Ó Briain and Grianán and Bill Whelan's soundtrack to *Dancing at Lughnasa*. His only solo album to date is the well-received **A Dark Horse**, a joyous swingalong release which blends elements of ragtime into some well-honed traditional tunes. Guests abound, such as Máirtín O'Connor and Frankie Gavin on "Mike Flanagan's" barndances while the strength of Murray's own compositions is revealed by the reel "The Dandy Brush". He and his wife Ann now co-run the fine pub Drowsey Maggie's in Martin's home town, Carrick-on-Suir, Co. Tipperary, and he can regularly be heard playing in sessions there.

⊙ **A Dark Horse**   Cross Border Media, 1996

The banjo/mandolin combination may not be everyone's cup of tea, but this one makes a fine brew.

Gerry O'Beirne

A familiar figure since the 1970s and his work in **Midnight Well**, **Gerry O'Beirne** is one of the most sought-after guitarists in Irish music. Over the years he's worked with some of the country's biggest names, including Mary Black, Sharon Shannon and Patrick Street and is garnering a growing reputation as a producer. Now based in Nashville, Gerry released his own long-awaited solo album, **Half Moon Bay**, in 1999. It's an absolute cracker for guitar-lovers as Gerry demonstrates his expertise on six- and twelve-string, national steel and slide varieties and even ukulele. Best of the instrumentals is "Off the Rocks at Clahane", where Gerry's rolls on the melody line enhance the maritime mood. And the best of his vocals is reserved for his most famous song, "Western Highway", which boosted Maura O'Connell's career and has been covered countless times.

⊙ **Half Moon Bay** own label, 1999

Exquisite guitar-playing and soulful singing.

Garry Ó Briain

A musician's musician, **Garry Ó Briain** (b. 1949 Dublin) is not only Ireland's pre-eminent exponent of the mandocello, but a notable instrument-maker, producer and arranger too. Ó Briain brings a wide range of influences to his music from his travels in Canada, Europe and the Middle East (where he first encountered the oud, an Arabic lute, which led him towards the mandocello). Since the 1970s, Ó Briain has featured in a number of influential bands (including Aengus, At the Racket, Buttons and Bows, Máirtín O'Connor's Chatterbox, and Skylark) and collaborated as musician or producer with singers and musicians as wide-ranging as James Keane, Pádraigín Ní Uallacháin and Len Graham, Dordán and The Clancy Brothers. Gary also studied fiddle-making and, for many years, has been based in North Clare where he established an instrument workshop. Experimental by inclination, his 1998 album **Fís – Carolan's Dream** saw him revisiting some of the composer's lesser-known works with an invigorating panache, utilizing musicians of the calibre of Nollaig Casey, Martin Murray and Laoise Kelly, to produce glorious confirmation of Carolan's melodic strengths.

⊙ **Fís – Carolan's Dream** Gael-Linn, 1998

Carolan revitalized with ingenuity and infinite grace.

Gerry O'Connor

Reckoned to be the fastest banjo plucker in the West, **Four Men and a Dog** stalwart **Gerry O'Connor** never lets speed serve as a substitute for quality as his playing on "Cam A' Lochaigh", the opening track of his latest CD **Myriad**, amply demonstrates. It's hard to conceive, but there is really only one tenor banjo player plucking away on these reels with such flair and not a small army tucked away in the studio. Family tradition determined that Gerry should be a fid-dle player and he was given a fiddle when he was still too young to hold it properly. Though he made progress on the instrument, hearing a banjo player in the local Barge Inn in Garrykennedy, Co. Tipperary, completely won him over and he was soon beginning a life-long love affair with the instrument. **Myriad** was recorded over a five-year period on the rare occasions that Four Men and a Dog were not on tour. Nevertheless, there's a remarkable constancy

HEIDI PEARSON

and cohesion to the album (half the tracks are O'Connor originals) which takes in a traditional jazz jam and some atmospheric dobro-playing from the wonderfully-named Randall Rainwater before Gerry returns to his roots with "The Garrykennedy Set", where he's accompanied by father Liam on fiddle and brother Michael on accordion.

⊙ **Myriad** Compass Records, 1999

Stunning, virtuoso brilliance from Gerry "Banjo" O'Connor made this one of the best albums of 1999.

Tommy O'Sullivan

An impressively quick and percussive guitarist with dextrous chord and barré techniques, **Tommy O'Sullivan** was born in London in 1961 and spent his first eleven years there before returning with his parents to their native Dingle Peninsula in Co. Kerry. His guitar skills were honed when he returned to London in the early 1980s and became a mainstay of the Irish music circuit, playing with Crannog and the legendary Jimmy Power among many others. In the early 1990s he was a member of **Skellig**, but since then his skills as an accompanist have been heavily in demand, notably on Paddy Keenan's **Na Keen Affair** album and on the piper's tours. Now back in Dingle and a member of **Sliabh Notes** Tommy can regularly be found accompanying **Séamus Begley** and giving air to his own emotive singing voice. Tommy's only solo album so far is the self-released **Legacy** cassette where he's equally at home demonstrating his finger-picking skills.

▦ **Legacy** own label, 1993

A strong album of expertly played tunes – catch Tommy in Dingle's An Droichead Beag for a copy.

John Rea

A rarity in twentieth-century Irish music, the hammer dulcimer's modern master was **John Rea**, born in 1922 near Glenarm in the Glens of Antrim. His father taught all six of his sons the fiddle but, in the absence of an instrument for John (the youngest), his elder brother Alex made him a dulcimer – a two-octave version, strung with piano wire, which John played with two other pieces of wire, bent and bound with darning wool. Much of his repertoire was inherited from his father who knew many of the jigs attributed to the eighteenth-century uilleann piper, William Jackson. Like many Antrim musicians, Scotland's proximity and strong cultural ties with the Glens also influenced his playing. Rea was a sailor for many years, latterly working on tugs in Belfast Harbour before returning to Glenarm where he died in 1983. His 1976 LP **Drops of Brandy** recorded with Fermanagh piper **Sean McAloon**, has been out-of-print for many years and the only currently available recordings are on the cassette **The Irish Hammered Dulcimer**, a reissue of a 1979 Topic LP (tracks from both albums appear on the Temple CD **Irish Traditional Music**). Well worth seeking out, Rea's sprightly renditions of a variety of tunes have an extraordinary precision, for instance on the strathspey, "Lady Anne Hope". Of the few Irish musicians now playing the hammer dulcimer, **Barry Carroll** (from Lisburn, Co. Antrim) was inspired to learn after seeing Rea in action. The results can be heard on **The Long Finger** (1992) recorded with the Derry uilleann piper Joe McHugh. Barry also features on Sharon Shannon's **Each Little Thing** album.

The Irish Hammered Dulcimer   Ossian Publications, 1979

A true original in inspired form.

Colin Reid

Described by no less than Bert Jansch as "myself and John Renbourn fused together", the young guitarist from Belfast, **Colin Reid** has (along with Scotland's Tony McManus) breathed new life into the finger-style gui-

tar. Reid was around the music scene for a while (and features on Niamh Parsons' first album) before heading off for London for a year's formal training on the electric guitar. Returning home, he purchased an acoustic guitar and began working on honing his technique. He is now one of the most accomplished guitarists around and his 1998 self-titled debut album represents an undoubted watershed in modern guitar playing. Varied tunings abound and influences are evident from many fields, but there's an undeniable Irish edge to Reid's playing. The appropriately-titled "Frantic", for instance, is rapidly improvised around a recognizable reel, while "Across the Fields" could easily be an Irish air.

⊙ **Colin Reid**   Veesik Records, 1998

Dexterous isn't sufficient praise, this man surely has more than ten fingers.

Uilleann pipers

Adapted from the Irish war pipes (a slightly larger version of the Scottish Highland bagpipes), the uilleann pipes began to appear in the early 1700s, though the form known today was first developed several decades later. The price of a set of uilleann pipes was well beyond the means of most people and, for some time, they remained largely the province of the gentry (hence the name "gentlemen pipers"). A full set today will cost several thousand pounds and most players begin on a cheaper practice set, consisting simply of bag and chanter.

The name "uilleann" (pronounced illun or ill-yun, depending on local dialects) derives from the Irish word for elbow. Played while seated, a bellows fixed under one arm drives air through a leather bag set under the other. Connected to the bag is a chanter, made of hardwood, which rests on the piper's right knee. The chanter has a double reed and a range of two octaves. Pressing the chanter's end against the knee allows the piper to stop the natural legato effect and produce a staccato style. Resting on the pipers' legs are the drones and regulators, and a full set has three of each – tenor, baritone and bass – tuned an octave apart. Drones can be switched on or off and the regulators have metal keys which sound a note when pressed with the side of the hand. (Some still refer to the instrument as the "union" pipes, referring to the link between the chanter and regulator.) Pipes are distinguished between those in concert pitch (D) and "flat" pitch – set one or more semitones lower – preferred by players seeking a more mellow tone.

A piper's playing style is described as either "open" (legato) or

"tight" (staccato). The former was favoured by the travelling piper
Johnny Doran who was a huge influence on today's best exponent
of the legato style, **Paddy Keenan**. The most prolific "tight" player is
Paddy's great friend **Finbar Furey** (see p.194), whose sound was
described by fellow-piper Pat Mitchell as resembling "pistol shots".
Undoubtedly the most celebrated and significant figure in the development of piping in the twentieth century was **Leo Rowsome**,
whose use of the regulators for harmonic and percussive effect was
exceptional. Another key character was **Seán Reid** who, in addition
to leading the Tulla Céilí Band, played a fundamental role in the continuation of the tradition during CCÉ's early years and proposed the
formation of a specialist organization for pipers. When this was finally
set up, as Na Píobairí Uilleann in 1968, the result was a remarkable
resurgence of interest in the pipes which shows no sign of abating.
(One outstanding modern piper not included in the following pages is
Brian McNamara who is
discussed in the "Families
section" on p.261.)

Uilleann piping is well represented by compilation
discs covering virtually the
whole of the twentieth century. **The Gentleman Pipers**
boasts twenty-five tracks
from many vinyl albums now
almost impossible to find
while **The Drones and the
Chanters** is a remarkable
testament to the pipers who formed Na Píobairí Uilleann and inspired
the art's latterday revival (a second volume was devoted to piping in

the 1990s). **The Piper's Rock** is a ground-breaking album of young players, one of whom, Gabriel McKeon, recently joined forces with the album's producer, P.J. Curtis, to deliver the most up-to-date survey, **A New Dawn**, featuring pipers from the latest generation (but also including a spectacular recording of "The Shaskeen" by Patsy Touhey from the early years of the twentieth century).

⊙ **The Gentleman Pipers**   Globestyle, 1920s–70s

Classic piping from the Topic archive, including William Jackson and Liam Walsh from the early twentieth century.

⊙ **The Drones and the Chanters Vols 1 and 2** Claddagh, 1971 and 1994

The first album includes Leo Rowsome, Tommy Reck and Dan Dowd, the second looks at Ronan Browne, Liam Ó Flynn and Seán Potts.

⊙ **The Piper's Rock**   Mulligan, 1978

This superb collection of young uilleann pipers features Davy Spillane, Mick O'Brien, Gabriel McKeon and Robbie Hannan.

⊙ **A New Dawn**   Na Píobairí Uilleann, 1999

A showcase which presents six of the best young pipers around today.

Peter Browne

Peter Browne is one of several past students of Leo Rowsome who went on to become significant pipers in their own right. In the 1970s, he co-founded the short-lived **1691** and later rejoined some of its members (Matt Molloy and Tríona Ní Dhomhnaill) in **The Bothy Band**, stepping in to replace Paddy Keenan. His playing with the band can be heard on the **BBC Radio 1 in Concert** album. In the subsequent decade, Peter worked closely with **Philip King**, playing pipes, flute and whistle, and collaborating on two, sadly, long-deleted albums, **Rince Gréagach** (1981) and **Seacht Nóiméad Deag Chun a Seacht** (1983) and has also featured on recordings by Mary Black and Mick Hanly among many others. Nowadays, he is better known as a

KEVIN ROWSOME

Leo Rowsome (left) with Peter Browne

broadcaster specializing in traditional music programmes, and has unearthed several major recordings from the RTÉ archive, including the essential Pádraig O'Keeffe collection (see p.347).

⊙ **BBC Radio 1 in Concert Album**   Windsong, 1978

Two Bothy Band concerts, the earlier featuring Peter in fine form at Birmingham Town Hall in 1976.

Ronan Browne

Dubliner **Ronan Browne**'s grandmother was **Delia Murphy**, the queen of balladeering, and her grandson can sometimes be heard providing the bass parts for **Cran**'s exquisite vocal harmonies, though he's much better known for his uilleann piping and flute playing. At seven he began lessons at The Pipers' Club and soon demonstrated a prodigious talent. Willie Clancy, Séamus Ennis and Johnny Doran were early influences but his musical journey has also absorbed the contrasting fiddle styles of Denis Murphy and Tommy Potts. Love of the fiddle has continued and Ronan has often played as a duo with **Kevin Glackin**. Indeed, his 1993 album **The South West Wind** saw him working as another pairing with the Co. Clare fiddle master **Peadar O'Loughlin**. It's a scintillating record, deriving several tunes from Willie Clancy plus an egregious version of "The Connaught Heifers" learned from the piping of Tommy Reck. Since then Ronan has toured with **Afro Celt Sound System** and featured on their albums, and played or recorded with a host of other names from Elvis Costello to Breton harper Alan Stivell.

⊙ **The South West Wind**   Claddagh, 1993

The music of West Clare runs through Peadar O'Loughlin's veins and he found an fine collaborator in Ronan Browne.

Willie Clancy

Among all the piping greats of the twentieth century, none is remembered with as much affection or respect as **Willie Clancy**. The writer and fellow piper Pat Mitchell described him as "a man who embodied everything that was good and noble and generous in the old Irish tradition". Clancy's original connection with that tradition came through two key sources. One was the music of the renowned blind piper **Garret Barry**, a long-time friend of his father's and a regular visitor to the Clancy household in Miltown Malbay, Co. Clare. Through his father's playing, on flute and concertina, and his many stories about Barry, Clancy, born on Christmas Eve, 1918, became closely familiar with Barry's music even before he began playing himself, starting with the tin whistle, aged five, then progressing on to the concert flute, on which his style was heavily influenced by piping techniques. The other key encounter in his musical development was with **Johnny Doran**, the first time being when the legendary travelling piper played a nearby race-meeting in 1936. So entranced was Clancy that he would follow Doran's caravan around the county at every opportunity, and it was through Doran's brother Felix that he acquired his first practice set of pipes, in 1938. The local West Clare fiddle style was also a significant influence, particularly the playing of Scully Casey and his son **Bobby**.

In between his work as a master carpenter, and playing the flute at house-dances, weddings and wakes, alongside Bobby Casey or piper and flute player **Martin Talty**, Clancy slowly taught himself to master the pipes, acquiring his first full set around 1940. In 1947, Séan Reid, then working for Clare County Council, drove Clancy, Martin Rochford and Paddy O'Donoghue to Dublin to compete at that year's Oireachtas, where Clancy won first prize. As celebrated as he was now becoming, there was no money in traditional music during this period, and insufficient other work at home, so in 1951 Clancy moved to Dublin in search of employment. He got to know many of the city's leading pipers including **Séamus Ennis**, **John Potts** and **Tommy Reck**, absorbing their tight-fingered method into his own legato technique, the resulting hybrid later coming to be identified as "the Clancy style". He also joined Leo Rowsome's quartet for several radio broadcasts.

A shortage of work saw Clancy and Casey move to London in 1953, where Willy renewed his acquaintance with Ennis, becoming a well-known figure on the expat Irish music scene until called home by his father's death in 1957. By this time, the Irish cultural climate was beginning to create a more conducive environment for Clancy's gifts. A series of recordings for Gael-Linn in the late 1950s won him national recognition and, over the next decade and a half, Miltown Malbay and its surrounding area became known as a mecca for traditional musicians, with Clancy very much at the heart of the sessions that took place in Friel's bar. Thanks in no small part to Clancy's personal warmth, wit and wisdom, as well as his music, those sessions attracted many a distinguished visitor over the years, including Paddy Moloney, Christy Moore and Paul Brady.

In addition to his playing, Clancy developed an interest in pipe- and reed-making, using his carpentry skills to teach himself these aspects of the instrument, and was in the process of establishing a business in this line at the time of his sudden and premature death in January 1973. His funeral was among the biggest ever witnessed in the traditional music community, and within months of his death plans were being drawn up for an annual teaching festival in his honour. Scoil Samraidh Willie Clancy is now the biggest such event in Ireland, attracting thousands of visitors as well as participants to Miltown Malbay each July for a week-long feast of non-stop music-making (see p.573).

Combining elements from the "lonesome" West Clare sound of Garret Barry, the magnificent wildness of Johnny Doran and Ennis's sparing use of the regulators with a bright, keen gaiety very much in keeping with his own personality, Clancy's playing – especially in the slow airs – was also deeply informed by his love for the Irish language, which he once described as "the greatest music of all". His music is preserved primarily on three recordings – **The Minstrel From Clare** (1964), divided equally between his piping, singing and whistle playing, and the posthumously-released **The Pipering of Willie Clancy Vols 1 & 2**, compiled from recordings he made for RTÉ between 1958 and 1972 including his versions of tunes learned from

Garret Barry ("Garret Barry's Mazurka", "The Fowler on the Moor"), Johnny Doran ("My Love Is In America", "The Steampacket"), Séamus Ennis and others.

⊙ **The Pipering of Willie Clancy, Vols 1 & 2**   Claddagh, 1958–72

This 42-track companion set shows off Clancy's "pipering" in all its glory.

Johnny and Felix Doran

Just as music itself, in many of the folk tales enshrined in traditional tunes and songs, is often invested with supernatural properties, so the lives of some traditional musicians take on a quality of myth, even magic. The great uilleann piper **Johnny Doran** was one such: his travelling heritage, his tragic untimely death, but most of all the mesmerizing power of his playing, all lent his story an aura of otherworldly mystique. Along with his younger brother **Felix**, also a hugely gifted player, Doran was the last in a long and illustrious line of professional travelling musicians which included his maternal grandfather John Cash – one of the great pipers of the nineteenth century. Born in 1907, he grew up within a culture that valued music, piping especially, as the highest of callings. When in his early twenties, Johnny taught Felix – eight years younger – to play, not long before the elder brother answered the call of the road.

Although their family roots were in Co. Wicklow – and despite their nomadic lifestyle – both brothers' favourite haunts were in Co. Clare. The paucity of pipers in the county belied the instrument's former local dominance until around the beginning of the twentieth century, but it guaranteed a warm welcome when Johnny's brightly-decorated

FOLK ROOTS ARCHIVE

Johnny Doran (right), with Pat Cash and son

horse caravan first rolled up in the early 1930s. A teenage Willie Clancy, entranced by Doran's playing, would often follow him around the county, from house-dance to horse fair, football game to hurling match, later acquiring his first set of practice pipes from Felix.

Wherever he went, though, Johnny's magic touch on the pipes ensured him a good living, supplemented by horse-trading. A small but charismatic figure, who played standing up for greater impact, he was also reputedly in the habit of playing out in the fields after dark, for the delectation of the little people. More certain is the fact that those who heard him first-hand, including Clancy, Seán Reid, Martin Rochford and Martin Talty, consistently talked of falling into a kind of spellbound trance, such was the fiery magnificence of his music.

In 1947, at the instigation of his old friend, fiddler and concertina player John Kelly, Johnny entered a studio for the first and only time, recording nine acetate discs for the Irish Folklore Commission. Forty years on, these were remastered and issued as **The Bunch Of Keys**. Even given the technical limitations of the time, Doran's bravura handling of chanter, drones and regulators, creating endlessly varied configurations of melody, harmony and rhythm, legato and staccato fingering, shine resplendently through in classic reels and jigs including "Rakish Paddy", "My Love Is In America", "Coppers and Brass" and "The Rambling Pitchfork", while slow airs like "An Chúileann" allow one to linger on the profound emotional depths he brought to their execution.

Less than a year after the recordings were made, a wall collapsed on Johnny's caravan during a storm, leaving him crippled and in steadily deteriorating health. He died in 1950, but his legacy lives on through successive generations, including Finbar Furey, Davy Spillane and, in particular, Paddy Keenan, who continues to play many of Doran's tunes and settings today.

By the time of Johnny's death, Felix was prospering both musically – like his brother, being much in demand on his travels to play at local gatherings and dances – and commercially, dealing in horses and scrap metal. After winning the All-Ireland piping prize at Mullingar in 1963, he fetched up in the haulage business in Manchester, where he became wealthy enough to buy first a silver-plated set of pipes from Leo Rowsome, and then an all-silver set commissioned from a German mechanic. His death in 1972 was followed by one of the largest funerals Wicklow had ever seen. Though falling marginally short of Johnny's wild transcendent genius, his playing was by any other standards exceptional, as is richly apparent from his sole extant recording, **Last of the Travelling Pipers**, which includes a live version of his celebrated showstopper, "The Fox Chase".

🎵 **The Bunch of Keys**   Comhairle Bhéaloideas Éireann, 1947

Containing the authentic sound of a bygone age and a player of true genius in Johnny Doran.

🎵 **Last of the Travelling Pipers**   Ossian Publications, 1965–67

Truly the last of his kind, Felix Doran was a remarkable piper in his own right, as these recordings demonstrate.

Séamus Ennis

Though remembered primarily for his exceptional prowess on the pipes, **Séamus Ennis** was also a talented singer and tin-whistle player, a leading traditional music collector, broadcaster and song translator, and possessed such fluency in Irish that, on his field trips, he could switch between different regional dialects depending on the locality he was researching. Each of these skills drew on and informed the others, all contributing to Ennis's monumental standing within the twentieth-century history of Irish music.

He was born in 1919 in Jamestown, Finglas, Co. Dublin, and would later recall the sound of his father's pipes among his earliest memories. James Ennis, who had learned from the renowned Co. Meath piper **Nicholas Markey**, was a prize-winning musician on several instruments, as well as a champion dancer, and the family home was a frequent gathering-place for leading players. Séamus attended both English- and Irish-language schools, with the latter grounding being reinforced by family visits to the Connemara Gaeltacht. He first picked up the pipes aged thirteen and, despite receiving little or no formal tuition, developed a virtually fully formed style by the time he reached his early twenties.

Ennis's first job was with the Three Candles Press, where he learned staff notation and music transcription – vital skills in his subsequent work – before being hired as a music collector by the Irish Folklore Commission in 1942. These early field trips, taking in the Scottish Highlands as well as much of Ireland, quickly revealed his gift for establishing an easy rapport with his subjects and his phenomenal memory for tunes. The trips produced the first of his seminal music and song collections, among his richest sources being the singers **Colm Ó Caodháin** and **Elizabeth Cronin**. Employed by Radio Éireann as an Outside Broadcast Officer in 1947, he exhibited a similar flair for producing and presenting documentary programmes, among them two surviving shows on sean-nós singing. His programmes were among the first to bring the music of rural Ireland to an urban audience, and enabled musicians in different parts of the country to hear other regional styles. He moved to London in 1951 to join a landmark BBC collection project covering all four countries of the British Isles.

During these years he worked extensively alongside the legendary American collector Alan Lomax – some of these recordings having recently been reissued as part of **The Alan Lomax Collection: Classic Ballads of Britain and Ireland, Vols 1 and 2** – and presented the BBC's ground-breaking weekly traditional-music programme *As I Roved Out*. The timing of these projects and the skill of the collectors involved (who included Ewan MacColl, Peter Kennedy and Hamish Henderson) was of immeasurable importance in preserving a vast store of traditional material, much of it gathered from older singers and players in rural areas being transformed by continuing waves of emigration.

By the time Ennis returned to Ireland, after finishing with the BBC in 1958, the first stirrings of the folk revival were just around the corner, and during the 1960s and '70s he combined freelance broadcasting work with what gradually became a full-time career as a professional musician and lecturer. In addition to playing throughout Ireland, driving around with hair-raising haphazardness in his Ford Zephyr, he also appeared at the 1964 Newport Folk Festival in the US, and performed at the inaugural meeting of Na Píobairí Uilleann in 1968. During the early 1970s he shared a flat with **Liam O'Flynn**, becoming a mentor to the younger piper and playing alongside him in the **Halfpenny Bridge Quartet**, also featuring fiddler **Séan Keane** and accordionist **Tommy Grogan**. In 1975, having bought a plot of land on what had once been his grandparents' farm, he moved "home" to Naul, Co. Dublin, living there in a caravan while continuing to travel for concerts and lectures, until his death from cancer in 1982.

Besides the overall balance of delicacy, finesse and livewire exuberance in Ennis's piping, his style included a number of signature touches that render it instantly recognizable to this day. His unusually long wrists and fingers enabled him to exceed the instrument's normal physical constraints, by reaching into the third octave of the chanter, and setting deeper regulator chords against the melody. Other hallmarks included his full forearm roll, or "shiver" on the high E and F, his distinctively stuttering cran and the double-note illusion of his "ghost D", while his masterly slow air playing was richly informed by his understanding of traditional song and the Irish language.

Ennis made many recordings during his lifetime, among them **The Bonny Bunch of Roses** (1959), which also included his singing and whistle playing, **The Pure Drop** (1973) and **The Fox Chase** (1978), the latter featuring his famous version of the showpiece title track. It also appears on **Forty Years Of Irish Piping** (1977), along with several other of his best-known sets, including "The Silver Spear", "Salamanca" and "Don Niperi Septo". **The Return From Fingal**, compiled by Peter Browne from 40 years' worth of archive material, is generally regarded as the definitive collection. Revealing both the consistencies and the developments in Ennis's playing, it includes classic renditions of "Bonny Kate" and "The Milliner's Daughter" complemented by a few examples of his vibrant singing.

⊙ The Return From Fingal   RTÉ, 1940–80

A resplendent overview of Ennis's brilliant career despite some distinctly crackly tracks.

⊙ Forty Years of Irish Piping   Green Linnet, 1937–77

Once again the recording quality is poor but this is still definitively and gloriously Ennis.

Robbie Hannan

Born in Belfast, **Robbie Hannan** was raised a few miles to the east in Holywood, Co. Down and is currently Curator of Music at the Ulster Folk and Transport Museum in nearby Cultra. Inspired by listening to Paddy Moloney and Liam O'Flynn, he took up the pipes himself and received early encouragement from the Co. Fermanagh piper Seán MacAloon, then resident in Belfast. A regular at Willie Clancy Week since the late 1970s, Robbie has since developed into one of Ireland's foremost pipers. His repertory reflects his own keen interest in the fiddle music of Donegal and a sample of this can be heard on his, so far, only solo release **Traditional Irish Music Played on the Uilleann Pipes**. Robbie's inspired rendition of the Doherty-associated jig "Darby Gallagher's" segues seamlessly into "An Buachalillin Buí", one of the "Lark in the Morning" family of jigs learned from the playing of Séamus Ennis. Robbie's adroit fingering embellishes but never overwhelms his material, an accomplishment recognized by the many musicians who have sought his accompaniment on their own recordings, most notably **Paddy Glackin** with whom Robbie released the exhilarating **Séidéan Sí** in 1994.

⊙ **Traditional Irish Music Played on the Uilleann Pipes**   Claddagh, 1990

Donegal-inspired piping from one of Ireland's contemporary greats.

Tommy Keane

For a while in the 1980s, **Tommy Keane** (b. 1953, Waterford) was probably the best-known uilleann piper in the UK, thanks to his appearance on The Pogues album **Rum**, **Sodomy and the Lash**. During a seven-year stint in London he was a regular performer on the Irish music scene, a member of the **Thatch Céilí Band** which twice won the All-Ireland title and also provided music for the infamous first production of *The Romans in Britain*. Also adept on fiddle, flute and bodhrán, Tommy's 1991 solo release **The Piper's Apron** showcases his own flowing, legato-style piping which hits delightful heights on the reels "Big Pat/Billy Brocker's". There's also the first sighting of a musical duet with his wife **Jacqueline McCarthy** whose concertina follows Tommy note-for-note on "The Maids of Mont Cisco/The Crooked Road". Now living in Galway, their musical partnership came to full fruition on their joint album **The Wind Among the Reeds**, on which helpfully all the tunes are sourced. Tommy also produced and plays on Jacqueline's recent solo album, **The Hidden Note**.

⊙ **The Wind Among the Reeds**   Maree Music, 1996

Perfect pipes and concertina from the Galway-based couple, plus a
helping hand from Alec Finn's bouzouki.

Paddy Keenan

S ome have called **Paddy Keenan** "Johnny Doran incarnate", to
others he's known as "the pipers' piper" while, in the notorious
words of one reviewer, he's "the Jimi Hendrix of the uilleann pipes".
Together with his trademark wide-brimmed hats, Paddy Keenan's

piping is instantly recognizable, a consummate
blend of fast-paced, tight
fingering on the chanter in
the Doran "open" style
with a sublimely skilled –
and often understated –
harmonic accompaniment
on the regulators. Added
to this, his matchless skill
as an improviser and the
sheer soul of his perfor-
mances have made Paddy
Keenan one of the most exciting players of the last 50 years – in Irish
music and in any genre.

   Paddy was born in Trim, Co. Meath in 1950 into a travelling family
where both music and the upholding of the piping tradition took centre stage. His father, John, was a skilled piper and equally adept on
the flute and banjo, while his mother, Mary, was an able accordionist

and banjo player. Paddy's early years were spent travelling before the family settled in the Ballyfermot area of Dublin, where a close neighbour was Ted Furey (father of Finbar and Eddie). After learning the whistle, Paddy began playing pipes at the age of ten, receiving lessons from his father who also taught Finbar for several years. Paddy's first major performance was a travellers' benefit at the Gaiety Theatre, though he had been busking with his banjo-playing elder brother Johnny, for several years and had formed a band with him (plus singer Liam Weldon and singer/guitarist Johnny Flood) which played at The Swamp Club. Father John joined on pipes and mandolin and they became the "house band" of The Pavees Club run by John and based in Slattery's, Capel Street, a venue which soon became one of *the* places to play in Dublin.

Paddy's musical interests have always been eclectic and the late 1960s saw him learning blues on the guitar and busking in London. He abandoned traditional music for several years, enjoying a hippie lifestyle and joining a skiffle band called **The Blacksmiths** recording one long-forgotten album. Back in Ireland, he returned to the pipes and the limelight as a member of **The Bothy Band**. Desire to innovate rather than re-create saw him reject the chance to join Moving Hearts and he spent spells in the 1980s living in Brittany and Clonakilty, Co. Cork. Finally returning to music, he toured the US in 1991 and settled there the following year. He has been based in Massachusetts ever since, gigging regularly and often touring internationally.

An official reissue of Paddy Keenan's astonishing eponymous debut LP is long overdue, but the original vinyl is well worth seeking out. As Séamus Ennis writes in the sleeve notes "In the first rushing, I thought it was Doran who was playing!" Keenan's solo-playing is unstoppable, but fiddler **Paddy Glackin** matches him in a virtuoso duetted rendition of the reels "The Humours of Ballyconnell" and "Toss the Feathers" and elsewhere Paddy's brothers Johnny and Thomas provide spirited assistance on banjo and whistle, respectively. Keenan and Glackin reconvened in 1978 for the exceptional **Doublin'** album, featuring some of the most astounding duets ever recorded, before Paddy released his own solo album, **Poirt An Phíobaire** (1983), produced by Nicky Ryan (later of Enya fame). The piper's especial fondness for Brittany is represented by the slow air "Jezaique" and there's a broader sensitivity to the record as a whole, though Paddy still lets rip on reels like "The Maid Behind the Bar" and, especially, the wondrously sonorant "Collier's" (with guitarist Arty McGlynn providing able support). Devotees had to endure a Keenan-less fourteen years before the release of the self-produced **Ná Keen Affair** on his own HoT Conya Records and the wait proved inestimably worthwhile. Recorded in both Newfoundland and Ireland, the album demonstrated without doubt that Paddy is still the hottest piper on the planet. There's a super-group outing on a set of reels ("The Corner House/Paddy Taylor's/Reavey's") where McGlynn's driving guitar sets the scene for the flying fiddle of Tommy Peoples before Keenan makes his grand entry. Elsewhere, Paddy joins forces with fiddler Séamus Creagh and Niall Vallely's concertina (the latter producing a humdinger solo on "Scotch Mary").

⊙ **Poirt An Phíobaire**   Gael-Linn, 1983

It sounds simple – just pipes, whistles and guitar – but Keenan and McGlynn redefine virtuosity.

⊙ **Ná Keen Affair**   HoT Conya Records, 1997

The maestro returns in all his glory.

Tommy Martin

Dubliner Tommy Martin (b. 1972) progressed from the whistle to the uilleann pipes at the age of twelve. Almost five years of tuition from Mick O'Brien left a lasting impression, while listening to older pipers, such as the Dorans and Leo Rowsome, has influenced his repertoire. Tommy participated in a CCÉ tour of North America in the early 1990s and appeared on the subsequent **Erin's Green Shore** album. Since turning professional in 1995, he has continued to tour extensively, travelling as far afield as Asia and New Zealand. In 1999 he appeared on fiddler **Brendan Lynch**'s **Tunes from the Hearth** album and released his own **Uilleann Piper** the following year. It is a brave young piper who opens his first album with two tunes ("The Dawn"/"Buckley's Fancy") associated with Leo Rowsome, but there is no doubt that Tommy has the skills to get away with it. Unsurprisingly, there are strong echoes of O'Brien in his playing, especially in his use of crisp triplets; at other times he can sound like Davy Spillane, especially on the reel "The Jolly Tinker", but he proves he's his own man with a great version of "The Shaskeen" reel.

⊙ **Uilleann Piper**   own label, 2000

On the evidence of this debut recording, Tommy is a young piper with a promising future.

Declan Masterson

Dublin uilleann piper **Declan Masterson**'s credits are illustrious: he's been a member of Moving Hearts; played with Patrick Street and Christy Moore; featured in *Riverdance* and on soundtracks such as *The Secret of Roan Inish*, and recorded and performed with symphony orchestras. He learned his early music from his uncle, Jimmy Reilly and was also influenced by **John Kelly** and the fiddler Conor Tully. Declan's albums over the years have revealed a remarkable divergence and eclecticism. **Tropical Trad** (1993) kicks off with a bouncy Caribbean-inspired duet with fellow Moving Heart Keith Donald on saxophone, while his more recent self-produced **Fionnuisce/Fairwater** (1996) sees the multitracked Masterson trying his hand at everything from concertina to mandolin. Best of the bunch is undoubtedly his solo pipes album **Deireadh an Fhómair** (1990) where he demonstrates a delicate mastery of touch and sound across a wide spectrum of tunes from the sublime elegance of the slow air "Bean Dubh an Ghleanna" to the bouncy resonance of the set dance "Cúlú Napoleon" (popularized by The Chieftains as "Bonaparte's Retreat").

⊙ **Deireadh an Fhómair**　　　　　　　　　　　　Gael-Linn, 1990

Undisputably one of the best pipers around, this is a glorious expression of Masterson's skills and range.

Seán McAloon

Based in Belfast for many years, **Seán McAloon** (1930–98) was one of the North's most illustrious pipers. Born in Roslea, Co. Fermanagh, he began playing the whistle before progressing to the fiddle. Michael Coleman's records were a huge influence on his development, but it was his first hearing of the uilleann pipes which shaped his musical destiny. As he remarked himself, "After that I was gone daft on pipe music". Seán eventually acquired his own set from Crowley, the Cork pipe-maker, developing his skills on these before exchanging them with Leo Rowsome for a set of the illustrious man's own making. Seán was a farmer until 1964 before trying his luck as a musician first in the US and then in Dublin. He returned to the North in 1966 working in Belfast for the Corporation's Parks Department. He soon became well-known in the city's music circles, forming a remarkable partnership with the dulcimer-player **John Rea** and becoming an inspiration to a younger generation of pipers. With Rea, McAloon recorded the remarkable **Drops of Brandy**, the first album to feature the rare partnership of pipes and dulcimer. Seán also solos on both concert and flat pipes, using the latter's mellow tone to evocative effect on the air "Blind Mary". His fiddle gets an airing too, producing effortless rolls on the reels "Crowley's Nos. 1 & 2".

> ⊙ **Drops of Brandy**   Topic, 1976

McAloon and Rea, two of the North's great musicians, solo and combine with ease and grace.

Joe and Antoinette McKenna

The unique uilleann pipes and harp combination of **Joe** and **Antoinette McKenna** has produced some of the most distinctive sounding traditional music over the last twenty-five years. Both Dubliners, Joe was born into a well-known Liberties piping family and studied at The Pipers' Club, where he was taught by Leo Rowsome, and gradually developed a characteristically light and lyrical style augmented by delicate use of the regulators. He is also an able whistler, accordionist and pianist. Antoinette is a member of the Bergen family and continues its strong line of singers, but she is equally renowned as one of the first modern harpers to apply the instrument to traditional music. The pair first recorded in 1978,

Traditional Music of Ireland, and followed this with a number of other successful releases, including **Farewell to Fine Weather** (1984) and **Magenta Music** (1991). Selections from their back catalogue are collated on **The Best of Joe and Antoinette McKenna** on which their refined interaction can be heard on tunes like the march "The Eagle's Whistle". In the 1990s the McKennas formed the group **Sean Nua** with a second piper, Joe McHugh (also bouzouki and keyboard), and flute, whistle and clarinet player Gerry O'Donnell. Still gossamer-like in substance – especially the whistle-harp duet on the waltz-time "Clara's Vale" – the album features one of the finest of Antoinette's own songs, "Ó Ró Song of the Sea".

⊙ Sean Nua   Shanachie, 1993

From "old to new" justly summarizes this adventurous album by the McKennas and friends.

Pat Mitchell

Dublin-born Pat Mitchell began playing the pipes after receiving a set as a 21st birthday present from his parents. There had been little traditional music in his own family, though the blind piper **Dinny Delaney** (c. 1836–1919) was a distant relation (known in his last years as "The Rebel Piper" after being arrested for playing "seditious tunes" in 1916). Pat took lessons from Leo Rowsome and discussed techniques with other pipers, while his wife, Brid, helped his developing repertoire through a present of Breandán Breathnach's initial *Ceol Rince na hÉireann* (Dance Music of Ireland) collection. Breathnach himself loaned tapes of rare Edison cylinder recordings which included Dinny Delaney material. Meeting Willie Clancy at Miltown Malbay in 1966 sparked a friendship that lasted until the great piper's death in

1973. Pat was involved in the founding of Na Píobairí Uilleann in 1968 which later published his transcriptions of some of Clancy's tunes as *The Dance Music of Willie Clancy* (reissued by Ossian Publications, Cork) and, in 1986, his highly influential collaboration with fellow piper **Jackie Small**, *The Piping of Patsy Touhey*. 1976 saw his only solo release to date, **Uilleann Pipes**, though he does also feature on **Folk and Dance Music of Ireland** (see p.43). A passionate and gifted piper, Mitchell blends the tight-fingering technique he initially adopted with the looser open style associated with Clancy. His playing bristles with energy and tunes include several obscurities, such as a highly ornamental version of "Frieze Britches", in the Garret Barry style.

📼 **Uilleann Pipes** — Ossian Publications, 1976

A spell-binding mix of open and tight playing make this one of the classics of contemporary piping.

Neil Mulligan

Neil Mulligan's life has revolved around traditional music almost ever since the day he was born in Dublin in 1955. His father, **Tom** (1916–84), was a fiddler from Barnacoola, Co. Leitrim who heard the pipes for the first time when he saw Leo Rowsome play in 1932. Three years later he came to work in Dublin, acquired his own set of pipes and met fellow piper Tommy Reck (who became a close friend) and both became involved in the Pipers' Club. Tom married Catherine McMahon, from Beale, Co. Kerry, and the pair set up house in North Dublin. By the time Neil was born, his home was so often visited by musicians that **Séamus Ennis**, himself a regular caller, dubbed it the "Rotary Club". It was Ennis, indeed, who gave Neil his nickname of Neillidh, in honour of the great fiddler Neillidh

Boyle. After learning the whistle, Neil began playing the uilleann pipes at the age of eleven, initially under his father's tutelage, but later attending Leo Rowsome's classes at the School of Music, soon augmented by Saturday lessons at The Pipers' Club. Neil won both under-14 and under-18 All Ireland titles, but gave up competition after the latter victory in 1970, preferring not to vie for honours with his friends.

Instead he broadened his musical education through visits around the country with his father (who had by now returned to the fiddle), meeting and playing with some of the legends of traditional music – Willie Clancy, Lad O'Beirne, Felix Doran, **Joe Heaney** and many others – while Séamus Ennis remained a constant influence. Father and son performed in concerts organized by Heaney and played together for the last time at the singer's funeral in 1984 just two days before Tom Mulligan's own death.

Though retaining his day job, Neil has continued to play and tour whenever he can and has remained active in Na Píobairí Uilleann since its foundation. Although his brothers Alfie and Tom (who runs the excellent Cobblestone music pub in Smithfield, Dublin) are also both fine musicians, only Neil has recorded, releasing two superb examples of the piper's art – **Barr Na Cúille** in 1991 (named after his father's birthplace) and **The Leitrim Thrush** six years later. On both, the great warmth of his character and his love for the tradition imbue his pipes to thrilling effect. While absolute mastery is evident throughout his playing of dance tunes, it is Neil's reverence for the sean-nós song tradition which informs the majestic grace of his renditions of slow airs such as "Curachaí na Trá Báine" (learned from Joe Heaney) or "Bean Dubh an Ghleanna" (from Seán 'ac Dhonncha). His ornamentation is as clear and powerful as you could ever wish to hear and the dexterity of his fingering is thrilling. Fittingly, **The Leitrim Thrush** closes with two reels from Tom, recorded in 1982.

⊙ The Leitrim Thrush   Spring Records, 1997

Neil takes his pipes to uncharted territories in this marvellous recording.

Mick O'Brien

Another of the young pipers to feature on **The Piper's Rock** (see p.396), Dubliner Mick O'Brien took up the pipes at the age of nine under Leon Rowsome (Leo's son) at The Pipers' Club. In his teens he was a successful hurler and made the full county side, piping taking a back seat for a while. He returned to piping in the 1980s, releasing **The Flags of Dublin** (1980) with fiddler Paddy Glackin and playing with the band **Oscine** and **Boys of the Lough** (including their most recent album **The West of Ireland**). Mick has featured in the RTÉ Orchestra's performance of Charlie Lennon's *Island Wedding*, but nowadays can be more often heard in continental Europe where he is a member of the band **Callino** and also regularly tours as a soloist and teacher. A devotee of the Patsy Touhey "close fingered" piping style, Mick plays both concert and flat pipes on his CD **May Morning Dew**, employing elegant use of drones and regulators on "Statia Donnelly's" jig and achieving a dolorous majesty on the title track air. More recently Mick was the featured performer on **The Ancient Voice of Ireland** (1999) where his exceptional technique is wasted on "haunting melodies" for the tourist trade.

| ⊙ **May Morning Dew** | own label, 1990s |

O'Brien's piping in all its many-splendoured colours.

Tomás Ó Canaínn

One of traditional music's most illustrious theoreticians and practitioners is the Derry-born uilleann piper, accordionist and singer **Tomás Ó Canaínn** (b. 1930). Author of *Traditional Music in Ireland* and co-author of an acclaimed biography of Seán Ó Riada, *A Shaol agus a Shaothar*, Tomás's published music collections include *Traditional Slow Airs of Ireland*. After a spell in England, where he was a founder member of the **Liverpool Céilí Band**, Ó Canaínn moved to Cork and was, for several years, Dean of Engineering at the University where he also continued Ó Riada's Irish music lectures after his death in 1971 and taught pipes in the Cork School of Music. A past All-Ireland champion piper known as "The Pennyburn Piper" (after the area of Derry city where he was reared), Tomás formed one of the 1970s most popular groups, **Na Filí**, with fiddler **Matt Cranitch** and whistler **Tom Barry**. Since its demise, he's continued to be active in traditional music and has released two albums: a solo recording, **With Pipe and Song** (1980), and **Uilleann Pipes** (1998) in collaboration with cellist, flute player and fellow-piper **Neil Martin**. Ó Canaínn plays a number of his own compositions, including "Planxty Montenotte" (on which he's joined by his three daughters) and produces some sumptuous piping of slow airs, especially "Aisling Gheal", with Martin's cello adding an extra resonance. There's some good singing too, and collectors of odd tune titles will appreciate "The Pratie in the Gander's Whole", renamed by James McPeake.

⊙ **Uilleann Pipes**   Outlet, 1998

A fine collection, impeccably played and sung by one of traditional music's literati in harness with Neil Martin.

Liam O'Flynn

A survey of **Liam O'Flynn**'s piping career offers a powerful refutation of purist notions that traditional music should be kept hermetically sheltered from the supposedly corrupting taint of other genres and styles. Having helped invent the very concept of the modern traditional band during his days with **Planxty**, O'Flynn has worked with pop stars and poets, film directors and classical orchestras, all the while exhibiting an unerring, almost uncanny ability to preserve the integrity of his instrument's voice.

Though he was born in Co. Kildare, in 1945, O'Flynn's true musical roots lie in Co. Clare, the birthplace of his piano-playing mother who was a cousin of the famed fiddler Junior Crehan. Introduced to the pipes by a family friend, Liam quickly revealed an outstanding natural talent, going on to study with Leo Rowsome. Through his Clare connections, he also got to know Willie Clancy (who once owned O'Flynn's current Rowsome set of pipes), another formative influence was Séamus Ennis, whose antique Coyne set O'Flynn also inherited.

It was through playing at sessions in the neighbouring Kildare village of Prosperous that O'Flynn first met **Christy Moore**, **Dónal Lunny** and **Andy Irvine**, his colleagues in the line-up that would catapult all four to international prominence, Planxty. Towards the end of his time with the band, his ground-breaking soloist's role in Shaun Davey's **The Brendan Voyage** (1980), one of the first compositions ever to combine traditional instruments and orchestra, introduced him (and his instrument) to a whole different audience.

O'Flynn has continued to pursue new avenues ever since, among them several more collaborations with Davey, and a number of film scores, notably for *Cal* (1984), with Mark Knopfler, and *The Field* (1990). He's guested on albums by the likes of Kate Bush, Enya, the Everly Brothers and Sinéad O'Connor, as well as with many leading top artists, formed a much-fêted performance partnership with Nobel Laureate Séamus Heaney, and developed a burgeoning interest in other European "Celtic" traditions, especially Galician music. Towards the end of the 1980s, he also released his own first two albums – his eponymous debut (1988), featuring several ex-Planxty pals, followed by **The Fine Art of Piping** (1989), both essentially re-underlining his traditional credentials as a solo artist, while subtly revealing the influence of his musical travels.

It was during the 1990s, though, that O'Flynn's solo work took on a new pre-eminence. **Out To An Other Side** (1993) blended ancient classic tunes and songs, Davey compositions, and semi-orchestral arrangements with marvellous subtlety and sensitivity, while **The Given Note** (1995) swung the pendulum masterfully back towards a more traditional approach, also developing that Galician connection with guests from the band Milladoiro. **The Piper's Call** (1998), however, triumphantly united the best of both predecessors. Its range of complementing contrasts are exemplified in "An Droichead" (The Bridge), a regal slow march composed for Irish President Mary McAleese's inauguration, with Mark Knopfler on electric guitar, the rambunctious seven-part jig "The Gold Ring", featuring fiddler Seán Keane in dazzling form, and the slow air "Bean Dubh an Ghleanna" (Dark Woman of the Glen), gorgeously arranged by Mícheál Ó Súilleabháin for the Irish Chamber Orchestra.

Among all the plaudits O'Flynn has received, it's perhaps Séamus Heaney who has most eloquently defined the "forcefield" his playing creates: "Behind these tunes you can hear freedom as well as discipline, elegy as well as elation, a longing for solitude as well as a love of the seisiun." The great thing is, too, that the trajectory of O'Flynn's career so far suggests he's only now approaching the true peak of his powers.

⊙ **The Piper's Call**   Tara, 1998

A wise and wonderful album, from the most significant piper of his generation assisted by a dream team of accompanists.

Christy O'Leary

Although **Christy O'Leary**'s primary roots lie in Co. Kerry, the life and career of this widely respected piper, singer and multi-instrumentalist (he also plays fiddle, tin whistle and harmonica) have seen him roving far and wide from this home territory. Born in Dublin, he received piping tuition from Mícheál Ó Riabhaigh of the Cork Pipers' Club after the family moved back to Kenmare, Co. Kerry; Willie Clancy and Séamus Ennis were his other main influences. He started performing professionally aged twelve, with his elder brother Tim, later joining **De Dannan** as lead singer from 1979–81. Membership of Irish/Scots outfit **Boys of the Lough** for twelve years, prompted a move to Edinburgh, where the group were based. Solo since 1997, and having married a Swede in 1992, he now divides his

time mainly between Scotland and Sweden – hence the title of his first solo album, **The Northern Bridge** (1997), a mainly song-based collection of both Irish and Scandinavian material. The mix produces some interesting results: "Norwegian Wedding March/Slängpolska efter Lungström", played on pipes and whistle, lends a distinct

Kerry flavour to these Nordic tunes, while O'Leary and his brother's buzzing twin fiddles on a set of slides produce an effect, reminiscent of the double-strung Norwegian hardanger fiddle. In pride of place, however, is O'Leary's sweet, gentle, naturally authoritative singing – poignantly woebegone on Jimmy Mo "Mhíle Stór", supple and sprightly on "The Trip Over the Mountain" – with excellent accompaniment throughout, led by ex-Boys of the Lough colleague **Chris Newman** on guitar, mandolin and bass.

⊙ **The Northern Bridge**   Old Bridge Music, 1997

A long overdue solo debut, offering a finely-wrought and absorbingly varied introduction to O'Leary's multiple talents.

Mícheál and Eoin Ó Riabhaigh

F ormed in 1898, the Cork Pipers' Club is the oldest organization of its kind in Ireland, but fell into abeyance between the 1930s and 1963 when it was revived by **Mícheál Ó Riabhaigh** (1911–76). Both here and at his later classes at the Cork School of Music, the dynamic Ó Riabhaigh sparked a remarkable revival of interest in the uilleann pipes. First taught by the Cork pipe-maker Tadgh Crowley, Mícheál came under the influence of Leo Rowsome during a spell working in Dublin, and would later emulate the master by achieving fame through his own radio broadcasts. He also was often invited to appear at European festivals and one such, at Quimper in 1960, led to his appearance playing a selection of airs on an obscure 10" LP, **Les Irlandais aux Fêtes de Cornouaille**, one of his few surviving recordings.

Many of Mícheál's pupils have become skilled and successful pipers, including his son **Eoin Ó Riabhaigh**. A past All-Ireland champion at both Junior and Senior levels, Eoin has been piping since 1968 and made his first broadcast soon afterwards at the age of ten. One of the young musicians featured on **The Piper's Rock**, Eoin has subsequently appeared on a host of albums by artists as varied as Dolores Keane, Matt Cranitch and Iris DeMent – the latter appearance reflecting his long-term interest in American roots music. His own debut album is **Tiomnacht/Handed On** (2000), a stunning homage to his father and one of the finest recordings of uilleann piping released in recent years. By turns forceful and delicate, Eoin has taken the uilleann pipes to new heights through his extraordinary

imagination and humour. While his father is a major source of material, including an unstoppable couple of marches, "O'Neill's/I Won't Be
a Nun" (on which he is joined by six other pipers), Eoin's other treats
include a dazzling rendition of the reels "A Rainy Day/Ellie Curran's"
and a show-stopping "Bluegrass in the Backwoods" – an American
reel penned by the bluegrass star, Kenny Baker.

⊙ **Tiomnacht**   Gael-Linn, 2000

A glorious tribute to his father and incontestible proof of the
strength of Eoin's own piping.

Jerry O'Sullivan

The uilleann pipes' power to captivate has been well-document-
ed and, once hooked, few pipers are keen to get over their
addiction. **Jerry O'Sullivan**'s fascination was triggered at an early
age by hearing a record featuring the Longford piper, Peter Carberry.
Born in Manhattan, New York in 1959, his enthusiasm was nourished
by holidays visiting relatives in Ireland, seeing pipers in action and listening to the records of Séamus Ennis, Leo Rowsome, Willie Clancy,
Liam O'Flynn's work in Planxty and, above all, Johnny Doran. He
began playing in 1975 and has since risen to become the most
prominent piper in the US, featuring on records by performers as
diverse as Dolly Parton, Sinéad O'Connor and Joanie Madden. He's
figured on soundtracks, in world premiere performances of Patrick
Cassidy's orchestral compositions and even in TV commercials for
Pizza Hut! While Jerry's musical influences include East Galway flute
playing and the Clare fiddler **Séamus Connolly**, he sees the pipes as
a medium for exploring his own broader interests – so while the presence of a gospel song, a jazz ballad and works by Bach on his most

recent CD, **The Gift** may strike traditionalists as perverse, they certainly demonstrate the instrument's versatility. Purists would almost certainly be placated, however, by the warm power of his playing, with Connolly, on a set of jigs.

⊙ **The Gift**   Shanachie, 1998

Multifaceted music from the tasteful O'Sullivan.

Tommy Reck

O ne of the best-known and most popular uilleann pipers of the revival years, **Tommy Reck** (1922–91) owed his earliest influences to the songs of his Wicklow-born mother and the music of his fife-playing father from Wexford. Raised in the Liberties area of Dublin, Tommy was taught pipes by **John Potts** (father of fiddler Tommy) and **Leo Rowsome**, both of whom reinforced the Wexford link. While Leo's playing leaned towards the legato style, Tommy opted for Potts' tighter approach and developed an individual, highly articulate method which involved switching between the bass and two smaller regulators to provide what he described as a "cross beat" accompaniment. He appears on **The Drones and the Chanters Vol. 1** (see p.396) playing three tunes on a set of pipes made in the eighteenth century by Timothy Kenna, including a stunningly precise version of "The Scholar" reel. His only solo album was **The Stone in the Field** where his unaccompanied playing of the flat pipes, tuned in B♭ and employing full use of the regulators, captures all the mellow harmonies associated with the instrument. The jigs "Rose in the Heather/The Wandering Minstrel" are utterly magnetic and there are a couple of stunning polkas too.

⌗ **The Stone in the Field**   Green Linnet, 1977

The sheer unadulterated mastery of Reck's piping in glorious full flow.

The Rowsomes

By its very nature, traditional music is passed on from generation to generation and no Irish family better illustrates this than the **Rowsomes**. It all began with **Samuel Rowsome senior** (b.1820) from Ballintore Ferns, Co. Wexford. In *Irish Minstrels and Musicians*, Francis O'Neill recounts that he was "A piper of acknowledged ability...no less skilful in equipping and repairing the instrument from bellows to reeds". These skills were passed on to his sons **John** (who emigrated to Canada in the 1920s), **Thomas** (a noted concert performer) and **William**. The last-named moved to Dublin where he set up a pipe-making workshop in Harolds Cross. It was here that his son **Leo** (1903–70) took his first steps to becoming one of Ireland's most esteemed uilleann pipe-makers. Inheriting the family's playing talents, Leo progressed so rapidly that he was appointed uilleann pipes teacher at the Dublin School of Music when only sixteen, holding the part-time post until his death fifty-one years later.

When William died in 1925, Leo took over the business, finding time to manufacture a set of concert pipes for himself which are generally reckoned never to have been matched for their quality of tone. In the early 1920s he became the first piper to broadcast on Irish radio and increased his popularity through regular appearances at concerts around the country. His first recordings, which appeared in the mid-1920s, were collated by Topic in the 1970s and are now available as a single CD, **Classics of Irish Piping**. As the piper Seán

Reid once wrote, Leo Rowsome "was the exponent par excellence of an authentic, full flowing style of piping", and his recordings more than amply demonstrate the phenomenal range of his playing alongside his ability to imbue his music with the joyful exuberance that was such an inspiration to others. The brilliance of Leo's style lay in its apparent relaxed simplicity, the way he allowed the melody to pour forth while his commanding and compact use of the regulators provided the harmony. He was no less a master of the cran, that fluttering and highly difficult staccato effect used on the chanter's low D. As an organizer, he revived the Dublin Pipers' Club in 1936, along with his brother **Tom** helped found CCÉ, and was (with Séamus Ennis) one of the first patrons of Na Píobairí Uilleann on its formation in 1968. By then he had already released the first-ever vinyl album of uilleann piping, naturally called **Rí na bPíobairí** (The King of the Pipers), which featured a classic rendition of "The Fox Chase".

KEVIN ROWSOME

Leo Rowsome and his son Leon

Leo had suffered serious illness in 1956, but, on recovery, returned to playing, cementing his international reputation with a concert at Carnegie Hall in 1968 and, the following year, performing "The Fox Chase" with the Radio Éireann Symphony Orchestra. Though he died in 1970, his legacy endures, thanks to his recordings and the regular reprinting of his piping tutor and through his many pupils (including Paddy Moloney, Liam Ó Flynn and Willie Clancy). His son **Leon** (1936–94), inherited the pipe-making business and was also a notable musician in his own right, performing solo internationally and recording two albums of piping. **Liam** (1939–97) was a talented fiddler who played with the Castle Céilí Band in the 1960s, while daughter **Helena** is another fine piper and CCÉ activist. Nowadays, Leon's son **Kevin** has already developed a grand reputation as a piper and pipe-maker and plays sets made by both his great-grandfather, William, and his grandfather, Leo, on his excellent album **The Rowsome Tradition**.

⊙ **Classics of Irish Piping**   Topic, 1920s–44

Absolutely essential collection of Leo Rowsome's 78rpm recordings.

⊙ **Rí na bPíobairí**   Claddagh, 1959

Claddagh's first-ever release and a milestone in the history of Irish music recording.

⊙ **The Rowsome Tradition**   own label, 1999

Kevin Rowsome's own majestic piping is augmented by wonderful home tapes of Leo and Leon from 1957.

Davy Spillane

In the 1970s Horslips experimented with uilleann pipes in a rock band setting with mixed degrees of success. It took **Moving**

Hearts and the astonishing talent of **Davy Spillane** to demonstrate exactly what could be achieved in a rock context. Softly spoken and shy offstage, Davy was a pivotal figure in the band's music. While all whirled around him, he sat centre-stage quietly concentrating on producing some of the most enthralling sounds imaginable. Born in Dublin in 1959, Davy was a relative latecomer to tradi-

STEVE GILLETT

tional music and his ears were only opened when he joined a beginner's tin whistle class at secondary school. A quick learner, he began playing the pipes at thirteen, influenced at first by Séamus Ennis, then later by both Paddy Keenan and Johnny Doran, adopting the latter's "open" mode of playing which he retains to this day. The young Spillane was recorded in 1977 for **The Piper's Rock** (see p.396), playing a set of concert pipes made by William Rowsome c. 1880. By then he was already making a name for himself on the Dublin circuit, leading eventually to his membership of Moving Hearts. Spillane's first solo album **Out of the Air** (1988) showcased his then live band, appropriately recorded for BBC Radio One sessions, and also included a guest appearance by Donegal bluesman, Rory Gallagher. **Atlantic Bridge** (1988) rapidly followed and it's largely self-penned compositions demonstrated further eclectic tastes. Though it included a stunning solo "Tribute to Johnny Doran", the album's orientations drifted between bluegrass (courtesy of Bela Fleck's banjo and Jerry Holland's dobro) and an apparent infatuation with the pipes' potential to sound lonesome and ethereal. 1990's **Shadow Hunter**, again produced by P.J. Curtis, is Davy's strongest album, beginning with a low whistle duet with Christy Moore's bodhrán before Spillane lets rip on the pipes over a basic Bo Diddley-style guitar riff on "Lucy's Tune/Indiana Drones". There's a jazzy feel to the pipes on "Watching the Clock" and **Seán Tyrrell** provides atmospheric vocals on "Walker in the Snow" and W.B. Yeats's "The Host of the Air".

By now Davy had become increasingly involved in pipe-making and had relocated to Co. Clare. The light in Clare has its own special qualities, especially at dawn and dusk in The Burren where the sun's rise and fall contrasts vividly with the stones' dark-grey mass. Much of this was reflected in Davy's last major label outing, **A Place Among the Stones** (1994), on which titles such as "Darklight", "Western Whisper", "Near the Horizon" and, of course, the title track itself evoke a suitable air of wonder. Davy's most recent release, 1998's **Sea of Dreams** mined this vein ever deeper, producing textured, ambient strata, where mood dominates and the pace sometimes drifts towards the funereal.

⊙ **Shadow Hunter**   Tara, 1990

At the peak of his powers, Spillane can still cook up a storm.

Patsy Touhey

The sight of **Patsy Touhey**'s comic vaudeville antics apparently drove tenor John McCormack to leave the US in disgust, but those interested in the history of uilleann piping should not be similarly dissuaded. Born near Loughrea, Co. Galway, in 1865, Patsy's family emigrated ten years later. His father, James, himself a piper, died in 1882, but not before passing on the rudiments of his skills to his son who also became a professional piper, touring US music halls with his wife Mary, a dancer, appearing in comic sketches, and, most notably, playing at the Chicago World's Fair in 1893. He began recording in 1901 and all his surviving studio ventures are gathered together on **The Piping of Patsy Touhey** which provides an enduring sample of his skilful playing in the typically tight, staccato style then common amongst Connacht pipers. Described by O'Neill as "the genial, unobliging and unaffected wizard of the Irish pipes", Touhey died in 1923. Pat Mitchell and Jackie Small, themselves notable pipers, have written the admirable *The Piping of Patsy Touhey* (1976) which includes a detailed account of his technique and tune transcriptions for those keen to replicate his playing.

▦ **The Piping of Patsy Touhey**   Na Píobairí Uilleann, early 1900s

Cylinder and early 78rpm recordings of the first great twentieth-century piper.

Flute players and whistlers

The flute is currently enjoying a degree of popularity second only to the fiddle as the adult instrument of choice. Though it certainly entered the country during the 1700s, it was not commonly used in traditional music until the latter part of the following century, largely because mass production led to a reduction in prices. Flutes are usually made out of ebony, blackwood or rosewood and come in a variety of forms, though the basic playing principle remains the same. Holding the tube horizontally, the player places the lower lip against a hole in the instrument and blows across it, altering the pitch by fingering the holes, or keys, along its length.

Simple flutes have six or, more usually, eight holes, and chromatic notes are produced by cross-fingering (partly covering the hole). The more sophisticated instruments incorporate a system devised by the German flute-maker Theobald Boehm in the 1840s where between four and eight keys are used to cover an additional set of holes, accurately placed to produce a full chromatic scale in the eight-keyed version. Since all the chromatic notes are rarely required in traditional music, most players plump for the simple system. Simple flutes have a range of one octave, though higher pitches can be achieved by overblowing, whilst a standard concert flute has a range of over three octaves. Most simple flutes are nowadays tuned in D.

The area most strongly associated with the instrument is the northern part of the Connacht province, consisting of the counties of Roscommon, Sligo and Leitrim. Sligo's flute players tend to be Ireland's most flamboyant, employing a technique involving deep breaths and consequent long phrases, characterized by an abundance of downwards rolls and triplets (see p.28). The most renowned purveyors of the Sligo flute style are **Matt Molloy** (from neighbouring Roscommon) and **Séamus Tansey**. The lighter, jauntier style of neighbouring Leitrim is best exemplified by the American 78s of flute player **John McKenna** (from Arigna, just across the Leitrim border with Roscommon), who played in an energetic and relatively unornamented fashion. Co. Fermanagh's flute players, notably **Cathal McConnell**, bear many similarities to their Leitrim neighbours, while the slightly eerie sound of East Galway owes much to the influence of uilleann piping.

Simple to learn and cheap to purchase, the tin whistle is often a traditional musician's first instrument. It consists of a metal tube – plastic versions also exist – perforated by six finger-holes and a mouthpiece through which air is blown. Covering the holes changes the pitch and overblowing extends the instrument's range. The oldest brand still available is the Clarke's original, manufactured since 1843. The most common versions are pitched in D (but are available in many other keys) including the low whistles which are increasingly prevalent, partly through their use in *Riverdance*. The tin whistle's fortunes were substantially revived by **Paddy Moloney** and **Seán Potts** of The Chieftans while **Mary Bergin** and **Séan Ryan** are regarded as the most exciting contemporary players. **Cormac Breatnach** and **Eoin Duignan** are both innovative low whistlers, and the instrument has been taken up by several uilleann pipers, notably **Davy Spillane** (see p.429).

No record company has issued a compilation of contemporary flute playing but Harry Bradshaw has remastered some of the best examples of early recordings on the excellent **Fluters of Old Erin**. Tin-whistle enthusiasts should look no further than **Totally Traditional Tin Whistles** which showcases some of the latter half of the twentieth century's major talents.

▦ **Fluters of Old Erin**   Viva Voce, 1920s–30s

A collection of remastered 78s from John McKenna and lesser-known players like Tom Doyle, Tom Morrison and John Sheridan.

⊙ **Totally Traditional Tin Whistles**   Ossian Publications, 1960s–80s

Drawn from Ossian's back catalogue, this features Josie McDermott, Cathal McConnell, the Russells and Willie Clancy.

Mary Bergin

I t's entirely apt that **Mary Bergin**'s two albums to date are unassumingly entitled **Feadóga Stáin** ("tin whistle") and **Feadóga Stáin 2** (1979 and 1992). No fanfare, frills or gimmicks, just the tin whistle being most purely and richly itself, bubbling with artless vitality, unerringly sure in cadence and weight, airily uncluttered yet replete with filigree ornamentation. The development of Bergin's style was significantly informed by the older players and repertoires she encountered growing up, amid a musically inclined family in Co. Dublin. It was hearing Willie Clancy play at an Oireachtas concert that fired her enthusiasm for the tin whistle, while visitors to the family home included the renowned Kathleen Harrington and Elizabeth Crotty, whose example helped inspire her to begin attending sessions and fleadhanna (she won the All-Ireland Senior tin-whistle title in 1968), where in turn she met more musicians who helped shape her repertoire, such as the blind whistle player Terry Horan. At the same time, the new-minted freshness and joie de vivre of her playing continue to evoke the revelatory excitement she and her musical contemporaries experienced as young adults amidst the 1960s/70s folk revival.

That Bergin hasn't recorded more is due mainly to a combination of family responsibilities and teaching commitments – she is much in demand as a whistle tutor, both privately and in schools around Spiddal, Co. Galway, where she's lived since the late 1970s – and she also performs with the traditional/baroque quartet **Dordán**. Despite this scant studio output, the definitive status of her debut album, in particular, as well as her live performances – usually with De Dannan's bouzouki player Alec Finn – ensures Bergin's continued standing as one of today's most respected tin-whistle exponents. Tracks like the reel set "Mick Hand's/The Reel of Mullinavat" or the jigs "Tom Billy's/The Langstern Pony" highlight her playing's sure equilibrium between quicksilver suppleness and rock-steady timing, her strong yet dainty tone and vibrant dynamic range. Elsewhere, the elegantly measured, gravely playful hornpipes "Garraí na bhFeileoig/Miss Galvin" and two contrasting slow airs – the understated intensity of "Liam Ó Raghallaigh", as against the richly lyrical "Mo Mhuirnín Bán" – reveal the breadth of her command.

⊙ **Feadóga Stáin**   Gael-Linn, 1979

Bergin's entrancing playing, accompanied by Alec Finn and Johnny "Ringo" McDonagh, makes for a classic whistle album.

Turlach Boylan

Houston, Texas may be one of the last places in the US you would expect to find an active Irish flute player, but that is where **Turlach Boylan** (from Glenullin, Co. Derry) has based himself since 1989. The eldest of seven musical siblings, Turlach was taught by the well-respected John Kennedy (from Co. Antrim) and won the All Ireland Senior slow-air competition in 1986. Since then he has developed a graceful style characterized by a relaxed confidence. Nowadays, he can be found leading a regular session in Houston and guesting occasionally with **The Texas Chainsaw Céilí Band**. When, in 1999, he set up Big Plain Records to promote Irish music in the US, his first release was his own **The Tidy Cottage** featuring his sister **Sheila** on fiddle, brother **Ruairí** on flute as well as Gerry O'Beirne on guitar and three-time US national mandolin champion, Dave Peters. The general breeziness of the album is exemplified by his duet with Sheila on "Seámus Quinn's/The Blackthorn Stick/Rosewood" and a gorgeous solo reading of "Johnny's Wedding".

⊙ **The Tidy Cottage**	Big Plain Records, 1999

Animated, infectious playing at just the right tempo, and a grand variety of tunes.

Harry Bradley

The city of Belfast has produced a mysteriously large supply of wonderful flute players and – though now resident in Galway – **Harry Bradley** is one of the best. Like another Belfast man Marcas Ó Murchú, Bradley extracts astonishing volume from his instrument, but, thankfully, shares Ó Murchú's subtlety. On **Bad Turns & Horseshoe Bends** (1999) tunes are drawn from a wide range of sources, including fiddlers Tommy Gunn (Boys of the Lough) and Proinsías Ó Maonaigh, while the flute playing of Séamus Tansey, John McKenna

Harry Bradley
Bad Turns &
Horse-shoe
Bends

and John Joe Gardiner offers another rich vein of material. Harry also uses the sharper-sounding marching band flutes for "Belfast March", a popular local session tune, and "The Horse-shoe Bend", named after a notorious local accident black spot. Overall, it's an album pulsating with energy, characterized by the sheer lyricism of Bradley's playing and able, understated assistance from Déanta's Eoghan O'Brien (guitar, harp), Davy Graham (mandocello) and Séamus O'Kane (bodhrán).

⊙ Bad Turns & Horse-shoe Bends   Outlet, 1999

Not just one to watch for the future, be there with Harry now!

Cormac Breatnach

J ustly regarded as one of the most innovative and stylish contemporary whistlers and flute players, **Cormac Breatnach**'s talents have been heavily in demand since the 1980s. Born in Dublin in 1963 and brought up in an Irish- and Spanish-speaking household (his middle name is Juan), Cormac's track record includes The Dónal Lunny Band, Méristem (with Máire Breatnach – no relation) and **Deiseal**. He has also guested on many recordings and soundtracks (including *Riverdance*), and his contribution to Brendan Power's **Blow In** album is particularly worth checking out. Once described as "the fresh prince of jazzy jigs", Cormac released his own-label debut album **Musical Journey** in 1999. Featuring an all-star cast (including Steve Cooney, Karen Tweed, Kevin Glackin and former Deiseal colleague, Niall Ó Callanain) it blends traditional tunes, Cormac's own compositions and songs in Irish and Spanish, all bound together by his own both rhapsodic and invigorating playing and tasteful infusions from other idioms.

⊙ **Musical Journey**   Dioscaí Mandala, 1999

Classy playing and elegant singing from one of Ireland's most imaginative musicians.

Vincent Broderick

O ne of the grand old men of Irish music, flute player **Vincent Broderick** was born in 1920 near Loughrea, Co. Galway. Adopting the East Galway style, Vincent began playing on an instrument donated by a local priest and, along with his similarly endowed brother Paddy, soon became a popular player at house dances. The only flute player to have won an All-Ireland title on an instrument of his own making and with his own composition, Vincent subsequently moved to Dublin and became a popular mainstay of sessions in the city. A fine composer, too, he published 68 of his tunes as *The Turoe Stone* and an identically titled cassette contains 32 of these. Accompanied by sons **Lawrence** on flute, **Des** on fiddle and the notable Cavan fiddler **Antóin Mac Gabhain**, Vincent's compositions belie the recency of their origins in a timeless flow of magical musicianship and provide some imaginative new titles at the same time – "The Plasterer's Dream" and "The Whistler at the Wake" being two enduring examples.

📼 **The Turoe Stone**   CCÉ, 1992

You don't have to be immured in the tradition to write grand music, but Vincent proves that it sure does help!

Conor Byrne

Conor Byrne was taught by Cian O'Sullivan and Paul McGrattan and cites Matt Molloy as a major influence. A Dubliner from Inchicore, he's the son of the singer Eilís Moore and the nephew of both Christy Moore and Luka Bloom. His album credits include Máire Breatnach's **Angels' Candles** and, more recently, the English guitarist John Renbourn's **Traveller's Prayer**. On his own solo album, **Wind Dancer**, the distinguished guests include Dervish's Cathy Jordan, who sings a spine-tingling version of "The Emigrant's Farewell", and Luka Bloom, who not only produced the album, but plays guitar and offers his own vocal tribute to Micho Russell in the "Hands of a Farmer" (there's also a guest spot for the bodhrán of Christy Moore). Byrne's own playing is vibrant, melancholic and at its most mellifluous on "The Coolea Jig". Singing, however, is not his forte, though his misguided rendition of Louis Armstrong's "We Have All the Time in the World" is, fortunately, both brief and the last track!

⊙ **Wind Dancer**   own label, 1998

Versatile playing from Byrne, plus a major contribution from Luka Bloom.

Paddy Carty

"The Carty Flow" might sound like the name of a reel, but was in fact the oft-used description of the tidal stream of notes that poured from the flute of **Paddy Carty** (1929–85) from Rafford, Co. Galway. Listen to "The Day I Met Tom Moylan/Ships A-Sailing" (two reels from the O'Neill collection) on **Traditional Irish Music** and you'll hear its perfect operation. Though self-taught, Carty developed a combination of relaxed breathing and sensitive fingering which allowed him to produce three or four bars of note-filled music without a break. Like many before him, he started on tin whistle, learning tunes from his parents, local musicians and then records (notably the Ballinakill Céilí Band) before graduating first to the fife and then to an old-style eight-keyed, open-holed concert flute. Paddy joined the **Aughrim Slopes Céilí Band** in the late 1940s whose founder was the influential fiddler **Paddy Fahy**. Subsequently, seeking more volume, he experimented with a metal Boehm-system flute, before settling on a Radcliffe Model whose power and simple fingering system still allowed him to play in a variety of keys. So successful was the adaptation that he won the All-Ireland title in 1960, 1961 and 1963 and also twice as a member of the **Leitrim Céilí Band**. Sadly, the night Paddy reputedly played "The Pigeon on a Gate" in three different keys has not been recorded but **Traditional Irish Music** is a delight from start to finish, even if accompanist, banjo-player Mick O'Connor appears to have been recorded underneath a blanket.

⊙ Traditional Irish Music   Shanachie, 1970

"The Carty Flow" in rampant form.

Séamus Cooley

Younger brother of the legendary accordionist, Joe Cooley, from Peterswell, Co. Galway, **Séamus** (1929–97) was himself a superb musician. Apart from Joe, the greatest influence on his musical development was fellow flute player Jim Fahey from nearby Derrawee whose music possessed a graceful lyricism. Séamus joined Joe in the **Tulla Céilí Band** when he was sixteen and spent four years with the band before emigrating to London with his brother in 1949. Here Séamus developed his talents in the company of many other fine émigré musicians, returning to Ireland in 1955 and settling in Co. Meath where he struck up a partnership with fiddler **Jim O'Leary**, winning the All-Ireland duet competition in 1957. Séamus continued to play with the Tulla at competitions and concerts and toured the US with the band in 1958 where they recorded an album for Shamrock Records. Deciding to stay in America, he eventually joined Joe in Chicago where the pair played together regularly and co-founded the **Glenside Céilí Band**. While Joe moved to San Francisco in 1965, Séamus remained in the Windy City often appearing at festivals with his wife, sean-nós singer **Mary McDonagh**, and striking up a partnership with the locally-born fiddler **John McGreevy**. The latter pairing produced the grand **McGreevy and Cooley** in 1974 which features superb duets and some excellent solo tunes from Cooley's wooden flute. Séamus was a restrained player in terms of ornamentation and tended to eschew rolls in favour of additional melody notes, as can be heard on his graceful legato version of the reels "Skylark/Roaring Meg". Perhaps best of all, however, is the sheer verve of his playing in tandem with Johnny on a tune from his Tulla days, "Tim Maloney's" coupled with his brother's famous reel, "Cooley's". Séamus moved back to Peterswell in 1985 and continued to make wonderful music until his death in 1997.

McGreevy and Cooley　　　　　　　　　Cló Iar-Chonnachta, 1974

A gem of an album from two of the finest musicians of their epoch.

Eamonn Cotter

One of Clare's best-known flute players (and a respected maker too), **Eamonn Cotter** grew up in Ennis where his mother was a piano teacher. By the time he went to college in the early 1970s he was a proficient tin whistler, but switched to a wooden Hawkes flute because the college's céilí band had a dearth of players at that time. Eamonn's own breezy style acknowledges the influence of Matt Molloy and Paddy Carty and, after moving to Kilmaley in 1984, following studies at Limerick School of Music, he played regularly with fiddler and piper **Peadar O'Loughlin**. In 1989, Eamonn was invited to join **Shaskeen** and has remained a fixture in the band ever since with many international tours under his belt. Unsurprisingly, he has only managed time for one solo album, 1996's **Traditional Music from County Clare**. The combination of Cotter's sparkling playing and a rather too bouncy piano accompaniment is not always effective and the best cuts are those recorded with guitarist **Randal Bays**, such as the jig "Old Grey Goose", though Eamonn's most delicious playing is reserved for a stunning rendition of "The Stoney Steps".

⊙ **Traditional Music from County Clare**   own label, 1996

A skilled and stylish player who deserves a better setting for his abilities to really shine.

Kevin Crawford

Acclaimed as one of the best of the new breed of flute and whistle players through his work in **Lúnasa**, **Grianán** and **Moving Cloud**, **Kevin Crawford** was born and brought up in Birmingham, though his heart has always yearned for West Clare (where his mother's family originates). Summers spent in Miltown Malbay set his head reeling with the music of Junior Crehan, Bobby Casey and many others and – back home in Birmingham – he gradually began to make contact with Irish musicians and to build on the early repertoire he had acquired from his late Uncle Michael. Though the city is not renowned for its traditional Irish music, there were still plenty of musicians around and their various origins and related styles expanded the base of Kevin's knowledge. Eventually, Clare's magnetism proved too strong and an impromptu trip in 1988 led to permanent residency. Kevin's recordings include **Raise the Rafters**, as part of a trio with long-time collaborator accordionist **P.J. King** and singer-guitarist **Martin O'Malley**, and his own highly-recommended solo release **'D' Flute Album**. Those familiar with his ebullient performance on Lúnasa's **Otherworld** will be enthused by the sheer range of his playing, best revealed in the evocative slow air "Season of Mists" and the subsequent wittiness of his renditions of reels by Maurice Lennon and Connie O'Connell.

⊙ **'D' Flute Album**   Green Linnet, 1995

A punning title from a new modern master.

John Doonan

John Doonan was born to Irish parents in Hebburn, Co. Durham, in the northeast of England, where his father was a respected traditional fiddler. John followed suit at an early age, but also learned mandolin, piano and flute (though he was forced to switch to piccolo to make himself heard in his father's céilí band!). Though he won the All-Ireland flute title in 1964, John has always been regarded as one of the best players for dancing and was much sought after as an accompanist for competitions, a duty once described by his contemporary, the London-based fiddler, Jimmy Power, as "one of the most tiresome tasks in the field of Irish music". Both John's recordings **Flute for the Feis** and **At the Feis** demonstrate that he took the task very seriously indeed. The latter, subtitled "Irish Traditional Dance Music in Strict Tempo" is still available and highly recommended. While the measured pace is constant, Doonan's lyrical style soars above it, his wooden flute achieving simple majesty on reels, set dances and hornpipes, but most magically on the slow jigs "The Idle Road/The Frost is All Over/The Black Rogue". John's piccolo can also be heard on **The Lark in the Clear Air** (see p.43).

📼 At the Feis	Ossian Publications, 1978

One of the best of its kind, featuring lively, controlled playing by a real craftsman.

Eoin Duignan

O ne-time member of **Wild Geese**, Dublin-born low whistler and uilleann piper **Eoin Duignan** now lives in West Kerry though the inspiration he brings to his music is more cosmopolitan. His first solo album **Coumineol** appeared in 1994 and since then he's composed the music for the National Folk Theatre's show *Immrama* and for John Boorman's film *Angela Mooney Dies Again*. Most of the tunes on his second album, the snazzily-packaged **Ancient Rite**, are self-penned and draw on influences as wide-ranging as Hungarian folk music ("Road to Budapest") and his own travels in East Asia ("The Taipei Jig"). Highlights include an atmospheric duet with Máire Breatnach's viola on the slip jig "Barefoot" and joyous unaccompanied call-and-reply singing by Eoin's mother Muireann and sister

Gobnait on his grandfather's song "Táimse agus Máire". You can catch Eoin playing regularly in Dingle and should definitely do so.

⊙ **Ancient Rite**   OAC, 1999

Atmospheric, carefree whistling and piping with a touch of roguishness from the eloquent Duignan.

Packie Duignan

A wall plaque in the centre of the village of Drumshanbo, Co. Leitrim commemorates the life of the acclaimed local flute player, **Packie Duignan** who died in 1992 aged 69. Packie was born and lived just over the border in Arigna, Co. Roscommon and worked in the coal mines there into his fifties. Though his own family loved a song, there were few musicians in Packie's background and his greatest musical influence came from hearing the 78s of Leitrim flute player **John McKenna** who recorded some 60 sides in New York between 1921 and 1937. Much of Packie's own repertoire, first on the whistle and later the concert flute, was "inherited" from McKenna and, not unnaturally, he also acquired something of his predecessor's forcefully direct style. Packie played in Drumshanbo's **Shannon Star Ceili Band** for fifteen years, but is best remembered by many for his regular playing in the village pubs with fiddler **Séamus Horan** and, later, bouzouki player **Ciaran Emmett**. The sessions were often unforgettable especially if, in Ciaran's words, a bunch of "top-class cowboys" had turned up. Collaboration with Horan produced Packie's only album, the effervescent **Traditional Music from County Leitrim**, includes several tunes from McKenna and a piece forever associated with Duignan, naturally called "Packie Duignan's Reel". It's hard to imagine a finer flute–fiddle combination than this pair and their recording encapsulates all the lilt and lyricism of the Leitrim style.

📷 **Traditional Music from County Leitrim**　Ossian Publications, 1978

Duignan's blithe flute and with Séamus Horan's tasteful fiddle make the perfect pairing.

Seamus Egan

Winner of All-Ireland championships on four different instruments (tin whistle, flute, tenor banjo and mandolin), the prodigiously-talented **Seamus Egan** was born in Hatboro, Philadelphia in 1971, but raised in Co. Mayo between 1973 and 1980. Seamus featured in the **Green Fields of America** tour with Eileen Ivers and Robbie O'Connell while still in his teens and released his first, self-titled, album, at the age of seventeen. Since then he has gone on to make **3 Way Street** and co-founded the US's most prestigious traditional group, the phenomenal **Solas**. His musical and

production credits are legion, while his compositional skills have been demonstrated by his soundtrack for the film *The Brothers McMullen* and the score for Jean Butler's *Dancing on Dangerous Ground*. His own second album, **A Week in January**, appeared in 1990, extending his debut's discernible eclecticism with a set of Cape Breton reels, and backing musicians as varied as an Appalachian-style five-string banjo player and a classical cellist. Seamus's most recent offering **When Juniper Sleeps** (1996) demonstrates further skills, though he abandons the banjo for finger-style guitar on such tracks as a jazz-phrased rendition of "The Mason's Apron/My Love is in America". Guitar features on seven of the thirteen cuts, while elsewhere its Egan's stylish flute and whistles which dominate proceedings. There's a dreamy feel to much of the album, courtesy of his own mood-saturated compositions and arrangements, though "The Czar of Munster" features a wild banjo breakout. Guests include fellow Solas members John Doyle and Win Horan.

⊙ **When Juniper Sleeps**   Shanachie, 1996

A largely laid-back set of tunes from the exceptional Egan, ideal for a lazy Sunday.

Kevin Henry

The survival and strength of Irish music in America owes much to people like **Kevin Henry**. Like many a young Irishman, he worked as a migrant labourer in England, before trying his luck first in Canada and then the US. His journey ended in Chicago, largely because of its connections with the great collector Chief O'Neill (see p.13), but, finding little Irish music there he helped to form the

Chicago chapter of the Irish Musicians' Association in 1956 whose efforts revitalized traditional music in the city. Kevin himself was born in 1929 near Tubbercurry, Co. Sligo, an area noted for its flute players and their characteristic "flow and rush" staccato manner of playing. Kevin inherited the style when he progressed from tin whistle to flute in his teens, and acquired his early repertoire by listening to local musicians and attending dances and competitions. He had played the dance halls in England too, turning to the war pipes to make himself heard above the crowd. Ironically, much of the material that he chose for his debut CD **One's Own Place – A Family Tradition** (1998) was not included in O'Neill's massive collection (largely because the Chief seems to have overlooked much of Connacht's music) but you can hear some fine renditions of the reels, double jigs and hornpipes which he neglected, a tremendous 1962 archive recording of Kevin's fiddle-playing older brother Johnny, and perhaps best of all "Rex", one of several narrative recitations where Kevin maintains an almost extinct tradition.

⊙ One's Own Place – A Family Tradition　　　　　　　　BogFire, 1998

Wit, wisdom and grand music from a scion of Sligo – a tremendous recording!

Peter Horan and Fred Finn

The flute of **Peter Horan** (b. 1926) and fiddle of the late **Fred Finn** (1919–86) formed one of traditional music's most renowned and durable partnerships. Both from Killavil, Co. Sligo, they began playing together as a regular duo in 1959. Though Peter is also a fine fiddler (heavily indebted to Michael Coleman), his flute playing is rapid and rolled in a unique version of the florid and flamboyant South Sligo style. Those used to Matt Molloy will marvel at the ornamentation that Peter employs seemingly by finger work and the tip of his tongue in conjunction. As evidence, seek out the pair's recording, **Music of Sligo**, which features a noteworthy example of the Horan style in his renditions of "The Boys of the Lough/The Devils of Dublin". The album also includes the tune most usually associated with Finn and Horan, "The Killavil Jig", and a couple of well-known reels, "Wynne's No. 1 and No. 2", from fiddler Martin Wynne. Both Fred and Peter were members of the **Coleman Country Céilí Band**, which recorded and toured in the US, and Peter continues to play actively today.

🎞 **Music of Sligo**   CCÉ, 1988

A memorable duo caught in the act shortly before Fred Finn's untimely death.

Niall Keegan

The flute-playing talents of **Niall Keegan** (born St Albans, England) first gained recognition when he was a member of one of London's best-known céilí bands, St. Colmcille's and the young Niall can be heard playing solo on **From a Distant Shore** (see p.276). A one-time regular at London sessions, he's now based in Limerick where he runs the Masters programme in Traditional Music with bodhrán-player and singer, **Sandra Joyce**. Niall's stupendous debut album, **Don't Touch the Elk**, was recorded live at the University's World Music Centre with the assistance of **Verena Cummins** (piano) and Reeltime's **Chris Kelly** (guitar). Keegan's playing throughout is breezy and effortless though his jazz influences and love of Tommy Potts' music mean that he's willing to confront risks that might deter others. Keegan's mentor, Mícheál Ó Súilleabháin, guests on piano on the waltz "La Botte à Frissons", but the most intriguing track here is the duet with Sandra Joyce "Killybegs Chinese Meal Reel/Jota de Mahía", the first tune a paean to Donegal's culinary delights and co-written on their honeymoon. Niall and Sandra now play together as the duo **Neilí go Deazz**.

⊙ **Don't Touch the Elk**   Elk Records, 1999

A magical, powerful, free-flowing work from the ever-inventive Keegan.

Barry Kerr

The Kerr family runs one of the North's premier music venues, The Céilí House in Lurgan, Co. Armagh, the ideal environment for a young musician's education. Now in his twenties, Barry is one of the most precociously talented flute and low whistle players of his generation as well as no mean hand on the pipes. There's a touch of Séamus Tansey's Sligo lilt and sway to Barry's playing and no surprise that the flute master has been a major influence and, indeed, provides the sleeve notes for the younger man's exquisite debut album **The Three Sisters**. Barry draws inspiration widely, however: there are a couple of beefy tunes learned from Ronan Browne (splendid flute and whistle on "Ronan's March" and chirpy pipes on "Bush in Bloom"), a lively whistled reel associated with the great Leitrim flute player John McKenna and a resonant air, "Tuirse Mo Chroí", learned from the singing of Mairéad Ní Mhaonaigh. Keep your eyes peeled for Barry, you'll not be disappointed!

⊙ **The Three Sisters**   Spring Records, 1998

Lively, unfeasibly mature music from one of the North's rising stars.

Emer Mayock

R ecent **Afro Celt Sound System** recruit, **Emer Mayock** burst onto the traditional scene with **Merry Bits of Timber**, one of the brightest albums of 1996, although those who had already witnessed the young flute and whistle player in sessions were not in the least surprised. Born in Ross West, Co. Mayo, she's an equally proficient player on uilleann pipes and fiddle, but lets her flute and whistle do the work on **Merry Bits of Timber**, an outstanding and eclectic set of tunes, some self-penned like the elegiac "Great Denmark Street" and others from Cork and Donegal. Her duetting with fiddler **Kevin O'Connor** on "John Doherty's" is inspirational, and overall this is an album that justly links the words "living" and "tradition"!

⊙ **Merry Bits of Timber**   Key Records, 1996

Thoroughly delightful music from start to end by the prodigious Mayock.

Cathal McConnell

D on't be fooled by the celebrated air of bespectacled confusion: this Co. Fermanagh musician is widely ranked by connoisseurs as one of the most authentic yet distinctive exponents in his fields of singing, flute and whistle, as well as being a noted collector of old and rare songs and tunes. The product of a long line of flute players, **Cathal McConnell** inherited his love of song from his father, taking up the whistle at eleven and flute at fifteen, and was also influenced in his early years by such local luminaries as John Joe Maguire, Tommy Gunn and Mick Hoy. He won All-Ireland titles in flute and tin whistle as an eighteen-year-old in 1962, honing his skills in various céilí bands before co-founding **Boys of the Lough**, with whom he still plays, in 1967. In addition to over twenty recordings with the band, he has brought out two acclaimed solo albums: the Fermanagh-based **On Lough Erne's Shore** (1978) and **Long Expectant Comes at Last** (2000). The latter showcases McConnell's intimate, minutely modulated singing and robust yet delicate touch on flute and whistle in the company of some thirty guest artists – including Richard and Linda Thompson, Len Graham, Charlie Lennon, Solas's Win Horan, and

Compass Records

Cherish The Ladies' Joanie Madden – and blending unadorned traditional arrangements with more adventurous takes on his mainly Ulster-sourced material.

⊙ **Long Expectant Comes At Last**   Compass Records, 2000

Provides a satisfying cross-section of McConnell's strengths, both as an old-time traditionalist and a subtly innovative modern virtuoso.

Josie McDermott

One of the most eclectic and talented musicians and singers in the history of Irish traditional music, **Josie McDermott** once remarked, "If you put a good céilí band, a good traditional jazz band, a good country and western band and a small orchestra in four halls…I'd want to hear the four of them". Born in 1925, Josie lived all his life in the townland of Coolmeen in Co. Sligo, a mile across the border from the Co. Roscommon town of Ballyfarnan. The area might have been rich in the tradition, but there was little actual music in Josie's family, though his mother sang and could knock out a tune on the concertina. However, the nearby Butler home was a well-known céilí house and Josie heard much of his first music here, though it was from local fiddler James Flynn that he acquired his early repertoire, and from the radio and gramophone that he broadened his musical education. Though Josie began playing the jew's harp and tin whistle at an early age he first "trod the boards" at 14 when he began singing with a local dance band. Subsidizing his income by various labouring jobs, over the years he taught himself to play the trumpet, tenor and alto saxophones, fife and concert flute. In all, he played in around ten modern dance bands, while also acquiring a considerable reputation for his traditional playing, singing and lilting.

When Josie lost his eyesight in 1962 it proved no hindrance to his music and in 1964 he joined **Sonny Flynn's Céilí Band** and, subsequently, **Flynn's Men**, a "weddings, parties, anything" band whose range covered most popular styles and with whom he spent more than a decade. At the same time he was winning All-Ireland championships on the whistle and alto sax in the miscellaneous instruments section (both 1964), lilting (1967) and flute (1974), though, to his great regret, he was only ever runner-up (on three occasions) in the ballad-singing. Josie died in 1992, and Ballyfarnan commemorates his memory with an annual festival weekend in early May. His only traditional release, **Darby's Farewell**, was recorded by **Robin Morton** for Topic in 1976 and is a wonderful memento of the man. McDermott's flute and whistle playing on tunes, both familiar and self-composed, is as bright and airy as a fine May morning and – despite additional influences – reflects the strength of the local tradition exemplified too by his own song "Ballad of the O'Carolan Country".

⊙ **Darby's Farewell**   Ossian Publications, 1976

Includes several of Josie's own compositions such as "Trip to Birmingham" and "Peg McGrath's Reel".

Catherine McEvoy

Nowadays, there are plenty of outstanding women flute players around, such as Emer Mayock or The London Lasses' Sharon Whelton, but they were few and far between when **Catherine McEvoy** recorded with **Macalla** in the 1980s. Born in Birmingham, England, but long based in Ireland, Catherine plays in the North Connacht style, popularized by Matt Molloy, but brings her own fresh take to the music through a clear grounding in the importance of pace and melody and her own adroit technical ability. Her only solo album to date is the magical **Traditional Music in the Sligo-Roscommon Style**, where her accompanist is the notable US-based pianist **Felix Dolan**. Best of all the tunes, perhaps, is her characteristically bright rendition of "The Heather Breeze", a reel which requires good breath and finger control to encompass its almost two-octave range. Catherine's playing is immaculate throughout, always allowing the tune to take the wheel and a model of excellence for those tempted to learn the instrument.

⊙ **Traditional Music in the Sligo-Roscommon Style**   Cló Iar-Chonnachta, 1996

Rich-voiced and ever eloquent, this is flute playing of the highest order sympathetically accompanied by Felix Dolan.

Michael McGoldrick

Acheerfully self-confessed "folk tart", thanks to his multiple involvements with different bands, this young flute player, whistler and uilleann piper has also made a name as one of the most gifted and creative instrumentalists to emerge during the 1990s. Born into the thriving cultural enclave of Manchester's Irish community, **Mike McGoldrick** began playing as a child, at fifteen joining local folk-rock act **Toss the Feathers**, who built up a substantial live following at home and on the Continent during the late 1980s and '90s. McGoldrick remained with the line-up for over a decade while simultaneously immersing himself in the full wealth of music his home town had to offer, from jazz clubs to cutting-edge dance-floor sounds. Having won the BBC Young Tradition Award in 1995, he further underlined his traditional credentials with a brilliantly authoritative debut album **Morning Rory** (1996) which highlights his quicksilver phrasing, sure rhythmic control and exhilarating expressive energy. A founder member of both **Flook** and **Lúnasa**, he has also toured with the **Afro Celt Sound System**, but has lately been working more under his own name, while continuing as a semi-permanent guest with the Scottish band Capercaillie.

Mike's stunning second release **Fused** (2000), features an extensive all-star guest list drawn from the cream of young Irish and Scottish players, including fiddler **Dezi Donnelly**, accordionist **Alan**

Kelly, Flook's bodhrán virtuoso **John Joe Kelly** and singers **Karen Matheson** (from Capercaillie) and **Karan Casey**. The kind of cross-genre fusion referred to by the album's title has been a major feature of musical developments throughout the "Celtic" world over the last decade or so, but it remains rare indeed for such seemingly disparate elements as those found on **Fused** – folk, jazz-funk, hip-hop, traditional instruments alongside drum-loops, a brass section and wah-wah guitar – to be so sensitively and seamlessly integrated. Despite the album's emphatically contemporary feel, well over half the tunes are traditional while most of the rest are written by McGoldrick himself. The pièce de resistance is the all-traditional reel set "Fisher Street" which opens with a lissom, bubbling flute melody over minimal guitar and percussion, before evolving into a superbly slinky jazz/funk/folk workout without any whiff of strain or artifice.

⊙ **Fused**   Vertical Records, 2000

A marvellously fruitful union between his traditional Irish roots and cosmopolitan Mancunian upbringing.

Paul McGrattan

Though flute player **Paul McGrattan** is from Dublin's Northside, his influences are drawn from all over the country. Early encouragement came from his uncle, Paddy Tracey, from East Galway, while near neighbours Dubliner **Seán Potts** and **John Egan** (from Co. Sligo) provided later lessons. Holidays in Southwest Donegal saw him meet and hear renowned fiddlers such as Con Cassidy and James Byrne and catalysed an enduring interest in the region's styles. Paul's musical partnership with fiddler **Paul O'Shaughnessy** dates from the mid-1980s, based on their common love of the Donegal music and the discovery that they shared much of John Egan's repertoire, and the pair are now both members of **Beginish**. Egan's influence can be heard on McGrattan's solo album **The Frost is All Over**, not only in the selection of tunes, but in the buoyant Sligo touch that Paul brings to his playing. There's also a rare guest appearance from Matt Molloy and the pair duet adventurously on "Byrne's Hornpipes". The two Pauls can also be found in powerful tandem on **Within a Mile of Dublin** (1995).

⊙ **The Frost is All Over**   Claddagh, 1992

McGrattan pays homage to his early mentors, including a perky rendition of "Tracey's Jig", on this stylish flute special.

John McKenna

The American recordings of flute player **John McKenna** (1880–1947) were hugely influential in his time and continue to enthuse musicians to this day. Born in Tents, near the village of Tarmon, Co. Leitrim (an area with a strong musical tradition firmly focused on the flute) McKenna worked as a weighmaster at the Arigna coal mines before marrying in 1909 and emigrating, first to Scotland and then to New York. McKenna secured a job with the New York Fire Department, a post he was to hold until 1927 when, following his wife Mary Jane's death, he resigned in order to look after his six children. Although he played with a variety of accompanists, he notably preferred duets and his most celebrated partner was the great Sligo fiddler, James Morrison – an outstanding example of their collaboration being the reels "The Tailor's Thimble/The Red Haired Lass". McKenna's brilliant, compulsive style was also well-suited to polkas and he had a predilection for running slip jigs and double jigs together. He only returned once to Ireland (a 1938 visit which involved a live radio broadcast), but his renown as a flute player of the highest order remains undiminished.

McKenna cut some 60 sides for a variety of labels between 1921 and 1937 (the earliest bearing the name "Firepatrolman John McKenna"), and a fine selection of them features on **His Original Recordings**, a cassette produced by the John McKenna Traditional Society. Established to honour his memory, the society erected a memorial to McKenna in Tarmon in 1980 and holds an annual festival in his name.

His Original Recordings   John McKenna Traditional Society, 1921–37

Masterful playing, essential listening and a mandatory component of all flute-lovers' collections.

Matt Molloy

A pioneering and uniquely inspirational figure in the modern development of the Irish flute, **Matt Molloy** remains the benchmark against whom other players of the instrument are most often judged. Born in 1947 in Ballaghadereen, Co. Roscommon amidst the rich fiddle/flute heartland of North Connacht, Molloy inherited a family tradition of flute playing stretching back several generations. After starting out in the fife and drum band at National School, he was taught mainly by his father, going on to win a clutch of Fleadh Cheoil and Oireachtas titles in his teens. He attributes his highly personalized style, heavily informed by piping techniques as well as his native regional traditions, to the sheer numbers of players around him during his youth: "You had to have something of character in your music to be noticed at all, so I started chasing after playing tunes that nobody played on the flute – fiddle tunes, accordion tunes, piping tunes. I just messed around trying out what could be done – and I'm still messing."

After leaving school, Molloy moved to Dublin to work for Aer Lingus, swiftly becoming immersed in the capital's burgeoning session scene, playing regularly with Liam O'Flynn, Paddy Moloney, Tommy Peoples and Charlie Lennon. Abandoning the day-job in 1974 to co-found **The Bothy Band**, he was a key force in the line-up until their demise in 1979, after which he briefly joined the reformed **Planxty**, before Moloney snapped him up to replace Michael Tubridy in **The Chieftains**, with whom he has played ever since. Besides his many recordings with these groups, he has made four solo albums, the first of which, his self-titled debut (1976), remains one of the most influential traditional flute albums. Backed solely by Dónal Lunny on bouzouki and guitar, the album showcased Matt's astonishing technique and control as he rolled through a series of joyful jigs and reels and offered his hallmark rendition of "The Lament for Staker Wallace". **The Heathery Breeze** (1981) repeated the format, while **Stony Steps** (1988) is, if anything, beefier, thanks to the addition of a second accompanist, guitarist Arty McGlynn.

By now The Chieftains' international profile left little time for individual projects and it was to be almost a decade before Matt's most recent release **Shadows on Stone** (1997). Still spaciously uncluttered, this features a glittering guest-list that includes Christy Moore on bodhrán, guitarists Arty McGlynn and Steve Cooney, and fiddlers Frankie Gavin and Ciarán Tourish. The extended mini-suite "Music of the Seals", featuring Altan's Mairéad Ní Mhaonaigh as the seal's voice, is the showpiece of this outstanding collection. Although these four albums reveal a steady maturing and refining of his style, most of Matt's signature touches are present from the first: his use of pip-ing-style crans, rolls, triplets and cuts, his even, subtly accented rhythmic approach, his bending of notes to embellish the melodies of jigs and reels, as well as the tremendous sensitivity and depth of feeling he brings to his material.

Other albums include a celebrated 1978 collaboration **Molloy/ Brady/Peoples** (with **Paul Brady** and **Tommy Peoples**) another with fiddler **Seán Keane**, **Contentment is Wealth** (1985), and still another with Keane and **Liam O'Flynn**, **The Fire Aflame** (1992). Since the early 1990s Molloy has made his home in Westport, Co. Mayo, where he runs a pub unsurprisingly celebrated as a magnet for musicians, which provided the setting for the excellent session-style album **Music At Matt Molloy's** (1992). In 1999, his achievements were for-mally recognized when he was named as Traditional Musician of the Year by the Irish TV station TG4.

⊙ Matt Molloy	Mulligan, 1976

A glorious, inspirational album, showcasing not only Molloy's astonishing technical ability but the sheer joy of his playing.

⊙ Shadows on Stone	Virgin, 1997

There are no weak moments but look out for the set headed by the slip-jig "A Fig For A Kiss" and the spine-tingling solo "The Banshee".

Laurence Nugent

Another in the North's rich store of flute players, **Laurence Nugent** comes from Lack, Co. Fermanagh. His father, **Seán**, was an eminent fiddler and accordionist, All-Ireland champion in his time and for many years leader of the Pride of Erin Céilí Band. Emigrating to the US in the late 1980s, Laurence has been based in

Chicago since 1992, though returned home to win his own All-Ireland titles in 1994 and the following year. His exuberant style of flute and tin-whistle playing, often fun-packed with frills and frolics in a style redolent of fellow Fermanagh man Cathal McConnell, has shone over two excellent albums. The first, **Traditional Irish Music on Flute and Tin Whistle** (1996) features other major Irish-American names, such as Liz Carroll and Andy McGann, but is notable for an ebullient duet with Seán on "The Mossy Banks/The High Hills of Larghey" recorded shortly before his father's death. **Two by Two** (1998) includes another splendid duet, this time with fiddler Kevin Burke on the well-known reel "Within a Mile of Dublin". **The Windy Gap** (2000) is undoubtedly Lawrence's most assured release to date, commencing with a gorgeously eerie reading of "Paddy Fahy's" jig and including yet another stunning duet, this time with fellow flute player Kevin Henry on a set of reels. Guitarist Dennis Cahill is on splendid form on many of the tracks and is sometimes joined by his long-time partner Martin Hayes on fiddle.

⊙ **The Windy Gap**   Shanachie, 2000

A marvellous, elegant album whose star cast also includes uilleann piper Paddy Keenan and the bodhrán maestro Jimmy Higgins.

Colm O'Donnell

An accomplished flute player from South Sligo, **Colm O'Donnell** (b. 1962) is also a superb and eloquent vocalist and can often be found singing or playing at local sessions when not running his farm in Kilmactigue. Starting at the age of eleven on the tin whistle, he didn't get his first flute until he was 16 and, when he was skilful enough to play at competitions acquired the sobriquet "The Spoke" in recognition of his instrument's wooden origins (the spoke of a cart). Since then he's won three All-Ireland Senior singing titles, toured both the UK and US with CCÉ, recorded two solo cassettes, featured on two recordings by the Michael Coleman Heritage Centre in Gurteen and taught at Tubbercurry's South Sligo Summer School. His polished debut CD, **Farewell to Evening Dances** (1999) is well worth acquiring both for its delightful and stylish flute-playing, especially on the slow air "An Tonn Amplach", and for the emotive strength of Colm's sweet tenor voice.

⊙ Farewell to Evening Dances   BogFire, 1999

A welcome release from one of Sligo's most polished musicians.

Conal Ó Gráda

Highly proficient on both the concert flute and fife, **Conal Ó Gráda** (b. 1961) began playing traditional music through the local Cork Pipers Club, the oldest of its kind in Ireland. Séamus Creagh and Jackie Daly's sessions at the Country Club often spilled over into his parents' house and the young Conal soon became a regular player on the Cork circuit where he learned much from the Clare flute player Séamus Mac Mathúna (then working as Cork and Kerry organizer for The Gaelic League). Conal appeared on Jackie Daly's **Eavesdropper** album and piper Eoin O'Riabhaigh's **Tiomnacht**. His own album, **The Top of Coom** (1990), a grand selection of tunes drawn from many sources, still sounds like a breath of fresh air more than a decade after its release with Conal's rapid, driving style always spirited but precise. Highlights include the reel "O'Connell's Trip to Parliament" (celebrating Daniel O'Connell's famous victory at the 1828 Clare by-election), learned from the Sligo flute player, Patsy Hanly, and the even older seventeenth-century "The Cuckoo's Nest". Sensitive accompaniment comes from Arty McGlynn (guitar), Colm Murphy (bodhrán), Seán Ó Loingsigh (bouzouki) and Bernadette McCarthy (piano).

⊙ **The Top of Coom**   Claddagh, 1990

Unforgettable, joyful music from one of the true individuals of the flute.

Marcas Ó Murchú

Marcas Ó Murchú's flute and whistle bristle with exhilaration and, though he is generally reckoned to be one of the loudest players around, he makes joyful music that never reveals signs of force or haste nor loses touch with his love of the tradition. Though born in West Belfast in 1961, his style is deeply rooted in the Leitrim–Roscommon region where his parents originated. Marcas was given his first tin whistle by Francie McPeake III, progressing to the flute at the age of fifteen when his elder brother Mícheál gave him a copy of Ó Riada's **Gaiety** album. His love of singing derives, in part, from his father, Alf, who won Oireachtas competitions for sean-nós singing. In Belfast (where the Unionist *News Letter* once described him as a "talented tootler") he encountered musicians of the calibre of Seán McAloon and Tommy Maguire while acquiring some of his huge repertoire directly from his distant cousin **Josie McDermott** and **Packie Duignan** – two major influences on his development. Marcas's solo album, **Ó Bhéal go Béal** (1997), is a diamond from start to finish, despite coming in at an awesome seventy-one minutes. His singing is delightful (especially on "An Bhanaltra", a song praising whiskey) while his flute (whether keyed or keyless) is simply the epitome of excellence, other highlights include a planxty learned from Josie McDermott on which Eoghan O'Brien's harp adds subtle shades to Marcas's playing. Though nowadays based in Derry, if you hear a flute on the streets of Ballyshannon at the August festival (or at many others, for that matter), follow your ears – it's almost certainly Marcas.

⊙ **Ó Bhéal go Béal**   Cló Iar-Chonnachta, 1997

Graced by a superb photograph and detailed bilingual notes, this is compelling, enthralling, ground-breaking music.

Seán Potts

Founder member of **The Chieftains**, with whom he remained until the late 1970s and recorded eight albums, tin whistler and uilleann piper **Seán Potts** comes from one of Dublin's most illustrious music-making families. His grandfather was the renowned uilleann piper, John Potts, originally from Co. Wexford, while his uncle was the innovative fiddler, Tommy Potts. Seán's father, Eddie, was also a fine piper, an ability which was inherited by his son and grandson, Seán Óg Potts, while to this day Seán continues to play a leading role in Na Píobairí Uilleann. Seán's sublime whistling skills have been demonstrated on a number of recordings, not least the album **Tin Whistles** (1974) which he released with old friend **Paddy Moloney** aided by the

bodhrán of Peadar Mercier. The album is a whistler's heaven, featuring some astonishing interplay between the pair, not least on an alarming version of the reel, "Julia Delaney", which at times resembles a jazz jam session, but never loses the thread of the melody. Seán solos on a magical rendition of the lament, "Jimmy Mo Mhile Stór", and together with Paddy, blows some astonishing versions of jigs (a superb "The Gander in the Pratie Hole") and reels, while waxing lyrically on slow airs and a Carolan tune, "Pléaráca An Ruarcaigh". Seán went on to form the group **Bakerswell** in the 1980s.

⊙ Tin Whistles   Shanachie, 1974

One of the best whistle albums ever recorded from two of the greatest players.

Seán Ryan

The blithe tin and wooden whistles of **Seán Ryan** have graced many a Galway session and his albums reveal a diversity to his music much broader than the average player. His 1989 debut **Siúil Uait – Take the Air** is as bright and refreshing as a mountain spring.

Listen to the reel, "Belles of Tipperary", where Seán makes his whistle cry like a bird, or the sheer jauntiness of "The Whistling Postman" jig, the title for once conjuring up an apposite image. There are slides, single jigs, airs and waltzes too and both production and accompaniment (by the likes of Johnny McDonagh, Arty McGlynn and Caroline Lavelle, whose cello provides a resonant backdrop for "Kerry Cow") are outstanding. If you're hooked on this one, then the follow-up **Cliaraí Ceoil – Minstrel's Fancy** (1994) should be high on your shopping list too.

⊙ **Siúil Uait**   Gael-Linn, 1989

Fabulous music from one of Ireland's most illustrious whistlers.

Séamus Tansey

O ne of the most important postwar champions of the Sligo flute tradition, Gurteen-born **Seamus Tansey** possesses a distinctively dramatic, heavily ornamented playing style, vibrantly informed by an encyclopedic knowledge of his native local heritage. He is also unusual among traditional musicians in drawing explicit, often outspoken connections between the music's history and his own nationalist convictions, both in his detailed, vividly evocative accounts of the tunes he plays and in his book, *The Bardic Apostles of Innisfree* (1999), the first in a projected trilogy recalling the lives of Sligo musicians.

Tansey was born in 1943, directly connected through his fiddle-playing mother, a first cousin of Sligo legends Kathleen Harrington and John Joe Gardiner, into the region's musical heartland, although much of his early learning, on tin whistle, came from migrant labourers working around his home. Having acquired his first flute in 1961,

TEMPLE RECORDS

he won the All-Ireland title four years later, going on to produce several albums between 1970 and 1981, including **Séamus Tansey and Eddie Corcoran** (1970), **King of the Concert Flute** (1976) and **Seamus Tansey** (1981), most of them now difficult to obtain. There followed a protracted recording silence that came to a welcome end when Robin Morton, formerly of The Boys of the Lough and now MD of the Scottish folk label Temple Records, persuaded him into the studio for **Easter Snow** (1997). Standout tracks include the beautifully wrought title air and the similarly compelling "Lament for the Death of Staker Wallace", together with the fierce, fiery tune sets "Dillon's Favourite/The Bag O'Spuds", and the two jigs paired as "Famine Requiem". His subsequent recording with fiddler **Jim McKillop**, **To Hell With the Begrudgers** (1999) also won widespread praise.

⊙ **Easter Snow**   Temple, 1997

An album which showcases Tansey's playfully capricious yet tautly controlled phrasing and his crisp yet supple rhythmic drive.

Paddy Taylor

There's many an Irish tune which carries the name of a particular musician and some of the most frequently played are the jigs associated with the flute player from Loughill, Co. Limerick, **Paddy Taylor** (1912–76). Over many years of playing, Paddy developed into one of the most alluring musicians around. The first music he heard was from his mother, Honora (a renowned concertina player) but both Paddy and his brothers took up the flute, perhaps hoping to emulate Honora's father, Patrick Hanley, a fine player and composer.

Based in London from the early 1930s, Paddy spent his days working as a lighting engineer on films and later TV, while his evenings were devoted to playing music. He was a member of **Frank Lee's Tara Band**, where he acquired a taste for playing airs from Larry Hogan from Cork and subsequently played in **The Garryowen Band** (alongside many famous émigrés) making his first broadcast with the band on Irish radio in 1938. Paddy's flute was regularly heard in London's Irish pubs during the 1950s and following decade and he, and his wife May, were involved in establishing the city's first CCÉ branch. He was often seen too at festivals and competitions, and indeed twice won prizes at An t-Oireachtas.

Paddy entered the studios as early as 1939 to record with Leo Rowsome (among others), but surprisingly does not feature on any of the currently available releases from the London Irish archives, such as **Paddy In the Smoke**. However, he was recorded by Peter

Kennedy in 1956 and plays and talks enthrallingly about his music on the Folktrax cassette **Rolling in the Ryegrass**. His absence from the mainstream recording industry was rectified by his own charming album, **The Boy in the Gap**, originally issued in 1974. Playing unaccompanied music of the highest calibre, Paddy infuses his music with subtle shades of grace and gusto. Two of the single jigs, "Taylor's Fancy" and "The Limerick Jig" were learned from his mother while his grandfather also features in the polka, "Hanley's Delight". Taylor's playing of airs is phenomenal and there are four stupendous examples. Paddy and May's children were excellent musicians too and their son **Kevin** (1944–98), a piano-accordionist and pianist, recorded **Irish Traditional Music** for Brendan Mulkere's Inchecronin label.

📷 **The Boy in the Gap**   Claddagh, 1974

Subtitled "Traditional Music from Limerick and Clare", this is in the all-time top ten of traditional flute albums.

Michael Tubridy

Though an accomplished performer on several instruments (including concertina, fife, bombarde and bodhrán) **Michael Tubridy** is best known for his flute and, like many Clare musicians, favours the more simple and direct tunes. Born in Ballykett, near Kilrush, West Clare in 1935 into a family where music was fundamental to life, his first instrument was the tin whistle. House dances were a regular feature in his community and Michael himself is a noted traditional step dancer and has produced the first tutor on the subject. After moving to Dublin in the 1950s to study civil engineering at University College, he became a familiar figure in the city's music scene. His notably rhythmical style of flute playing (as suited to set-dancing) made him a natural choice for **Ceoltóirí Chualann** and he was a founder member of **The Chieftains**, remaining with the group for more than a decade. Paddy Moloney shared production with Michael on his only album to date – 1978's **The Eagle's Whistle**. It's notable as possibly the first traditional album where all the instruments are played by the same person, but also for the sumptuous sound of Tubridy's flute, particularly on a series of slip jigs sparked by the opener, "The Humours of Derrykissane".

⊙ **The Eagle's Whistle**   Claddagh, 1978

Classy flute and whistles from a compelling musician.

Desi Wilkinson

Desi Wilkinson is one of Ireland's best-known contemporary flute players – thanks, in part, to his membership of **Cran** – and one of its most cosmopolitan musicians. Brought up in South Belfast, his parents were country people and neither played an instrument although his mother loved dancing and singing. Desi's enthusiasm for music was stimulated by regular visits to the fiddler Tommy Gunn (one of the founders of Boys of the Lough) whose wife Sheila ran a guesthouse popular with musicians. Here Desi met and heard a number of players, including another Lough Boy, Cathal McConnell, who inspired him to learn the flute, travelling with him to Dublin to advise on a purchase. Though Desi was now playing with other musicians on the Belfast scene, his own love of music's lyrical capacities directed him towards the flute players of North Connacht, such as Peter Horan and Josie McDermott.

Travels to Brittany saw Desi strike up an enduring friendship with the influential Breton flute player Jean-Michel Veillon and for a period in the 1990s he lived and worked in the region, teaching himself the clarinet for playing Breton music. During this time Desi participated in the pan-European music project, *Hent St. Jakez*, which followed the medieval pilgrimage to Santiago de Compostela and resulted in a CD of the same name in 1993. By then he had already recorded **Cosa gan Bhroga** (1986), with fiddler **Gerry O'Connor** and singer **Eithne Ní Uallacháin** closely followed by his own superb **The Three Piece Flute**. This begins with a startling introduction: the sound of footsteps, joined by one whistle, then another and embellished by lilting – all performed by Desi as he creates his own session rendition of "Stoney Steps". The tunes, whether drawn from Connacht, Brittany or Ulster, are all coloured by Desi's trademark mix of wit and lyricism Apart from flutes and whistles, there's a fine song, "The Rose of Ardee", learned from the Co. Louth singer, **Finbar Boyle**, and Desi also demonstrates his prowess on the highland bagpipes on a couple of marches. A new album, **Shady Woods**, was in the offing at the time of writing.

⊙ **The Three Piece Flute**   own label, 1987

Thankfully rescued from the vinyl graveyard, Desi can do no wrong on this marvellous, fun-packed album.

Accordionists

Notoriously described by Seán Ó Riada as "designed by foreigners for the use of peasants with neither the time, inclination nor application for a worthier instrument", the button accordion and other members of the "free reed" family of bellows-operated instruments have, nevertheless, become an essential part of traditional music. Often collectively referred to as "melodeons", there are significant differences between the simple ten-button melodeon and two-, three- or even five-row button accordion. However, all work on the same principle of squeezing bellows to force air through a set of metal reeds. Buttons or keys are used to select which reed or reeds should sound, and each reed can produce two separate notes depending on whether air is pulled or pushed through it.

The ten-button melodeon, available usually in D or G, encompasses a range of three octaves while its few bass buttons offer some scope for harmonization. Despite its limitations, it has a deserved reputation as one of the best instruments for dance accompaniment. The favourite form of accordion, as popularized by **Sharon Shannon**, consists of two rows of treble buttons for the right hand and eight bass buttons for the left. Such instruments usually have several reeds per note and, though these may be tuned in various ways, the current fashion is to have pairs of reeds tuned exactly the same to produce a clear sound. The two most popular types of two-row accordion are the B/C and the C#/D (the letters referring to the home note of each row). The acclaimed B/C accordionist **Joe Burke** plays across the rows with frequent use of rolls and much melodic variation. In contrast, the C#/D player focuses on just one of the rows employing what is sometimes known as the "press and draw" method because the bellows need to be used in order to produce adjacent notes. Like the simple melodeon, this means that the C#/D style is essentially rhythmic, as opposed to the more legato style of the B/C system.

Though the piano accordion has featured in many céilí bands, it remains much derided in traditional circles. The reasons for this are that insensitive players often employ the bass buttons excessively, thus drowning out the rest of the musicians, whilst clumsy accordionists often "play between the cracks" (hit two notes simultaneously). Fortunately, there are some highly-skilled exponents around, including **Alan Kelly** and **Karen Tweed**.

Only a small range of accordion compilations exits, but our selection covers many of the great players of recent times. **The Master's Choice** features early recordings by **Joe Derrane** and his mentor **Jerry O'Brien** together with some **Bobby Gardiner** tracks from the early 1960s. **Pure Irish Traditional Accordion Session** draws on the Outlet label's archive of recordings from the 1970s and 1980s, while the best all-round collection is **The Big Squeeze**, which covers some of the biggest contemporary names.

⊙ **The Master's Choice**   Beaumex, 1946–62

An absolute must for fans of accordion history consists of recordings by Joe Derrane, Jerry O'Brien and Bobby Gardiner.

⊙ **Pure Irish Traditional Accordion Session**   Outlet, 1970s–80s

Four of the best from the Outlet archives – Finbarr Dwyer, Kevin Loughlin, John Whelan and the mighty Joe Burke.

⊙ **The Big Squeeze**   Green Linnet, 1980s

This great compilation boasts Joe Burke, as well as the Sliabh Luachra maestro, Jackie Daly, and the superb James Keane.

Paul Brock

Like Paddy (Nenagh) O'Brien, button accordionist **Paul Brock** (b. 1944, Athlone, Co. Westmeath) has a close affinity to the fiddle, while his playing style and choice of material often evokes the golden era of the dance bands. Beginning on the single-row melodeon as a boy, he acquired his early repertoire from Frank Dolphin, a fiddler from Co. Sligo, whose stock of 78s augmented Paul's own radio listening. Paul later mastered two-, three- and five-row boxes and, in 1986, demonstrated his expertise in collaboration with fiddler Frankie Gavin on their superb **Ómós do Joe Cooley**, a homage to the great accordionist. Though he has an especial affection for jazz and classical music, Paul's own 1992 solo album, **Mo Chairdín** saw him returning again to the 78s era with bright and breezy renditions of "Devine's", once recorded by a young Joe Derrane, and the set dance "The Blackbird", harking back to John J. Kimmel's 1919 recording. Brock is assisted by fellow members of the modern céilí band he founded, **Moving Cloud**, and his duet with fiddler Maeve Donnelly on "The Kildare Fancy" hornpipe would fill dance floors anywhere.

⊙ Mo Chairdín   Gael-Linn, 1992

Brock digs down deep to the roots and produces a modern masterpiece of accordion music.

Joe Burke

With his full Father Christmas beard, his famously twinkling wit, and above all his consummate mastery of the two-row B/C accordion, **Joe Burke** (b. 1939) has attained living-legend status both as a torch-bearer from the past and a pioneering influence on successive generations. The seeds of his long and distinguished career, now spanning six decades, were sown during the early 1940s in Kilnadeema, near Loughrea, Co. Galway, when Joe's accordionist uncle Pat Burke played his then four-year-old nephew the old march "Let Erin Remember". Burke was soon "mad into it", listening voraciously to 78s of Michael Coleman, Paddy O'Brien and Westmeath box player Michael Grogan, rubbing shoulders with Kevin Keegan, Joe Cooley and Paddy Fahy at local sessions. He won the All-Ireland Senior button-accordion titles in 1959 and 1960, scoring a double that first year as a member of the **Leitrim Céilí Band,** with whom he worked the London Irish dance circuit.

A 1961 tour of the US led to an extended sojourn there until 1965, during which time he recorded the seminally magnificent **A Tribute to Michael Coleman** (1966), with fiddler **Andy McGann** (an ex-pupil of Coleman's) and pianist **Felix Dolan**; the trio would later reunite for **The Funny Reel** (1979). Irish airplay for the Coleman record consolidated Burke's reputation on returning home, after which he toured for several years with fiddler **Seán Maguire**, a justly feted pairing immortalized on **Two Champions** (1971). From his first solo release **Galway's Own Joe Burke** (1971), to his most recent **The Bucks of Oranmore** (1996), Burke has continued to beguile and dazzle fans old and new with his technical supremacy, rhythmic dynamism and easy handling of complex variations and phrasing. While Paddy O'Brien's 78s revitalized interest in the B/C accordion in the 1950s, it was Joe's effervescent rolling style which galvanized a small army of aspiring box-players into action over the subsequent two decades and established the B/C as the pre-eminent version until recent times. Joe is also an imaginative flute and whistle player and his album **The Tailor's Choice** (1983), with harper **Máire Ní Chathasaigh**, is a fine display of his abilities. Joe continues to play and tour regularly with his wife, the guitarist and accordion player, **Anne Conroy**.

⊙ **A Tribute to Michael Coleman**   Green Linnet, 1966

This established Burke and his partners Andy McGann and Felix Dolan as three of the tradition's most gifted musicians.

⊙ **The Bucks of Oranmore**   Green Linnet, 1996

The title tune will always be associated with Joe but there's lots more treats on offer.

Dermot Byrne

The fiddle holds sway in Donegal and button accordionists are thin on the ground (except on Tory Island). Fortunately, Altan's formidable **Dermot Byrne** fully compensates for the dearth and is also a dab hand on the single-row melodeon. Raised near Buncrana, Dermot spent much time as a youngster in his father's birthplace, the hamlet of Teelin in the shadow of Slieve League and its majestic sea-cliffs. Here he heard the unique fiddle-playing style of Con Cassidy, with other fiddlers, especially James Byrne and Tommy Peoples, also providing inspiration. The result was that Dermot has become a latter-day Paddy (Nenagh) O'Brien – extending the accordion's range to encompass the frills and ornamentation of the local fiddle styles. He first recorded with **Altan** in 1990, becoming a full-time band member by 1996's **Blackwater** album. A year earlier he released his only solo release to date, the eponymous **Dermot Byrne** with the assistance of Stephen Cooney, Trevor Hutchinson and Dónal Lunny. Recorded live around Co. Cork, it's recommendable for the sheer verve of Byrne's playing including a wondrous virtuoso solo performance of the Brazilian tune "Tico, Tico".

There's no more wondrous sight than Dermot in full flow and this CD fully captures the experience.

Aidan Coffey

Born in 1962, near Bunmahon, Co. Waterford, it wasn't until his late teens that **Aidan Coffey** began to play the instrument that made his name. His family wasn't especially musical, but Aidan learned piano-accordion and tin whistle at school, had classical piano lessons and later tried his hand at both the bagpipes and uilleann pipes. Turning eventually to the B/C accordion, he began playing at sessions, picking up a repertoire, including Waterford polkas, and travelling to fleadhanna, often competing as a duo with septuagenarian fiddler Tommy Norris. In the 1980s Aidan moved to Cork to study microbiology (leading ultimately to a PhD) and began playing regularly with musicians such as Matt Cranitch, Vince Milne and his ensuing musical partner, **Séamus Creagh**. He also switched to the C#/D system which required different fingering, but gave him his characteristic fluid, rhythmic sound. He was still a postgraduate student when invited to join **De Dannan** in 1988, appearing on **A Jacket of Batteries** and **½ Set in Harlem**, and recording **Irlande** with Frankie Gavin and Arty McGlynn. However, Aidan's liking for accordion–fiddle duets, saw the beginning of a long partnership with Séamus Creagh in 1992 – thankfully recorded for our repeated enjoyment. Assisted by Séan Ó Loinsigh's attentive bouzouki, Creagh and Coffey weave fiddle and reeds together through a delightful series of tunes. Aidan proves himself a wizard of the polka through a couple learned from Johnny O'Leary's playing. There are plenty of snappy jigs and hornpipes, a couple of fine slides and the pair bow out with a formidable brace of reels, "Mulqueen's" (also known as "Free and Easy" and "The Kerry Lasses") and a version of Neillidh Boyle's much-adapted "The Moving Cloud".

⊙ **Séamus Creagh, Aidan Coffey**   Ossian Publications, 1999

Coffey and Creagh play a blinder and the sleeve notes here are also exemplary.

Verena Commins and Julie Langan

A s fresh as a May morning's dew and as frisky as a fawn, **Fonnchaoi** is the stunning debut album by the Galway-based button accordion and fiddle pairing of **Verena Commins** and **Julie Langan** who have played together since first meeting in Miltown Malbay in 1996. Before then Julie toured regularly with her schoolmate, harper Laoise Kelly, but she has also played with Kevin Burke, Anam, Thom Moore and the singer/songwriter John Hoban. Verena's recording credits include fiddler Kevin O'Connor's **From the Chest** and a notable appearance as piano accompanist on Niall Keegan's **Don't Touch the Elk**, while she also currently plays the box with the band **Faolán**. **Fonnchaoi** is an assured and mature album which starts off with a sparkling rendition of Jackie Daly's "The Fly-Fishing Reel" before embarking on a voyage across music associated with many other traditional greats, such as the Leitrim flute player, Josie McDermott, and Galway's own Jackie Small. Both players have strong Co. Mayo connections (Julie was born in Newport and Verena's parents moved to England from Mayo) and there's a set of

Mayo tunes including "The Maids of Castlebar", while the best of Verena's own compositions is the perky "The Slippy Wet Jig".

⊙ **Fonnchaoi**   Fonnchaoi Records, 2000

An effervescent album of delights from the excellent Commins and Langan.

The Connollys

Known as the "King of the Melodeon", **Johnny Connolly** is a native Irish speaker from the now deserted island of Inis Bearacháin off the coast of Connemara. Like many others, he heard his first music from 78s and began playing the melodeon at around nine years old. In his late teens he went to work on building sites in the north of England where he first learned English and married his wife, Patricia. On returning to Ireland in 1976, the pair and their two children settled near Spiddal, Co. Galway, where Johnny was persuaded to try his hand at the double-row accordion which he played for several years before returning to the single-row melodeon, because he found it more suited to his fundamentally rhythmic style. The melodeon is, of course, ideal for accompanying dancing and Connemara places heavy demands on accompanists as Bobby Gardiner once found when the dancers had him playing "Miss McLeod's" until sheer exhaustion set in after 45 minutes! Johnny is an exceptional accompanist and has recorded his own four-cassette set **Popular Céilí Dances**, but he's also extremely adept in playing tunes in a variety of keys, producing an ever melodious, never monotonous sound, despite the instrument's limitations. His first solo album, the critically acclaimed **An tOileán Aerach** (1993) featured no fewer than forty-two tunes, many drawn from his childhood repertoire, and he subsequently recorded **Bruach**

na Carra Léith with the distinguished local sean-nós singer **Johnny Mháirtín Learaí**. 1998 saw his gem of an album, **Drioball na Fáinleoige**, where Connolly's spirited, nimble playing is accompanied by Charlie Lennon and Steve Cooney, though there's also a relaxed duet with fiddler Nóirín Ní Ghrádaigh and Johnny's "party-piece", the song "Johnny Seoighe" (from Carna, Connemara).

Johnny's son, **Johnny Óg**, was born in England and began playing the B/C two-row button accordion at seven, soon after the family's homecoming, although he nowadays favours the C#/D variety. Johnny Óg joined **Na hAncairí**, the enduring Connemara dance hall band led by John Beag, when he was fourteen and stayed eight years, playing guitar and bass too. Joe Burke had been his idol, but seeing Dermot Byrne play one night in Spiddal inspired a changed view of the accordion. Since then he's appeared on Anam's debut album and has been a regular member of singer Seán Keane's touring band, while also working as a duo with fellow band member, banjo player and pianist **Brian McGrath** with whom he recorded **Dreaming up the Tunes** (1998). The title comes from a request tunes put to Charlie Lennon who promised that he might dream up a few and promptly did so. The album's jaunty mood is exemplified by the closing track, a Coleman barn dance, and the pair's playing is as tight as they come. Brian also supplies some dazzling plectrum-work on "Mick O'Connor's", two favourite reels associated with the London-based banjo player.

⊙ **Drioball na Fáinleoige**   Cló Iar-Chonnachta, 1998

Watching the quiet, unassuming Johnny Connolly play is sheer joy and this fully reproduces all his zest and finesse.

⊙ **Dreaming up the Tunes**   Cló Iar-Chonnachta, 1998

Johnny Óg Connolly and Brian McGrath provide taut, considered playing throughout this fine album.

Joe Cooley

Describing **Joe Cooley** as a legend is a little like calling water wet. Indeed, with his homecoming in 1972, the button-accordionist achieved near-messianic status and today, almost thirty years after his death the following year, mere mention of his name is guaranteed to bring a smile and an appreciative nod from those who knew him. There are many stories about Cooley and his astonishing prowess on the accordion, but the bare bones of his life are as follows. Born in 1924 in Peterswell, Co. Galway, he grew up in a house where music was as much a matter of life as food and drink. Both parents played the melodeon and the young Joe, and his elder brothers were encouraged to learn music too, especially to play for the dancers who would come to the house most evenings. A block-layer by trade and an itinerant by nature, Cooley first moved to Co. Clare, playing dances around the county with the fiddler **Joe Leary**, and spending a spell in the Tulla Céilí Band with his accordionist contemporary and friend **Paddy O'Brien**. He moved to Dublin and then London, emigrating to the US in 1954, living in various cities before ending up in Chicago where he was joined by his flute playing younger brother, **Séamus**. Together they broadcast regularly on radio and formed the popular **Glenside Céilí Band**. While Séamus remained in Chicago, Joe moved to San Francisco living there from 1965 until 1972, teaching music and playing regularly with fellow Galway accordionist Kevin Keegan and the Clare-born flute and fiddle player Joe Murtagh.

Joe Cooley played a D/D♯ accordion in the old "press and draw" style and made music that was simply inspirational, not least to dancers; music with a twinkle in its eye and sheer abandon in its spirit. In defiance of the instrument's limitations, its supposed inexpressive

nature, his tunes, often albeit in major keys, possess a wild and powerful enchantment. Simply entitled **Cooley**, his only album was released
posthumously in 1975 and included recordings from several sessions.
The first consists of eight tunes recorded at Lahiff's Bar in his home village of Peterswell, a month before Cooley died, where he is accompa-

nied by his brother **Jack** on
bodhrán and **Des Mulkere**
on banjo, while snatches of
an interview with the great
man appear between tracks.
Tony MacMahon, who was
himself given his first accordion by Joe, was responsible
for this recording and notes
that so many turned up to
hear him, that "those who
couldn't get in pressed their
faces to the dripping

November window panes". You can hear the reason why as Joe
launches into "The Wise Maid" and those luckily inside the bar whoop
their appreciation. The sparkling versions of "The Blackthorn" and "The
Boyne Hunt" were performed in another Galway bar in July, 1972
(again with Mulkere) while the remaining tracks, from Chicago in 1962
and Dublin in 1963, include a stunningly definitive version of "The
Bucks of Oranmore". A master of his craft, ever-willing to share his
music, Joe Cooley died in December, 1973, at the age of forty-nine.

⊙ **Cooley**   Gael-Linn, 1962–73

Emphatic proof of the sheer majesty and emotional power of
Cooley's music – utterly essential.

Jackie Daly

Though actually from Kanturk, Co. Cork, about twenty miles east of the region, accordionist and concertinist **Jackie Daly** is one of the key figures in bringing the music of Sliabh Luachra to its current level of popularity while also featuring in several of Ireland's most significant traditional bands. Born in 1945, and, encouraged by his melodeon-playing father, Jackie took up the tin whistle and harmonica aged ten, later progressing to the accordion. His main musical education took place at the crossroads dances held each Sunday at Knocknacolan near his home, learning tunes mainly from the gatherings' regular fiddler, Jim Keefe, himself a pupil of the Sliabh Luacra fiddle master, Pádraig O'Keefe. Eventually, Jackie joined the group and played with them for a couple of years.

Five years working in Holland put music on hold until he returned to Ireland in 1973, winning the All-Ireland Senior accordion competition the following year. He then hooked up with Cork-based fiddler **Séamus Creagh**, a ten-year partnership that produced the seminal 1977 album **Jackie Daly agus Séamus Creagh** (see p.301), one of the first to introduce the Sliabh Luachra style to a wider audience. Another key recording in this vein was Daly's solo debut the same year, **Music From Sliabh Luachra** (1977), both albums highlighting Daly's old-style "press and draw" technique on his C#/D instrument, and his influentially distinctive "dry" tuning.

Then followed a four-album stint with **De Dannan**, beginning with **The Mist Covered Mountain** (1980), during which time Jackie took time out to record another much-admired duo album, **Eavesdropper** (1981), with fiddler **Kevin Burke**, and play with Dolores Keane in **Reel Union** and **Kinvara**. Since the mid-1980s, apart from a brief stint in **Arcady**, Daly's duties have divided between **Buttons and Bows** the band he formed with fiddlers Séamus and Manus McGuire and man-docello player Garry Ó Briain, and the supergroup **Patrick Street**, which reunited Jackie and Kevin Burke alongside Andy Irvine and Arty McGlynn. Known not only for his mastery of the C#/D accordion, but also for his experimentation with tunings and reeds, Jackie finally released a second solo album, **Many's A Wild Night** (1995), which explored his customary territory of polkas, slides, reels, jigs and horn-pipes, along with several of his own compositions.

⊙ Music From Sliabh Luachra   Green Linnet, 1977

From sparklingly vivacious dance tunes to masterly slow airs, unaccompanied accordion has rarely sounded so sweet.

Joe Derrane

Joe Derrane – the boy wonder of the button accordion – was born in Boston, Massachusetts in March, 1930, to a mother from Co. Roscommon and a father from Inis Mór in the Aran Islands. Influenced by **John J. Kimmel**'s recordings and studying first the melodeon then the C#/D accordion under the acclaimed Jerry O'Brien from Kinsale, Co. Cork, Derrane acquired a dazzling profi-ciency, characterized by the rapid cascades of triplets and rolls which seemed to teem from his flowing fingers. His early renown was acquired through the sixteen recordings he made in Boston for the Copley label during 1946–47 (reissued as **Irish Accordion**) which, though then regarded as the acme of accordion achievement, in fact owed a considerable debt to the 78s recorded by Kimmel.

The decline of Boston's Irish dance-hall scene in the early 1950s saw Joe embarking on a long alternative musical career, first on piano accordion and later synthesizer, which encompassed many of the changes in popular music over the following decades. However, others never forgot his traditional playing and he made a surprise and acclaimed return to the fold in May, 1994, at the Irish Folk Festival, Wolf Trap, Virginia, once again playing button-accordion. His revitalized solo career has seen him perform in places as far afield as Alaska and Inis Mór and produce two fine albums for Green Linnet, **Give Us Another** and **Return to Inis Mór** (the latter with Carl Hession). 1998 saw his stunning debut for Shanachie, **The Tie That Binds**. Now using a 23-button C#/D accordion, Derrane's playing on the reels "The Pullet and the Cock/Banjo Man" achieves heights few other performers would dare to attempt.

⊙ Irish Accordion	Beaumex, 1946–47

The teenage star's early recordings compiled on one grand disc.

⊙ The Tie That Binds	Shanachie, 1998

Still on top form more than fifty years later, Derrane's fingers don't so much produce a river as a torrent of sound!

Tom Doherty

Born in 1913 in the village of Mountcharles a few miles west of Donegal town, melodeon player **Tom Doherty** retained a connection with the pre-recorded era. He began playing the melodeon at the age of six and acquired most of his repertoire before the arrival of radio in the county in the late 1920s. Tom spent years working in Scotland as a migrant labourer before emigrating to the US in 1948 and settling in Brooklyn, marrying, and working in a cold-storage factory. After a brief spell playing for céilís, he left the professional music scene until his own retirement from work coincided with the late 1970s traditional revival in New York. Returning to performance, often with his daughter **Maureen** (later of Cherish the Ladies) on flute, he finally recorded an album, **Take the Bull by the Horns**, a sparkling collection of predominantly Donegal dance tunes, including highlands and Germans learned from his parents almost 80 years earlier. Sadly, Tom died a couple of years ago, but this, his sole record, is a superb memorial to bygone times and includes what is possibly the only available recording of highlands played on a melodeon.

⊙ **Take the Bull by the Horns**   Green Linnet, 1993

Donegal dance music played with verve and style by a master of the melodeon.

Finbarr Dwyer

The **Dwyers** from Cailroe near Castletownbere are one of Co. Cork's well-known musical families and, probably, their most famed member is the button accordionist, **Finbarr** now based in Slough, England. Both his parents and brothers Michael and Richard played the instrument (while brother John is a noted fiddler and composer) and Finbarr, in his time, won both the All-Ireland and All-Britain Senior titles. A multiskilled musician (including both acoustic and pedal-steel guitars, fiddle, piano and whistle), Finbarr recorded prolifically in the 1970s and 1980s in a rolling style which might seem familiar to Joe Burke fans simply because Joe recorded several of Finbarr's tunes. Little is currently available on compact disc, though on **Pure Traditional Irish Accordion Music** Finbarr's three-row accordion is accompanied by Teresa McMahon's very hopalong piano. Information provided on the tunes is scanty and, for some mysterious reason, the artwork includes a picture of Killarney's Bunratty Castle. Finbarr's playing may seem quaintly dated to ears attuned to, say, Dermot Byrne or Conor McCarthy, but there's no doubting his ability on tunes like the jig "Frieze Breeches" (listed as "The Fries Breeches" for all chip lovers), ornamented by an impressive range of triplets. His own well-known reel "Finbarr Dwyer's No.2" is also included.

⊙ **Pure Traditional Irish Accordion Music**　　　　　Outlet, 1980s

Spirited playing ever easy on the ear.

Patty Furlong

Button accordionist **Patty Furlong** (née Conway) recorded as long ago as 1977 when, as one of Martin Mulvihill's pupils, she soloed on **Irish Music: The Living Tradition**, an album overseen by the notable Bronx-based teacher. By then she was already an adept performer on the C#/D box having won the under-fifteen All-Ireland title in 1975. She had been inspired by her father Jimmy Conway, from Castlebar, Co. Mayo, who favoured the Derrane style (see p.485) and encouraged by her mother Peggy. In the mid-1980s, Patty became one of the original members of the **Cherish the Ladies** entourage, appearing on their first album, and has been a prominent figure on the Irish-American music scene ever since. A regular session in the 1990s spawned the band **Atlantic Bridge**, which also featured a certain **Karan Casey** on vocals, and, in 1995, Patty joined **The Chieftains** for three of their East Coast concerts and a TV appearance – recognition indeed! Wider acclaim should result from her wonderful solo debut, **Traditional Irish Music Played on Button Accordion**, a sparkling selection of tunes played with all the esprit of her acknowledged influence, **Jackie Daly**. Listen to the polkas "Nell

Fee's/I'll Buy Boots for Maggie" and hear an inventive, polished musician at the peak of her powers.

⦿ **Traditional Irish Music Played on Button Accordion**   own label, 1999

The press and draw style thrives in this splendid collection of tunes from Ireland, Scotland and Cape Breton.

John Joe Gannon

The button accordion playing of **John Joe Gannon** (b. 1915, near Streamstown, Co. Westmeath) is imbued with the spirit of a bygone age. His father, James, was a talented melodeon player and carried a store of tunes, some of which were reckoned to be unique to the area. John Joe inherited both his father's skills and his style, becoming a familiar figure in musical and dance hall circles after joining one of Ireland's most popular céilí bands, the **Moate,** in 1936 and recording with them. Moving to Dublin in 1949, he joined the equally illustrious **Kincora Céilí Band**, founded and led by fiddler Kathleen Harrington, and was often heard playing at clubs like the Church

Street. In 1996, John Joe recorded the aptly-titled **A Blast from the Past**, an unaccompanied album of tunes drenched with the tide of history from the opening fling associated with his father, "James

Gannon's", to the closing waltz from Michael Coleman. Tunes both familiar ("Drops of Brandy", "Tell Her I Am") and less so ("The Quarrelsome Piper", "The Kingston") roll from his fingers with an infectious, foot-tapping joy.

⊙ A Blast from the Past   CCÉ, 1996

A real treasure – no more, no less.

Bobby Gardiner

Acclaimed button accordionist, **Bobby Gardiner** (b. 1939) hails from Aughdarra, near Lisdoonvarra, Co. Clare. His mother played concertina and melodeon and uncles and brothers were musical too, so Bobby had much assistance when he began learning the concertina before moving on to the accordion when he had managed to save enough money to buy one. Developing increased proficiency through playing at house dances, Bobby first brought his music to a wider audience through the **Kilfenora Céilí Band** in the 1950s, joining the Armagh-based **Malachy Sweeney** band later in the decade. Emigrating to Connecticut in 1960, he worked on the railroad, encountered Joe Cooley at sessions and played with the **Jack Wade Céilí Band.** Such exposure brought recognition of his abilities and he recorded **Memories of Clare** two volumes of rolling accordion music. In 1963, he was drafted into the US Army, but on his discharge returned to work and make music in the Catskills until deciding to move back to Tipperary in 1970. Resuming a home-based career as musician and teacher, though frequently participating in CCÉ's international tours, Bobby was later recruited by Mícheál Ó Súilleabháin when the latter was establishing University College Cork's traditional music programme. This resulted in the 1993 album

The Master's Choice, a fine record marred, in part, by some inappropriate synthesizer accompaniment. Far better is the more recent **The Clare Shout**, on which Bobby plays melodeon assisted by Mel Mercier's bodhrán and a host of set and step dancers. He also unleashes his lilting skills, learned originally from John Joseph Clair of Liscannor, and delivered here with remarkable flair and humour.

⊙ **Memories of Clare**   Beaumex, 1962

Youthful, spirited, surging music from Bobby at 23.

⊙ **The Clare Shout**   own label, 1998

Almost 40 years on, Gardiner plays what he does best, inspired dance music.

James Keane

The first accordionist **James Keane** remembers meeting was Joe Cooley. Born in 1948 in Drimnagh, Co. Dublin, James was six at the time and Cooley's performance left an abiding impression. Both James's parents were fiddlers (his elder brother Seán would follow suit and become a fixture in The Chieftains) but the young James started picking out tunes on his uncle's C#/D box before being bought his own Paolo Soprani. Sadly, when he felt sufficiently proficient to play in a session at The Pipers' Club he discovered that he couldn't join in as he was still playing in C#/D fashion on his new B/C box! He proved quick to adapt, however, winning the All-Ireland Junior title at 15 and the Senior title for the following three years, the first time such a feat had ever been achieved. His reputation blossomed through both membership of the **Castle Céilí** band from 1960 to 1968 and through sessioning on an unparalleled level – indeed, the

Dublin papers once reported him playing in thirteen different venues on a single night! For a while in the 1960s James shared a Dublin flat with **Paul Brady** and **Mick Moloney** and both still recognize the huge influence he had on the development of their own musical careers. However, all was to change in 1967, when he toured the US for three weeks with the **Loughrea Céilí Band** (whose members also included **Joe Burke** and **Paddy Carty**). For James returned the following year to set up residence in New York and soon after married Theresa O'Shea, from Co. Kerry. Apart from a brief spell in Canada and regular trips back to Dublin, they've lived in the US ever since with James cementing his reputation there as the accordionists' accordionist.

Despite the acclaim, James's recording career has been sparse until late. His 1970s album for Rex Records, **The Irish Accordion of James Keane** is long out-of-print and there was a lengthy gap between **Roll Away the Reel World** (1980), made with **Mick Moloney** and brother Seán, and his "come-back" **That's the Spirit** (1993). Since then, however, he's released the splendid **With Friends Like These** (1998) – the friends being Tommy Peoples, Paddy Glackin, Kevin Conneff, Matt Molloy, Garry Ó Briain and Liam O'Flynn – and the highly recommended **Sweeter as the Years Roll By** (1999). Recorded at Liam Clancy's Ring studio, the latter is a conscious attempt to bridge "the musical gap between young Ireland and a Dublin box player who left over thirty years ago" and features the youthful energies of nephews Padraic and Darach Keane (fiddles), Danú's Donnchadh Gough (bodhrán), concertina-player Aoife O'Connor plus her brother Liam's band Turas. There's also a spot for brother Seán on a sparkling set of reels, but the real joy is James's own sensational musicianship. On the album's outstanding closing track, the slow air "Paddy's Rambles Through the Park", associated with John Doherty, he squeezes such mournful expressiveness from his accordion that it appears to have acquired a soul of its own. A maestro at work!

⊙ **With Friends Like These**   Green Linnet, 1998

Supergroup outings in the rock world are often disastrous, but not this album from Keane and some of Ireland's other traditional greats.

Alan Kelly

The piano accordion is scorned by some traditional purists as an instrument incapable of producing the necessary subtleties while others believe that it's just too damned loud. However, in the hands of a master like **Alan Kelly** such criticism can be tossed out with the feathers. Born in Roscommon, but now Galway-based, the young piano accordionist has long been noted for his exhilarating live performances and his playing on Mike McGoldrick's **Morning Rory** caught many an ear. His own debut album **Out of the Blue** (1997) received generally ecstatic reviews and you can hear exactly why on tracks like "The Red Haired Lass" set of reels where Kelly's dexterity sets the keys a-flipping at a breathtaking pace as he negotiates rapid triplets, employs the odd chordal effect and virtually ignores the dreaded bass notes. Alan's father, Frank (himself winner of the 1964 All-Ireland Senior piano-accordion title), encouraged him to listen to as broad a range of musicians and idioms as possible and Alan's latest album, **Mosaic**, shows this eclecticism in operation. The initial track, "Salamanca Samba", composed by producer, Arty McGlynn, begins with a brass section riff, before Alan enters Jack Emblow style, suggesting he is about to embark on a wild version of "I've Got Rhythm", before settling down to a nifty reel. The remainder includes some of Alan's own tunes, together with one from Liz Carroll and some Scottish tunes (including "Campbeltown Loch I Wish You Were Whisky"). There's a good range of Irish dance music too, including a spirited duet with Alan's flute-playing brother, Jim, on "Martin Whynne's".

⊙ **Mosaic**   Tara, 2000

Kelly's flying fingers reclaim ground for the maligned piano accordion on this eclectic album.

John J. Kimmel

Among the twentieth century's great musical mysteries is – in the unbeatable words of Reg Hall – "how an American born of German parents in the old Dutch town of Brooklyn should have been attracted to Irish music and developed such an authentic style". Whatever the answer, **John J. Kimmel** (1866–1942) was one of the century's most prolific recording artists and, though he released many records in other musical genres (and played several other instruments), his recordings of Irish traditional music have had a lasting impact. Pictures usually show him clutching a one-row melodeon, but his use of triplets and a variety of keys means that he must sometimes also have used a two-row accordion. Kimmel's first release dates from 1903 and he was still recording almost thirty years later. Fifteen of these sides, the earliest dating from 1907, are collated on **Early Recordings of Irish Traditional Dance Music** and the sound may sometimes strike the unitiated listener as bearing a remarkable resemblance to a fairground organ. Nevertheless, despite the mystery surrounding Kimmel's interest in Irish music and his employment of accompanists apparently unfamiliar with the tradition, these are extraordinary recordings of tunes which still play a significant part in many musicians' repertoires.

> ⊙ **Early Recordings of**   Leader Records,1907–29
> **Irish Traditional Dance Music**

Required listening for all interested in the music's history and development.

Tony MacMahon

Button accordionist **Tony MacMahon** (b.1939, The Turnpike, Ennis, Co. Clare) is one of traditional music's most colourful, controversial and vital characters and a superb musician to boot. Over the last thirty years he has become well known to Irish television and radio audiences as a presenter and producer (in the latter role initiating seminal traditional music programmes such as *The Long Note* on radio and *The Pure Drop* and *Come West Along the Road* on TV), while acquiring a reputation as a fearsome defender of the core values of the tradition. It was his appearance and comments on an edition of *The Late Late Show* devoted to a discussion of the *River of Sound* series which led to the 1996 Crossroads Conference (see p.544), and his own paper, *Music of the powerful and majestic past*. Some have dismissed Tony as a backwoods conservative, but through his efforts a significant body of material has entered the public domain which might otherwise have been lost or forgotten (such as the recording of Joe Cooley on both disc and film). Contrarily, he has remarked that traditional music "isn't my favourite music and hasn't been for a long time" while his oft-quoted comment that there was "no boghole too deep for all the accordions in Ireland" indicates his sense of being entrapped by the instrument at which he is so adept. Known too for his radical politics, for a time he ran a weekly club in aid of the ANC and was a notable supporter of the H-Block hunger strikes.

Tony inherited his initial love for the music from his parents (his mother played the concertina) and visits to the family house from musicians such as Tommy Potts, Felix Doran and Joe Cooley. It was Joe who gave him his first accordion, a small piano model, and remained a lasting influence, while soon afterwards Seán Reid presented him with

a button version. In 1957 he moved to Dublin to train as a teacher and soon made contact with many musicians. An especial influence was John Kelly whose first advice was apparently "learn to smoke a pipe and drink a pint", while accordionist Sonny Brogan encouraged his development as a player. In 1963, on a transatlantic

trip, Tony hitched from Toronto to New York to see Seámus Ennis and spent a fortnight in the piper's flat mastering the art of playing slow airs. In the mid-1960s, Tony passed through London on his way to busk in France and Morocco and his visit coincided with the recording of **Paddy in the Smoke** (see p.358) in The Favourite pub. He appears on the album in cahoots with fiddlers Martin Byrnes and Andy Boyle, playing a very Cooleyesque couple of reels.

The appearance of his own, self-titled, debut album followed his return to Dublin and is one of Ireland's landmark releases. Dance tunes teem from his accordion with delightful abandon, while his playing of slow airs, especially "The Wounded Hussar" and "The Dear Irish Boy", is fired by a spellbinding passion. Next MacMahon helped form the original line-up of **The Bothy Band** but left shortly afterwards. There were no further solo albums until 2000, but 1985 saw him convene with concertina player **Noel Hill** and a group of set dancers in Dan O'Connell's pub in Knocknagree to record **I gCnoc na Graí**, an album pulsating with the raw vivacity of two maestros in their element. The pair repeated the format in a more formal setting in Dublin for **Aislingí Ceoil** (1993) with Iarla Ó Lionáird whom Tony had persuaded to return to singing. Again MacMahon and Hill reaped a bountiful harvest of reels and jigs together, but the heart is left longing for more of the former's slow air playing. His rendition of "Gol na mBan san Ár" leading into "Cnocán an Teampaill", a lament and old jig from a rarely played descriptive suite, "Máirseáll Alasdrum", evokes both the anguish expressed for the battle-fallen and a macabre determination to continue the struggle. **MacMahon From Clare** (2000) looks back over his long and illustrious career.

⊙ **Tony MacMahon**   Shanachie, 1972

A monumental album in the history of the accordion.

⊙ **I gCnoc na Graí**   Gael-Linn, 1985

Tremendous, foot-stomping music from MacMahon and Noel Hill – indisputably the ultimate live traditional music release.

Josephine Marsh

Those in the know have long wondered why Sharon Shannon gets all of the limelight when there's another gem of a Clare accordionist living just down the road. In a sense, it's an unfair comparison: Sharon's music grabs you by its sheer verve and energy, while the playing of her contemporary, **Josephine Marsh** (from Broadford, East Clare), creeps up on you surreptitiously and suddenly sets your toes a-tapping. Josephine favours the B/C Hohner Black Dot accordion and has a distinctive style based on a fluid lightness of touch that Sean Tyrrell describes aptly as "...so effortless, less of the head and more of the spirit". Unless you catch her playing in Ennis or touring with her own band, or obtain a copy of her rare cassette **To Meet a Friend** (recorded in 1990 with bouzouki player **Cyril O'Donoghue**) the easiest way to hear her is on her captivating eponymous solo album. The choice of tunes is varied and she's also not afraid to include her own compositions, like the waltz "Matthew's", named after her new-born nephew. The album's understated accompaniment is provided by brother Pat's bouzouki and guitar and Jim Higgins' piano while Cathy Custy's concertina adds weight to a set of polkas named after Jo's father, Paddy.

⊙ **Josephine Marsh**   Tara, 1996

The deftest of touches and the sweetest of tones produce a hot-buttered toast of an album!

Conor McCarthy

In addition to its legions of concertina players, Co. Clare has produced some stunning accordionists, including Sharon Shannon, Tony MacMahon and Jo Marsh, while Joe Cooley was an adopted son. A potential addition to that list is **Conor McCarthy** (b. 1967, Ennis), well known for his membership of The **Kilfenora Céilí Band** alongside his wife, fiddler **Annemarie McCormack**. Conor learned the accordion from his father, **Johnny**, a driving force in Ennis's music, though a typically relaxed player in the flowing style of Clare. Other musicians to have influenced Conor include the Kilfenora's fiddler, Michael Kelleher, a player with a natural "lift", as well as other fiddlers such as Tommy Potts and Martin Byrnes. Conor featured on two

Kilfenora albums before releasing **Ace and Deuce** in 1998 with Annemarie accompanied by the bouzouki and guitar player **Cyril O'Donoghue**. An album studded with remarkable interchanges, this whetted appetites for solo albums by both players and Conor's duly appeared in 2000 as **Selection Box**, featuring Alph Duggan's discriminating guitar and a guest appearance from Conor's father, Johnny. Conor's highly individual style employs a confident use of the bass, as on the aptly-named "My Left Hand" (featuring the reels "Hanley's Tweed/Paddy Fahy's"). He is also happy working his B/C box around minor keys and includes a remarkable D minor rendition of the jig "Banish Misfortune", replete with an onrush of rapid downward rolls. Air playing is Conor's forte too and there is an evocative version of "A Stór mo Chroi", plus a snatch of his father's own mastery of the form on "The Source".

⊙ **Selection Box**   Twin Records, 2000

McCarthy and Duggan provide lots of treats and none of the sweets nobody wants.

Mick Mulcahy

Button accordionist **Mick Mulcahy** from Brosna, Co. Kerry, learned his early music from his father and uncle, both accordionists, and by taping Ciarán Mac Mathúna's radio programmes. A spell working in London in the 1960s brought him into contact with many of the city's renowned Irish musicians and resulted in an enduring friendship with the banjo player, Mick O'Connor. Mulcahy's self-titled debut album appeared back in 1976 and aficionados of his relaxed but spirited style still await its CD reissue. Meanwhile, there's the comfort of his 1990 **Mick Mulcahy agus Cairde** (Mick Mulcahy and Friends) recorded with bodhrán-player **Mel Mercier**, **Mick O'Connor** on guitar and banjo, and Ennistymon (Co. Clare) fiddler **Joe Rynne**. There's all the informality of a fireside session here and Mick's easy, rolling pace helps to stoke the embers with a wonderful rendition of the jigs "Seán Ryan's/Charlie Mulvihill's", the standout cut from a panoply of excellent renditions. Another decade passed before the arrival of one of the surprise releases of 2000, **The Mulcahy Family**, featuring Mick and his teenage daughters **Michelle** (concertina and harp) and **Louise** (flute and uilleann pipes) and backing of the highest order from the bouzoukis of **Cyril O'Donoghue** and **Zan McLeod** plus **Mick Moloney**'s tenor banjo. While their father's in supreme form throughout, Michelle proves herself a stylish harper on the solo jigs "Vincent Broderick's/Jerry Holland's" and Louise solos with equal grace on a pair of rousing reels, "Father Kelly's/The Belles of Tipperary".

⊙ Mick Mulcahy agus Cairde   Gael-Linn, 1990

A delightful box of tricks from Mulcahy.

Paddy ("Nenagh") O'Brien

J ust as the 78s recorded by Coleman, Morrison and Killoran galvanized traditional music in the 1920s and 1930s, those released by **Paddy O'Brien** revolutionized button-accordion playing in the 1950s and his influence endures to this day. Born in Newtown, near Nenagh, Co. Tipperary, in 1922, his father **Dinny** (fiddle and concertina) was the leader of the local Bridge Céilí Band. Paddy began playing the fiddle at the age of seven and the two-row G/G# accordion at ten. At fourteen he made his first radio broadcast with his father and flute-player Bill Fahy and subsequently formed the **Lough Derg Ceili Band**. Changing to the B/C accordion at fifteen and playing with the **Aughrim Slopes Céilí Band** in the 1940s, his reputation spread quickly and he made his first recording in 1949: two reels, "Peter Street/Bonnie Kate", and two hornpipes, "Maguire's Fiddle/Wade Hampton", released back to back with four tunes by Belfast fiddler Seán Maguire. Paddy also occasionally played alongside **Joe Cooley** in the **Tulla Céilí Band** and they became good friends. When the two met head to head in the Senior solo competition at the Athlone Fleadh Cheoil in 1953, O'Brien won after a rerun but never again competed solo.

Before emigrating to the US in 1954, Paddy recorded the three 78s which were to have such an prolonged impact. Originally released by Columbia, five of the six sides are available on **The Banks of the Shannon** CD including the reels "Youghal Quay/The Rambling Sailor", the slip jigs "The Arragh Mountains/Father Burke's" and the hornpipe "The Banks of the Shannon". Sounding simple in theory, in practice Paddy's transposition of his fiddle-style to the two-row accordion was both remarkable and ingenious and harnessed much of the ornamentation and embellishment so beloved by fiddlers. Using fiddle keys rather than the "natural" tuning of the accordion, Paddy's dexterous fingers described up and down triplets and exceptionally precise five-note rolls, together with an understated use of simple grace notes, never before heard to such effect on the instrument. At 32, Paddy had transformed the sound of the accordion and, astonishingly, had done so on an instrument only recently acquired.

In the US Paddy worked as a bus driver and mechanic, shunning professional venues in favour of house sessions and céilís, eventually joining the renowned **New York Céilí Band** towards the end of the 1950s. Returning to Ireland in 1962, he first lived in Dublin, playing with the **Lough Gowna Céilí Band** (which also included Paddy Moloney), before moving back to Newtown with his wife and daughter in 1965. There he continued his exploration of the box's potential in partnership with fiddler **Séamus Connolly**. The pair formed **Inis Cealtra** with Peadar O'Loughlin (flute), Paddy Canny (fiddle) and George Byrt (piano), broadcasting several times on RTÉ radio before opting to continue as a duo. In 1973, Paddy and Séamus, assisted by **Charlie Lennon** recorded six tracks for CCÉ – the original **The Banks of the Shannon** release – which comprise the remainder of the 1993 CD (along with two later recordings by Séamus). When Séamus emigrated to the US in 1976, Paddy continued to play and teach until bedridden by a debilitating stroke in 1988. He had composed tunes for much of his life and even illness didn't deter him, his wife notating melodies at his bedside. Paddy died in 1991 but Nenagh honours him annually in late August with the Aonach Paddy O'Brien Festival. One CD may seem a small legacy for such an innovator, but fortunately many of his 200 or so tunes have been collected in *The Compositions of Paddy O'Brien* and his daughter **Eileen** (fiddle) and her long-time friend **Willie Fogarty** (accordion) have issued the excellent CD of the same name, including two of Paddy's most famous tunes, "Dinny O'Brien's" reel and "The Boys of Lough Gowna" double jig.

⦿ **The Banks of the Shannon**   Green Linnet, 1954–90

A quintessential landmark album with Séamus Connolly and Charlie Lennon.

Paddy ("Offaly") O'Brien

Known as Paddy "the Younger" or "Offaly" O'Brien to distinguish from his illustrious namesake, this button accordionist and musicologist (b. 1945 Daingean, Co. Offaly) has forged his own notable reputation. Paddy has a phenomenal memory for tunes and began collecting in his teens, making contact on his travels with many older players. Such encounters influenced his own distinctive style which, in part, reflected his desire to incorporate their expressiveness and sense of abandon into his own playing. Paddy moved to Dublin in the late 1960s where musicians such as the fiddlers John Kelly, Joe Ryan and Seán Keane encouraged his playing and he became a long-standing member of both the **Castle Céilí Band** and **Ceoltóirí Laighean**. During the 1970s Paddy twice won the All-

Ireland Senior accordion title. In 1978 he formed the trio **Bowhand** with fiddler **James Kelly** and guitarist **Dáithí Sproule**, recording two albums in the US, where – like both Kelly and Sproule – he decided to settle.

Based in Minneapolis since 1983, Paddy has continued to play, teach and augment his massive collection of tunes. These now number over three thousand, including many rarities and variations, and, in 1994, five hundred of them were collated as a set of twelve cassettes entitled **The Paddy O'Brien Tune Collection**. Astonishingly, until this production, all of the tunes were stored in Paddy's memory, though a score or so appear in Breandán Breathnach's *Ceil Rince na hÉireann* (Vols. 2 and 3). Though he has appeared on numerous recordings, including Breathnach's **Folk Music and Dances of Ireland** and a notable solo on Liam Weldon's **Dark Horse in the Wind**, Paddy has so far made just one album himself, **Stranger at the Gate** (1988), on which he was reunited with Dáithí Sproule. Paddy's playing of reels is always animated, using shrewd ornamentation and unpredictable flights of fancy, while jigs, such as the slip jig "Jimmy Power's Favourite", are played with a wonderful, gambolling zest. He's just as comfortably at home with slow airs, for instance "The Lament from Eoin Rhua" which he learned from Cathal McConnell.

⊙ **Stranger at the Gate**   Green Linnet, 1988

The pure drop from a hugely accomplished tune collector.

Máirtín O'Connor

Diversity has been long the hallmark of **Máirtín O'Connor**'s career. Playing a two-row D/D# accordion, he started out alongside singers Thom Moore and Janie Cribbs and guitarist Gerry

O'Beirne in the 1970s folk-rock outfit **Midnight Well**, going on to per-
form with the Boys of the Lough, Dolores Keane's Reel Union, De
Dannan, Skylark and the original *Riverdance* orchestra. While his
Lunny-produced solo debut **The Connachtman's Rambles** (1978)
was a largely traditional affair, his subsequent two recordings have
revealed a greater spirit of eclecticism. The splendidly effervescent
Perpetual Motion (1990), its title track derived from a piece by
Paganini, also takes in a Basque fandango, American ragtime, a
Ukrainian polka, French and Italian waltzes and a superb self-penned
Irish blues. The result is characterized not only by awesome technical
control, but an easy-going charm which banishes any suggestion of
gimmickry, the underlying swing and tone colour of O'Connor's style
creating a dynamic, often playful dialogue between Irish and other

folk traditions. **Chatterbox** (1993), entirely made up of O'Connor's own compositions, is equally mercurial in its range of flavours – Irish, Mediterranean, Balkan, American, classical. As on the previous album, an array of distinguished guests – including guitarists Steve Cooney, Jimmy Faulkner and Garry Ó Briain, fiddlers Ciaran Tourish, Nollaig Casey and Máire Breatnach, percussionist Tommy Hayes, and Micheál Ó Suilleabháin on piano – is artfully deployed.

⊙ Perpetual Motion   Claddagh, 1990

A marvellously winning blend of technical sophistication and infectious joie de vivre.

Johnny O'Leary

Johnny O'Leary, of the Sliabh Luachra accordionists, was born in 1924 in Maulykeavane. Though he moved to Gullane in 1949 he has been based in Rathmore since 1977 where he worked as a fitter for many years. Johnny started off on the melodeon, playing at first with his uncle Dan O'Leary, a fiddler, and with Dan's teacher, Tom Billy Murphy. Early encouragement came also from John Clifford who advised Johnny to obtain a C#/D accordion, a tuning which O'Leary has used to this day. At thirteen he began playing dance halls with **Denis Murphy**, a partnership which lasted for thirty-seven years until the great fiddler's death in 1974. The pair were recorded for radio by Séamus Ennis in 1949, just before Denis left for the US for the first time, and some of the tunes from this session are included in Murphy's **Music from Sliabh Luachra** album. Denis returned several times during the 1950s, before coming back for good in 1965, and he and Johnny played all around the country, regularly broadcasting on radio and TV. Johnny also enhanced his repertoire through his friendship with Pádraig O'Keeffe who had firm opinions on the accordion, as O'Leary has recalled. "Pádraig was never gone too much on that crossing or trebling of the keys. He always said if it was played properly the plain way that was the right way for music." In the 1950s Johnny also played in the Cliffords' **Star of Munster Band**, and later with Denis in the **Desmond Céilí Band**, but since 1966 his music has been a regular feature at Dan O'Connell's bar in Knocknagree.

Johnny's recorded output has been sparse. 1989's **The Trooper** is a record of his versatility, but the one to track down is the LP originally released in 1977 (later reissued on cassette by Ossian), **Music for the Set**. Recorded in O'Connell's Bar, it features the accordionist doing what he does best, accompanying dancers. Though Johnny knows more than two hundred reels and many of the slower hornpipes which O'Keeffe favoured, the bulk of his repertoire consists of polkas, slides and quicker hornpipes and this album contains a number of tunes of local origin, such as "The Scartaglen Slide". His playing is ever measured, but with a gregarious abandon inspired by the dancers and fellow musicians, including his daughter Ellen on tin whistle. Johnny is one of traditional music's true gentlemen and this is a splendid record of his talents. Transcriptions of almost 350 of the tunes in his repertoire appear in *Johnny O'Leary of Sliabh Luachra*.

📼 Music for the Set	Ossian Publications, 1977

Captured in his natural habitat, O'Leary's playing is pure dynamite.

Charlie Piggott

One of traditional music's most popular figures and a founder of **De Dannan**, **Charlie Piggott** was born in Cobh, Co. Cork, of Kerry parents, but has been based in Kinvara, Co. Galway, for many years. Equally adept on banjo, his main instrument with De Dannan on albums such as **The Star-Spangled Molly**, Charlie is now best known for his lilting accordion style. In the 1990s he formed **The Lonely Stranded Band** with the ace South Clare concertina player, **Miriam Collins**, and Waterford guitar and bouzouki man, **Joe Corcoran**, releasing a self-titled album for Cló Iar-Chonnachta in 1996. Now hooked up with the Kerry fiddler, **Gerry Harrington**, the pair have recently issued **The New Road**, a splendid album, crammed to the rafters with charm and guile. The tune selection is wide-ranging, though choices from Sliabh Luachra and counties Clare and Galway are prominent and indicative of the musicians' influences. Charlie demonstrates the strengths of his own solo playing on a lovely slow air, "Lament for Lugh Darcy", learned from the singing of Dolores Keane's father, Matt, while he and Gerry forge a powerful, ever-sensitive alliance on this thoughtful, enjoyable release. Charlie is also co-author (with Fintan Vallely) of *Blooming Meadows* (see p.591), a book which approaches perfection in presenting the spirit of traditional music through character sketches of some of its major personalities.

⊙ **The New Road**   Cló Iar-Chonnachta, 2000

Formidable playing, both solo and combined, from Charlie Piggott and Gerry Harrington – two master musicians.

John Regan

Long-time stalwart of the Dublin scene (where he's been based since 1966), button-accordionist **John Regan** hails from Drumcliffe, the village in North Sligo where W.B. Yeats is buried. His father Tommy played the melodeon, but John always fancied being an accordionist and learned the basics of the B/C style (which he still employs today) from Alfie Dineen of the Coleman Country Céilí Band. Once in Dublin, John began playing with the equally youthful **Mary Bergin** and **Paddy Glackin**, while visits to musical events around the country brought contact with an older generation. Throughout the years, however, John's style has never lost the exuberant spring to its step that he first heard from céilí bands at Drumcliffe for the summer carnival. His first album, **Slopes of Benbulben**, appeared in 1988 but it was eleven years before he released another, the rollicking **Let Down the Blade**, again with the assistance of **Mary Corcoran** on piano. Regan revives the partnership with Paddy Glackin, which won them All-Ireland titles three decades earlier, on rolling numbers like "The Tailor's Twist" hornpipe and adds a family feel in separate accordion duets with sons Colm and Dónal.

⊙ **Let Down the Blade**   Beaumex, 1999

John's regular appearances at Chief O'Neill's attracts a large, happy crowd and here's the reason why.

Sharon Shannon

Both live and on record, the unmistakeable, unadulterated joy that shines through **Sharon Shannon**'s playing has established the Clare-born accordionist, fiddler and whistle player among Irish music's most popular contemporary ambassadors. One of four musical siblings from Corofin – sister Mary plays with Bumblebees – she began playing whistle aged six, progressing to the accordion a few years later. Her teenage years were a virtually non-stop whirl of céilís, gigs and sessions at home, in Toonagh and Doolin, and later in Cork, where she soon abandoned her studies at University in favour of learning the fiddle. Following a brief spell in the band **Arcady**, a 1989 meeting with **The Waterboys** – then riding the crest of their **Fisherman's Blues** wave – led to Shannon joining them on tour for eighteen months and appearing on their **Room to Roam** album.

Shannon's own self-titled debut (1991), featuring U2's Adam Clayton, Dónal Lunny and The Waterboys on its guest list, fixed her solo star firmly in the ascendant. The iridescent, pealing tone, the buoyant but muscular swing and resonant depth that characterize her style are all abundantly in evidence, on an album that straddles traditional and contemporary approaches and incorporates American, Cajun, Canadian and Portuguese tunes alongside Irish material. This gift for pushing at traditional music's boundaries without compromising

HEIDI PEARSON

its spirit has continued to inform her development. Around half the material on her second album **Out the Gap** (1994) emerged from a collaboration with reggae producer Denis Bovell, a seemingly unlikely marriage of styles that sounds positively heaven-made, in tracks like the mellow, sauntering opener "Sparky", and the dynamic swagger of "The Mighty Sparrow". **Each Little Thing** (1997), although less overtly fusion-inclined (barring the beatbox backing on "The Bag of Cats"), continues to highlight Shannon's broadening range, for instance in a winsome version of Fleetwood Mac's "Never Going Back Again" or the Chilean tune "El Mercado Testaccio". Another standout is the thrillingly dynamic tune "Bonnie Mulligan's", with Shannon playing fiddle alongside Solas's Win Horan, which has since rapidly infiltrated the wider contemporary repertoire. Shannon's latest album **The Diamond Mountain Sessions** (2000) finds her exploring yet more new avenues, working with a diverse international array of guest singers and players including Galician piper Carlos Nunez and Irish balladeers John Hoban and Dessie O'Halloran. The six vocal tracks add up to a rather mixed bag, but the instrumentals – especially the title track and the fiery duet with Nunez on "A Costa De Galicia" – are a delight.

⊙ **Spellbound: The Best of Sharon Shannon**   Grapevine, 1989–97

An excellent retrospective, combining material from her first three albums alongside previously unreleased tracks.

Mary Staunton

Hailing from one of Ireland's less well-known Gaeltachts, Tourmakeady, Co. Mayo, button accordionist **Mary Staunton** grew up in a family with a long musical tradition: both her grandmother and mother were box players while her father played the fiddle. She started playing the accordion at the age of eight, first by the press and draw method (which she still sometimes employs) and later learning the B/C system. Mary began playing in sessions in her teens and, after a spell at college in Dublin, toured Britanny and Ireland before settling in Galway. Since then she's often sung and played with **Sharon Shannon**, appeared on **Kathleen Loughnane**'s **Affairs of the Harp** and is a member of the **Heritage Céilí Band** while also making appearances on both radio and TV. Her long-awaited solo album **Bright Early Mornings** was released to massive acclaim on her own label in 1998. Mary's astonishingly sensitive playing achieves its zenith on the emotive slow air "Inishcarra" while her singing is expressiveness incarnate, especially in the duet "What Would You Do Love?", performed with De Dannan's **Andrew Murray**. The strength of the album's supporting cast (Alec Finn, Frankie Lane, Steve Cooney, Sharon Shannon, Matt Cranitch, etc) underlines the esteem in which Mary is held by other musicians.

⊙ **Bright Early Mornings**   Fuschia Music, 1998

Subtitled simply "Songs and Tunes", this is a gorgeous album from a huge talent.

Karen Tweed

Piano-accordionist **Karen Tweed** has one of the most productive track records around: at one time she was simultaneously a member of the Northumbrian piper **Kathryn Tickell**'s band, English folk quartet **The Poozies** as well as **Sally Barker and The Rhythm**. Born to an English father and an Irish mother (from Co. Kerry), Karen was brought up in Northamptonshire and joined a local marching band at the age of 12. Her music teachers included button accordionist **John Whelan** and her perseverance and innate skill led to

HEIDI PEARSON

her winning five All-Ireland titles and appearing in the 1985 CCÉ tour of the US and Canada. Inspired by button accordionists such as Jackie Daly and Billy McComiskey, Karen's piano accordion style is characterized by a very light touch on the bass. You can hear this to grand effect on **The Silver Spire**, the second of two albums produced to accompany her book of Irish session tunes. This album has forty-six of them and it's a wonderful way of familiarizing yourself with some of the best-known melodies. Karen also appears on **From a Distant Shore** (see p.276) and is still a Poozies member, while also playing in the **Two Duos Quartet** and in the band **Swåp**, a part-Scandinavian foursome whose 1999 debut album **Swåp (Sic)** is well worth exploring.

⊙ **The Silver Spire**　　　　　　　Dave Mallinson Publications, 1994

Tunes from across the spectrum, played with impeccable dash and style.

John Whelan

The son of Irish parents (though born in Dunstable, England), when **John Whelan** arrived in the US in 1980 aged 20, he had already established a reputation as a precociously talented button accordionist having won the first of his seven All-Ireland Championships in 1970 and released his first solo LP, **Pride of Wexford**, when only fourteen. A second album didn't appear until 1986's outing with fiddler **Eileen Ivers**, **Fresh Takes**, and, though he can still cut the mustard on traditional tunes, John now concentrates more on his own compositions. His 1996 album, **Celtic Reflections – Misty-Eyed Mornings**, sees him skirting the fringes of "Celtic" New Age music, but avoiding the obvious pitfalls through the sheer brio of his melodies, his jaunty playing style and the adroit support of his guests (including Seamus Egan, Pat Kilbride and Jerry O'Sullivan). John also leads the prestigious **Kips Bay Céilí Band**, though don't be misled by its title as it sounds more like Moving Hearts than the Kilfenora!

⊙ **Celtic Reflections – Misty-Eyed Mornings**　　　　　Narada, 1996

Probably the best of Whelan's "Celtic" crossover albums for the Narada label.

Concertina players

The single-action version of the concertina known as the Anglo is the usual form found in Ireland. This consists of two hexagonal ends, each with ten or fifteen buttons, connected by a bellows which the player squeezes or pulls to produce the notes. Once extremely popular in England, cheap mass-produced concertinas arrived in Ireland by the end of the nineteenth century and soon attained prominence as an instrument for dance music. However, the emergence of the accordion in the 1920s led to its decline. The instrument's last bastion has remained Co. Clare and distinctive variations in playing style can still be found across the area. Why the concertina achieved such prominence in Clare remains open to conjecture. Suggestions include its proximity to the port of Limerick (where the instrument was stocked by ship's chandlers) and the presence of British Army bands in the county around the close of the nineteenth century. However, more likely reasons are the instrument's cheapness, its relative easiness to learn, and the fact that its loudness makes it ideal for laying down simple rhythms for dancing. Whatever the cause, the concertina became the main instrument for accompanying dancing in Clare and, unusually in a musical tradition dominated elsewhere by men, proved especially popular among the county's women. The numerous superb concertina players from Clare, include **Elizabeth Crotty** and **Noel Hill**

while other players to look out for (but not featured below) are Cathy Custy, Máirtín Fahy, Ann Droney, Mick Carrucan, Padraig Rynne (of Cían) and John MacMahon, while two of the most majestic players, the late **Tommy McCarthy** and his daughter **Jacqueline**, are included in the Families section (see p.257). From the North, Jason O'Rourke is another great player well worth hearing.

Terry Bingham

Though based in Doolin, Co. Clare for some years, concertina player **Terry Bingham** comes from Comber, Co. Down (also home to a famous strain of potato and a purpose-built B-movie cinema). There's neither starch nor shlock horror in Bingham's playing, but an airiness propelled by a touch of Northern drive (he cites Belfast fiddler Dermie Diamond as a major inspiration) and, of course, the influence of his father, Leslie, one of the region's most renowned flute players. Terry's relocation to Clare must have been fate since, when he started on the concertina at the age of twelve, the first tunes he learned were from a tape of concertina player **Chris Droney**. **Traditional Irish Music from Doolin Co. Clare** is the title of Bingham's solo album but it is a slight misnomer as these tunes come from all over Ireland. No matter, for whether playing a reel from Belmullet or a hornpipe from Belfast, Terry proves himself a mighty squeezebox exponent. Dermot Byrne joins in for a pulsating "The Durrow Reel" and there's also excellent support from Doolin regulars Mary Custy, Eoin O'Neill and Kevin Griffin.

⊙ **Traditional Irish Music from**   Ossian Publications, 1997
Doolin Co. Clare

Relaxed, stylish playing catches the Clare sea breeze.

Elizabeth Crotty

The doyenne of the Clare concertina is commemorated each August by a festival (Éigse Mrs Crotty) in the town of Kilrush. Born Elizabeth Markham in Gower, Cooraclare, West Clare in 1885, the youngest child in a large musical family, she began playing an older sister's concertina at a young age, picking out the melodies learned from her mother's fiddle. In an era when few women played publicly, she was to become a popular player at local house dances and for the sets (and was herself a fine dancer). On occasions she also played at American Wakes where migrants were given a grand send-off, indeed all her brothers and sisters, bar one, emigrated to the US. After marrying near neighbour Miko Crotty in 1914, the couple settled in Kilrush where Miko bought the pub (still known as Crotty's to this day) in which they spent the rest of their lives. Though she continued to play the concertina, little is known of her musical history until the late 1940s when she first broadcast with fiddler Kathleen Harrington for Radio Éireann.

Elizabeth Crotty

CONCERTINA MUSIC
FROM WEST CLARE

In 1954 the Clare branch of Comhaltas was founded and Mrs Crotty was its elected president, holding the post until her death in 1960. As a result she became a popular figure both at fleadhanna and was recorded by Ciarán Mac Mathúna at the 1960 Clare Fleadh

Cheoil. These and previous recordings from 1955 and 1957 constitute the wonderful collection **Concertina Music from West Clare**.
Her pub provided a fitting backdrop for the earliest recordings which
include duets with fiddlers **Paddy Canny**, **Aggie White** and **Denis
Murphy**, but it is Mrs Crotty's own unaccompanied playing that
catches the ear. Utterly rhythmic, simple and relatively unadorned
(though she occasionally played the higher parts of tunes in octaves),
it's an addictive brew which includes too many magical renditions to
list. However, her playing of "Geary's Reel" (sometimes known as
"Sporting Nell"), which she learned from a travelling fiddler, is especially infectious, while the duet with Denis Murphy on the reels, "The
Bird in the Bush/The Silver Spear", is just plain fun! Her distant
cousin, **Michael Tubridy**, supplies extremely detailed and informative
notes and, indeed, plays flute on the group tunes.

⊙ **Concertina Music from West Clare**   RTÉ, 1955–60

Diligently researched and remastered, these recordings capture
the spirit of West Clare with remarkable panache.

Chris Droney

Probably the only musician to have played for both the late
Cardinal Tómas Ó Fiaich and the Crown Prince and Princess of
Japan, **Chris Droney** (from Bell Harbour, North Clare) is pretty well
known among commoners too! Like his father, Jim, from whom he
learned to play, Chris is a concertina player with a natural aptitude for
accompanying set dancers. A member of various céilí bands, including the **Kilfenora**, Chris won a string of All-Ireland titles in the 1950s
and 1960s and regularly toured North America with CCÉ. Such exposure led to his album for Copley, **Irish Dance Music**, and, the follow-

ing decade, to a further release, **The Flowing Tide** (1975). While Chris continued to play and teach, most notably his daughter Ann and son Francis (both All-Ireland concertina champions too), it was another twenty years before **The Fertile Rock** appeared. Captivating in its deceptive simplicity, this sees him playing with that essential rhythmic flair needed for dancing, no better exemplified than on the hornpipes "The Stack of Wheat/The Killeigh" where the tune just seems to bounce merrily along on its way. When used at all, any ornamentation is itself rhythm-enhancing (often employing bellows and button clicks to punctuate notes) while **George Byrt** (pianist with the Tulla for 30 years) provides the simplest, and hence most effective, accompaniment.

⊙ **The Fertile Rock**   Cló Iar-Chonnachta, 1995

Exemplary concertina from the North Clare master, including some of his own fine compositions such as "The Bell Harbour Reel".

Noel Hill

No one has demonstrated the concertina's capacity nor defied its inherent limitations better than **Noel Hill**. Such has been the strength and persistence of his reputation that he seems to have been around forever. In fact he was born in 1958 in Caherea, a few miles southwest of Ennis. Young Noel's choice of instrument was inevitable – his parents, both sets of grandparents and various aunts and uncles all played the concertina – and he too found an immediate affinity with the instrument. Encouragement and a repertoire came from his mother, his uncle Paddy and from the renowned **Paddy Murphy** from nearby Connolly. The family home's reputation as a music house also drew musicians of the calibre of fiddlers

Paddy Canny and Peadar O'Loughlin and piper Seán Reid. As a result Noel's repertoire burgeoned in tandem with his rapidly developing technical ability.

At one of Frank Custy's music classes Noel met fiddler **Tony Linnane** (from Corofin) and the two formed a lasting musical bond.

For a while they partnered Kieran Hanrahan and Tony Callanan in the band **Inchiquin**, recording an album in 1976, before the latter pair left to form Stockton's Wing. After that Barry Moore (aka **Luka Bloom**) joined for a brief period on guitar, but had left by the time Noel and Tony recorded the staggering **Noel Hill and Tony Linnane** with the assistance of Alec Finn, Matt Molloy and Mícheál Ó Domhnaill. The pair's duets sound as fresh as the day they were recorded, but Noel's solo "A Pigeon on the Gate" would alone have enhanced his reputation. Hill and Linnane toured regularly during the next few years, and appeared on Christy Moore's **The Iron Behind the Velvet** and **Planxty**'s **The Woman I Loved So Well**, before Noel moved to Dublin and Tony decided to remain in Clare, working outside music but still playing sessions.

Noel ploughed a lonely furrow as Ireland's first professional concertina player but managed to record another classic album, **I gCnoc na Graí** (see p.497), in consort with button accordionist **Tony**

MacMahon and a group of dancers in Dan O'Connell's famed pub, Knocknagree. Noel and Tony reconvened in 1993 with singer **Iarla Ó Lionáird** in Dublin for another tremendous live release, **Aislingí Ceoil/Music of Dreams**, but by then Noel had already recorded his definitive statement. **The Irish Concertina** appeared in 1988 but its impact on the traditional musical world reverberates to this day. As a whole, this is the work of a man demonstrating his vast love and huge understanding of the music (described in characteristic modesty as "my humble effort") while its individual parts are a joyous exhibition of technical mastery. Aided by Charlie Lennon's piano accompaniment, Hill's music is grace and charm incarnate and the album is a crucial purchase for anyone wishing to comprehend the essence of Ireland.

⊙ **Noel Hill and Tony Linnane**   Tara, 1979

An astonishingly complete debut from a symbiotic pairing.

⊙ **The Irish Concertina**   Claddagh, 1988

Sheer alchemy produces a near-perfect release.

Mary Mac Namara

In *Notes from the Heart*, P.J. Curtis recounts how the young concertina player, **Mary Mac Namara** discovered a different musical world when she moved to Dublin in 1978. Attending a session at the Comhaltas headquarters in Monkstown, she found herself unable to join in because she knew none of the tunes, since her own repertoire consisted only of tunes popular in her native East Clare. The next day she bought a copy of O'Neill's *1001* and began learning a new repertoire (while continuing to prefer her original stock). Mary was born in Tulla into a musical family: her brother Andrew is an especially skilled accordion player while the legendary **Tony MacMahon** is her uncle. She first began by learning the accordion, before her father (also called Andrew) gave her a concertina to "break in" for her great-aunt. Mary was around ten years of age and her father, seeing her prowess and himself a concertina man, purchased a three-row Wheatstone pitched in C and G for her which she still plays today.

In the early 1980s Mary recorded with the women's ensemble **Macalla**, and her first solo album, **Traditional Music from East Clare**, appeared in 1994.

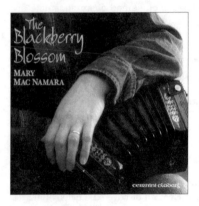

Firmly focused on the music of East Clare, it draws its huge strengths from Mary's thorough grounding in the tradition, her admiration for the concertina player John Naughton and her own confident, sublime music-making. Fiddle playing dominates East Clare's music and the album featured local notables, P.J. and Martin Hayes. Six years elapsed before fans of her inspiring music were able to greet **The Blackberry Blossom**, another stylish showcase for Mary's phenomenal music. At times heart-rending (an awesome slow reading of the reel "The Stone in the Field"), at others soaring skywards with the joy of a lark (the contagious "Paddy Kelly's" reel), this oozes magnificence throughout.

⊙ **The Blackberry Blossom**   Claddagh, 2000

A connoisseur's concertina player unleashes her remarkable talents.

Robin Morton

Known widely as a founder member of **Boys of the Lough**, with whom he played until 1979, **Robin Morton** (b. 1939, Portadown, Co. Armagh) has contributed significantly to the continuation of both Irish and Scottish musical traditions. Robin sang and played English concertina and bodhrán with the Boys while also pursuing an active interest in the Ulster song tradition. He made many recordings in the field, including singers such as Robert Cinnamond and John Maguire (whose autobiography he also edited) while his researches reached fruition in the book *Folksongs Sung in Ulster* (1970). On top of this he has produced a number of important albums, including Josie McDermott's **Darby's Farewell**, and has put his experience to wider use through the foundation of his Temple Records label based in Edinburgh where he also ran the Folk Festival for a spell in the 1980s. The only release under Robin's name is the essential **An Irish Jubilee**, recorded with long-time collaborator **Cathal McConnell** in 1969, a gentle, fluent album which draws upon the pair's great love and understanding of Northern song. Robin himself sings songs from Armagh ("The Hiring Fair at Hamiltownsbawn") and Tyrone ("On the Banks of a River Near Blackwatertown") with an eloquent resonance while his instrumental duets with McConnell are distinguished by their effective simplicity.

▭ **An Irish Jubilee**   Ossian Publications, 1969

A recording (with Cathal McConnell) that simply, yet gloriously, embodies the powers of the tradition.

Gearóid Ó hAllmhuráin

Author of *A Pocket History of Irish Music* (see p.591) and an esteemed ethnomusicologist now lecturing at the University of San Francisco, Ennis-born **Gearóid Ó hAllmhuráin** is also a top-notch concertina player. Another of Frank Custy's many pupils, Gearóid's first instrument was the whistle before moving on to the accordion followed, in 1974, by the uilleann pipes where he came under the spell of Seán Reid. By then, Ó hAllmhuráin was attending Reid's alma mater, Queen's University, Belfast, and beginning his long interest in the effects of the Great Famine and its diaspora on Irish traditional music and culture. When Reid died in 1978 Gearóid was persuaded to try a few tunes on an old concertina at his funeral

and, as he puts it himself, "has never looked back", winning five All-Ireland titles and enjoying a spell in the **Kilfenora Céilí Band**. The first album to bear his name was 1996's **Traditional Music from Clare and Beyond**, notable not merely for his own fine playing (with guest fiddlers Martin Hayes and Peter O'Loughlin) but for

CELTIC CROSSINGS

also reintroducing the legendary fiddler Paddy Canny to the recording studio after almost forty years' absence. Of significant merit too
is **Tracin'** reuniting Gearóid with the French fiddler (and East Galway
specialist) **Patrick Ourceau** with whom he had first played in Paris in
1985.

⊙ Traditional Music from Clare and Beyond   Celtic Crossings, 1996

A warm-spirited album, grandly delivered by Gearóid and
illustrious friends.

Bernard O'Sullivan and Tommy McMahon

The area around Cooraclare and Kilmihil in southwest Co. Clare
has produced many superb concertina players, all seemingly
skilled accompanists for dancing. Tommy McCarthy (see p.257) was
probably the most widely known, but other renowned players include
Bernard O'Sullivan and **Tommy McMahon**. Farmers and near
neighbours, they were raised in an area rich in music and dancing.
Bernard learned several tunes from his mother (who also played the
concertina) but even more from the late **Stack Ryan**, from the townland of Leitrim in Co. Clare, whose own repertoire drew on local
tunes as well as those learned from travelling players and the gramophone. Bernard passed on many of these melodies to the much
younger Tommy who had been playing since the age of four. Tommy
went on to major competitive success, winning the All-Ireland Senior
championship three times running in the early 1970s.

The pair were recorded together in 1974 for the superb **Clare
Concertinas**, one of the few albums to feature concertina duets. The

breadth of their combined repertoires is astonishing and includes many of the tunes they would play at dances. These include popular local settings of set dances, such as "Rodney's Glory" and "Mount Fabus Hunt" (a variation of "The Hunt", found in O'Neill's *1001*). You'll also find the very familiar waltz, "Over the Waves" (once often heard at fairgrounds), and a range of polkas, jigs and reels all played, whether solo or paired, with considerable swing and sway – sometimes in unison and sometimes "bassed". Maintaining a strong rhythm is at the core of their music and the tunes are delivered with minimal ornamentation but with a constant sweetness of sound and the lightest of touches.

⊙ **Clare Concertinas** — Green Linnet, 1975

An outstanding collection of local tunes and variants from two masters of the instrument.

Niall Vallely

The rolls and trills of **Niall Vallely**'s concertina have long held a pivotal role in **Nomos**, the band he co-founded, while his appearances on others artists' albums (most notably his stunning performance of "Scotch Mary" on Paddy Keenan's **Ná Keen Affair**) whetted the appetite for his own debut release. A member of one of Irish music's modern dynasties, the Vallelys from Armagh, Niall began playing the concertina at seven under the tutelage of his parents, Brian and Eithne. In the succeeding couple of decades, he has developed an inimitable style, (whether playing C/G, C#/G# or B♭/F concertinas) whose only point of comparison is with the intricate ornamentation of Joe Derrane's accordion playing. The solo album **Beyond Words** (on Niall's own label) encapsulates the breathtaking range of his playing whether on his own compositions, such as "The Pitbull Spiders", or his arrangements of traditional tunes like the Tommy Potts-inspired "Rakish Paddy", and the musical eclecticism derived in part from his studies and work with Mícheál Ó Súilleabháin. Nomos colleagues Frank Torpey (bodhrán) and Gerry McKee (bouzouki) play a significant "holding" role in the overall sound and it's hard to imagine more sensitive bass-playing than Noel Barrett's.

⊙ **Beyond Words**   Beyond Records, 1999

Valley's talent is staggering and this is as intoxicating as a crate of Jameson's.

Harmonica players

Variously-known as the mouth organ, tin sandwich and even, inexplicably, French fiddle, the harmonica is another free reed instrument where blowing into or sucking air through a hole produces different notes. The instrument comes in a range of formats and sizes: some, such as the octave and tremolo have two sets of reeds per note, in the former's case tuned an octave apart, while the latter has one set tuned slightly sharper. The diatonic, commonly used in blues music, has a single set of reeds whereas the chromatic has a button on the side enabling the player to produce sharps and flats. Harmonicas are available in many different keys, so players who don't play the chromatic harmonica tend to carry several around. Once extremely common, thanks to its cheapness, the harmonica's fortunes were essentially revived by the late **Phil Murphy** and his sons **John** and **Pip** who played as a trio, using all types of the instrument except the chromatic. In contrast, **Eddie Clarke** played a chromatic, but kept the button pressed in the whole time, releasing it only to produce quick rolls. The best-known modern diatonic player is **Brendan Power** while **Mick Kinsella** is currently developing a glowing reputation. An older, and unjustly overlooked, player, **Noel Pepper**, features on the Globestyle **In the Smoke** CD of London-Irish musicians.

Tommy Basker

The astonishing **Tommy Basker** (1923–99) was a truly unique player who could produce swaths of sound from his tremolo harmonica. One of seven brothers, he was born and raised in North Sydney, the largest town in "The Northside" of Cape Breton Island, an area long associated with the island's Irish music. His father Alex played the harmonica too and encouraged Tommy to buy one. As he progressed he learned from the island's vast store of Irish and Scottish music and developed a fondness for Michael Coleman's playing, learning his tune settings in the company of the fiddler **Johnny Wilmot**. In 1940 Tommy moved to New Waterford to become a miner (an occupation which did not seem to harm the power of his lungs) and continued his development in the company of many musicians. Wilmot was there too and, in the 1950s, the pair travelled together to Boston for sessions (including some with Joe Derrane) and later that decade recorded 78s which have been reissued as Johnny Wilmot's **Another Side of Cape Breton** (see p.287).

Tommy remained a popular figure for the rest of his life and, in 1994, recorded his own album, **The Tin Sandwich**, with simple piano or guitar accompaniment. Unlike many modern players, he tended to use the back of his throat to create tonal variation and the result can be spellbinding. Irish tunes are well represented by hornpipes, like "The Liverpool/McDermott's" (from Coleman), reels, such as "The Mullingar Races" (from Paddy Killoran), and jigs, notably "Devine's Favourite" (from Joe Derrane), all played with exceptional energy and rhythm.

⊙ **The Tin Sandwich**   Silver Apple Music, 1994

Marvellous exuberance from Tommy Basker, a true original.

Eddie Clarke

O ne of Ireland's finest exponents of the chromatic harmonica, **Eddie Clarke** (b. 1945, Virginia, Co. Cavan) became well-known in the 1970s through his partnership with Co. Clare fiddler, **Joe Ryan**, winning the Oireachtas duet competition in 1972. The pair recorded the superb **Crossroads** album in 1981 which features unison playing so accomplished that it is sometimes hard to distinguish fiddle from reeds, whether on slow reels like "John Joe Gannon's" or a riotous rendition of "Rakish Paddy". Try also to lay your hands on a copy of **Sailing into Walpole's Marsh** recorded by the foursome who undertook the 1976 USA Bicentennial tour: Eddie along with singers **Seán Corcoran** and **Mairéad Ní Dhomhnaill**, and fiddler **Maeve Donnelly**. Eddie's on particularly grand form in an evanescent duet with Maeve ("The Girl that Broke My Heart/Sailing into Walpole's Marsh") where his powerful playing is almost accordion-like in its strength.

⊙ Crossroads	Green Linnet, 1981

The combination of Eddie and Joe Ryan is, undoubtedly, the best fiddle and harmonica pairing ever recorded.

Phil, John and Pip Murphy

I n the hands of a genius like **Phil Murphy**, the harmonica became a marvellous conduit for literally breathtaking skill. Born in 1917 in Ballygow, Bannow, Co. Wexford, an area then rich in traditional music, his mother presented him with his first harmonica when he was eight and Phil progressed rapidly, becoming a popular figure at house dances and also sometimes accompanying Mummers' plays.

Phil usually played a tremolo harmonica and invented a technique which blended melody lines of tunes with a rhythmic vamping accompaniment essential for dancing. He passed his skills on to his sons **John**, who favours a ten-hole diatonic for solos (sometimes using a technique he describes as "a fierce suck"), and Phil (known as **Pip**). Phil senior won the All-Ireland title three years running (1969–71) and both sons later became champions in their turn. The trio appeared on **Kevin Burke**'s 1987 album **Up Close**, but their own and only album **The Trip to Cullenstown** is a gem. Though individ-

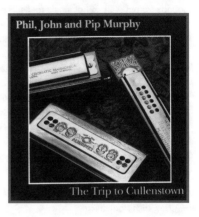

Phil, John and Pip Murphy

The Trip to Cullenstown

ual solo tracks sparkle with energy, it's the arrangements of the duets and trios which characterize their innovation. Try "The Ballygow Reel" – on which Phil demonstrates all his virtuosity – which runs into a trio performance of "The Trip to Cullenstown" with Phil now accompanying the others an octave below on a chromatic. Phil died in July, 1989, three weeks after the recording, though his life is commemorated in a music weekend held in his honour each July in Carrick-on-Bannow.

⊙ **The Trip to Cullenstown**   Gael-Linn, 1991

Devastating musicianship and imaginative settings make this the album for the instrument's fans.

Brendan Power

Noted for his dismantling and retuning of harmonicas, New Zealander **Brendan Power** obtains an extraordinary range of sounds from a mere set of single reeds. His familial roots are partly in Co. Waterford, whence his grandfather originated, but any mouth harp player is but a step away from the blues and Power's genius is to marry the labial dexterity required for playing traditional tunes with the essential bends and slurs that characterize the blues harmonica. Using the single-reed diatonic and chromatic instruments, he manages to generate an ingenious, but remarkably natural, Irish sound. This attained its undoubted apogee in his wonderfully soulful reading of "My Lagan Love" on his 1994 album **New Irish Harmonica**. More recently, he's released **Blow In** which, while including soundtrack pieces for the Irish film *Guiltrip*, has probably the first ever chromatic harmonica/whistle duet of "The Bucks of Oranmore" with **Cormac Breatnach** on whistle as partner.

⊙ **New Irish Harmonica**   Punch Music, 1994

Exactly as the title suggests, Power breaks new ground on this fabulous album.

Percussionists

J okes about the bodhrán are legion ("What do you call someone who hangs around musicians?", "A bodhrán player") and
there is certainly no more maligned traditional instrument –
legend has it that Seámus Ennis recommended that it should be
played with a penknife! The reason for its widespread vilification is
the belief that most bodhrán players are either rhythmically chal-
lenged, musically insensitive or both. A simple frame drum, the
bodhrán looks (and actually is) quite easy to play but the problem is
that it requires a thorough understanding of the music to play it well.
Until the 1960s, when **Sean Ó Riada** pioneered the bodhrán with
Ceoltóirí Chualann, the drum rarely featured in traditional music and
was primarily associated with the arcane ritual of the Wren Boys on
December 26th, St Stephen's Day. Older versions of the bodhrán
often had jingles inserted in the frame, like a tambourine, but these
have virtually disappeared and today most instruments consist of a
circular frame, a stretched skin held down by metal rivets around the
rim and cross-bars at the back. Bodhrán players use a multiplicity of
techniques to produce rhythmic and tonal variety. Some hold the
drum by the crossbars while others press the non-beating hand
against the underside of the skin to dampen the sound. Beating
sticks (beaters) come in a range of shapes and sizes, some with a
thong attached to the centre through which the middle finger passes,
while some players even use a hairbrush or a drummer's "brushes".
Others, of course, just use the hand to produce a variety of slaps or
knuckle-shots, sometimes also employing the holding hand to add
greater impact. Lastly, the frame, rim and rivets may all be struck to

produce further tonal contrasts. A number of bands feature outstanding bodhrán players, none better than Flook's awe-inspiring **John Joe Kelly**. Others to look out for include The Chieftains' **Kevin Conneff**, Danú's mighty **Donnchadh Gough** and, of course, **Christy Moore** and **Dónal Lunny**.

Bones have been employed as a percussion instrument for thousands of years. The use of a pair of rib-bones from a cow or sheep, pared down to resemble sticks and dried out, is still popular among bones players, but "synthetic" bones made from hardwoods or plastic resins are also available. Held loosely in the hand, the bones are struck together by shaking the wrist to and fro, producing a triplet of clicks. Single shakes and wilder flourishes can be used to generate variation. Ó Riada used a contrasting bones and bodhrán combination with Ceoltóirí Chualann and **Peadar Mercier** continued to demonstrate their versatility with The Chieftains. Currently, **Tommy Hayes**, **Cathy Jordan** and **Johnny McDonagh** are the most well-known bones merchants. Hayes is also a superb spoons player, hitting a loosely-held pair of spoons against various parts of his legs to produce changes in tone. Other forms of impromptu percussion can regularly be heard at sessions, such as bottle-clicking and the rattling of loose change.

Sometimes called the "jaw's harp" and also known as the "trump" in some parts of Ireland, the jew's harp is one of the simplest of all instruments. It consists of a metal frame to which a thin, flexible tongue of metal has been attached. The frame is held in the mouth and sounds are produced by flicking the metal tongue with a finger. There is no variation in pitch, but different tones can be produced by changing the shape of the mouth, moving the hand cupping the instrument or adjusting the tongue or throat. **Tommy Hayes** first revived the instrument with Stockton's Wing and continues to be its best-known exponent. Earlier, in the 1960s, the **Wright Brothers**, from Leicester in England, played dance tunes as a jew's harp trio to remarkable effect (see **The Lark in the Clear Air**, p.43).

Junior Davey

Son of fiddler Andrew Davey, **Junior Davey** hails from the very heart of Michael Coleman country, Gurteen in Co. Sligo. A bodhrán player of the highest order (he won All-Ireland titles in 1990 and 1993), his skills have been heavily in demand and seen him feature with many musicians, including **the Swallow's Tail Céilí Band** and a recent appearance on **Síona**'s album **Launching the Boat**. Davey's strength lies in his ability to achieve subtle gradations of tone, timbre and volume and the full range of his skills can be heard on **Skin and Bow**, the album he recorded with Bunninaden fiddler, Declan Folan. Declan plays in the South Sligo style (influenced by Andy Davey who appears on a couple of tracks) but his playing is unquestionably enhanced by the subtlety of Junior's bodhrán. If you think you're resistant to the bodhrán's charms, then listen to Junior's effortlessly imaginative solo before he and Declan break into "The Donegal Reel".

⊙ Skin and Bow   Sound Records, 1990s

The inspired combination of Davey and Declan Folan is well supported by some fine guitar from Shane McGowan.

Ray Gallen

A bodhrán-player for more than twenty years, **Ray Gallen** is many a musician's first choice as accompanist, noted for both

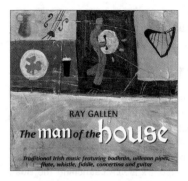

RAY GALLEN

The man *of the* house

Traditional Irish music featuring bodhrán, uilleann pipes, flute, whistle, fiddle, concertina and guitar

his steady rhythm and bursts of solo virtuosity. He's figured on many albums (including Cran's debut and Paul Bradley's **Atlantic Roar**) as well as touring with the likes of Lá Lugh and working as a TV and radio presenter. His own bodhrán tutorial, **Celtic Beat**, is available on CD and video while his debut album, **The Man of the House**, appeared in 1997. Consisting almost entirely of duets (with occasional added guitar from **Paul McSherry**), it offers Ray the chance to show off his skills in the company of piper **John McSherry** (a tremendous rendition of "The Dublin Reel/The Reconciliation"), concertina player **Jason O'Rourke**, fiddler **Brian McAteer** and a rare appearance by **Neil Martin** (usually known for his cello) on pipes and whistle.

⊙ The Man of the House   Outlet, 1997

Belfast's most renowned bodhrán player in an excellent showcase of his skills.

Tommy Hayes

Memorably described by *Melody Maker*'s Colin Irwin as "the most spectacular bodhrán player I have ever seen", West Limerick born **Tommy Hayes** first caught the eye as a founding member of **Stockton's Wing**, where he virtually reinvented the jew's harp as a traditional instrument. After six years with the band, Tommy moved to the USA in 1984, recording with the band **Puck Fair**, and he consolidating his reputation as one of contemporary music's most adept percussionists. Since returning to live in Co. Galway in 1989 (and later East Clare) Hayes has added to his prestige in numerous ways. His album and touring credits could fill a book and include appearances with Sinéad O'Connor, De Dannan, Altan, Davy Spillane, Martin Hayes, Christy Moore and many others. Tommy was the original percussionist in *Riverdance* and has also composed music for productions of *MacBeth* and *Playboy of the Western World* at Dublin's Abbey Theatre as well as *Territorial Claims* for the Limerick-based dance troupe DAGDA, not forgetting several film credits.

A notable teacher, Tommy has also found time to release a bodhrán tutorial video and record two of his own albums. 1986's **An Rás** is the more solidly traditional of the two, though Tommy's interest in jazz is highlighted by the astounding arrangement of John Coltrane's classic "Mr. P.C." on which Brian Dunning provides a stunning flute solo. The experimental **A Room in the North** sees Tommy investigating rhythm through a huge range of instruments, including a return to the jew's harp. One of the outstanding tracks, "Nagrisad", is a remarkable 48-beat hand-clapped rhythmic cycle derived from the Nubian musician Hamza Ali Din; there's also a fine duet with Ronan Browne's whistle on "The Pigeon on the Gate/The Copper Plate/Callaghan's" where Tommy cracks the bones as well as you'll ever hear. If you want to learn how to play the spoons, Tommy's advice is to experiment in producing tonal variation by using the fleshier parts of your legs!

⊙ **An Rás**   Mulligan, 1986

Percussionists may prefer the more adventurous A Room in the North, but this is the one for budding bodhrán players.

Jimmy Higgins

Well known to US audiences, thanks to his role in American *Riverdance* tours, Galway man **Jim Higgins** has been based in Los Angeles for several years with his wife, fiddler and tin whistler, **Breda Smyth**. A versatile multi-instrumentalist, Jimmy's bodhrán and piano playing has popped up on many albums, including Seán Keane's **Turn a Phrase**, Jo Marsh's solo album, John Faulkner's **Nomads** and, most notably, on Altan's **Runaway Sunday**. He's also worked with musicians and bands as varied as Máirtín O'Connor, Len Graham's Skylark, Carl Hession, Sliabh Notes, Galway rock band The Stunning (with whom he also played trumpet and flügelhorn) and appears on the soundtrack album to *Some Mother's Son*. For a while too, Jim was a member of **The Lahawns** and the band's only album **Live at Winkles** is the best place to hear an extended sample of his skills on bodhrán, snare drum and piano too.

⊙ **Live at Winkles** own label, 1997

Variable sound but still a fine session from The Lahawns driven forward by Higgins' astute use of skin and frame.

Johnny "Ringo" McDonagh

Probably the best-known bodhrán player in Ireland, **Johnny McDonagh** from Galway city first came to prominence as a founding and long-serving member of **De Dannan**. A dab hand on the goatskin, he is also a skillful bones player and has been much in demand as an accompanist for the last 25 years, appearing on albums by Altan, Eileen Ivers, Mike Oldfield, Cathal Hayden, Seán Ryan, Seán Keane (the singer) and Mary Bergin. Simply describing

Johnny as a bodhrán player, however, fails to convey what he brings to the music nor does it do justice to his impressive skills on bones and triangle (for the latter listen to "McLaughlin's Flings" on De Dannan's **How the West Was Won** compilation). Johnny's presence added an extra dimension to De Dannan's sound. His playing on "Ríl an Spidéal" or "Anthem for Ireland" (both from **Anthem**) initially sounds like straightforward accompaniment, closer examination reveals an astounding degree of polyrhythmic subtlety and tonal variation. In live performance, Johnny often embellishes his playing through striking the drum's wooden frame, a technique known as a "rim shot", producing a sharper, harder sound. He continues to explore percussive potentials through his own band, **Arcady**, and there's no better example of his bones-playing (sounding remarkably like castanets) on the opening tune on their **Many Happy Returns** album, the reel "The Watchmaker", which turns into a stunning flight of bodhrán fancy on the change into "The Milliner's Daughter".

⊙ **Many Happy Returns**   Dara, 1996

McDonagh's playing on the reels "Brid Harper's/Dennis Langton's" is perfection – a must for all bodhrán students.

Peadar and Mel Mercier

In his heyday, in the 1960s and 1970s, the late **Peadar Mercier** was the most famous exponent of both bodhrán and bones, while the family tradition continues through his son **Mel** who is rapidly acquiring a similar stature. Peadar's fame arose through his membership first of Ceoltóirí Chualann after replacing Ronnie McShane in Ó Riada's ensemble. The composer viewed the instrument's "random frequencies" as "richer than those of even the orchestral bass drum" and was an exponent himself. Peadar subsequently joined **The Chieftains** for **Chieftains 2** and remained a member until 1976 when he, in turn, was replaced by Kevin Conneff. A most outstanding example of his playing of both bodhrán and bones can be heard on the reel "Drowsey Maggie", found on **Chieftains 4**, where he uses an apparently simple drum pattern both to introduce and maintain the rhythm, later turning to an almost replicated pattern on the bones. Peadar featured on many other recordings, including Tommy Peoples' **Master Irish Fiddle Player**, Paddy Taylor's **Boy in the Gap** and Dolores Keane's **There Was a Maid**.

Mel Mercier (b. 1959, Dublin) is an innovative bodhrán player who utilizes the two-sides of the stick by means of an attached strap circling the middle finger while his other hand dampens the skin to create changes in tone and pitch. He has a wide interest in world music, especially Indian percussion and is an adept performer on the tablas. Based at the University of Limerick, Mel has featured on many of Mícheál Ó Súilleabháin's recordings, most notably **The Dolphin's Way** and **Casaidh**, and also played on albums as diverse as Mary Black's **Holy Ground** and Bill Whelan's **Seville Suite**. He also produced and plays on Áine Uí Cheallaigh's album while a rare duet between father and son features in the recording of John Cage's **Roaratorio**, an avant-garde, multimedia work inspired by James Joyce's *Finnegan's Wake*.

Colm Murphy

A bodhrán-player with the lightest of touches, **Colm Murphy** began honing his skills in his native Cork in the company of contemporaries such as uilleann piper Eoin Ó Riabhaigh and flute player Conál Ó Gráda. His textured rhythms and tonal variety were first heard on **Daly and Creagh**'s hallmark album and he has subsequently appeared on many others, enjoying a long association with Frankie Gavin and Alec Finn in **De Dannan**. While more than capable of maintaining a beat Murphy's forte is to create rhythmic patterns, sometimes contrapuntal or syncopated, which add a greater richness to the music. His own album **An Bodhrán – The Irish Drum** is a delight and includes combinations with all his old

LIVING TRADITION

muckers, though the undoubted highlight is a wild whistle and drum duet with Frankie Gavin on the reels "The London Lasses/The Glass of Beer/Dickie Dwyer's", recorded live before an exhilarated Dutch audience. As a Cork man, Colm is equally at home on both slides and – that deterrent to most bodhrán players – the polka.

⊙ **An Bodhrán**   Gael-Linn, 1996

Seemingly effortless, intricate yet never over-elaborate percussion work from one of the bodhrán's best.

Other major figures

This section brings together a number of influential, and sometimes controversial, figures who do not fit readily into other categories. Foremost among these is **Seán Ó Riada** whose traditional music ensemble, Ceoltóirí Chualann, was the prototype for its direct offshoot, The Chieftains, and groups like Planxty and The Bothy Band – although some have argued that the ballad boom and the rock scene were no less potent influences on the development of group playing. Ó Riada was also a composer but he only rarely employed traditional musical elements in his music, perhaps to avoid the pitfalls of earlier Irish classical composers like Sir Charles Stanford who tended to use it simply as a means of introducing an element of local colour into their work. The contemporary composer **Shaun Davey** adopted a less superficial approach in his suite **The Brendan Voyage** (1980) which effectively combined the uilleann pipes with an orchestra. A similar, but more wide-ranging, integration of traditional and classical instruments was employed by **Bill Whelan** in his score for the hugely successful **Riverdance** (1995). This dance extravaganza, conceived as interval entertainment during Ireland's hosting of the 1994 Eurovision Song Contest, helped to make Irish music a global phenomenon and created an international star out of its principal dancer **Michael Flatley**.

P.J. Curtis

P.J. Curtis sports a coat of many talents. A published playwright and novelist, he also wrote a superb account of the music of Co. Clare in *Notes from the Heart* (see p.590) and, encouraged a wider interest in world music through a series of acclaimed radio shows. In childhood, he was fascinated by country music (and later spent a lengthy spell in Nashville), blues, jazz and R&B, and developed an enduring affection for Elvis Presley. From Kilnaboy, Co. Clare, he purchased one of the first guitars in the county and his musical interests continued to grow – a conversation with P.J. can encompass everything from Portuguese fado singers to Hawaiian slat-key guitar.

It was while working in England as an RAF air traffic controller that the magnetic sound of Liam O'Flynn's pipes on the radio drew him back to Ireland where he became sound man and roadie for the newly-formed Bothy Band. Learning from their studio work, he produced his first album, **The Piper's Rock**, in 1978 (see p.396) commencing a career which has spanned a further 44 albums, including classics by Altan, Maura O'Connell, Freddie White, Stockton's Wing, Seán Tyrrell and, most recently, Mick Hanly. His first radio show, RTÉ's *Roots of Rock*, came in 1980 and he has broadcast regularly ever since (currently on Lyric FM and RTÉ Radio 1). Now back in Clare (because "I nourish on something here that I don't get anywhere else") he was a leading force in the successful campaign to protect The Burren from industrial devastation, bringing many local musicians on board through production of **The Sound on Stone** compilation album.

Tradition and Innovation

Irish music may be a playground, but it also became a battle-field during the 1990s with purists attempting to construct barricades against the twin onslaughts of innovation and external influence. Acting as a catalyst were two television series, 1991's *Bringing It All Back Home* (produced by the BBC) and *A River of Sound*, a co-production by RTÉ and the BBC broadcast in 1995. Both were the brainchildren of **Philip King** and **Nuala O'Connor** of Hummingbird Productions, while the latter programme was scripted and presented by **Mícheál Ó Súilleabháin**.

The thesis put forward on *Bringing It All Back Home* was that Irish traditional music had been a major influence on the development of popular music in the US. Both the programme and the subsequent album release, attempted to demonstrate the argument by, sometimes contrived, cross-fertilization between the traditions, such as The Everly Brothers singing "Rose Connolly".

A River of Sound provoked a far greater kerfuffle. Its major critics, such as accordionist **Tony MacMahon**, levelled the charge that the series' attempt to demonstrate innovation and versatility in modern Irish music through the half-baked opinions of a succession of rock stars, shamefully ignored the century's major traditional musicians. The rallying cry of the purists has always been Breandán Breathnach's definition of traditional music as the art of solo performance, and they saw experimentation as the bastard offspring of people who had no respect for the tradition. The upshot of the debate was the 1996 **Crossroads Conference**, the proceedings of which make vital reading for anyone seeking to examine the complexities of music in Ireland today (see p.591).

Much as the purist position must be respected, it is questionable whether it is tenable to ignore the realities of a multimedia, Web-conscious world where the possibility of a musician inhabiting a cultural vacuum is lower than Leitrim's chances of winning the All-Ireland Senior Hurling Championship. While the song tradition has always been inspired by contemporary events, instrumentalists have readily incorporated other idioms into their playing. Uilleann piper Paddy Keenan's notorious infiltration of "How Much is that Doggie in the Window?" into his playing is one extreme example, while Connemara's idiosyncratic adaptation of country and western is another.

Fashions in music (and we're not talking about Aran sweaters) have also stimulated concern. Currently, sessions and ensemble playing dominate the traditional scene and many groups show an alarming tendency towards velocity for its own sake, either to demonstrate technical prowess or to win over the attention of a pub's clientele. This undermines one of the fundamental elements of the tradition: when musicians are simply trying to keep up with the melody, the opportunity for individual expression evaporates. Such melodic embellishment lies at the heart of Ireland's music, but already there are signs of a backlash. Certain groups, such as **Providence**, seem to be returning to the core values of the tradition where a tune's melody is seen to have primacy above all other concerns.

Shaun Davey

When the orchestral suite **The Brendan Voyage** was recorded in 1980, the interest and acclaim that it generated brought its composer **Shaun Davey** (b. 1946, Cultra, Co. Down) firmly into the spotlight. The inspiration for the piece was Tim Severin's account of his attempt to replicate St Brendan's supposed sixth-century voyage across the Atlantic to America in a leather boat. It was the young composer's first attempt to grapple with a full orchestral work, but his decision to symbolize the boat by the sound of the uilleann pipes and his choice of Liam O'Flynn as soloist added a powerful and poignant dimension to the score. Since then Davey has continued to explore key moments and turning points in Irish history such as **Granuaile** (1986), featuring his future wife, Rita Connolly, and **The Relief of Derry Symphony** (1992). His other compositions, such as the "Concerto for Two Harps"

and "A Choral Symphony", have been performed by the National Symphony Orchestra and RTÉ Concert Orchestra and he has worked for the Abbey and Gate theatres in Dublin and the Royal Shakespeare Company, written many TV and film scores (including 1998's *Waking Ned*) and produced albums by Sonny Condell, Liam O'Flynn and Rita Connolly. In 1994 he revised and remastered **The Pilgrim**, originally released in 1984, to incorporate a more recent

1990 performance in Glasgow. The result is a dazzling evocation of the medieval Celtic world with O'Flynn, Connolly and Iarla Ó Lionáird adding new depths to the suite's earlier performance at the Lorient Interceltic Festival, 1983. Davey's composition of the theme tune to the popular BBC TV series *Ballykissangel* brought his music to an even larger audience.

⊙ **The Brendan Voyage**   Tara, 1980

Stunning in concept and delivery thanks, in part, to Liam O'Flynn's majestic uilleann piping.

⊙ **The Pilgrim**   Tara, 1994

Another epic from Davey's pen, embellished by the voices of Rita Connolly and Iarla Ó Lionáird.

Michael Flatley

The astonishing success of **Michael Flatley**'s dancing skills has propelled him to the dizzy heights of international celebrity and vast personal wealth, complete with multiple luxury homes, yacht, private jet, Ferraris and a fondness for Chateau Latour – not forgetting the expensive lawsuits, the gossip-column inches and legs insured for $40 million. The son of Irish immigrants, Flatley was born in Chicago in 1958. After lessons at home from age four, he began attending the Dennis Dennehy School of Dance at eleven, meanwhile learning to play the flute on family trips home to Sligo. As a teenager, he swept the board at dance competitions either side of the Atlantic, in 1974 becoming the first American to take the World Irish Dancing Championships, as well as winning two All-Ireland titles on flute (not to mention the Chicago Golden Gloves boxing competition). His outstanding prowess on those soon-to-be very expensive feet steered him towards what commercial opportunities then existed for Irish dancers – teaching, touring with The Chieftains, entering the Guinness Book of Records as the world's fastest tapper. He also recorded a self-titled flute album in 1981 and although his playing is not that highly regarded, it has a distinguished champion in flute player Séamus Tansey.

In 1993, Flatley danced with **Jean Butler** as part of the Mayo 5000 celebrations. In the audience was one Moya Doherty, who cast the pair as leads in the hard-shoe showpiece she was planning as interval entertainment for the following year's Eurovision Song Contest in Dublin. The raw physicality of Flatley's performance, as well as his choreographic input, were major factors in *Riverdance*'s initial seismic impact, but within less than eighteen months he had departed from the show, following a dispute over contracts and royalties which was eventually settled out of court in 1999. In the interim, Flatley has floated not one but two of his own star vehicles on the post-*Riverdance* market. *Lord of the Dance*, performed to a score by Ronan Hardiman, opened in July 1996; by 2000 its total gross, including prodigious video and CD sales, was reckoned at around £150 million. Hard on its heels, in 1998, came the £5 million *Feet of Flames*, another international hit, this time incorporating not only his terpsichorean talents but his flute playing ("the part where the women melt", according to the show's publicity), while a Hollywood biopic, *Dream Dancer*, is said to be in the pipeline. Now approaching middle age, Flatley may have to contemplate hanging up his shoes ere long – but at least he can count on a comfortable retirement.

| ⊙ **Michael Flatley** | Son Records, 1981 |

Sligo-style flute in much the same mould as his dancing – flashy, florid and extremely fast.

Philip King

Having grown up on a varied musical diet of late-60s pop, Clancys-style ballads and classical recordings, before studying trumpet at University College Cork during the tail-end of Seán Ó Riada's lectureship there, **Philip King** certainly had the grounding for a wide-ranging musical career. He first made his mark as a singer, songwriter and harmonica player with the much-loved **Scullion** in the 1970s and early '80s and made two fine albums with uilleann piper Peter Browne – **Rince Gréagach** (1981) and **Seacht Nóiméad Deag Chun a Seacht** (1983). These days, however, he is better known as a director, with Nuala O'Connor and Kieran Corrigan, of Hummingbird Productions, the independent TV production company responsible for a string of critically and popularly acclaimed music-based documentaries since its foundation in 1987. The outfit's debut project was in 1991 with *Bringing it All Back Home*, a five-part BBC series tracing the influence of Irish music in US country, folk and rock traditions (see p.544). Other major productions since then have included *A River of Sound* (1994), an exploration by **Mícheal Ó Súilleabháin** of Irish music's history and evolution for RTÉ and the BBC (see p.544); *Christy* (1994), a highly-praised profile of Christy Moore, and the TV film *Keeping Time* (1999), celebrating the performance partnership of poet Séamus Heaney and piper Liam O'Flynn.

In recent years, King has been increasingly in demand as a festival producer, having programmed the *From the Heart* Irish music festival at London's Barbican Centre in 1997 and 1999, and been extensively involved in the "Island – Arts From Ireland Festival" in Washington during 2000. His deep-seated love and understanding of Irish traditional music, coupled with his background as a performer, contribute to a visual and creative sensitivity in his handling of musical subjects that unfortunately remains all too rare in the world of TV.

Peadar Ó Riada

As the son of the late great Seán Ó Riada, you might have thought **Peadar Ó Riada** would avoid a musical career, given the size of the footsteps in which he'd be following. Instead, however, the composer, arranger, choirmaster and multi-instrumentalist (on concertina, piano, harmonium, whistle and accordion) sums up his philosophy thus: "I am not the composer, but a window through which the voice of my people may sometimes be heard. I am grateful for this honour." How you respond to this statement, taken from the sleeve notes of Ó Riada's most recent album **Winds – Gentle Whisper** (1996), will probably have a significant bearing on whether you find his music – a diverse but overridingly earnest collage of traditional, classical, Eastern, avant-garde and jazz elements – profound or pretentious.

Peadar was still a small child when his father moved the family from Dublin to Cúil Aodha, Co. Cork, in order to immerse himself in the culture of the Gaeltacht. Nearly forty years later, Peadar still lives in the old family home, directing the Irish-language choir his father established, leading them each Sunday in the Mass his father wrote. Along with "found sounds", his children's voices, and incidental background noises, the choir also feature frequently on his recordings – the others being **Nollag** (1993) and **Amidst These Hills** (1994). The latter (financed in part by Christy Moore and U2) includes an Indian-tinged aural backdrop to a tapestry exhibition, a small boy's wavery singing backed by the Cúil Aodha choir, and an epic battle lament played on tin whistle and bones. Besides his musical explorations, Ó Riada also runs a small TV production company, Dord, freelances in print and radio journalism, and keeps bees, while his other credits include the string arrangements for The Pogues' **Peace and Love** album, and as producer/arranger on **Seven Steps to Mercy**, by his former Cúil Aodha neighbour Iarla Ó Lionáird.

⊙ **Amidst These Hills**   Bar/None Records, 1994

Provides just some of the many facets of Ó Riada's distinctive vision.

Seán Ó Riada

There's often an element of fairy lore woven into the histories of Ireland's musical heroes, and that of **Seán Ó Riada** – musician, composer, broadcaster, arranger, scholar and all-round visionary instigator – is no exception. Several accounts of his life refer to an aisling, or prophetic dream-vision, that the then John Reidy experienced while living in Paris during the mid-1950s. Eking a living playing jazz piano and freelancing for French radio, he was suddenly fired by a new and overriding vocation, to devote himself to the indigenous culture of his own country. "I'd rather be breaking stones in Ireland," he declared, "than be the richest man living in Europe."

Ó Riada was born in Cork city in 1931, growing up in his father's Garda posting of Adare, Co. Limerick. As a child, he quickly displayed exceptional academic and musical promise, becoming fluent in the Irish language, winning a secondary-school scholarship at eleven and matriculating at sixteen. He entered University College Cork to study classics in 1948, switching to music after two years, while playing piano in local dance bands to supplement his income. On graduating he was appointed assistant director of music at Radio Éireann, a largely bureaucratic post of which Ó Riada soon sickened, prompting his departure for Paris in 1955. On his return in 1957, he became musical director of Dublin's Abbey Theatre, the seedbed for his pioneering "folk chamber orchestra" **Ceoltóirí Chualann**. Originally assembled for a production of Bryan McMahon's *Song of the Anvil*, the group gave its first performance proper at the Shelbourne Hotel in

1959. It featured many of Ireland's top traditional musicians, including, at various times, piper Paddy Moloney, fiddlers Seán Keane and Martin Fay, Michael Tubridy on flute, Seán Potts on whistle, and singers Seán Ó Sé and Darach Ó Catháin. Ó Riada himself played bodhrán and harpsichord, the latter adopted as the nearest extant approximation to the old wire-strung harp.

By adapting classical and jazz ensemble formats to traditional music, and thus adapting traditional music to the concert-hall stage, Ó Riada – as he began styling himself around this time – instigated a revolution in the way Irish music was performed and perceived, simultaneously bringing it back into the cultural mainstream, while lending it a new-found credibility even in highbrow circles. Ceoltóirí Chualann's ensemble structure enabled different instrumental and harmonic permutations to be highlighted within a performance, creating the essential prototype for successive folk groups, from The Chieftains – an early Ceoltóirí Chualann offshoot – onwards. Ceoltóirí Chualann were also among the first to introduce the bodhrán into the modern instrumental repertoire, and to revive the work of eighteenth-century harper/composers, notably Carolan.

The year after Ceoltóirí Chualann's concert debut, *Mise Éire* (I Am Ireland), one of the first-ever Irish-made films, was released. This documentary chronicle of Ireland's independence struggle was accompanied by Ó Riada's orchestral arrangements of classic traditional song airs. Both film and soundtrack became a potent focus of national pride, turning Ó Riada into a household name. His scores for *Mise Éire*'s follow-up, *Saoirse* (Freedom) and – with Ceoltóirí Chualann – the screen version of Synge's *Playboy of the Western World*, achieved similar impact. Ceoltóirí Chualann's 1961 Radio Éireann series *Fleadh Choil an Raidió and Reacaireact an Riadaigh* won them further nationwide acclaim, as did their several recordings for Gael-Linn, among which the live concert set **Ó Riada sa Gaiety** (1969) best captures them at their peak. This live recording of a concert celebrating the bicentenary of Ulster poet Peadar Ó Doirnín, featuring singer Seán Ó Sé, immortalizes the full flowering of Ó Riada's ensemble model for traditional music. It also records the premiere of his own setting for one of Ó Doirnín's poems, in the song "Mna na hÉireann" (Women of Ireland), which would later become The Chieftains' first international hit.

In 1962, Ó Riada resigned from the Abbey and moved his family to the West Cork Gaeltacht of Cúil Aodha – ten miles from his mother's birthplace – following his appointment as a music lecturer at University College Cork, where he is remembered as an eloquent and inspiring teacher. He formed a male voice choir in Cúil Aodha, for whom he composed a Mass in Irish – still widely sung today – based on sean-nós singing, also becoming an important lobbyist for the promotion of Irish language and culture. He continued commuting to Dublin, writing and presenting the landmark Radio Éireann series *Our Musical Heritage*, exploring the history and diversity of Irish traditional music. By the end of the decade, however, his health was deteriorating badly, and Ceoltóirí Chualann's disbandment in 1970 was probably due as much to his being too weak to travel for concerts, as to the stated reason that the experiment had run its course.

In August 1971, just weeks before he died, Ó Riada and Paddy Moloney visited the home of Claddagh Records founder Garech Browne in the Wicklow mountains. There, according to Chieftains' biographer John Glatt, he "poured his heart and guts" into fourteen traditional dance tunes, harp pieces and song airs, played on Browne's antique harpsichord and recorded as **Ó Riada's Farewell** (1972). Some have speculated that the marked shift in musical approach on this album derived from his recent acquisition of a traditional harp, as distinct from the modern gut-strung version he despised, thus giving him a much closer technical understanding of the old harp music he loved. The music's eerily poignant passion, grandeur and sweetness serve as both an apposite valediction, and a tantalizing indication that Ó Riada's musical ambitions were far from exhausted. Following his death in early October, the thousands-strong crowds at his funeral in Cúil Aodha represented a national expression of gratitude to the man who'd done so much to give Ireland's music back to its people.

| ⊙ Ó Riada sa Gaiety | Gael-Linn, 1969 |

The best album of Ceoltóirí Chualann, one of Ó Riada's most
significant achievements.

| ⊙ Ó Riada's Farewell | Claddagh, 1972 |

Ó Riada's leave-taking, performed on solo harpsichord, draws on
virtually every aspect of his life and study.

Mícheál Ó Súilleabháin

One of the most eminent contemporary figures in defining and
exploring the interface between traditional and classical music,
the Co. Waterford-born composer, pianist and musicologist **Mícheál
Ó Súilleabháin** has also played a key role in expanding traditional
music's place and status within Ireland's universities. Much of his
career, in fact, has been spent among the groves of academe, predominantly at University College Cork, where he studied under Seán
Ó Riada – still cited as his primary formative influence – before writing his doctoral thesis on the music of fiddler Tommy Potts at
Queen's University in Belfast. Back at UCC, from 1975 to 1993, he
was instrumental in establishing the Music Department as the first in
the country to work towards integrating traditional and classical students through a joint curriculum, also spending a semester as Visiting
Professor at Boston College, where he founded an Irish music
archive. He moved to Limerick University in 1994 to take up its
newly-established Chair of Music, there setting up the Irish World
Music Centre as a hub of research and development in Irish and
Irish-related music around the world. In 2000, the Centre was named
as a core unit in the multisite Irish Academy of Performing Arts. Ó
Súilleabháin was also assistant editor on Aloys Fleischmann's

mammoth collection project, *Sources of Irish Traditional Music* (1999), and in 1995 wrote and presented the TV series *A River of Sound* (see p.544) exploring the roots and evolution of traditional music – partly through interviews with mainstream stars like Van Morrison and The Cranberries' Dolores O'Riordan – and helping to trigger a national debate on the subject.

Ó Súilleabháin's own compositions and recordings span a broad array of performance formats. His self-titled 1976 debut comprised solo pieces played on five different types of keyboard; **Óró Damhnaigh** (1977) featured a traditional-style line-up of fellow Waterford musicians; while **Becoming** (1998) has as its centrepiece a new composition written to accompany a 1925 silent movie, *Irish Destiny* featuring Ó Súilleabháin on piano with the Irish Chamber Orchestra. His music – both traditional and classical – is informed by an in-depth historical understanding, leading him away from attempting to blend the two directly, to an approach better likened to a dialogue, while his Hiberno-Jazz outfit, founded in 1993, aims to stake out some meeting-place between Irish, classical, jazz and world music forms. As a performer, he has developed a highly individual, distinctively Irish piano style, substantially shaped by his many arrangements of traditional tunes for the instrument. Though he has always eschewed any ivory-tower or highbrow persona, probably his most populist venture was his dreamy composition "Lumen", penned as the interval entertainment for the 1995 Eurovision Song Contest in Dublin, while more recently a commission from the Cork International Choral Festival saw him venturing into vocal composition with "Maranata", premiered by the National Chamber Choir in May 2000.

⊙ **Between Worlds**   Virgin, 1995

This aptly titled compilation mines several earlier albums to illustrate the range and the continuities in Ó Súilleabháin's work.

Bill Whelan and Riverdance

Seven minutes that shook the world…In an Irish musical context, this is no exaggeration of *Riverdance*'s impact, right from its original incarnation as an interval item during Ireland's hosting of the 1994 Eurovision Song Contest. The subsequent hike in profile and income of composer **Bill Whelan**, from a well-respected but publicly little-known composer, producer and session musician to the author of Ireland's biggest ever cultural export was actually a culmination of developments that had long been taking shape in his work.

Whelan's career up to that point had been a widely varied one, including two years' touring and recording with **Planxty**, composer-in-residence at the Abbey Theatre's annual Yeats festival, plus film and TV scores, and production credits on albums by Andy Irvine, Patrick Street, Stockton's Wing and The Dubliners. The Planxty/Irvine connection, especially his involvement in the latter's 1992 **East Wind**

REDFERNS

Riverdance in full spate

album with Davy Spillane, first brought him into contact with the East European rhythms he would later cross-fertilize with Irish idioms when composing *Riverdance*, and with Bulgarian multi-instrumentalist Nikola Parov, who performed in the original full-length show.

It was following the premiere of Whelan's large-scale work **The Spirit of Mayo** (1993) that he was approached by Eurovision producer Moya Doherty to compose an intermission showpiece for the programme, her only stipulation being that it involve a large corps of hard-shoe Irish dancers. The impact of *Riverdance*'s inaugural airing, with its unapologetic musical fusion of traditional and modern, Irish and international, together with its dazzling reinvention of a hitherto much-derided dance form, was immediate and electrifying. Although Ireland's official Eurovision entry, "Rock'n'Roll Kids", actually won the contest, it was kept off the top of the country's charts by the *Riverdance* single, which stayed at #1 for eighteen weeks.

By the time it finally slipped, plans for a full-length show, co-created by Whelan, Doherty and John McColgan, were already well under way, resulting in a production that incorporated American, Spanish and even Russian folk-dance traditions. From its original five-week run at Dublin's Point Theatre in February 1995, *Riverdance* has now swelled to encompass three full touring companies around the world while launching the solo careers of its original lead dancers, **Michael Flatley** and Jean Butler. Needless to say, the show has had its detractors because of its supposed corruption of authentic Irish music and dance forms with alien influences, but this is to ignore the extent to which both score and choreography do draw on traditional idioms, a bias which is arguably *Riverdance*'s greatest strength.

⊙ **Riverdance**   Celtic Heartbeat, 1995

This 1995 version captures the initial, raw-edged excitement of the then-fledgling show.

Listings

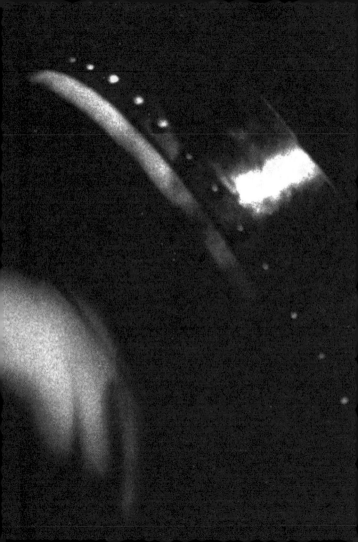

Sessions around Ireland

R egular sessions can be found throughout the year in Dublin, Belfast and most of the large towns and cities, while the summer months from June to August are the best in the rural areas, especially in the counties on the western seaboard. So, with apologies to certain counties in the Leinster and the Ulster provinces, our listings focus on the more active musical areas and tourist centres. Bear in mind that venues sometimes change and sessions may move to another night of the week. The simplest ways to find a session are to ask the locals, buy the local newspaper or listings magazine where available (see p.584) or consult the Tourist Office.

Telephoning Ireland and Northern Ireland

All telephone numbers included in these listings are prefixed by the local dialling code. If you're calling from abroad you should dial the international code – 00 353 for the Republic or 00 44 for Northern Ireland – followed by the local code minus the initial zero, and then the subscriber number. While calls from Northern Ireland to the Republic require the full international code, those from the Republic to the North only need 048 followed by the local code (omitting the initial zero) and number.

IRISH COUNTIES

N

Donegal
Derry
Antrim
Tyrone
BELFAST
Farmanagh
Armagh
Down
Silgo
Monaghan
Mayo
Leitrim
Cavan
Roscommon
Longford
Louth
Meath
Westmeath
DUBLIN
Galway
Offaly
Dublin
Clare
Kildare
Laois
Wicklow
Carlow
Limerick
Tipperary
Kilkenny
Wexford
Waterford
Kerry
Cork
Cork

0   25 miles

The Republic

Clare

The county town, **Ennis**, is awash with music during the summer months and good bets are *Ciaran's* on Francis St, *Cruises* on Abbey St (which has music every night of the year), *Mary Kearney's* in nearby Lifford and the Clare CCÉ headquarters at *Cois na hAbhna* on Gort Rd. Out of town, both **Bunratty** and **Crusheen** offer possibilities. The West is equally replete and the villages of **Carrigaholt**, **Cooraclare** and **Doonbeg** are good bets, while **Kilkee** has the estimable *Crotty's* and *The Way Inn*. In and around The Burren, **Corofin** and **Ennistymon** are grand at the weekend while **Kilfenora** offers both *Linnane's* and *Vaughan's*. Then, of course, there's always **Doolin** where music's possible any night of the year, though many musicians now avoid the influx of tourists. In the east of Clare, **Feakle**, **Killaloe** and **Tulla** might make a more authentic alternative.

Cork

You can usually find music in the city of **Cork** most nights; particular favourites include *An Spailpín Fánach* (South Main St), *The Lobby Bar* (Union Quay), *An Crúiscín Lán* and *Gable's* (both on Douglas St). Around the county, **Midleton**, **Kinsale**, **Clonakilty** and **Castletownbere** all have regular sessions and, then, of course there's the legendary *Dan O'Connell's* in **Knocknagree** in the northwest.

Donegal

Sessions abound in the county during the summer. Head for the Glencolmcille peninsula where there's usually something happening in

Kilcar, **Carrick** and **Glencolmcille** at weekends while, to the north, at least one of **Ardara's** thirteen pubs will be hosting music. Inland, **Glenties** has regular sessions at the *Highlands Hotel* and nearby *Glen Tavern* in **Tangaveane,** while **Dungloe** and **Annagry** are worth trying in The Rosses area. **Arranmore Island** can be lively while the **Gweedore** area includes excellent sessions at *Tessie's* in **Meenaleck** (also home to *Leo's* pub of Clannad fame) and **Bunbeg** where *Húdaí Beag's* is a must on Mondays. The craic can be as wild as the landscape on **Tory Island** while the Cloghaneely area offers plenty of choice in **Gortahork** and **Falcarragh**. Near Mount Errigal, *Ionad Cois Locha* regularly hosts concerts and, the county's largest town, **Letterkenny**, boasts many venues. The **Rosguill** peninsula houses a couple of grand session pubs and, finally, Inishowen has **Clonmany**, **Ballyliffin** and one of the best venues in Ireland, *McGrory's* at **Culdaff**.

Dublin

The Republic's capital has some of the best and some of the direst sessions in the country and seekers of good music are strongly advised to avoid the tourist areas, especially Temple Bar, and consult the listings magazines (see p.584) for details of gigs in the larger venues. Currently, the favourites on the **Northside** are *Hughes* on Chancery St (especially Fri nights) and *The Cobblestone*, further west on King St, which has superb sessions nightly and on Sunday afternoons. Just down Smithfield from here is *Chief O'Neill's Hotel* which has great music in a swish, modernist setting midweek and occasional concerts. Popular choices **south of the Liffey** include the *Brazen Head*, Lower Bridge St and the *Porterhouse*, Parliament St. No first stay in Dublin is complete without a visit to *O'Donoghue's*, Merrion Row, once home to The Dubliners, while a little further south, *The Harcourt Hotel*, Harcourt St, hosts major names on Monday nights and has a Tuesday night session. If you really do fancy a tour of Temple Bar's pubs, then one way of doing it is to join the **Musical Pub Crawl**, which meets 7.30pm at *Oliver St. John Gogarty's*, Fleet St, Temple Bar (May–Oct every night; Nov & Feb–April Fri & Sat only; tickets can be prebooked at the Suffolk St Tourist Office). Bear in mind that the same musicians accompany you on your trip. Lastly, Comhaltas Ceoltóirí Éireann regulalry presents music at its **Culturlann na hÉireann** centre, next to its headquarters in Belgrave Square, Monkstown. Ignore the costumes and trappings – the music can be tremendous.

Galway

A lively university city, **Galway** offers some tremendous venues for traditional music, such as *Roisín Dubh* (which also hosts gigs), *The Crane*, *The King's Head* and *Taafe's* while ballad lovers should head for *An Púcan*. Also worth checking is *Aras na Gael*, a music and theatre centre, run by Irish language enthusiasts, with sessions three nights a week. **Kinvara**, to the south, is home to more than a few musicians and the *Auld Plaid Shawl* and *Winkles* are great for the craic (and the latter for set dancing too). Heading westwards from the city, *Hughes'* bar in **Spiddal** is where De Dannan was formed and, deeper into **Connemara**, the area around **Carna** and **Glinsk** is strong in sean-nós singing and you just might strike lucky. Connemara's largest town, **Clifden**, has several session possibilities while **Inishbofin** island includes *Miko's* and the *Doonmore Hotel*. Lastly, once the day-trippers have left, the pubs of the **Aran Islands** really do come to life.

Kerry

Knowing music lovers head for the Dingle peninsula. In **Dingle** town itself *An Droichead Beag* and *Flaherty's* are essential destinations, while impromptu sessions are always a possibility in **Ballyferriter** and **Ballydavid**. **Tralee** is a good bet, especially *Betty's Bar* and occasional concerts at *Síamsa Tíre* (The National Folk Theatre), or *The Tankard* in nearby **Fenit**. In north Kerry, **Listowel**'s always worth a stop, but there's regular music too in **Ballybunion**. Back south, many of **Killarney**'s pubs and hotels offer a sterilized musical brew for tourists and its better to head for the **Ring of Kerry** where **Glenbeigh**, inland **Glencar**, **Cahersiveen**, **Waterville** and **Kenmare** all have sessions in summer. Lastly, Sliabh Luachra fans should head for **Castleisland** and bars such as *Tagney's*.

Leitrim

One of Ireland's smallest counties is also a Country and Irish hotbed, as a glance at the local *Observer* will prove. However, **Drumshanbo** is usually a safe bet for a high-quality session. Elsewhere, **Carrick-on-Shannon**'s pubs cater for a younger, dance-oriented crowd, though *Cryan's* is always a possibility and, out of town, there's *Anderson's Thatch Pub*. Elsewhere, try **Kiltyclogher** on the Fermanagh border while the *North Leitrim Glens Centre* in nearby **Manorhamilton** occasionally hosts major names.

Limerick

The 1990s saw a remarkable revival in **Limerick** city's musical fortunes, thanks in part to the development of the University's *World Music Centre*. The excellent *Dolan's* has music every night and there are plenty of other sessions around at bars like *Nancy Blake's*, *Hogan's* and *Hanratty's*. Elsewhere around the county, **Abbeyfeale** in the very southwest has the fine *Central Lounge*, while **Adare** (closer to Limerick on the N21) usually has music at weekends. To the east of Limerick, **Castleconnell** is a good option midweek while **Foynes**, to the west, has the excellent *Shannon House*.

Mayo

Westport has a variety of sessions, at *Henehan's*, *The West*, *The Towers* and, of course, nightly at *Matt Molloy's* (owned by The Chieftains' flute player). In the north, **Belmullet** and the riverside town of **Ballina** can be lively while inland **Castlebar** (especially *Johnnie McHale's*) and **Cong** (nightly at *Bannagher's Hotel*) offer musical opportunities.

Sligo

Lovers of the local fiddle and flute styles should head to the county's southern region and, particularly **Gurteen**, where the *Coleman Centre* hosts music throughout the summer. The bars here can be lively too and in **Tubbercurry** to the west. **Sligo** town itself is a music fan's dream and it's usually possible to find at least one worthy session here any night of the week (even Mondays!).

Tipperary

Surprisingly, Tipperary has more sessions than other more tourist-centred counties. Starting in the county's east, *Drowsey Maggie's* in **Carrick-on-Suir**, co-run by fiddler and mandolin-player, Martin Murray, is a definite must with sessions five nights a week. The larger towns of **Clonmel** and **Cahir** have several options, while Tipperary's major tourist trap, **Cashel**, includes the excellent *Feehan's*. In the county's north, *Kenyon's* in **Nenagh** is home to the acclaimed *Nenagh Singers' Circle*.

Waterford

The music scene here is pretty animated and not least in **Waterford** city itself. *Doolan's* on George St has music every night, while other good places include *Croker's*, *Muldoon's* and the *Bridge Hotel* for Monday night set-dancing. In the west of the county **Dungarvan** has weekend sessions at bars such as *Bean a'Leanna* while nearby **An Rinn** (Ring), in the Déise Gaeltacht, is pretty active – try *Mooney's*, *Tígh an Cheoil* or the *Marine*.

Wexford

A county once rich in traditional music, Wexford can still provide a grand night's entertainment. **Wexford** town itself has regular sessions at *Ó Faoláin's*, *The Centenary Stores* and *The Sky and the Ground*. Elsewhere, **New Ross** offers a couple of good summer bets in *The Mariners* and *Mannion's* and there's usually something happening in **Enniscorthy** (venue for the Fleadh Cheoil in both 1999 and 2000).

Wicklow

Sparse pickings, unfortunately, though **Bray**'s proximity to Dublin means that a session can be found in at least one of the bars most nights of the week (especially at *The Mayfair Hotel* and *Clancy's* bar). **Wicklow** town and **Arklow**, further down the coast, also have music in high summer.

Northern Ireland

Antrim

Belfast has a number of regular sessions and places to look out for include *The Hercules*, *The John Hewitt*, the *Kitchen Bar*, *Madden's*, *The Menagerie* and, in the docklands area, *Pat's Bar* and *The Rotterdam*. Outside Belfast, traditional sessions hug doggedly to the coast. Heading northwards, stopping places might include **Millbay** (on Islandmagee), *Black's* in **Carnlough**, the essential *Johnny Joe's* in **Cushendall** and several options in **Ballycastle** (including *The Central Bar* and *McCarroll's*). Two notable inland exceptions are *The Skerry* in isolated **Newtowncrommelin** and *The Cross Keys* between Portglenone and Toome (badly damaged by fire in 2000, but likely to be restored in the near future).

Armagh

The Céilí House in **Lurgan** has rapidly become one of the North's best venues and attracts major names from around the island. Otherwise, head for the south of the county and the villages of **Mullaghbane** (which has *O'Hanlon's* and the *Tí Chulainn Cultural Centre*) and nearby **Forkhill** (*The Welcome Inn* and *The Forge*). For a Sunday afternoon treat of music and tea, there's *Hearty's Folk Cottage* at **Glassdrummond**, on the way to Crossmaglen.

Derry

Derry city's traditional scene is not what it was, but you can usually find something happening in the pubs along Waterloo St or at

Salgado's, Water St, which sometimes hosts major names. Elsewhere, *Owen's* in **Limavady** is a possibility, but the most reliable venue is *The Anchor* in **Portstewart**.

Down

Down's options are relatively limited and include: *Fealty's* in **Bangor**, the singalong specializing *Fiddlers Green* in **Portaferry** (at the very tip of the Ards peninsula) and the Saltwater Brigg a little to the north on the road to **Kircubbin**. **Downpatrick** has the excellent *Speedy Mullan's*, while around the Mourne coast, there's usually something to be found in **Rostrevor** or Warrenpoint. Lastly, *The Cove* or *Nan Rice's* are the best bets in **Newry**.

Fermanagh

Pretty quiet for most of the week, **Enniskillen**'s bars such as The Crow's Nest, Mulligan's or Pat's offer a good chance of a session at the weekend. Otherwise, head northwest to **Derrygonnelly** or the pottery town of **Belleek** where there is usually activity at the weekends.

Tyrone

Once a strong fiddling county and sparsely populated with the exception of **Omagh** or the towns near Lough Neagh, Tyrone has become rather a dry region for sessions. In Omagh itself, the local CCÉ's Dún Úladh Cultural Centre hosts regular events and a few bars, such as Bogan's, hold sessions. On the way to from Omagh to Cookstown, the An Créagan Visitor Centre is also a regular venue.

Festivals and schools

All the major events and schools are listed here, while most towns and villages also have their own street festivals which will almost always include traditional music. Both Bord Fáilte (the Irish Tourist Board) and the Northern Ireland Tourist Board publish an annual calendar of events: their Web sites are Ⓦ *www.travel.ie* and Ⓦ *www.ni-tourism.com*. Dates of events may vary slightly from year to year.

As part of Comhaltas Ceoltóirí Éireann's international competition scheme, each of the 32 counties holds an annual Fleadh Cheoil. The first of these takes place in mid-April, while most occur in May and June. Winners next compete at the four provincial Fleadhanna Cheoil in July leading to the Fleadh Cheoil na hÉireann at the end of August where they are joined by winners of the British, US and other international championships. Venues for all of these events usually change on an annual basis. CCÉ's Web site at Ⓦ *www.comhaltas.com* is the best place to check first.

For major summer schools such as Scoil Samhraidh Willie Clancy, it is advisable to register (and pay) as far in advance as possible. Tuition fees are usually remarkably low, ranging from IR£10–£20 for a weekend and IR£35–£60 for a longer school, while festivals may only charge for specific events. For details of accommodation contact the school and local tourist office.

As far as possible, web page or email addresses have been provided in these listings. However, some events only advertise a telephone number. Please consider that this is often the number of a private individual.

March

St. Patrick's Day (March 17);
Ⓦ *www.stpatricksday.ie*
Events throughout Ireland.

Fourth weekend

Sean-Nós Cois Life, Dublin;
Ⓣ 01/280 4023
Specialist event including singing classes and storytelling workshops.

April

Fourth weekend

Edward Bunting Annual Harp Festival, Mullaghbane, Co. Armagh (venue may vary);
Ⓦ *patricia@armaghpipers .freeserve.co.uk*
Traditional harp and singing workshops, concerts and sessions, run by the Armagh Harpers' Association.

May

First weekend

Féile na nDéise, Dungarvan, Co. Waterford;
Ⓦ *tiodgar@indigo.ie*
Waterford's main event, with a huge number of shows and activities.

Josie McDermott Memorial Festival, Ballyfarnon, Co. Roscommon; Ⓣ 078/47096
Annual festival commemorating the great Sligo flute player, including lots of planned events, workshops and sessions and a major flute competition.

Fourth weekend

Fleadh Nua, Ennis, Co. Clare;
Ⓦ *www.ctr.com/fleadh*
One of the year's biggest traditional music festivals with around fifty events, including sessions, workshops, a

celebrity concert, nightly céilís
and the national dancing
championships.

June

First weekend

**Clare Festival of Traditional
Singing**, Ennistymon, Co. Clare;
Ⓦ *www.iol.ie/~clarelib*
A weekend of singing which in
2000 focused on religious song;
features a closing concert with
some of the contemporary
greats.

Second week

Fleadh Amhrán agus Rince,
Ballycastle, Co. Antrim;
Ⓣ 028/2076 3703
Hugely popular festival in one
of the North's traditional music
towns – lots of sessions and
concerts.

**Tommy Makem International
Song School**, Mullaghbane, Co.
Armagh; Ⓦ *www.tculainn.ie*
Important new summer school
focussing on singing, with
classes, workshops, concerts
and sessions.

Fourth weekend

An Chúirt Chruitireachta,
Termonfeckin, Co. Louth;
Ⓦ *www.harp.net/cnac/cnac.htm*
A major annual residential event
for harpers, includes concerts,
workshops and classes.

July

First week

Scoil Samhraidh Willie Clancy,
Miltown Malbay, Co. Clare;
Ⓣ 065/708 4148 or 708 4281
Known as "Willie Week", this is
the major summer school of the
year. With classes in virtually
every instrument, it attracts
around 1000 students and
many renowned tutors.
Highlights include a week-long
céilí programme and
instrumental recitals by the top
names. Prospective students
need to register and secure
accommodation well in advance.

Second week

**Blas International Summer
School**, Irish World Music Centre,
University of Limerick, Limerick;

Ⓦ *www.ul.ie/~iwmc/blas/*
Rapidly rising event which has
become the next stop for many
musicians after Willie Week;
consists of more than fifty
events including lectures,
concerts, workshops and plenty
of sessions around town.

South Sligo Summer School,
Tubbercurry, Co. Sligo;
Ⓦ *www.sssschool.org*
Another hugely popular school,
running since 1987 and offering
tuition in most instruments and
set dancing, plus lectures,
recitals and a nightly céilí;
welcomes all ages and abilities.

Third week

Joe Mooney Summer School of Traditional Music, Song and Dance, Drumshanbo, Co. Leitrim; Ⓦ *www.indigo.ie/~davebird/joemooney/*
Large and popular summer
school including a huge range
of workshops and plenty of
recitals and sessions.

Fourth week

Fiddlers' Green Festival, Rostrevor, Co. Down;

Ⓦ *dnausers.d-n-a.net/fiddlers.green/*
Major music festival attracting
lots of big names with concerts
and sessions around the town.

James Morrison Traditional Music Festival, Riverstown, Co. Sligo; ⓣ 071/65082
Founded in 1991, this
commemorates the great
fiddler and attracts many
musicians to its workshops,
sessions and concerts.

August

First week

Donegal Fiddlers Summer School, Glencolmcille, Co. Donegal; Ⓔ *dldclk1@iol.ie*
Long-standing and very popular
school promoting the county's
fiddle tradition, aimed at those
living in Donegal and other
interested fiddlers; includes
workshops and recitals, plus
lots of sessions in the village.

O'Carolan Summer School + Harp and Traditional Music Festival, Keadue, Co. Roscommon;

ⓔ *ocarolan@oceanfree.net*
Five days of workshops
(beginning at the very end of
July) in most instruments,
singing and set dancing,
culminating in a weekend
festival featuring a major harp
competition.

Scoil Acla na Mílaoise, Achill
Island, Co. Mayo;

ⓦ *www.scoilacla.com/*
Almost two-week-long school
with classes in most
instruments, sean-nós singing
and nightly events.

First weekend

**Ballyshannon Folk and
Traditional Music Festival**,
Ballyshannon, Co. Donegal;

ⓦ *www.donegalbay.ie*
Long-standing major festival
focused on the town's hilly
streets and concerts in the
marquee. Altan regularly top
the bill.

**Caherciveen Celtic Music
Festival**, Caherciveen, Co.
Kerry; ⓦ *www*
.celticmusicfestival.com
Busking, workshops and
concerts usually featuring
some big names from

traditional music and crossover performers.

Second week

**Bray International Festival of
Dance and Music**, Bray, Co.
Wicklow;

ⓔ *sparksmurpy@eircom.net*
Firmly focused on traditional
music and one of the most
popular festivals on the east
coast.

**Féile An Phobail – West Belfast
Community Festival**, Belfast;

ⓦ *www.irish-culture.com*
One of the North's major
community festivals with
plenty of traditional music.

Second weekend

**Feakle International
Traditional Music Festival**,
Feakle, Co. Clare; ⓣ 061/924332
or 924288
One of the county's biggest
festivals, includes many events
and classes.

Third week

Aonach Paddy O'Brien,
Nenagh, Co. Tipperary;

W *www.iol.ie/~aonach*

One of Ireland's major festivals, held in honour of the great accordionist. Fifty events – concerts, sessions and workshops

Fonn Traditional Music Summer School, Galway;

E *gsitm@indigo.ie*

Workshops and masterclasses in song, music and dance, hosted by the Galway School of Irish Traditional Music and usually kicked off by a major-name concert.

Third weekend

Eigse Mrs Crotty Traditional Music Festival, Kilrush, Co, Clare; W *www.clare.local .ie\kilrush*

Annual event commemorating the illustrious concertina player; includes special classes on the instrument plus lots of other action.

Fourth week

Scoil Éigse, Venue varies each year according to the location of the Fleadh Cheoil na hÉireann; W *www.comhaltas.com*

Annual school in the week prior to the Fleadh Cheoil na hÉireann and held in the same town, organized by CCÉ, includes a comprehensive range of classes in music, usually only open to those who can already play reasonably well. Requires booking at least three weeks in advance.

Fourth weekend

Fleadh Cheoil na hÉireann, changeable venue;

W *www.fleadhcheoil.com*

Winners of provincial fleadhanna (plus those from abroad) compete for the All-Ireland titles at Junior and Senior level in a comprehensive range of categories. Attracts many other singers, musicians and dancers.

September

First week

Coleman Traditional Festival, Gurteen, Co. Sligo;

W *www.colemanirishmusic.com*

Concerts, sessions, céilís and more in the heart of Coleman country.

Cork Folk Festival, Cork;
Ⓦ *www.aardvark.ie*
Thirty events including
sessions, concerts and
workshops.

Second weekend

Dingle Music Festival, Dingle,
Co. Kerry; Ⓣ 066/915 2411
A weekend of gigs featuring
major names, many of whom
can also be found sessioning in
the town's pubs.

Fourth weekend

Music under the Mountains,
Hollywood, Co. Wicklow;
Ⓔ *bonfiels@gofree.indigo.ie*
A weekend of concerts, sessions
and workshops featuring many
leading names.

October

First weekend

**Slieve Gullion Festival of
Traditional Singing**,
Mullaghbane, Co. Armagh;
Ⓔ *gerry.ohanlon@btinternet.com*
Eight musical events, including

concerts, lectures and informal
sessions.

Fourth weekend

An tOireachtas, venue varies;
Ⓦ *www.indigo.ie/egt/ighlin
/oireachtas*
Prestigious annual competition
organized by Conradh na
Gaeilge (The Gaelic League),
celebrating the arts among
Irish-speaking communities –
150 separate competitions, the
highlight being the Corn Uí
Riada, the most valued award
for sean-nós singing.

November

Second weekend

Ennis Trad Festival, Ennis, Co.
Clare; Ⓦ *www.clarenet.ie/ennis
/novtradfest*
A grand weekend of concerts
and over 100 sessions in 20
venues around the town; runs
Thurs–Sun.

Third week

**William Kennedy International
Festival of Piping**, Armagh, Co.

Armagh; ⓔ *jbv @ukgateway.net*
Focuses on all forms of pipes
worldwide and includes
everything from lectures to
sessions and recitals.

December

**Frankie Kennedy Winter
School**, Gweedore, Co.
Donegal; ⓔ *gearoidm@iol.ie*

The major winter event,
running from the end of
December into the New Year,
celebrates the late Altan flute-
player and features many
workshops, concerts and
sessions. Requires booking
some time in advance and
arranging your own
accommodation.

Record shops

Only specialist record stores in the main towns and tourist areas have been included in these listings. You'll find branches of major chains, such as HMV, Tower and Virgin, in most of the major cities and Ireland's own Dolphin and Golden Discs around Dublin (and the latter in Belfast too). Most musical instrument shops also stock CDs.

The Republic

Clare

The Knotted Chord Music Store, Cook's Lane, Ennis;
Ⓣ 065/682 2152;
Ⓦ *www.knotted-chord.com*
Excellent store, specializing in traditional, folk and world music in various formats, plus videos, tutors and related books.

Magnetic Music, Fisherstreet, Doolin; Ⓣ 065/707 4988;
Ⓦ *www.magnetic-music.com*
Recently established complex containing record store, crêperie and restaurant.

Cork

The Living Tradition, 40 MacCurtain St, Cork;
Ⓣ 021/502040;
Ⓦ *www.thelivingtradition.com*
Ossian Publications' retail outlet located north of the river is firmly focused on traditional music stocking a grand range of CDs, cassettes and books (studies, collections, tutorials) and also selling tin whistles and bodhráns.

Donegal

Melody Maker, Castle St, Donegal town; ⊤ 073/22326. Handily placed in the town centre, Melody Maker has a great range of Irish music on CD and cassette.

Dublin

Celtic Note, 27–29 Nassau St, Dublin 2; ⊤ 01/670 4157; Ⓦ *www.celticnote.ie* Facing Trinity's southern walls, Celtic Note's stock ranges from traditional music to Country and Irish CDs; also has a range of videos and sometimes hosts lunchtime concerts.

Claddagh Records, 2 Cecilia St, Temple Bar, Dublin 2; ⊤ 01/677 0262; Ⓦ *indigo.ie/~claddagh* Claddagh's enormous range of traditional releases includes many hard-to-find CDs and cassettes. Highly knowledgable staff provide helpful advice. Also operates a mail-order service

Secret Book and Record Store, 15a Wicklow St, Dublin 2; ⊤ 01/679 7272 The best place to hunt down rare folk and traditional vinyl.

Galway

Mulligan, 5 Middle St Court, Galway; ⊤ 091/564961; Ⓦ *indigo.ie/~mulligan* Reckoned to have the largest stock of Irish and Scottish traditional music in the country, including CDs, cassettes and vinyl.

Zhivago, Shop St, Galway; ⊤ 091/564198. Claims to be the largest music shop in the west of Ireland. Sells tapes, CDs, videos, tin whistles, bodhráns and song books.

Kerry

Lee Records, The Island Centre, Main St, Castleisland, ⊤ 066/42580; and 11 The Mall, Tralee, ⊤ 066/27589 General record store whose branches stock a grand range of Irish music.

Waterford

Sinnott's Music Shop, 3
Michael St, Waterford;
☎ 051/875622

Easy to locate in the centre of
town, Sinnott's stocks a very
broad range of releases.

Northern Ireland

Belfast

Cultúrlann MacAdam Ó Fiach,
216 Falls Rd, Belfast;
☎ 028/9096 4180
West Belfast arts and cultural
centre whose shop is
recommended for both books
and traditional CDs; also hosts
music events.

Good Vibrations, 54 Howard St,
Belfast; ☎ 028/9031 4888

New releases and many bargain
reductions; stocks CDs,
cassettes and vinyl.

Derry

Sounds Around, 24 Waterloo
St, Derry; ☎ 028/7128 8890
Wide-ranging stock with plenty
of rare traditional vinyl.

Media

This section provides information on the many radio stations and televison channels which schedule traditional music, listings and specialist music magazines. In addition, The Music Network (Ⓦ *www.musicnetwork.ie*) publishes the comprehensive *Irish Music Handbook*, a huge, 400-page directory listing festivals, schools, instrument suppliers and manufacturers, venues, etc. Its companion *Directory of Musicians in Ireland* contains contact information and profiles for 1600 musicians, from the worlds of traditional, jazz and classical music.

Radio

The best and most reliable source of traditional music and song programmes is **Raidió na Gaeltachta**, the Irish language station known as RnaG, broadcasting on 92.9–94.4 and 102.7 FM (Ⓦ *www.rnag.ie*). The national network stations **RTÉ Radio 1 and 2FM** (Ⓦ *www.rte.ie*) regularly feature traditional programmes, such as the long-standing Saturday night mainstay, *Céilí House* at 9.30pm. Full details of programmes and frequencies are available in the weekly *RTÉ Guide* and national newspapers. The national commercial station is **Lyric FM** (Ⓦ *www.lyricfm.ie*) and one programme to look out for is P.J. Curtis's *Reels to Ragas*, every Wednesday night at 7pm.

A reliable gateway to information on local radio stations is Ⓦ *www.medialive.ie/radio/local-commercial/local.html*. Most of the local stations regularly broadcasting traditional music are in the western counties. Specialist shows are listed here, but many stations include the music in their schedules throughout the day. Remember that local stations have a limited range.

Both **Cork** stations **96FM** and **County Sound** (103 FM) schedule traditional music (Ⓦ *www.96fm.ie* or see the *Irish Examiner* for details). **Radio Kerry** (96.2–97.7 FM) has *Trad Tradhnona* on Mondays from 9pm to 10pm, and a regular céilí band slot at 8pm on Fridays. **Connemara Community Radio** (87.8 and 106.1 FM; Ⓦ *connemara.irish-music.net*) is a reliable source – watch out for the weekly *Lift the Latch*. Monday nights on **Limerick 95FM** feature three hours of *Rambling House* from 7pm. **Clare FM** (95.2–96.4) broadcasts traditional music each weekday night from 7pm, often presented by the singer Tim Dennehy and has a highly informative website (Ⓦ *www.clarefm.ie*). Further north, **Highland Radio** covers **Donegal** on 95.2 FM (western) and 103.3 FM (northern), with information available at Ⓦ *www.highlandradio.com*.

Inland, **Tipperary Mid-West Radio** (104.8 FM) has a number of programmes, including *The Crooked Road* (Thursdays 9pm, Sundays 8am) and a regular CCÉ show (Mondays 6.30pm). Nearby **Tipp FM** (97.1 and 103.9 FM) has a weekly morning show on Sundays 11am–2pm. **Radio Kilkenny** (96, 96.6 and 106.3 FM) features a traditional music show on Fridays and Sundays from 8pm to 9pm. In the south, **WLR FM** in **Waterford** (97.5 FM) showcases *Open Door* (Sundays 10–11pm).

Dublin's airwaves are awash with rock, pop and techno, but one notable exception is **Raidió na Life** (102 FM), the capital's Irish language station.

National radio in Northern Ireland is provided by the BBC and its programmes on **Radios 1 to 5** only rarely cover Irish music. Local coverage is provided by **BBC Radio Ulster** and **BBC Foyle** (based in Derry) and details of programmes are available in newspapers. Norhern Ireland's commercial stations show little interest in traditional music.

Television

TV schedules change regularly, so keep your eyes on the newspaper listings. The Republic's national Irish language channel **TG4** regularly broadcasts traditional music shows, while **RTÉ 1 and Network 2** do so intermittently and the commercial **TV3** hardly at all. **Northern Ireland** is covered by **BBC Northern Ireland** and the commercial **UTV**; both take most of their schedules from the BBC and ITV, while the few locally-made programmes occasionally cover music.

Magazines and newspapers

Outside the major cities, the most valuable source of information is the local newspaper, usually published towards the end of the week. Most have an entertainments page, consisting of a collation of advertisements with sometimes editorial content previewing events.

Copies of the few free listing magazines can usually be found in pubs, clubs, record stores, arts centres, cafes and local tourist offices. All magazines are published fortnightly, unless stated otherwise.

Dublin is covered by the expansive and well-written free newspaper, *The Event Guide*. Its session listings are not comprehensive, but major events are always included. *In Dublin* (IR£1.95) is more tourist-centred, but does include some music listings. Cork has *The*

Cork List which, like the similar *List Galway*, provides pretty detailed information on events in the respective cities. A newcomer further north is the monthly *What's On in Donegal*, which is based in Letterkenny and focuses mainly on the town itself. Lastly, Belfast has *The Big List* with extensive music listings, including some in other parts of Northern Ireland.

Articles and reviews can often also be found in the Republic's national newspapers, such as *The Irish Times*, *The Irish Independent*, *The Irish Examiner* and Dublin's *Evening Herald*. In the North occasional articles appear in the *Irish News* and the *Belfast Telegraph*.

Irish magazines

Hot Press, fortnightly, IR£1.95; Ⓦ *www.hot-press.com*
Ireland's only national rock magazine also regularly reviews traditional albums, has articles on leading singers and musicians and provides extensive listings of forthcoming gigs around the country. Also publishes annually *The Hot Press Yearbook* listing contacts for bands, shops, venues, etc. and established The Hot Press Hall of Fame.

Irish Music Magazine, monthly (except Jan), IR£1.95; Ⓦ *www.mayo-ireland .ie/irishmusic.htm*
IMM is the best source of information on new releases and up-and-coming singers and musicians with occasional features on tuition and tune tips; also includes session listings around Ireland and details of forthcoming events.

The Journal of Music in Ireland, bimonthly, IR£2.95; Ⓦ *www.thejmi.com*
A new journal drawing together the best writing on Ireland's classical, jazz and traditional music and featuring stimulating and sometimes provocative articles and reviews.

Treoir, quarterly; Ⓦ *www.comhaltas.com*
Comhaltas Ceoltóirí Éireann's journal is available to members only. Articles appear in both

Irish and English and the focus is usually discursive and scholastic, and sometimes extremely cogent.

UK and US magazines

Dirty Linen, bimonthly, $5; Ⓦ *www.dirtylinen.com*
General roots music magazine: well written, provocative and usually with an astonishing number of CD reviews.

Fiddler Magazine, quarterly, $5; Ⓦ *www.fiddle.com*
Specialist magazine, excellently written and diligently researched, often featuring articles on Irish musicians.

fRoots, monthly, £3.50; Ⓦ *www.froots.demon.co.uk*
Formerly *Folk Roots*, this excellent world music magazine celebrated its 20th anniversary in 2000 and continues to provide comprehensive coverage.

The Living Tradition; bimonthly, £2.50; Ⓦ *www.folkmusic.net*
Uniformally excellent, free-thinking magazine covering Scottish, Irish and related traditions. Worth purchasing just for its letters page.

Resources and organizations

Both specialist and general traditional music organizations and resources are included in this section. All are best accessed initially via their Web sites (where available).

Cairde na Cruite, 50 Wyvern, Killiney, Co. Dublin; Ⓦ *www.harp.net/cnac/cnac.htm* CnaC ("Friends of the Harp"), founded in 1960, promotes the Irish harp through activities, which include an annual summer school (see p.573), teaching and publishing books of graded pieces.

Cairdeas na bhFidleiri, Tullyhorkey, Ballyshannon, Co. Donegal; Ⓔ *dldclk1@iol.ie* Promotes (and thereby helps to maintain) the Donegal fiddle tradition through classes, workshops, its summer school in Glencolmcille (see p.574) and its annual gathering of fiddlers in Glenties each October.

Ceol, Smithfield Village, Dublin 7; Ⓦ *www.ceol.ie* An essential part of any traditional music enthusiast's visit to Ireland, Ceol (part of the Chief O'Neill hotel complex) celebrates the living tradition through an entertaining range of interactive displays and film presentations. There's also an excellent shop attached. Open Mon–Sat 9.30am–6pm, Sun 12–7pm; IR£3.95.

Coleman Irish Music Centre, Gurteen, Co. Sligo; Ⓦ *www.colemanirishmusic.com* A community-based enterprise celebrating the fiddler Michael Coleman and the music of Sligo, including a visitor centre, theatre, music school and (at nearby Knockgraine) a full-scale replica of the Coleman family home. The music archive contains a comprehensive collection of music and recordings from the county.

Comhaltas Ceoltóirí Éireann,

Belgrave Square, Monkstown, Co. Dublin; Ⓦ *www. comhaltas.com*
Celebrating its fiftieth anniversary in 2001, CCÉ is the foremost organization promoting Irish song, music and dance with 400 branches worldwide. Its cultural centre, Cultúlann na hÉireann, provides an information service and music archives, runs classes and courses, and offers entertainment throughout the summer. CCÉ organizes 44 Fleadhanna Cheoil, culminating in the All-Ireland championships in late August. Its quarterly magazine is *Treoir* and it also publishes cassettes, CDs and tutors.

Cumann Cheol Tíre Éireann,

15 Henrietta St, Dublin 1; Ⓣ 01/873 0093
The Folk Music Society of Ireland, founded in 1971, focuses on the study of traditional music and its practice, largely through lectures, seminars and recitals during the winter months.

Irish Traditional Music Archive,

63 Merrion Square, Dublin 2; Ⓦ *www.itma.ie*
Established in 1987, ITMA is a splendid resource for anyone with a serious interest in traditional music. General collections include: a vast range of recordings: song, music and dance collections and studies; reference material and periodicals; videos; ephemera, etc. Many special collections have been donated to the Archive, including field recordings and transcriptions. ITMA also makes its own recordings of musicians and dancers. ITMA's email address is for internal use only. Archive open 10am–1pm and 2–4pm, Mon–Fri.

Music Network, The Coach

House, Dublin Castle, Dublin 2; Ⓦ *www.musicnetwork.ie*
Ireland's national music development organization, aiming to provide access to music for people in the context

of their own communities. Publishes *The Irish Music Handbook* and the *Directory of Musicians in Ireland* plus the quarterly newsletter *Musiclinks*.

Na Píobairí Uilleann, 15 Henrietta St, Dublin 1; Ⓦ *www.iol.ie/~npupipes/npuhome.htm*

Founded in 1968, NPU promotes the playing of the uilleann pipes. It organizes classes and recitals, produces a range of publications (including a magazine *An Píobaire*), recordings and videos, runs an archive and provides support through its membership network. Its Web site offers a vast range of information, including a list of current pipe-makers. Only pipers are eligible for full membership (IR£20 pa).

Ulstersongs, 10 Apollo Walk, Portrush, Co. Antrim, Northern Ireland, BT56 8HQ; Ⓦ *www.ulstersongs.com*

Singer/collector John Moulden's laudable initiative promoting the social, unaccompanied singing tradition of (mainly) the North of Ireland through its own publications and sale of books (both studies and collections), cassettes, CDs and vinyl, including much rare and deleted material.

Selected reading

Breandán Breathnach, *Folk Music and Dances of Ireland* (Ossian Publications).
Breathnach's classic analysis of the structure of Irish music is still essential reading. A companion CD features all the songs and tunes from the book's closing section.

Nicholas Carolan, *A Harvest Saved: Francis O'Neill and Irish Music in Chicago* (Ossian Publications).
A detailed account of O'Neill's role in the preservation of the tradition, with many historical photographs and tune transcriptions.

Ciaran Carson, *Irish Traditional Music* (Appletree Press).
Though dating from 1986, this slim, pocket-sized book is still the best brief introduction to the instruments and music.

Ciaran Carson, *Last Night's Fun* (Pimlico).
Carson's lyrical prose captures the spirit and atmosphere of the music with style and zest whether tracing a tune's origins, seeking out the best sessions or simply telling a tale.

P.J. Curtis, *Notes from the Heart* (Poolbeg).
The opening chapters provide an admirable overview of the music's twentieth-century developments while the remainder focuses on major figures of Co. Clare.

Allen Feldman and Eamonn O'Doherty, *The Northern Fiddler* (Blackstaff Press).
Feldman's 1979 study of the fiddle traditions of Donegal and Tyrone enlivened by O'Doherty's great photos.

Caoimhín MacAoidh, *Between the Jigs and the Reels: The Donegal Fiddle Tradition* (Drumlin Publications).
A marvellous book which captures the richness of the county's musical heritage.

Christy McNamara and Peter Woods, *The Living Note: Heartbeat of Irish Music* (O'Brien Press).
Sumptuously illustrated account of the role Irish music plays in people's lives, told by the participants themselves.

Christy Moore, *One Voice – My Life in Song* (Hodder & Stoughton).
Innovative and forthright as ever, Christy tells a powerful tale of his life, loves and commitments.

Nuala O'Connor, *Bringing It All Back Home* (Merlin Publishing).
Originally published to accompany the 1991 TV series, this recently updated book remains an enthralling and controversial account of the influence of Irish music on other cultures.

Gearóid Ó hAllmhuráin, *A Pocket History of Irish Traditional Music* (O'Brien Press).
The author's own research into the impact of the Irish diaspora on music around the world forms some of the best sections of this informative account.

Fintan Vallely (ed.), *The Companion to Irish Traditional Music* (Cork University Press).
An indispensable A–Z providing copious accounts of the music's form, style and qualities and brief biographies of many key participants.

Fintan Vallely et al (eds.), *Crosbhealach an Cheoil – The Crossroads Conference 1996* (Whinstone Music).
Stimulating and controversial selection of papers examining the conflict between tradition and change in contemporary Irish music.

Fintan Vallely and Charlie Piggott, *Blooming Meadows: The World of Irish Traditional Musicians* (Town House & Country House).
For the feel of the music, turn to this glorious book, based on interviews with singers and musicians and written with a deep affection.

Index

M

Sorted

ROUGH GUIDES